Flexible
Working Hours

Flexible Working Hours
An Innovation in the Quality of Work Life

BY
SIMCHA RONEN, PH.D.
Associate Professor of
Management and Organizational Behavior
Graduate School of Business Administration
New York University

McGRAW-HILL BOOK COMPANY

New York   St. Louis   San Francisco   Auckland
Bogotá   Hamburg   Johannesburg   London
Madrid   Mexico   Montreal   New Delhi
Panama   Paris   São Paulo
Singapore   Sydney   Tokyo
Toronto

Library of Congress Cataloging in Publication Data
Ronen, Simcha, 1935–
Flexible working hours.

Bibliography: p.
Includes index.
1. Hours of labor, Flexible—United States.
I. Title.
HD5109.2.U5R66   331.25′72′0973   80-14614
ISBN   0-07-053607-4

1234567890   KPKP   8987654321

The editors for this book were Robert L. Davidson and Christine M.
Ulwick, the designer was Mark E. Safran, and the production
supervisor was Teresa F. Leaden. It was set in Roma by ComCom.

Printed and bound by The Kingsport Press.

To Freddy, Benzy, and Vered
for teaching me the value of flexitime

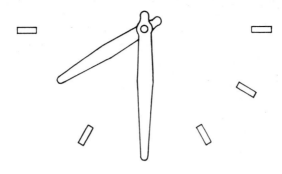

Contents

Part 4   Flexible Working Hours and the Labor Force

Part 5   Considerations for Effective Implementation

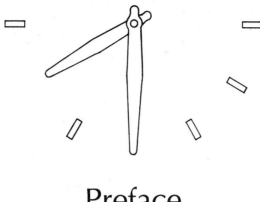

Preface

The last decade has witnessed a proliferation of ideas aimed at countering sagging productivity and decreased job satisfaction in industry. Creative organizations are searching for innovations that will improve the effectiveness of their production and service processes. These efforts have been accompanied by the growing awareness that many traditional management practices are no longer appropriate: the employee must be considered an individual with special needs instead of a cog in the machinery of the organization.

Consequently, work scheduling innovations have begun to receive serious consideration as a means by which individual needs and organizational effectiveness can be enhanced. Although the consideration of alternatives is limited in some cases by factors such as production processes, task interdependence, union contracts, and federal and state legislation, creative managers not bound by the constraints of traditional management philosophy have found sufficient opportunity for modifying the fixed work schedule. Listed below are a few examples of organizations which have already initiated innovative schedules:

- The French Peugeot-Citroen car manufacturer is experimenting with alternative work schedules by allowing 1620 employees additional days off which can be taken periodically, accumulated to be used for an extended leave in mid-career, or credited toward an early retirement.

- One of duPont's plants, located in Athens, Georgia, is operating on weekends by employing part-time workers, the majority of whom are students from the University of Georgia.

- Honeywell Corporation has a "mothers' shift" at one Massachusetts plant. Women work hours which coincide with the hours their children attend school. Students replace mothers during summer vacations.

- The Kingsbury Machine Tool Corporation located in Keene, New Hampshire, implemented a flexible work hours program for almost a thousand manufacturing and clerical employees. Employees can choose their daily arrival and departure times within a flexband of 1 hour in the morning and the afternoon. Both the day and the night shifts utilize flexible schedules.

Employees must work a total of 40 hours per week; they are allowed to accumulate credit hours and to take off one morning or afternoon during any day of the week.

These examples represent special applications of alternative work schedules; the more accepted and popularized alternatives include the compressed or 4-day week, part-time work and job sharing, and the many variations of flexible work hours. Each of these schedules includes a variation in one or both of two dimensions of work scheduling. The first is the *number* of hours worked during a given period of time, usually a day. The second is the *timing* of these hours of work, that is, when the required number of hours are scheduled within the work period. The number of hours required is a decision that is rarely left to the individual employee: it is usually a result either of a legal provision or of a particular organizational policy. Timing, on the other hand, is an area where the individual can be given some freedom of choice, although the organizational constraints and task characteristics will determine the level of flexibility. These two dimensions are the constraints determining which alternative work-scheduling variations are feasible.

On a personal level, I have witnessed the growing concern of managers over decreased employee productivity and the interest in quality-of-work-life issues as a response to the problem. Many employees have expressed to me their frustrations arising from the limitations placed on their lives by the dictates of the work schedules. Within this context, it seems appropriate to me that flexitime should be seriously considered by the management of organizations as we enter the 1980s. Flexitime represents an organizational change which can address the concerns expressed by both managers and employees: it represents an improvement in quality of work life for employees *as well as* potential improved performance levels within the organization.

My chief purpose in writing this book is to present the available results of flexitime to the manager and "organizational expert" in order to provide some basis for evaluating the applicability of the system with respect to each of these issues. In other words, I hope to provide you, the reader, with enough information to help you evaluate the potential of flexitime in your organization. Along with results from the field, I have tried to anchor the relevant concepts in appropriate psychological and organizational behavior theory to provide a basis for predicting results of future implementations. In addition, a review of the practical considerations involved in the implementation process is included, emphasizing the applied orientation of the book.

In general, this book is meant primarily as a *resource* on flexible work schedules. Sufficient interest has been demonstrated in this type of schedule to justify its treatment to the exclusion of other alternatives, such as the compressed work week and job sharing. An attempt is made here to provide all of the information available which can help managers or consultants evaluate the appropriateness of flexitime for a particular organizational unit. For students of organizational behavior and change, this book should provide a complete description of the change process, possible outcomes, and their implications.

Part 1 provides an analysis of the potential behavioral and attitudinal causes and outcomes for the individual and the implications for organizational effectiveness. Basic definitions of terms and related concepts in the use of flexitime are followed by detailed descriptions of possible variations in the schedule.

Part 2 encompasses potential advantages and disadvantages for each sector influenced by the implementation of a flexible schedule. These sectors include employees of the sponsoring organization, the management of the organization, and society in general.

Part 3 describes field results from flexitime installations in Europe and in the public and private sectors in the United States. Extensive data from many companies have been collected and compiled here and reported in terms of the system's impact on the individual and on the organization. In addition, two comprehensive case studies are included—one each from the public and private sectors—in order to provide the reader with an idea of the actual process of implementation of and experience with flexitime. A chapter on the effects of flexitime on transportation has also been included in Part 3.

Part 4 describes the potential and actual implications of a flexible schedule on various segments of the labor force. A chapter is devoted to each of the following: first-line supervisors, unions, and female employees.

Part 5 is devoted to a discussion of considerations for effective implementation of flexible work hours. This part begins with a chapter describing the prerequisites for effecting change within an organization and includes extensive checklists enumerating the process in detail. This is followed by chapters on legal and contractual considerations and the selection of time-recording systems.

ACKNOWLEDGMENTS

A book of this nature, which presents data from a myriad of sources, is the cooperative effort of many individuals. It is difficult to know where to begin in acknowledging the important contributions of all those who participated in this effort. I am most indebted to the following people, and wish to express my gratitude to each of them.

Three individuals from the Civil Service Commission (now the Office of Personnel Management), Barbara Fiss, Tom Cowley, and John J. Burns, gave me access to the records of those federal agencies that had implemented and conducted studies on flexitime. They also provided valuable information and comments on the case study for the public sector. A tribute goes to the federal agencies themselves that, in the early 1970s, were among the first organizations in the United States willing to consider flexitime as a beneficial intervention for employees. Several of these agencies were generous in forwarding their data directly to me for my research.

From the private sector, Maureen E. McCarthy, of the National Council for Alternative Work Patterns, Inc., was most generous in allowing me access to extensive lists of companies on flexitime. I would also like to express my thanks to each of the companies that responded to my request for information and provided the materials for the short case studies. These include: Jim G. DeMayo and Maurice A. Cayer, J.C. Penney; Marlene C. Goldberg, John Hancock Mutual Life Insurance Co.; Dr. Michael A. Hopp, Control Data Corporation; Jerome F. Perrone, Pitney Bowes; Roger W. Hetherman, Kingbury Machine Tool Corporation; Linda J. Villane, Exxon; Gilberta N. Fouquet, Sandoz, Inc.; Joe Wolzansky, Westinghouse Electric Corporation; and John Flaherty, Hewlett-Packard. I would especially like to thank Richard J. Hilles for his time and access to information that enabled me to write the extensive case study on the SmithKline Corporation.

Three people were most helpful in providing advice and critiques on the European Chapter:

Archibald A. Evans, Bernhard Teriet, and Denise LeCoultre. Data in the chapter on transportation were contributed by Carl S. Selinger, Walter Colvin, and Charles Fausti of the Port Authority of New York and New Jersey. I am particularly grateful to Bernard Keppler of Interflex, and Heinz Hengstler and Richard F. Martel of the Hecon Corporation for the time and materials contributed for the chapter on time-recording systems.

The staff at McGraw-Hill requires a special note of thanks for their help, support, and attention to detail in the production of the book. My gratitude goes to Robert L. Davidson, Christine Ulwick, Joan Zseleczky, and Mark Safran.

The New York University Management Department was most helpful in providing support services. To my colleagues, I am thankful for the constructive and supportive climate. I am also thankful to Susan Hollander Weisberg, Andrea Agolia, Linda Sherman, and Valery Pitt for their cheerful and willing help in typing endless drafts and complicated tables.

There are several individuals who contributed their special resources and talents, without whom the book would not have been possible. To Allen Kraut, I owe more than gratitude, for it is he who, in 1974, encouraged me to pursue flexitime as an area of research. He has been a continuous source of support as a colleague and as a friend. Gerald Schilian and Deborah Watarz not only contributed their time and professional expertise as attorneys to the chapter on legal and contractual considerations, but were always more than generous with their support and special friendship. My students, John Cloonan, Pat Kunkel, and Ely Weitz made invaluable contributions to the research and preparation of material for different areas. One person deserves a special note: Sophia B. Primps, in her capacity as my research assistant, contributed her time and talent far beyond the call of duty. Her unique qualities, diligence, and resiliency, which were consistently combined with humor, were invaluable. Martha Yevin receives my thanks for her meticulous editing and polishing of the final draft. This group formed the "team" that was responsible for the richness of the work experience that, I hope, was felt by all who were involved. It is rare to have the opportunity to work with a team in such an atmosphere of trust and cooperation. The high level of sharing and support we achieved was very special to me.

SIMCHA RONEN

PART 1

Theoretical Basis and Definitions

Introduction

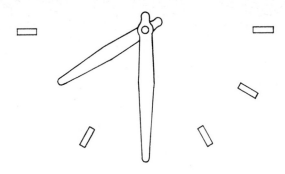

Introduction

Alternative work schedules, and in particular flexitime, have been extensively employed in Europe and the United States, although they are still considered by many managers to be only remote possibilities for their organizations. Despite these reservations, the appeal, popularity, and acceptability of the flexible hours concept is increasing. Before examining the trends in American life, and more particularly, trends in the work force which have created an environment conducive to the acceptance of flexible scheduling, it is important to examine the historical development of fixed work schedules and the societal values they represent.

The preindustrial eighteenth century was characterized by the self-employed, independent farmer or craftsman who possessed a unique style of work and a special set of attitudes and values often described as the "frontier spirit." He himself was responsible for all managerial duties, including planning, organizing, coordinating, and controlling. Employees were usually family members or outsiders incorporated into the family. Because they had a stake in making the enterprise successful, motivation was high. In fact, it was often the case that success meant survival, whereas failure meant death, if not literally, then at least to their way of life. The farmer or craftsman had complete control over his workday and the autonomy to be able to consider and accommodate the various domains of his life—work, family, and leisure activities. There was little separation between these domains, especially if family members were members of the enterprise. The dichotomy between work and nonwork was further diminished by the extremely high interdependence among members of the group or family unit; effective cooperation was a necessity for a successful outcome.

In contrast, the industrial revolution brought a shift *away* from the frontier values of independence and autonomy. Rapid industrial expansion in large cities combined with the closing of the frontier to the thousands of arriving immigrants created a population which was highly dependent on an impersonal work organization for its most basic needs. The management philosophy of the typical organization embraced the idea that efficient production systems were based on the well-coordinated activities of employees who performed fractionated, simply defined tasks in a highly structured and centralized organization. Be-

3

cause the employee was viewed as part of the machinery of the organization, there was no consideration of, or room for, variability in individual needs and expectations. Rigid, standardized work schedules were quite consistent with this philosophy of the work organization and the employee's position in it. Imbalance existed in the sense that the individual employee was truly dependent on the organization for basic economic security, but the organization was not equally dependent on that employee. The economic insecurity of the urban poor was such that the need for employment gave the organization a great deal of power over the individual. The most obvious example of this power was the long hours extracted for relatively low wages.

Another important factor contributing to the domination of the organization was the subservience of the industrial labor force to the clock. An emphasis on efficiency has caused a regularity and immutability in the schedules which govern businesses and institutions. Such schedules are clearly suited to the convenience of organizational functioning rather than the satisfaction of human beings. Within this context, it has become clear that most individuals perceive themselves as exchanging time for money. In many cases, time is the criterion for remuneration rather than the exchange of skills. Thus, it is not surprising that wasting time is considered a "sin." Indulgence in nonproductive activity is the prerogative of children, according to the Protestant ethic.

Half a century later, by the mid-twentieth century, a generation of economic stability brought about a decrease in perceived economic dependence on the organization by the individual. This change in the balance of power between the organization and the employee has been enhanced by labor reform resulting from the union movement and intervention by the government in the form of legislation to protect the worker. By the late 1970s, economic conditions and the changed values of employees and employers had created a work environment conducive to the consideration of flexitime.

Specifically, the rigid scheduling required by organizations has been recently challenged by the new generation, objecting to the notion of the irreversible characteristic of time. Instead of focusing on the future and considering the present as a preparatory stage, younger people tend to emphasize the present and concentrate on experiencing the here and now. Thus, the utlilization of time available may be considered either as a corridor to future growth or as a chance for immediate gratification, depending upon the age group or generational viewpoint. Indulging in the here and now rather than postponing gratification should be the prerogative of the individual employee, according to these new values. The recognition of inter- and intraindividual differences in the utilization of time requires an increased level of choice within the organization if the individual is to be able to gratify his desires. Otherwise, organizational requirements may result in aggressive attitudes and behavior directed toward the frustration-imposing organization. No wonder that the clock has become the symbol of the exploiter, and fixed working hours one of the obstacles to the achievement of pleasure. This perception is compounded by the increased number and availability of leisure activities: "There are so many more things to do—and less time to do them!"

Another important impetus for the acceptance of flexibility in the work schedule is the increased complexity for the individual in managing his own life, coordinating work and nonwork domains. The result has been stress-producing conflict between workers and management, employee discontent, and frustration. For example, one survey indicates that job satisfaction has significantly decreased over the last 8 years for most employees. Another survey revealed that most individuals spend approximately 33 percent of their time on work and work-related activities and only 29 percent on home and leisure activities. The implications of these two sets of statistics are disturbing: the employee spends one-third of his time in a work situation which is increasingly unsatisfactory to him. The negative consequences of this unhappiness will be manifested in the organization as well as in the individual's other life domains, such as his family and leisure activities.

In addition to pressures from within—from employees—the public has begun to demand increased availability and flexibility from the organization. For example, consumers have demanded that the retail and banking industries increase their hours to accommodate those who work the traditional hours that conflict with the times when these facilities are normally open for business. Many of these services are now available at night and on Sundays, or even 24 hours per day. The consequence of increasing the interface with the environment through extended hours is flexibility *within* the organization in the scheduling of employees. Rigid work schedules for employees inside the organization are somewhat inconsistent with the relaxing of the traditional hours of availability to clients. Further, the sheer increase in the number of hours during which the store is staffed allows, if not encourages, variations in the typical workday. Under the traditional system, the employee's work schedule was equated with the organization's workday. As the organization increases its frontal hours of availability, this is no longer the case. The result of these combined pressures from employees within the organization and clients external to the organization have created conditions more conducive to the consideration of flexitime.

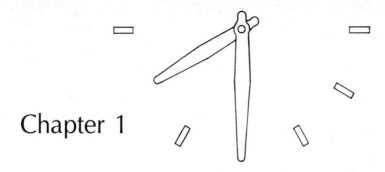

Chapter 1

Quality of Life and Individual Differences

QUALITY OF LIFE

The economic prosperity during the last two decades has given rise to an unprecedented affluence for many individuals in America today. Although not all economic necessities have been provided for the entire population, an increasing number of individuals now have the economic security to shift personal priorities to objectives which are not strictly economic in nature. This shift in priorities is influencing the components of the individual's quality of life, inasmuch as increased economic security has allowed the individual to invest in *himself.* Attention to self-development and self-improvement has stimulated the expectation that the individual be treated as a unique entity by society in general, and by the employing organization in particular.

Concurrently, increasing attention is being given to the understanding of people in our society. Social and economic indicators of national well-being, such as gross national product and employment level, are being supplemented by audits of the individual's subjective experience. This orientation toward psychological issues reflects the growing interest in determining the sources of dissatisfaction and maladaptive behavior as well as the sources of satisfaction and fulfillment in one's life domains, or regions of experience. Research studies have categorized these life domains as follows:

1. Physical and material well-being, including material comfort, health, and personal safety

2. Relationships with other people, including family, children, and close friends

3. Social, community, and civic activity such as clubs, religious associations, public affairs, and political activities

4. Personal development and fulfillment in the forms of learning, developing self-awareness, heightening expressive abilities, and seeking interesting and rewarding work

5. Recreational and physical activities[1]

These domains encompass all aspects of the individual's life situation. Their examination and measurement provide a better understanding of an individual's behavior in terms of choices made within a domain, such as job or career choice; the interaction between domains, such as the interaction between family and work responsibilities; and the level of personal commitment to each.

For the purpose of this book, the two relevant domains will be defined as work and nonwork. These represent combinations of the five domains listed above. Several factors may influence the individual's allocation of resources in these two areas: cultural and societal values, group references, personal and family characteristics, socioeconomic status, personal resources, and life/career stage. As a result of the interaction between these factors, a decision will be made by the individual about the level and type of activity in each domain and the interaction between them. Personal fulfillment results from the level of success achieved in each domain consistent with the individual's values, and from the successful interaction between these domains, which depends on an acceptable allocation of resources. A sense of well-being at work might be termed job satisfaction, while the successful interaction between work and nonwork domains would contribute to life satisfaction. A level of satisfaction in one domain does not necessarily imply the same level of satisfaction in the other, nor is the direction of causality between differences in each domain completely understood. For example, the case is well known of the employee who may have an unhappy home life, but who is highly productive and seems to derive his sense of self-esteem and fulfillment through work. On the other hand, many have witnessed the employee with an unhappy home life whose effectiveness at work is diminished by the spillover effects from his life outside work. In the first case, quality of life in one domain serves to compensate for a lack in the other area. This idea of trade-offs between domains is known as the *compensatory* hypothesis.[2] The second case describes a direct relationship between the work and nonwork areas of experience; this is an example of the *spillover* hypothesis.[3] Although the direction of causality is not known, it is clear that the levels of well-being in both regions affect each other. Since the domains do interact, it follows that the overall quality of life will be higher in the absence of opposing pressures between them. In other words, a better fit between the two domains implies a more consistent, positive, integrated quality of life. Thus, personal characteristics and environmental pressures combine to produce a level of fit between the regions of experience of the individual. Changes in these factors alter the nature of the individual's experience and the relationship between domains. The end result, of course, is that the individual's quality of life or sense of well-being may be affected. These relationships are presented schematically in Figure 1-1.

With this in mind, it becomes important to explore social trends and changes in values influencing the quality of life. The following sections describe changes in the demographics of the labor force and in societal values which, through their impact on the work and nonwork domains, may result in a reduction of the level of fit.

CHANGES IN DEMOGRAPHICS

It is important to identify the changes in the composition of the work force and accompanying changes in societal expectations regarding the work experience. Clearly, changes in

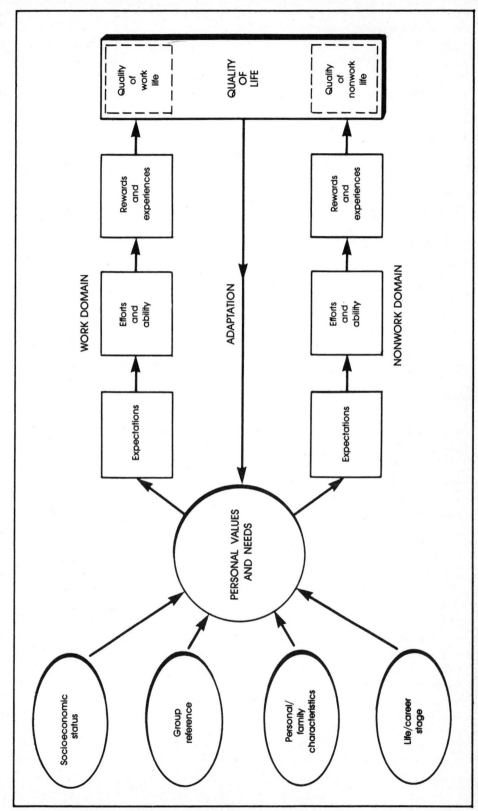

Figure 1-1 Individual differences and the quality of life.

expectations about organizational inputs and outcomes will alter their value to the individual. Adjusted expectations often require new or additional criteria for evaluating personal success in the work domain. The most recent and significant changes in the demographics and activities of the work force which may have influenced expectations are described below.

Age

The average age of employees during the decade 1970–1980 has decreased from 40 to 35. This decline is the result of large numbers of individuals born during the post-World War II baby boom who entered the work force during the 1970s. The clustering of this age group in the work force may mean intense competition for the existing number of jobs. Further, job advancement may be blocked by people only slightly older, instead of those from an older generation, delaying or diminishing the opportunity for promotion.

Women

The participation of women in the work force has increased dramatically in recent years. In 1977, women represented 41 percent of the work force in the United States; this percentage is double what it was in 1920. Further, as of 1976, wives were working in 49 percent of all families with husbands present. Changes in societal values have been an important factor in allowing and encouraging women to enter the work force.

Education

The levels of education of work force members is increasing. Currently, 50 percent of all high school graduates attend college. However, the emphasis on education as a *right* may have resulted in a generation of workers educated beyond the requirements of available jobs. Large numbers of workers may be destined to spend their work lives in occupational levels below their potential.

Additional Factors

The mobility of Americans has increased dramatically in the last decade. For example, a recent statistic indicates that 36 million Americans a year relocate, creating an enormous turnover in the work force. The unemployment rate has remained at a high level for the last several years, fluctuating between 6 and 7 percent.

Implications

In comparison to earlier decades, the work force of the 1980s will be younger, more mobile, and more educated. It will also contain proportionately more women than previously. However, the high expectations of youth, reinforced by higher education levels, may not be met because of job shortages. The competition for jobs, caused by a slumping economy and aggravated by the clustering of baby-boom entrants into the work force, will require a major readjustment for many. According to Peter Drucker:

> For the ones now entering the executive job market—the ones who are being offered high salaries—there is thus a huge and widening gap between their expectations and the reality they

will encounter. What they expect, quite understandably, is modeled after the experience of their older brothers, sisters and cousins. After all, they are at least as well educated, just as bright and eager. It's not their fault they were born five years later.[4]

For this group, the opportunity to advance to anticipated levels within the organization is seriously threatened. The frustration experienced as a result of unmet expectations may well jeopardize the future quality of work life. Further, overall productivity may suffer: the pressures and resentments felt by these individuals is typically directed against the organization.

For women, the economic pressure or personal desire to work often conflicts with the responsibilities felt toward husband and family. These pressures must be moderated in order to achieve some degree of fit between the work and nonwork domains. Although the increasing number of women entering the work force has required that organizations and families provide a more supportive environment for the working mother, there is still much to be accomplished before a fully supportive network is achieved.

It is apparent that changing demographics have influenced the work and nonwork domains of large segments of the population. This is only one source of change, however. Changes in societal values have also had an impact on expectations and attitudes which are reflected in the individual's evaluation of his own quality of life. The implications for the work force of these changes in values and attitudes toward work and leisure are described below.

CHANGES IN SOCIETAL VALUES

Perhaps the most current and pervasive change in values is reflected in the increased emphasis by society on organizations' accountability for their interaction with and impact on the environment and society. A current example is the requirement that organizations maintain and preserve the physical environment for society through pollution control. Another example is the demand for greater social responsibility as the organization conducts its exchange relationship with the labor force. Fewer and fewer employees view economic rewards as the sole motivation for working. More are demanding exposure to more challenging and interesting work—this is considered a right rather than a privilege by many. The organization is considered to be responsible for providing a work environment in which the employee has the opportunity to exercise control and autonomy through increased participation in decision-making processes and has access to inherently interesting and intrinsically rewarding work as well. In his view of the changing value systems of employees, Yankelovich refers to the "new breed" in America. He claims that they

> . . . often start a job willing to work hard and be productive. But if the job fails to meet their expectations—if it doesn't give them the incentives they are looking for—then they lose interest.
> . . . The preoccupation with self that is the hallmark of the New Breed values places the burden of providing incentives for hard work more squarely on the employer than under the old value system.[5]

The employee is focusing increasingly on fulfillment through the self instead of through identification with organizational or national institutions.

This emphasis on the intrinsic aspects of work, particularly among younger employees, has been expressed as a willingness to trade extrinsic for intrinsic work rewards. This is consistent with the concept of centrality of work life as expressed by many employees. Some researchers have reported that the primary source of fulfillment in an individual's life, especially those in higher job levels, is the work domain.[6] For example, many employees have been willing to trade higher income levels for more intrinsically satisfying work in making their choice of occupation.

A trend has been identified in the United States which emphasizes the importance of the quality of work life in the promotion of personal growth and development. Implied in the search for more intrinsic sources of well-being in the work domain is the recognition of the importance of the self as a resource to be developed to its full potential. An unprecedented degree of economic security since World War II has helped to create these somewhat egocentric values. In the rapidly growing field of psychology, self-actualizing theories of human behavior have emphasized the uniqueness of the individual and have fostered the development of the self based on criteria unrelated to one's economic status in society.

One effect of a generation of stability in our society has been the focus on individual development we have just described. Another corollary of the high standard of living achieved by Americans is the opportunity for the choice and acquisition of a wide variety of products and services. The ability to acquire is often considered a criterion for measuring success in our society. In fact, the pressure to acquire can be a source of frustration and tension, as well as of insecurity, for those who cannot indulge to the extent that they would like, in spite of their relatively high standard of living. The question then becomes whether individuals reach a saturation point where the further acquisition of goods carries only marginal reward value, compared to the frustration levels experienced because of an inability to acquire them. If this is so, one could argue that individuals may be willing to make a trade-off between acquisitions and the opportunity for autonomy in the work domain— especially if work is the central life interest. Research on current trends in the work force supports this hypothesis. We submit that it is the *marginal* addition to the acquisition ability of the individual that is subject to that trade-off, since a certain minimum base level of economic security and social acceptability is necessary before such trade-offs become evident.

Another important aspect of this shift in personal and societal values should be noted. As mentioned earlier, one criterion for the economic success of a society is the availability of goods for acquisition. A criterion which was implied is the availability of alternatives, the opportunity for the individual to choose between similar or equivalent goods. In terms of day to day economic transactions, the ability to choose is often taken for granted. The value of *choice* has been an important economic assumption in American society, highly promoted on all levels. Witness the protection of competition between producers of goods in the form of legislation against monopolistic practices, and the millions of dollars spent on product development, marketing, and advertising each year. In a society where the availability of alternatives is assumed, and the choice process is integrated into almost every aspect of day to day interactions, it is inconsistent that so little choice is available to the employee in his work situation. This is particularly apparent in the area of work scheduling, where it could be relatively easy to provide some degree of choice for the employee.

The various socialization processes an individual experiences create a conflict inside the formal work organization. Socialization during childhood and adolescence has prepared him for self-determination, autonomy, privacy, mastery over his environment, use of initiative, and an independent identity. These expectations are thwarted in the work domain, with negative consequences for both the employee and the organization. Pressures on industry for increased employee control and autonomy over the work process and environment are only now allowing some of these values to be expressed in the work place. This emphasis on choice in the work domain, along with the disenchantment with extrinsic rewards in both work and nonwork domains, has focused the attention of the individual squarely on the organization as a source of intrinsic rewards through heightened autonomy and self-determination.

Implications of Social Change

The dynamics of societal changes have been significant in their impact on the individual, his values, and decision-making processes. The pressures caused by these changes have resulted in a decline in the quality of life for many. The result has been that individuals displace the pressures they experience onto the organization, and demand help in the effort to reestablish and maintain a satisfying quality of life.

INDIVIDUAL DIFFERENCES

In the previous section we described the value of choice in our society, both as an underlying assumption of our economic system and as a criterion for economic success. This emphasis on the importance of choice is an expression of the value placed on the recognition of *individual difference*—a fundamental principle in a democratic society. In terms of quality of life, individual differences are reflected in the many facets brought to each domain by the individual reacting to environmental circumstances. Different individuals in the same environmental setting will not experience the same quality of life because of differences in personal resources, abilities, and expectations. Further, the *same* individual will not necessarily always react in the same way to environmental circumstances. In other words, behavior varies from one individual to another, as well as varying over time for the same individual.

It would be beyond the scope of a book on flexible work schedules to delve into all aspects of individual differences such as personality, cultural background, and heritage. However, two aspects of individual differences are particularly relevant to the flexitime concept, since they relate directly to the psychobiological impact of the passage of time on the individual. These two sources of individual difference are biological cycles called *circadian rhythms* and *life-cycle stages.* In any fixed work schedule, the implication of cycles which influence behavior is that low points in the cycle of the individual will coincide with work hours at some point. It is essential for the organization to recognize the existence and implications of these cycles and to help the individual to maintain effectiveness during these slumps. Appropriate flexibility within the organization can accommodate individual cycles.

Biological Cycles

Perhaps one of the most significant sources of variation in individual behavior is attributed to biological fluctuations in the state of the individual. Biologists have recognized the presence of daily cycles such as variations in temperature, heart rate, metabolic rate, and urine constitution. These cycles, called circadian rhythms, have been shown to be related to factors in the environment such as daylight and darkness, and temperature changes. For example, a typical circadian rhythm is the pattern of the heart rate over the course of a day: the heart rate is lowest during the night when sleep is deepest, rises rapidly during the early morning period, and peaks in the late afternoon or early evening, around the dinner hour. There are variations between individuals in the timing, extent, and duration of peak and low points.

These rhythms, particularly temperature and heart rates, have been shown to be significantly correlated with performance at work, where peaks in the circadian rhythms are related to periods of higher productivity or performance. Korman has explained the relationship between daily physiological cycles and the environmentally determined need to function effectively. He suggests that performance is related to level of arousal and is highest at moderate levels but tends to decrease in situations of low or very high arousal (see Figure 1-2).[7] For example, if one found oneself at a very low arousal level at work in the morning, behavior might be diverted from productive activity to drinking coffee, nibbling breakfast, visiting, or other actions designed to help increase the arousal level. If the individual indulges in this type of behavior each morning because his cycle is out of synchronization with the required work cycle, it is unlikely that he will achieve his productive potential.

On an inflexible schedule, the individual must either steer his behavior in order to elevate or depress his arousal level to conform to job demands or else succumb to his arousal level, foregoing an attempt to meet these demands. The amount and type of steering behavior will depend on job requirements, situational factors such as deadlines or other sources of pressure, and the biochemistry of the individual. Assuming for the moment that the individual's own internal governors are about as efficient in maintaining health and appropriate activity levels as any environmental supports or constraints we have yet devised, we submit that having to "hype" oneself up or down with coffee, alcohol, cigarettes, or other forms of arousal or depressive behavior diverts inappropriate amounts of attention and energy from work activities. Moreover, such unproductive forms of behavior may be costly to the organization in terms of morale and productivity.

One must consider variations in cycles among individuals, as well as the variations experienced by the individual within a typical workday. When one considers the inflexible work hours of most organizations, it is clear that human factors such as circadian rhythms have not been considered. Performance improvements might be significant if individuals were allowed to work according to their own cycles. From the individual's viewpoint, some autonomy in determining work schedules may provide the opportunity to arrange an improved fit between work and the biological cycle, assuming the individual is willing to coordinate peaks in his cycle with peak work demands. The result may be an overall improvement in the quality of life in general, as well as in the quality of work life in particular.

Life Stages

A second important aspect of individual differences is the cycles or stages through which an individual progresses during the course of his life. Recently, much attention has been devoted to the concept that individuals experience transitions during the course of their life which can substantially alter their behavior.[8] Recognition of these

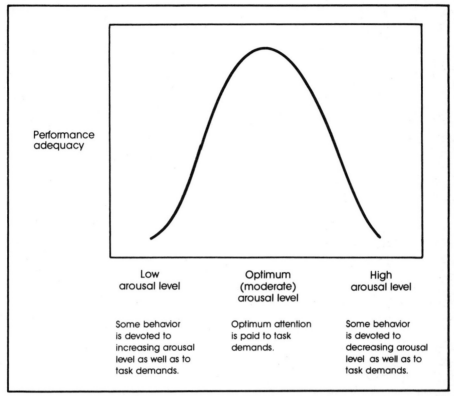

Low arousal level	Optimum (moderate) arousal level	High arousal level
Some behavior is devoted to increasing arousal level as well as to task demands.	Optimum attention is paid to task demands.	Some behavior is devoted to decreasing arousal level as well as to task demands.

Figure 1–2 The relationship between arousal level and performance. (Abraham K. Korman, *Organizational Behavior,* © 1977, p. 195. Reprinted by permission of Prentice Hall, Inc., Englewood Cliffs, New Jersey.)

concepts by the organization is essential to an understanding of individual differences and expectations.

Levinson describes two ideas central to the life-cycle concept. First is the idea of a process or journey. "To speak of a general human life cycle is to propose that the journey from birth to old age follows an underlying, universal pattern on which there are endless cultural and individual variations." Second, Levinson describes the cycles as seasons, each having its own distinctive character. "Every season is different from those that precede and follow it. . . ."[9]

Clearly, as the individual passes through various stages of his life, personal values and attitudes will change. Consequently, expectations about work, as well as the relationship and interaction between work and nonwork domains, may vary. For example, one might predict increased pressure for the allocation of resources to both domains during the years of parenthood, when the individual desires to spend time with his or her family as an active parent but also experiences pressure to work because of the financial needs of the family. In late adulthood, the work domain may become less important as children leave home and the individual considers retirement, or more important if the job is particularly rich in intrinsic awards. In Table 1-1 two charts from Cohen and Gadon have been adapted to create a

Table 1-1 A Model of How Career Stages and Processes Are Connected to Life Stages, Resulting in Variable Attitudes toward Desired Schedule and Amount of Work (*Continued*)

Age	Life Stages	Parallel Career Stages	Differential Effects of Life Stages on Men and Women in Regard to Time Availability and Desired Work Hours
16–22	Breaking out—experimentation with adulthood	Exploration—preparation for work	Part-time work, odd jobs, odd hours (after school, vacations)
22/23–28	Establishing self in the adult world Single—working Marriage—children	Establishment stage—mutual recruitment between the organization and the individual, acceptance and entry, levelling off, transfer and/or promotion	Willingness to work long hours, overtime, not weekends or evenings.
28–33	Age 30—time of transition Occupational change and divorce Financial needs begin to increase	Granting of tenure—evaluation by the organization of the individual leading to commitment to the individual, release or sidetracking	Men: long hours, take work home Women: drop out/part-time
30/33–40	Settling down Youngest child leaves home to enter school Commitments deepen to work, family	Maintenance—mid-career—self-reexamination in the presence of security; occurrence of mid-life crisis	Men If upwardly mobile, long hours, community work, flexibility If plateau in work, regular hours/second job, attention to family Women: Back into career, part or full time, shared jobs, flexible hours desired

16

40–45	Mid-life transition Children leaving home to enter adult world Reevaluation and commitment to life-style reordered priorities, then restabilization, no children at home	Maintenance—late career—teaching instead of striving, deceleration at work, growing interest in nonwork activities	Men: steady hours not as long— longer vacations, weekends, education for renewal, either evenings or on sabbatical Women: longer hours, perhaps flexibility
45–55	Restabilization Renewed interests, freedom from family responsibilities	Wish for more enriching personal life —renewal of important relationships Establishment of mentor-mentee relationships	Health problems may begin to emerge requiring reduced hours, increased interest in leisure
55–65	Anticipation of retirement	Decline—preparation for retirement increasing reliance on wisdom gleaned from experience, self-acceptance	Men and women: tapering to part time

SOURCE (Cohen, Gadon, *Alternative Work Schedules: Integrating Individual and Organizational Needs*, © 1978, Addison-Wesley Publishing Company, Inc., adaption from tables 2.1 and 2.2. Reprinted with permission.)

17

schema representing the individual's life stages, parallel career stages, and commensurate needs for differing work schedules at various points in the career. Also, men and women are differentiated with respect to scheduling needs; for example, during the period of transition around age 30, men typically work long hours in order to be granted "tenure" by the organization, while women often reduce their work schedule or drop out of the work force temporarily to assume child care responsibilities. Although these clear-cut differences between men and women are decreasing as women with children remain in the work force and men assume a more active role in child care, the situation described here still represents the majority of cases.

The work demands on individuals in most organizations assume no differences between individuals, or variations within the same individual in the life situation. For example, the same expectations are held of the young and old, married and single, childless and family-oriented. The organization has failed to realize the variability of the impact of the work domain on the self-esteem of the individual and his quality of life.

Alienation and Stress

Thus far we have emphasized the concept of individual differences in quality of life resulting from various environmental influences, including the work and nonwork domains as well as the life stage of the individual. One of the components of quality of life, in the context of work/nonwork domains, is the attitude—expressed as satisfaction or dissatisfaction—within each domain, and the degree of interaction between the two. Unhappiness or discontent in one area can have negative consequences for other areas, as well as for the quality of life in general.

Partly because of the changes in values we mentioned earlier and the lack of recognition of individual differences, a number of workers have reported a high level of discontent with their work domain. Neither job structure nor organizational climate, as reflected in the attitudes and policies of managers, has kept pace with the rapid change in employee aspirations and expectations. It is not uncommon to find the traditional manager, whose value system is still anchored in the Depression years of his childhood, surprised to discover that paying salaries and providing good working conditions and fringe benefits are not sufficient to satisfy employees or to increase motivational level.

For the individual, discontent can take many psychological forms, including frustration, demoralization, alienation, and stress. These processes threaten the physical and mental health of the employee. They take away from the individual his enjoyment of creativity at his work, diminish his personal happiness, disturb his personal growth, and disrupt his effectiveness as an employee. In short, his well-being is negatively affected. The next section presents a description of these processes and their impact on the individual in terms of his quality of life.

Alienation.   The term alienation is frequently encountered in descriptions of unhappy employees. An individual may experience alienation if he does not have sufficient control over his job or cannot satisfy his need for esteem, recognition, or fulfillment. The job-alienated individual is considered one for whom work is merely instrumental in obtaining more extrinsic or economic rewards. The sociological and psychological literature emphasizes the opposite concepts of involvement and alienation as functions of the degree of individual autonomy and control granted to the employee.[10] More specific symptoms of alienation include:

1. *Powerlessness:* existing when the individual does not have control over his work or job processes

2. *Meaninglessness:* referring to the employee's perception of his contribution to a final product

3. *Social alienation:* referring to the employee's feeling of exclusion from his work team or work-environment social group

4. *Self-estrangement:* referring to the employee's perception of his work as instrumental in obtaining extrinsic rewards, such as money, instead of intrinsic rewards, such as increased fulfillment of self-actualizing needs

The feeling of alienation results from the conflict between employees' expectations and values and the rewards (including intrinsic and extrinsic) derived from the employing organization. Walton describes employee needs as follows:

1. Employees want challenge and personal growth, but work tends to be simplified and specialties are used repeatedly in work assignments.

2. Employees want egalitarian treatment, but organizations are characterized by tall hierarchies, status differentials, and chains of command.

3. Employee commitment to an organization is increasingly influenced by the intrinsic value of the work itself, yet organization practices still emphasize material rewards and employment security, neglecting other employee concerns.

4. Employees want more attention to the emotional aspects of organization life, such as individual self-esteem, openness between people, and expressions of warmth, yet organizations emphasize rationality and seldom legitimize the emotional part of the organizational experience.[11]

The cost of negative feelings such as alienation may be high to the organization as well as to the individual. Walton suggested that "employee alienation affects productivity and reflects social costs incurred in the work place."[12] In addition to lost productivity, withdrawal behavior has real social costs for the organization as well as the individual. To summarize, most approaches consider individual autonomy, control and power over the work environment as basic preconditions for the removal of the state of alienation.

Stress. Since most adults spend at least half of their lives in work-related activities, social and psychological factors on the job, as well as physical conditions, may have a significant influence on employee health. One aspect of health directly related to these conditions is stress. Researchers have found that an increasing number of employees in America suffer from various symptoms which have been found to be related to stress.[13] These symptoms include interference with cardiovascular and gastrointestinal functioning as well as depression, insomnia, and irritability. Stress is caused by a combination of physical and psychological factors which can affect employee health, work effectiveness, and quality of life. Pinpointing the causes of stress has proven to be difficult, however. What may be a stressful situation to one individual may be inconsequential to another.

There is a potential for stress when an environmental situation is perceived as presenting a demand which threatens to exceed the person's capabilities and resources for meeting it, under conditions where he expects a substantial differential in the rewards and costs for meeting the demand versus not meeting it.[14] Within the work domain, stress refers to any characteristic of the environment which poses a threat to the well-being of the individual. There are at least two types of threat to the person: (1) demands which he may not be able to meet and (2) insufficient supplies to meet his needs. This discrepancy has been described as the degree of fit between the individual and his environment.

Sources of organization stress include lack of inclusion in the work group, changes in the organizational hierarchy, competition, and forms of role conflict, including ambiguity and overload (having too many roles). Table 1-2 presents several sources of stress resulting from the interaction between the individual and the environment. Hamner and Organ describe types of stress and then describe types of behavior which may be manifested as a result of the stress.

Although these descriptions are concerned with stress inducers *within* the work domain, the source of stress and its symptoms are not confined by this boundary. Conflicting role demands in the work and nonwork domains may be sources of stress for the individual. Further, stress induced in one region of experience may be displaced and manifested in another. For example, an employee under a stressful situation at work may take out his frustrations at home on his wife and children. On the other hand, stress introduced at home may be expressed as nonproductive or even destructive behavior at work.

It is clear that stress is a destructive force to the individual in terms of his personal health, and to the organization in terms of employee effectiveness. Organizations must recognize that stress is a problem and help employees to cope with stress by creating flexibility in situations in which employees are incapable of meeting all perceived obligations. Stress will continue to be a problem as long as organizations are rigid and inflexible in their demands.

Table 1-2   Sources, Forms, and Consequences of Psychological Stress in Organization.

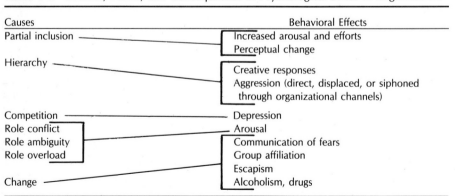

Causes	Behavioral Effects
Partial inclusion	Increased arousal and efforts
	Perceptual change
Hierarchy	Creative responses
	Aggression (direct, displaced, or siphoned through organizational channels)
Competition	Depression
Role conflict	Arousal
Role ambiguity	Communication of fears
Role overload	Group affiliation
	Escapism
Change	Alcoholism, drugs

SOURCE: Clay Hamner and Denins organ, *Organizational Behavior: An Applied Psychological Approach,* Dallas, Tex.: Business Publications, 1978, p.211. © 1978 by Business Publications, Inc.

NOTES

1. Flanagan, J. C. A research approach to improving our quality of life. *American Psychologist,* 1978, *33,* 138–147.

   Campbell, A., Converse, P. E., and Rodgers, W. *The quality of American life.* New York: Russell Sage Foundation, 1976.

   Dunnette, M. D., *Work and non work in the year 2001.* Monterey, Calif.: Brooks/Cole, 1973.

2. London, M., Crandall, R., and Seals, G. The contribution of job and leisure satisfaction to quality of life. *Journal of Applied Psychology,* 1977, *62,* 328–334.

3. Airis, B., and Barrett, G. V. Some relations between job and life satisfaction and job importance. *Journal of Applied Psychology,* 1972, *56,* 301–304.

   Kornhauser, A. *Mental health of the industrial worker.* New York: Wiley, 1965.

   Mansfield, R. Need satisfaction and need importance in and out of work. *Studies in Personnel Psychology,* 1972, *4,* 21–27.

   Near, J. P., Rice, R. W., and Hunt, R. G. Work and extra-work correlates of life and job satisfaction. *Academy of Management Journal,* 1978, *21,* 2, 248–264.

   Orpen, C. Work and nonwork satisfaction: A causal-correlational analysis. *Journal of Applied Psychology,* 1978, *63,* 530–532.

   Quinn, R. P., and Shepard, L. J. *The 1972–73 quality of employment survey.* Ann Arbor, Michigan: Institute for Social Research, University of Michigan, 1974.

   Quinn, R. P., Seashore, S. E., Mangione, T. W., Campbell, D. B., Staines, G. L., and McCullogh, M. R. *Survey of working conditions: Final report on Univariate and Bivariate Tables,* Document 2916–0001. Washington, D.C.: U.S. Government Printing Office, 1971.

   Stagner, R. *Humanizing programs: The impact of the affluent society.* San Francisco, Calif. Convention of the American Psychological Associations, August 1977.

4. Drucker, P. E. Baby-boom problem. *The Wall Street Journal,* February 5, 1979.

5. Yankelovich, D. Work values and the new breed. In C. Kerr and J. Rosow (Eds.), *Work in America: The decade ahead.* New York: Van Nostrand, 1979.

6. Dubin, J. Industrial workers' worlds: A study of the central life interests of industrial workers. *Social*

8. Cohen, A. R., and Gadon, H. *Alternative work schedules: Integrating individual and organizational needs.* Reading, Mass.: Addison-Wesley, 1978.

   Levinson, D. J. The mid-life transition: A period in adult psychological development. *Psychiatry,* 1977, *40,* 99–112.

   Schein, E. H. *1978 career dynamics: Matching individual and organizational needs.* Reading, Mass.: Addison-Wesley, 1978.

   Argyris, C. Personality and organization theory revisited. *Administrative Sciences Quarterly,* 1973, *18,* 141–167.

9. Levinson, D. J. *The seasons of a man's life.* New York: Ballantine Books, 1978, p. 6.

10. Kanungo, R. N. The concepts of alienation and involvement revisited. *Psychological Bulletin,* 1979, *86,* 199–138.

11. Walton, R. E. How to counter alienation in the plant. *Harvard Business Review,* November–December 1972, pp. 70–81.

12. Walton. How to counter alienation in the plant, p. 71.

13. Burke, W. W. (Ed.). *The cutting edge.* La Jolla, Calif.: University Associates Publishers, 1978.

French, J. R. P., and Caplan, R. P. *Organizational stress and individual strain: The failure of success.* New York: Amacom, 1972.

14. McGrath, J. E. Stress and behavior in organizations. In M. Dunnette (Ed.), *Handbook of industrial and organizational psychology.* Chicago: Rand McNally, 1976.

Stokols, B., Novac, R. W. Stokols, J., and Campbell, J. Traffic congestion, type A behavior, and stress. *Journal of Applied Psychology,* 1978, *63,* 4, 467–480.

Luthans, F. and Hodgetts, R. *Social issues in business.* New York: Macmillan, 1976.

Deehr, T. A., and Newman, J. R. Job stress and employee health. *Personnel Psychology,* 1978, *31,* 665–669.

Jenkins, C. D. Recent evidence supporting psychologic and social risk factors for coronary heart disease. *New England Journal of Medicine,* 1976.

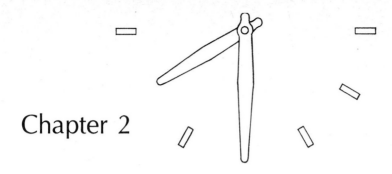

Chapter 2

Quality of Work Life and
Motivational Considerations

QUALITY OF WORK LIFE

The popularization of the movement for the improvement of quality of work life in America reflects the degree to which society has come to recognize the signs of employee discontent, such as alienation and stress, and changes in values, including the recognition of individual differences. The term *quality of work life* encompasses a full gamut of different approaches, prescriptions, and solutions for improving the total work environment with positive outcomes for the individual as well as the organization. It considers the organization as a sociotechnical system, integrating individuals and groups with the technology of goods and services offered. Thus, quality of work life refers to changes in both the sociology and technology of the work place. This suggests that the traditional antagonistic relationship between employer and employee needs reevaluation: quality of work life for employees and organizational effectiveness may not be mutually exclusive goals after all.

Defining Quality of Work Life

Researchers have attempted to define quality of work life more specifically by describing its components. For example, seven criteria for quality of work life have been described as:

1. Perception of adequate compensation

2. Safe and healthy working conditions

3. Opportunity to use and develop human capacities through autonomy, the acquistion of multiple skills, availability of information, performance of whole tasks, and opportunities for planning

4. Opportunity for continued growth and security

5. Social integration in the work organization, including freedom from prejudice, mobility, supportive primary groups, and interpersonal openness

6. Constitutionalism in the work organization, including privacy, free speech, equity, and due process

7. The social relevance of work, including social responsibility exhibited by organization members.[1]

These criteria focus on aspects of the individual's work experiences and work environment. In a similar vein, others have defined four principles which they feel are necessary to optimize employee well-being through the humanization of work. These include:

1. *Security:* freedom from fear and anxiety concerning health, safety, income, and future employment.

2. *Equity:* compensation commensurate with employees' perceived contributions

3. *Individuation:* conditions which will allow development of individuals' unique abilities and craftsmanship and will allow autonomy and learning

4. *Democracy:* a high level of participation by employees in decision making which involves their jobs and work environment[2]

Both sets of components described above include factors relating to conditions of employment as well as the work process itself. These may be considered the extrinsic and intrinsic aspects of the work domain. However, both typologies confine themselves strictly to aspects of the job or organization. Other approaches to the quality of work life focus on the characteristics of the individual worker. For example, quality of work has been defined as ''the degree to which members of a work organization are able to satisfy important personal needs through their experiences in the organization.''[3] This definition focuses on needs, and by implication, recognizes that needs will vary based on differences among individuals. Needs can vary both in terms of relative importance and level of satisfaction. Need theory would explain that these two aspects are related; that is, the less satisfied a need is, the more important it becomes. These two aspects of needs are reflected in factors in the work domain which influence the quality of work life. These factors are (1) those that affect the importance of a need to an individual and (2) those that satisfy or frustrate a need. The level of quality of work life is thus a product of the interaction between the individual's needs and the characteristics of the work environment.

The three viewpoints presented here describe criteria for the quality of work life on three levels: extrinsic aspects of the job or work environment, intrinsic aspects, and the needs of the employee. If the quality of work life is viewed as a product of the degree of fit between job aspects and individual needs, it follows that quality of work life must be assessed independently *for each employee.* For example, those in the same department working under the same manager cannot be assumed to have the same quality of work life. Individual differences with respect to needs, biological cycles, and factors from the nonwork domain all interact with those factors pertaining to the work domain, as described in the first two sets of principles above, to produce varying end results for each employee.

In the sections to follow, quality of work life will be presented in the context of a typical organization. Specifically, several activities which can be undertaken by the organization to improve the quality of work life are discussed, including participation, job redesign, and team building. These particular activities have been selected because they incorporate the concept of flexible scheduling as an integral part of their design.

Participation

Participation in the decision-making process has been widely recommended as a means of improving the quality of work life. However, when considering participation in the work place, one must differentiate between two levels. The first is horizontal participation, which means interaction between teams, co-workers, or peers. The second, vertical participation, is involvement in the decision-making process through interaction with one's superiors, and implies increasing vertical responsibility in areas otherwise controlled by the supervisor. Both types of participation are important components of the quality of work life. An organization which encourages both types will allow decision making at the lowest feasible hierarchical level, directly by the individuals affected by the decision, if possible. The implied goal is to provide an environment where an individual will have the freedom and autonomy to make choices which are related to his work environment and to improve the fit between his personality and the job demands as well as between his work and nonwork domains.

Participation in decision making strengthens the relationship between performance and the expectation of a satisfactory outcome through a better understanding of what the desired outcomes are and how they can be achieved.[4] Moreover, participation directs the energies of the employee work group toward the goals and objectives of the organization. A commitment to organization goals may result from the sense of ownership or proprietary rights achieved through the participation process. Perhaps most importantly, participation is consistent with American values such as equality, democracy, and individual dignity.

In granting the employee an opportunity to participate in the decision-making process, quality of work life is improved in two ways. First, the work environment is altered to a state which is more consistent with the employee's desires, because he has direct input or influence on the process itself, even if the sphere of influence is limited to his actual task or work group. Furthermore, the contribution of the worker representative or the collective opinion of the group can have influence far beyond that of the immediate work group. This is evident in the European concept of industrial democracy, or self-management, in which power is delegated to employees through participation in worker-management boards.

The second result of participation is the beneficial aspect of autonomy *itself*. In addition to providing the worker with greater control over his work situation, the opportunity to exercise autonomy is a source of self-esteem and actualization. There is little doubt that participation in decision making, as a means of exercising autonomy, has profound implications for the quality of work life.

Job Redesign

The need for efficiency in an industrialized society has resulted in the specialization of tasks and segmentation of work processes, necessitating high coordination and close control over employees. Research in the last two decades investigating the effects of this type of work environment on employee motivation, satisfaction, and performance has revealed negative consequences for the organization and a reduced quality of work life.[5] More recently, studies have demonstrated that there are ways to redesign jobs within the constraints of production requirements in order to enhance the quality of work life, while maintaining or increasing productivity.[6] The focus of the research has been on the need to increase the fit between the individual's personal characteristics and the job characteristics.

Job enrichment is a phrase used by many to describe aspects of job redesign which can activate desirable consequences. Typically, changes in the job under the rubric "job enrichment" include the assignment of additional responsibilities to employees for planning, setting up, and checking their own work; for making decisions about methods and procedures; for establishing their own work pace within certain limits; and for interacting directly with clients or other departments.[7]

Researchers in the field have described many elements of job enrichment or task restructuring. In one of the more well-known models, Hackman and Oldham have defined five components of job enrichment which they call *core job dimensions.* These include task variety, task identity (ability to relate the task to the whole), task significance, autonomy, and feedback. These job dimensions influence certain psychological states in the individual, which then result in personal and work outcomes such as internal work motivation, quality of performance, satisfaction, and low absenteeism and turnover. These outcomes have been summarized as the *motivating potential score* of the job, in an equation describing the interaction between the core job dimensions. This equation appears below:[8]

$$\text{Motivating potential score} = \left[\frac{\text{skill variety} + \text{task identity} + \text{task significance}}{3} \right] \times \text{autonomy} \times \text{feedback}$$

Providing job characteristics such as those described in this model will give individuals who wish it an opportunity for an experience which may enhance well-being through a fuller utilization of talents and capacities. Further, the greater degree of choice may enhance quality of work life through improved work-nonwork fit and an accompanying reduction in anxiety and stress. These choices will increase the opportunity for the individual to experience self-confidence, and derive self-esteem and fulfillment from his work.

Team Building

The scientific basis for the study of groups had its origins in the late 1930s with the investigations of social psychologist Kurt Lewin and his colleagues. They demonstrated that groups, through the perceptions and interactions of their members, take on a personality of their own. The group personality is characterized by such properties as cohesiveness, beliefs, values and norms, goals, and purposive direction. Group forces often override the desires of the individual member of the group. The dynamics of group interaction involve four important dimensions:

1. Common purpose or interest
2. Interdependence and psychological awareness of each other
3. Norms and values unique to the group which regulate the behavior of the members
4. Leadership style

The effectiveness and successful functional process of the group is largely a result of these variables.

The formation of groups, or teams, at work can be an important form of job enrichment for the individual. The Tavistock Institute in England has conducted extensive research on groups at work and their functioning within the context of the technology of the work place. Their invention of the phrase *sociotechnical systems* is an acknowledgment of the importance of aspects of social and group interaction as well as the technology of the work process. Their technique focuses on ways to alter work processes to encourage the team to maximize cooperation and enable members to learn a variety of skills, with the efficient production of the final product as the ultimate objective.

Additional Forms of Organizational Change.

Additional forms of organizational change which can be considered improvements in the quality of work life are profit sharing and stock options, participatory management and worker democracy, and management by objectives. One of the most inventive of the new ideas is the cafeteria-style fringe benefit plan, in which employees may put together their own packages of benefits, vacation time, and stock options, depending on their life-style and needs. In the following section we will examine a most important innovation in the quality of work life, flexitime.

Flexitime

Thus far we have described participation, job redesign, and team building as techniques for improving the quality of work life. These techniques focus on improvement through the alteration of the job itself to accommodate individual needs. However, the fact that individuals may vary in their needs is not sufficiently considered. Some sort of contingency design or flexibility within core job dimensions might help to improve outcomes for the individual and the organization by improving the fit between individual needs and job characteristics.

Although this concept may sound unfeasible, it is precisely the idea behind flexitime. Instead of the job design itself, flexitime focuses on the work schedule. It assumes that employees have differing needs and allows them to vary work schedules accordingly, within certain ranges and dimensions. Work hours may be varied in terms of the number of hours worked each day, depending on the type of schedule implemented, and in terms of when these hours are worked.

By allowing the employee to create a better fit between his individual needs and the work environment through scheduling, many other aspects of the work experience are affected. Flexitime has the potential to influence the degree of autonomy experienced by the employee through increased participation in decision making. Group cohesiveness and group orientation toward the organization's objectives may be enhanced, as employees find it necessary to interact in a cooperative mode to maintain work processes.

Further, in addition to its potential to improve the quality of work life, flexitime can help to improve the fit between the work and nonwork domains of the employee. The impact of flexitime on other aspects of work activity—specifically, its impact on the motivation level of the employee—is explored in the following section.

MOTIVATIONAL IMPLICATIONS OF FLEXITIME

Introduction

Thus far, we have emphasized that the individual holds certain values as a member of society at large as well as desires and expectations of the work organization. The fulfillment of these values and needs in the work and nonwork domains helps to determine the quality of life experienced by the individual. Since individuals vary with respect to these values and needs, they will vary in terms of what motivates them. This has important implications for motivating the individual in the organization. If management wishes to influence the employee's motivational system, it must understand the needs and values which prompt him to act with a certain level of force or energy in a given direction. Whether one explains it in terms of need theory, expectancy theory, or any of a host of other theories, it is essential to view the motivation process as unique to each individual. In many cases, motivation level is assessed for an entire work group or organization, as one might assess morale. Our perspective treats motivation as a reflection of one aspect of the individual's fit between needs and values in the work and nonwork domains. If the organization understands these needs and values, it will be better able to motivate the employee by energizing his efforts. The remainder of this chapter develops some of the theoretical aspects of flexitime and its potential for helping the organization to consider the individual in the motivation process.

Within the work domain, characteristics of the job can usually be classified into two categories: intrinsic and extrinsic. These categories are considered to be two different kinds of rewards or sources of motivation for the individual. The concept of *extrinsic outcomes* derives its impetus from incentives and rewards associated with the work setting, the job environment and conditions, and the tangible rewards such as pay and fringe benefits. For the attainment of these goals and rewards, the job is only an instrument, or interim step. In Maslow's hierarchy of needs, extrinsic rewards which would influence motivation levels are those which gratify basic needs of the individual, such as adequate shelter, food, and material goods, security benefits, and social interaction.[9] Herzberg calls these extrinsic aspects *hygienes,* and includes job components such as salary, work conditions, job security, company policy, supervision, interpersonal relations, and status. Unfulfilled expectations concerning these aspects are major contributors to job dissatisfaction.

Intrinsic outcomes are derived from the individual's willingness to invest effort in his job because he values the rewards and incentives that come to him through the performance of the work itself rather than the rewards (such as benefits) for which the work is instrumental. Herzberg calls intrinsic job factors *motivators,* as opposed to hygienes. Job factors which are considered motivators include the work process itself, achievement, autonomy, possibility of growth, and responsibility. Whereas hygienes can be sources of dissatisfaction, motivators can be sources of satisfaction. Within this dichotomous framework, we can investigate the effects of flexitime on the motivational system of the employee.

Extrinsic Outcomes

In the simplest sense, individually arranged flexible hours provide extrinsic rewards because basic work conditions are improved. For example, the employee may be more comfortable traveling to and from work because he can adjust his work schedule to avoid rush hour traffic or meet transportation schedules more easily. The employee can also come to work early or stay late, if he so desires, in order to take advantage of the quiet periods at the beginning and end of the workday, when the office is less crowded. Flexitime can reduce the anxiety associated with tardiness because the employee no longer has to be concerned with reprimands, or loss of pay or benefits. The reduction of tardiness should also help to improve interpersonal relations within the work group, specifically, supervisor-employee relations. Eliminating one aspect of the supervisor's authority role—the necessity for enforcing tardiness rules—may help to reduce friction between these two groups. (However, this factor can be effective only if supervisors are prepared to relinquish control in this area.)

When evaluating extrinsic rewards in the work environment as sources of motivation, it is important to note that in most organizations, these rewards are granted to the individual using criteria unrelated to individual performance. That is, the allocation of extrinsic rewards is usually not contingent upon the efforts of the individual. These extrinsic rewards are related to membership behavior instead of performance behavior. The individual is granted pay, security, insurance, and other benefits for being a member in good standing of the organization. This situation is probably most familiar in organizations which are unionized. For example, the most typical criterion for increased pay under a union contract is length of service; promotability is often determined by seniority.

With this in mind, the message transmitted by the organization to the employee through the adoption of flexitime is an important one. Under a fixed schedule, a premium is placed on membership behavior, specifically, punctuality and attendance, because of the necessity as perceived by management for monitoring this behavior. Membership behavior receives attention because it is the first step in achieving productive behavior, is more easily measured than productive behavior, and consequently is easier to reward. The unfortunate result, however, is a management focus on presence instead of performance. Under a flexitime system this focus should change: membership behavior becomes less of a criterion for reward. By allowing the employee to determine his own schedule, the organization delegates the responsibility for attendance to him, thereby eliminating the monitoring function of the supervisor. (This depends, of course, on the level of flexibility implemented by the organization.) The end result is a shift in focus from membership to performance behavior. This shift can be especially effective if the organization emphasizes that an important purpose of flexitime is to allow the individual to perform more effectively, and if it is able to change its reward structure to be more contingent upon performance. In contrast, the fixed time arrangement causes punitive rather than rewarding conditions. An employee is expected to arrive and leave on time, although he is rarely rewarded for it, but rather is punished if tardiness or short-term absence is too frequent. The responsibility delegated to the employee to set his arrival time and to be accountable for performance rather than punctuality has greater potential for a positive and more motivating reward system.

Flexibility in the working schedule may have an influence both on the structure of the job and on the fit between work and nonwork domains experienced by the individual. For some individuals, fit may represent minimal commitments at work and maximum commitments to the nonwork domain. Alternatively, others may concentrate their involvement at work, while still others try to minimize sacrifices in each domain. This view recognizes the fact that for some employees, work provides a major source of gratification, while for others, work is instrumental in satisfying other needs, such as pay, security, and social interaction.

From this perspective, flexitime accommodates the individual, wherever his needs may lie. The potential of flexitime to improve the individual's perception of his working conditions may thus improve his affective reactions, including level of identity with the organization. The outcome of this improved fit can be more positive attitudes such as increased job satisfaction and improved organizational climate. This implies an improvement in membership behavior, or a decrease in withdrawal behavior.

There is one negative aspect of flexitime with respect to its reward value. Research has demonstrated that most extrinsic rewards have a temporary effect on employees. For example, pay is quickly taken for granted as deserved by the employee, losing its value as a reward. Increases in pay have reward value at the time they are granted (depending, of course, upon the conditions of the raise), but reward value diminishes over time as the employee adjusts his perceptions and escalates his expectations regarding his new level of compensation. In light of this, the benefits of flexitime which are perceived as extrinsic—such as improved job conditions—may have a temporary effect. However, this should occur only when the system is fully accepted within a geographic area. According to equity theory, as long as the employee can compare himself favorably to others outside the organization not on flexitime, the perception of flexitime as a reward should be encouraged, and the positive effects felt toward the organization for implementing flexitime should remain.

Intrinsic Outcomes

Flexitime may be considered an intrinsic outcome for employees because the program increases employee responsibility, autonomy, and potential for personal growth. As mentioned earlier, Herzberg calls these aspects motivators. In terms of Maslow's need hierarchy, these factors contribute to the satisfaction of the higher order needs: esteem, autonomy, and self-actualization. More specifically, improvements in the intrinsic factors of the job stem from the following processes:

Increased autonomy and responsibility

Task accomplishment

Consideration of an individual as a holistic entity

Increased participation

Improved feedback

Reduction in cognitive dissonance

Increased job involvement

The Exercise of Autonomy and Responsibility.   The employee is given the opportunity to exercise autonomy in choosing his work schedule as well as in having the responsibility to ensure that the work is produced or task performed adequately and on time, within the chosen schedule. It should be clear, however, that the employee has autonomy over *when* he completes his work, but not over what he actually *does,* although flexitime may give the organization incentives to indirectly provide this latter kind of autonomy also. Increased autonomy can be a factor in helping the employee to fulfill self-actualization needs. The employee can alter his work schedule to accommodate the work process, coordinating the activities which are important to his growth, whether work related or external to the work environment. In this situation, the employee has the autonomy to make decisions, based on his own needs, whether they are internal or external to the organization and to his job requirements. The granting of autonomy is an acceptance of the fact that individuals have different needs and sources of rewards stemming from various aspects of work and life domains. The organization, by implementing flexitime, expresses trust in the employee and considers him a responsible agent. He controls his own schedule and is responsible for his own membership behavior.

Task Accomplishment.   Related to the concepts of autonomy and responsibility is the idea of task accomplishment. We mentioned earlier that flexitime reinforces performance instead of membership behavior. This focus on performance, along with the opportunity to choose a work schedule, allows the employee to plan his schedule in order to achieve certain objectives and goals, instead of planning around fixed events such as lunch or coffee breaks. Aside from eliminating the frustration of awkward points of interruption, the employee is given the opportunity to experience the sense of accomplishment associated with task completion. The ability or opportunity to plan time around task accomplishment is critical to the experience of intrinsic rewards from the work process.

Gratification of the Need to Be Treated as a Whole Person.   This means the recognition of needs in the nonwork domain as well as in the work environment. The holistic view of the employee implicitly recognizes individual differences. Flexitime is consistent with a holistic approach because it lets the employee include considerations arising from the nonwork domain in his decision making concerning work scheduling. The self-concept of the employee may be enhanced through the recognition of important needs outside the organization as well as at work, allowing him to cope more effectively with his life demands.

Participation—Especially Vertical—in the Decision-Making Process.   Increased cooperation and interaction between employees and supervisors may help improve relations through behavioral, attitudinal, and value changes on both sides. Participation encourages this interaction, resulting in more consistent goals and objectives in both groups. If employees have had the opportunity to participate in decision making, even in work scheduling, chances are greater that they will be committed to making the decision work through their own contributions. Thus, for the individual, participation means a better understanding of, and identification with, organization goals, enhancing feelings of accomplishment and improving employee-supervisor relations. Needless to say, this can also contribute to organizational effectiveness.

Feedback.   Feedback is an important aspect in the motivation process because it informs the employee whether his efforts are resulting in desired performance levels. Furthermore, feedback can be a form of intrinsic reward by itself, especially if the individual is highly involved in his job. Flexible work schedules have the *potential* to alter the nature of the feedback process through a change in styles of supervision. The fact that the supervisor's schedule may not exactly coincide with the employee's means that continuous monitoring is no longer possible. The supervisor must learn to delegate responsibility to accomplish a task to the employee and then provide feedback regarding the extent to which the goals were met. Feedback is thus associated with task accomplishment instead of less consequential interventions such as timekeeping throughout the course of a work period.

Reduced Cognitive Dissonance through the Resolution of Conflicting Values. The socialization process in our society emphasizes the importance of self-determination and freedom of choice. Within the organization, however, the individual is expected to behave as a dependent organization member; that is, at the most basic level, he exchanges the right to self-determination within the organization for a salary. As a consequence of socialization processes, the employee's self-image is that of a responsible adult, capable of managing his own time. This may contradict the organization's perception of him as an employee governed by the structure and rules to perform certain work processes within certain time frames. The employee must accept these conditions and internalize the values of the organization if he is to be a successful and effective member. Such conflicts in values or expectations experienced by individuals have been labeled *cognitive dissonance* by Festinger.[10] According to his theory, a person may experience dissonance when he maintains two contradictory cognitions or value systems. Dissonance is a stressful condition which must be resolved; the desire to reduce stress can be considered an internal state which motivates the individual.

In most organizations as they currently exist, the reduction of dissonance means either the rejection or diminished importance of either individual values or organizational values. Either of these alternatives would be destructive: the full acceptance of organizational reality may require a reduced self-image and impaired self-esteem; on the other hand, rejection of organization values implies a negative or aggressive reaction toward the organization, which comes to be perceived as an unjust agent.

Flexitime may help to reduce dissonance and the resulting anxiety in a less destructive manner than either of these two alternatives. The autonomy granted through the flexitime system reduces the threat to an employee's self-image by allowing some level of personal choice within the organization. The organization's perception of its employees as individuals, as represented by the decision to implement flexitime, may help to strengthen and reinforce self-esteem. In addition to reducing dissonance, the recognition that work behavior ought to be more consistent with the employee's needs and values may result in increased intrinsic job satisfaction, since negative feelings no longer interfere with the intrinsic experience of the work process. This potential reduction in dissonance also means improved organizational climate and an increased commitment to the organization itself. In general, individuals who perceive the availability of a higher level of choice in their actions will react with a higher level of satisfaction about their work behavior and its outcomes. It may be expected that such persons will be highly involved in their tasks and committed to the organization.

Job Involvement. Job involvement has been defined as the degree to which employees are ego-involved in their job, or the extent to which work is considered a central life interest. Using our domain concept, we may consider job involvement in terms of the contribution of the work domain to the overall quality of life experienced by the individual. In general, job-involved employees are considered to be highly motivated, taking pride in their actions. The components of job involvement have been summarized as consisting of personal characteristics and job characteristics.[11] The two personal characteristics usually associated with job involvement are self-esteem and ego-involvement. Both of these may be enhanced by providing the individual with the opportunity for self-determination at work. Highly intrinsically motivated employees are those who expect to satisfy the human needs for being competent and self-determined. Since job involvement is considered desirable, and autonomy contributes to job involvement, flexitime can be a possible enhancer of job involvement through its ability to increase autonomy. To the extent that flexitime recognizes individual differences and encourages control over scheduling, as well as over the work process, it can encourage job involvement.

If we consider an individual's self-image to be associated with the opportunity for self-determination, then the level of freedom provided to an individual in his work scheduling will greatly enhance his self-image. In general, we consider the job-involved person to be highly motivated, with a tendency to experience feelings of pride in his actions. To facilitate conditions conducive to the motivational aspects discussed, a supportive climate is necessary.

ORGANIZATIONAL CLIMATE

Organizational climate is seen as an enduring quality of the internal environment, specific to the organization, experienced by all members.[12] It is associated with the perceptions of employees about various attributes of the organization and its subsystems, as well as attributes of organization members. Some of the attributes used by researchers to measure climate have included:

1. Opportunity to participate in decisions concerning aspects of the job process, such as style of work, control of time, and sequence of tasks

2. Level of autonomy, responsibility, and independence

3. Degree of structure, consideration and support provided/imposed by supervisor—leadership style

4. Rewards provided by the organization and the attitudes of employees to these rewards

5. Opportunities for growth and development

6. Level of communication and dissemination of information

Others have grouped aspects of climate into three groups of organizational variables: structure, task activities, and interpersonal relations. These two categorizations of variables are quite similar, except that the former places heavier emphasis on aspects of employee growth and self-development.

Within this framework, to the extent that flexitime positively influences attributes of climate such as autonomy and participation in decision making, it can contribute to an improved organizational climate. More directly, flexitime has the potential to improve task activities and structure through job enrichment, and it will certainly influence interpersonal relations, especially those between supervisor and employee.

SUMMARY

In this chapter, we have tried to show how changes in societal values have created an emphasis on the development of the individual, and have led to a recognition of the problems facing him as he attempts to cope with increasing pressures in his life domains. These factors have been instrumental in the shift toward a focus on the person as a unique entity whose special needs must be considered by the work organization as well as by society. From there, we went on to describe the concept of quality of work life and some of the components which can help to improve the work domain for the individual. Flexitime was introduced as a quality of work life innovation that incorporates an acceptance and accommodation of individual differences into the work environment. As such, it has the potential to influence individual and organizational outcomes. For example, organizational effectiveness can be improved through the potential effects of flexitime on intrinsic and extrinsic outcomes, increasing employee motivation. Various sources of motivation were categorized into intrinsic and extrinsic components of the reward system. Other outcomes resulting from flexitime implementation are improved attitudes through the recognition of individual differences and the focus on the personal development of the employee.

Employees are satisfied to the extent that working conditions fulfill valued needs. It is suggested here that those employees for whom flexible schedules provide desirable conditions will experience greater job satisfaction. And indeed, this result has been verified. Moreover, flexitime implementation may help to improve membership behavior in terms of turnover and attendance. This type of behavior is closely related to attitudes—as job attitudes are improved, membership is likely to improve. Another consideration is the *direct* impact of flexitime on membership behavior. The elimination of tardiness and the granting of flexibility in the work scheduling shifts the focus away from membership to performance.

Figure 2-1 is a model representing the interaction between the influences on the organization and on the individual, and the potential outcomes resulting from the implementation of flexible work schedules. Organizational factors are subdivided into two general categories: climate and technology. Individual factors include value systems, family commitments, socioeconomic status, and leisure and recreational activities, among others.

Environmental influences represent inputs to the organization as well as to the situation of the individual. Outcomes are listed for both the individual and the organization as a result of the work process. Flexible work schedules can be considered a moderator, or catalyst, in the process through which the work organization and individual combine to achieve their desired ends.

The focus of this approach is the recognition that providing conditions for individual growth and reinforcing it may lead to improvements in the effectiveness of the organization while simultaneously providing an improved quality of work life for the individual through changes in behaviors as well as attitudes. Thus, it creates an atmosphere where *individual goals and organizational goals may coincide.* Such a progressive work environment, which will both enhance the fulfillment of individual goals and increase organizational effectiveness, requires a managerial philosophy that can provide the appropriate organizational climate. Flexitime may be an appropriate means to achieve a climate consistent with these goals because it helps to introduce *at all levels* in the organization the values necessary for quality of work life improvements. These values include the concepts we described earlier such as increased autonomy and participation in decision making, a holistic approach to the employee and his needs, and increased intrinsic rewards from job performance through job involvement and accomplishment. Results

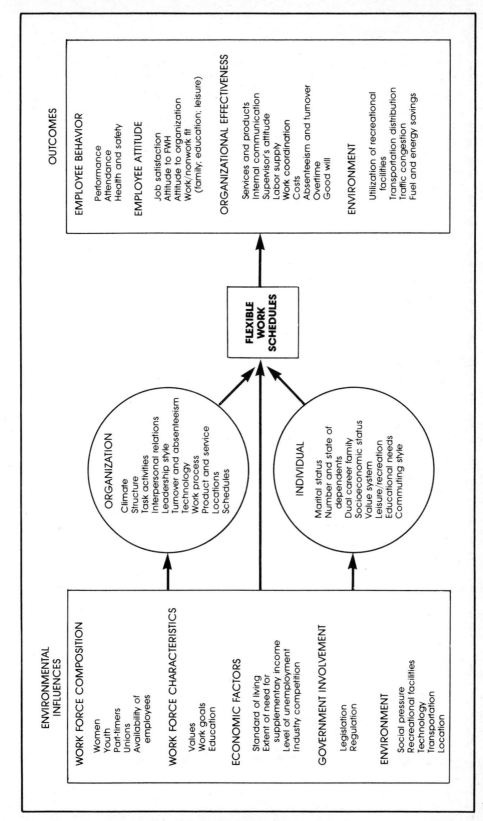

Figure 2-1 Antecedents and consequences of flexible work schedules.

consistent with these claims are reported in the findings from the public and private sectors (see Chapters 10 and 12).

Flexitime should represent to management an expression of a changing environment and a focus on individual needs. It is not, however, a technique to be considered in isolation. Implementing flexible work hours has to be viewed within the perspective of a supportive organizational climate conducive to *both* individual employee satisfaction *and* improved organizational effectiveness. Improvements in these two aspects can also have broad implications for society through the potential for a better quality of life.

NOTES

1. Walton, R. E. How to counter alienation in the plant. *Harvard Business Review,* November–December 1972, pp. 70–81.

   Walton R. E. Improving the quality of work life. *Harvard Business Review,* May–June 1974, p. 12.
2. Herrick, N. Q., and Maccoby, M. Humanizing work: A priority goal of the 1970's. In L. E. Davis and A. B. Cherns (Eds.), *The quality of working life.* New York: Free Press, 1975.
3. Suttle, J. L. Improving life at work—Problems and prospects. In J. R. Hackman and J. L. Suttle (Eds.), *Improving life at work.* Santa Monica, Calif.: Goodyear, 1977, p. 4.
4. Straus, G. Managerial practices. In J. R. Hackman and J. L. Suttle (Eds.), *Improving life at work.* Santa Monica, Calif.: Goodyear, 1977.
5. Sheppard, H. L., and Herrick, N. Q. *Where have all the robots gone?* New York: Free Press, 1972.

   Katzell, R. A., and Yankelovich, D. *Work, productivity, and job satisfaction.* New York: The Psychological Corporation, 1975.
6. Hackman, J. R. Work design. In J. R. Hackman and J. L. Suttle (Eds.), *Improving life at work.* Santa Monica, Calif.: Goodyear, 1977.
7. Herzberg, F., Mausner, B., and Snyderman, B. *The motivation to work* (2nd ed.). New York: Wiley, 1959.

   Herzberg, F. *Work and the nature of man.* Cleveland: World Publishing, 1966.

   Hackman, J. R. Work design. In J. R. Hackman and J. L. Suttle (Eds.), *Improving life at work.* Santa Monica, Calif.: Goodyear, 1977.
8. Hackman, J. R., and Oldham, G. R. Development of the job diagnostic survey. *Journal of Applied Psychology,* 1975, *60,* 159–170.
9. Maslow, A. H. *Motivation and personality.* New York: Harper, 1954.

   Maslow, A. H. A theory of human motivation. *Psychological Review,* 1943, *50,* 390–396.
10. Festinger, L. *A theory of cognitive dissonance.* Evanston, Ill.: Row, Peterson, 1957.

    Festinger, L., and Carlsmith, S. M. Cognitive consequences of forced compliance. *Journal of Abnormal and Social Psychology,* 1959, *58,* 203–210.
11. Rabinowitz, S., and Hall, D. T. Organizational research on job involvement. *Psychological Bulletin,* 1977, *84,* 265–288.

    Rabinowitz, S., Hall, D. T., and Goodale, J. G. Job scope and individual differences as predictors of job involvement: Independent or interactive? *Academy of Management Journal,* 1977, *20,* 273–281.
12. James, L. R., and Jones, A. P. Organizational climate; A review of theory in research, *Psychological Bulletin,* 1974, *81,* 1096–1112.

James, L. R., and Jones, A. P. Organizational structure—A review of structure dimensions and their conceptual relationship with individual attitudes and behavior. *Organizational Behavior and Human Performance,* 1976, *16,* 74–113.

James, L. R., Hater, J. F., Gent, M. J., and Bruni, J. R. Psychological climate column—Implications from cognition social learning theory and interactional psychology. *Personnel Psychology,* 1978, *31,* 783–813.

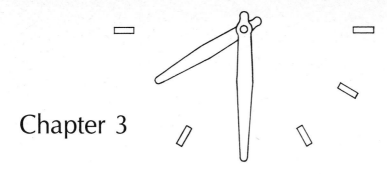

Chapter 3

Basic Definitions

INTRODUCTION

The concept of flexible working hours, or flexitime, appears in many forms, facilitating its adaptation to the unique needs of different organizations. The main objective of the method is to create an alternative to traditionally fixed work schedules through a system which grants the employee a certain freedom to choose his times of arrival and departure. The degree of variation possible in this choice is usually defined by the organization. The simplest variation of the system allows the employee to determine starting and finishing times within a certain time range set by the employer, provided that the employee works the contracted daily attendance hours. Conditions governing the degree of flexibility may include the total number of hours the company is operative during the day, the hours an employee is required to be present, and the level of interdependence between jobs, between departments, and with suppliers and customers.

It should be emphasized here that the choice given to the employee is restricted to variations in times present at work and the distribution of working hours, but does *not* apply to the total number of working hours required by the employment contract. This condition remains unaltered and is mandated by the organization. Further, flexitime will *not* alter current management policies regarding vacations or sick leave allowances.

CORE TIME

Core time refers to the mandatory attendance hours during which all employees are required to be present on the job. This block of time, established by the organization, does not apply to those who are ill, on vacation, or away on company business. The primary purpose of core hours is to establish times when normal channels of communication between individuals in the organization are open for the exchange of information. It also provides minimum coverage hours for servicing customers, dealing with the public, and scheduling deliveries from suppliers.

Instead of a continuous core time, extending throughout the entire day, greater flexibility can be provided by the organization if the core time is split into two periods, one in the morning and one in the afternoon, affording a flexible lunch period. The concept of two core times allows employees to extend their lunch break to several hours or to limit it a minimum amount of time (usually ½ hour). This variation allows employees to go home for lunch, attend to family chores, or go shopping. A more extreme option, called core time deviation (CTD), allows absence during core time. Usually the employee must obtain the supervisor's authorization for CTD and is required to make up the time within the same day during the flexible portion of the day. It should be stressed that absences during core time should be permissible only in cases of urgent personal need in order to ensure a minimum of abuse and preserve the purpose of core time.

FLEXIBLE TIME BANDS (FLEXBANDS)

Flexbands are periods of time during the workday during which employees may determine their own schedules of work time, provided they meet the firm's requirements for total hours on the job. Flexbands occur at the beginning and end of the day, and sometimes on either side of the lunch period. A typical flexband schedule is illustrated in Figure 3-1.

The length of the flexband determines the amount of flexibility allowed employees. For example, an organization may demand that employees work a total of 8 working hours daily and provide three flexbands—one in the morning (7–9 A.M.), one at lunch (12–2 P.M.), and the third at the end of the working day. If this third flexband extends from 3:30 to 7 P.M., an employee wishing to leave early in the afternoon could start his day at 7 A.M., take only ½ hour for lunch, and complete his working day at 3:30 P.M. Another employee might begin working at 9 A.M., take the 2 full hours for lunch, and complete his day at 7 P.M. However, the organization may wish to limit this last band to 2 hours, for example, from 4 to 6 P.M. Under this restriction, employee A cannot leave work before 4 P.M. and therefore may begin

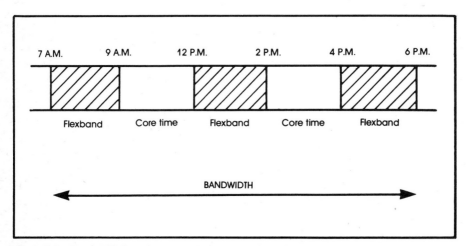

Figure 3–1   Bandwidth for a firm open 11 hours per day.

at 7:30 P.M., with ½ hour for lunch, or at 7 A.M., with 1-hour break. In this case, employee B, who started working at 9 A.M., is limited to a 1-hour lunch break if he is to complete the required number of hours of working time.

One more option for flexibility concerning the flexband, especially if the flexband is wide, is to allow the employee to take time off *within* the flexband. In other words, an employee may arrive at work, work for a period of time, leave work, and return all within a flexband. The approval or permission of the supervisor for absence during flexband periods is not usually required.

LUNCH BREAK

The traditional fixed working day provides for a fixed lunch break when the company stops most operations to enable employees to eat, rest, and refresh themselves. Although the laws in many states provide for a minimum of ½ hour for lunch for full-time employees, many organizations provide more than the minimum, scheduling 45-minute or one 1-hour lunch breaks. Flexitime systems allow variations in the type of midday breaks as follows:

Staggered Lunch Break

Different groups of employees stagger their lunch break period, providing station or office coverage throughout the day and relieving congestion in cafeteria facilities. Lunch times are either preassigned by the organization or decided by the members of a work team, but usually these assignments are permanent.

Semiflexible Lunch Break

The organization defines a shutdown period when all employees are required to stop work. Flexbands are established both before and after this required lunch break. The fixed period is not necessarily equal in length to the minimum lunch break prescribed by the organization. For example, the fixed period could be ½ hour, while the minimum period is 45 minutes. Any time worked during this fixed lunch break is not added to the employee's recorded hours of attendance. Semiflexible lunch schedules are often instituted to ease cafeteria overcrowding.

Flexible Lunch Break

A flexible lunch break requires that the organization define a midday flexband between two core periods. An employee is free to choose both the length and time of his break, as long as it falls between any minimum (usually ½ hour) and the maximum of the lunch flexband (usually about 2 hours in most organizations). Such a schedule is illustrated in Figure 3-2. This system is popular among workers since it allows them to use their lunch break to best suit their life-style. Some employees reduce their break to the minimum in order to be able to arrive later or go home earlier. Other workers who prefer to eat at home, schedule appointments, or go shopping during lunch benefit from the full 2-hour flexband. Another aspect of the midday flexband is the ability to schedule the time as well as duration of lunch. This allows employees to plan their lunch in order to avoid crowded eating facilities, or to meet friends from other organizations with different schedules. Finally, it allows employees to eat when they are hungry, instead of having to wait until a preassigned time.

WORKDAY SPAN (BANDWIDTH)

The working day span refers to the number of hours that the company is open, from the beginning of the morning flexband to the end of the evening flexband. The working day span can vary from 8 hours to a maximum of 24 hours. An 11-hour bandwidth is shown in Figure 3-1. The bandwidth, or the day span, is an important factor contributing to the level of flexibility of the system. Considerations governing the length of the bandwidth will be discussed later.

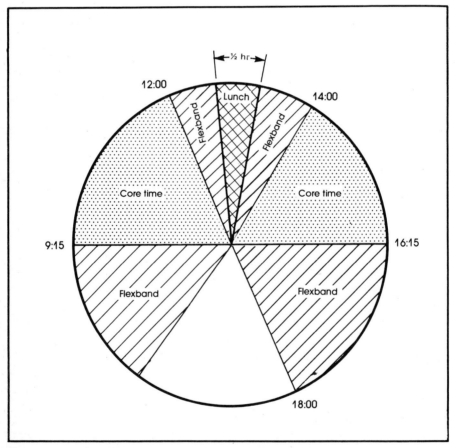

Figure 3–2 A chart illustrating one variation in flexible work schedules. In addition to the two flexbands at the beginning and close of the day, there is a flexband on either side of the required ½ hour lunch.

CONTRACTED ATTENDANCE HOURS

The variations in working schedules and the extent of the system's flexibility do not affect the basic total contractual attendance hours as stipulated in the individual contract of employment or relevant collective agreement. Employees are allowed to choose their preferred schedule within the options provided, as long as the completion of the contracted number of hours is guaranteed.

The idea of a contract implies a negotiation between the employer and the employee with some level of input from the employee. In most organizations, however, this is not the case. The contracted attendance hours are accepted as part of the work environment and responsibilities which an employee accepts in return for a wage or salary.

SETTLEMENT PERIOD

Under an FWH (flexible working hours) system, the actual number of hours worked may not exactly reflect the number of hours contracted to be worked within a specific period of time. The period over which the contracted number of hours must be delivered is called a settlement period. Depending on legal, contractual, and organizational constraints, the settlement period may vary from 1 working day, in which an employee has to work 8 hours, to a week or even a full month, or longer, which allows for conditions of maximum flexibility. Under a settlement period of 1 week, an employee must put in the contracted attendance hours (40 or 37 ½ hours are typical, depending upon the organization and the job).

The settlement period can be different from the accounting period, which is simply the standard of time used by an organization for the administrative purposes of calculating the wages of employees. For example, employees may receive their paycheck every 2 weeks (the accounting period), but must resolve their working hours each week (the settlement period). However, it is convenient to have the settlement period coincide with the accounting period used for calculating the employee's salary.

In flexitime systems where the settlement period exceeds 1 day, an array of options becomes available for the individual employee. Fundamentally, this flexibility results from a provision which allows the employee to work an undesignated number of hours during the day, provided he or she is present during the assigned core time. He or she may be absent during the flexband hours, working only during the core times, or present during both the flexbands and core time to compensate for absence on another day within the settlement period. The only requirement under these terms is the completion of the contracted hours by the end of the week.

CARRY-OVER (BANKING)

A desirable provision of the flexible working hours system allows an employee to carry over debit or credit hours from one settlement period to another. If, for example, the settlement period is 1 week and the contracted number of hours for this period is 40, the organization may allow its employees to work only 35 hours in one week and compensate for the debit of 5 hours during the next week by working 45 hours. These 5 debit hours are made up during the flexband periods.

Credit balances occur when an employee works for more than the contracted hours required and has no debit hours to make up. Credit balances are not overtime, but additional hours worked during one settlement period in exchange for hours taken off in subsequent periods. In most systems, employees must take their credit hours during the flexbands. For example, if an employee has a 4-hour credit in an organization which has a core time of 10 A.M. to 3 P.M. and requires 40 hours per week, the employee may choose to arrive at 10 A.M. on one day, take an hour lunch break, and leave at 3 P.M., working the equivalent of a 4-hour day. Or, he may choose to arrive at 8 A.M., take an hour lunch, and leave at 3 P.M. on 2 days during the week. He cannot, however, use his credit hours in the core time of 10 A.M. to 3 P.M.

Some organizations allow their employees the additional flexibility of being absent for one of two core periods during the day. This usually applies to organizations with two core periods and a flexible lunch hour. Workers thus have the right to a half day off, using their credit and debits within a settlement period.

The most flexible systems grant the employee the opportunity to take an entire day off, using banking. For example, if an employee has worked 40 hours by Thursday, he may take Friday off. Or, if he has worked 38 hours by Thursday, he may take Friday off and incur a 2-hour debit carried over into the following week, or settlement period. These types of credit leaves are granted only if the total number of credit leave units taken in a settlement period does not exceed a certain total which is predetermined by the organization. Note, however, that in order to implement such a system, flexbands must be wide enough to allow employees to accumulate sufficient credit hours during the settlement period.

The last variation can be equated with the popular compressed week schedule or 4-day workweek which has been experimented with widely in the United States. Permission to exercise this option may be incorporated into the flexitime system, but it usually requires approval by the immediate supervisor.

OVERTIME

The different possibilities of work scheduling require a clear and precise description of conditions which constitute overtime. Traditionally, overtime is defined as the time worked beyond the *normal* starting and finishing times, at the request of a supervisor. However, unlike fixed or staggered work schedules in which overtime can clearly and simply be defined, based on predetermined employee starting and quitting times, the definitions of overtime in a flexitime situation may take various forms, depending on the particular system in use. Overtime hours and appropriate compensation can be included in the system, but management and the employees should clarify and agree fully on the conditions which constitute overtime. An oversight or dispute on this issue may introduce volatile conditions which could threaten the smooth and satisfactory implementation of the system.

The requirements for determining overtime situations may include either or both of the following:

1. Initiation and authorization of overtime by supervisors

2. Predefined hours during the day which are charged as overtime either for an individual or for a work group as a whole
   The supervisor usually negotiates with the individual or the group to determine what these hours will be. Some organizations work out systems to define overtime hours according to deviations from average starting or quitting times, but these systems must be made known to employees in advance of the hours worked.

   Type and style of compensation for overtime should include one or more of the following:

1. Pay according to legal or contractual overtime rate

2. Credit hours to be added to the normal credit-debit balance for the settlement period

3. Credit hours to be deposited in a "special credit balance" from which credit leaves can be taken
Sometimes these credit hours are credited as time and a half or double time for overtime worked, in a similar manner as a wage rate.

   The complexity of defining overtime increases with the degree of flexibility allowed by the firm. In a flexible workday, presence at work may vary depending upon the flexband. For example, U.S. government employees, under present law, are limited to 8 hours of work daily as straight time. Any additional working hours in one day constitute overtime, since banking is not allowed. (A 1978 act provides for extended experimentation with flexitime and the compressed workweek in the federal work force.)

VARIABLE HOURS

This term has been assigned to a flexitime scheme where core time is not defined at all, although this variation may still incorporate other constraints such as the bandwidth. For example, a company may define a bandwidth of 6 A.M. to 6 P.M., and an appropriate settlement period, such as 8 hours daily, or 40 hours weekly. Within this bandwidth, an employee could come and go at any time, as long as he met the contracted number of hours required for the settlement period. It is most common to find this level of flexibility in a highly "organic" type of organization in which workers are extremely independent of one another in their task assignments and performance. A research and development firm would provide this type of environment.

TIME RECORDING

A time recording system is necessary to provide an accurate record for the employee *and* the employer of the actual hours the employee has worked within a specified period of time. Management has the responsibility to ensure that the employee has worked the contracted number of hours and that the laws governing the minimum and maximum number of working hours are enforced. Time recording also provides a basis of information which can be used in the settling of disputes over credit or debit balances. This protects the employee as well as the employer.

There are four alternatives which should be carefully evaluated when choosing a time-recording system. These alternatives are manual recording using time sheets, a time clock, a meter, or a computer-based system. Although a detailed description of time recording can be found in Chapter 19, a brief description of each type of recording system is included here.

A manual time-recording system usually means a daily or weekly log sheet on which each employee records his starting and stopping times. This information is then compiled by settlement period and by group or department for accounting purposes.

The simplest form of mechanical recording is the time clock and clock cards which employees use to "punch in." The chief advantage of the time clock system is that it provides a mechanical means of logging time while minimizing capital expenditures, although many employees resent having to clock in.

The concept of time recording using a meter has been the most popular and successful of recording systems used by companies implementing flexitime. The meter system provides a cumulative record of the amount of time worked within a settlement period. Further, it is popular with employees because the cumulative number avoids the invasion of privacy associated with a time clock, where starting and stopping times are registered.

Computerized attendance-recording systems represent the current state of the art in time recording. In a typical system, each employee has his own personalized plastic badge, similar to a credit card, which he inserts into a data terminal designed to read the coding on the badge. The computer then logs the time worked. This information is provided periodically to management and employees in the form of a computer printout.

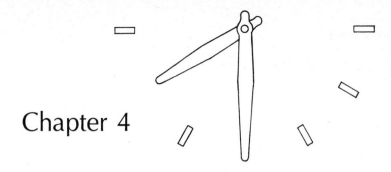

Chapter 4

Variations of Work Schedule Systems

INTRODUCTION

When considering the variations in the flexitime system, we shall categorize the alternatives within the context of legal and contractual constraints on overtime, as these are the major limiting factors in flexitime system design. In general, these constraints, insofar as overtime is concerned, are based on requirements that wage premiums be paid to certain employees who work in excess of defined work periods. They can be categorized into three broad areas:

1. Overtime premiums for work in excess of a stated number of *hours per day* (e.g., federal employees up to GS 10)

2. Overtime premiums for work in excess of stated *hours per week* (e.g., employees in private firms covered by the Fair Labor Standards Act)

3. No overtime premium for extra hours worked (e.g., management personnel)

Other constraints include shift differentials and Saturday, Sunday, and holiday premiums. (The full implications of legal limitations and new legislation are discussed in Chapter 18.)

These categorizations limit the application of the flexible working hours system in various ways. The first group, the "8-hour employees," can be permitted variations in FWH within one working day. The second group, the "40-hour employees," may benefit from variations allowing the carry-over of either debit or credit hours from one day to another, provided that 40 hours, or the specified contracted hours, are completed by the end of the workweek.

Paradoxically, the procurement of overtime pay for excess daily working hours, considered an achievement by unions, is now an obstacle to granting federal employees and those under union contract an important privilege which is in the interest of members and could be an improvement in working conditions.

VARIATIONS WITHIN A WORKING DAY
(8 HOURS)

The deciding factors for the level of flexibility of the system are management and employee needs and legal and contractual constraints. The length and number of core time periods per day and the length of the bandwidth are measures of the level of flexibility implemented within these constraints and considerations.

Fixed Working Schedule

The traditional working day, which is still the schedule for the majority of employees in the Western industrial world, is based on fixed starting and finishing times. In flexitime terminology, this schedule consists of perhaps 8 hours of core time with no flexbands. There are, however, a few minor variations within the 8-hour core time schedules.

Group Staggered Time.   In order to reduce the problems resulting from overly congested lines at the punch clock at starting and finishing times, long waits for elevators, and traffic jams in parking lots, various service and production organizations have assigned different starting times to different departments working at the same location. The assignment schedules for groups of employees are usually made by management—there is little or no employee choice involved. Differences in schedules may be based on 5-, 15-, or 30-minute intervals in arrival and departure times. Planning may include considerations such as elevator loads, the assignment of parking spaces, and traffic movement; for example, an FIFO system (first in is first out) might dictate parking assignments. Often, firms schedule arrival and departure times not only to alleviate congestion at the work site but to allow employees to avoid rush hour problems, whether they utilize private or public transportation.

One should note here that staggered time, although able to solve certain problems for the individual and his organization, does not consider private and family needs. For example, husbands and wives may now be on different schedules. This can cause difficulties in community and social commitments and may mean that they have less time to spend with each other and with their families. With co-workers arriving and leaving at different hours, car pool problems may be created. Problems with transportation may also arise if employees use buses or trains which run on specific schedules. For example, after the establishment of staggered hours, an employee may not leave the work site before 5:50 P.M., yet his train may leave at 5:45 P.M.

Staggered Lunch Break.   To avoid crowded facilities, elevator overload in large office buildings, and the crowding of neighborhood restaurants and coffee shops, management may wish to assign different lunch hours to different departments. In this case, the length of the lunch break is constant and varies only in starting time. The intervals between lunch schedules for various groups may range from a few minutes to half an hour. Employees may also be required to stagger their lunch break in order to provide constant job coverage throughout the day, thereby ensuring continuity in a particular process or service.

Staggered Time during the Summer Season.   A few organizations provide a different working schedule for the summer season. These variations may include earlier arrival and, therefore, earlier departure times. Many possibilities are feasible for summertime work schedules, although these variations are still institutionalized changes which basically require fixed attendance hours.

Variable Schedule

In this model, employees are permitted to determine their starting and quitting times within certain limitations. The decisions may be made individually or in groups. After employees have chosen their alternative, that schedule becomes fixed for a preassigned period—usually the duration of the accounting period. Under the Office of Personnel Management (formerly the U.S. Civil Service Commission) guidelines, this type of schedule is termed a *tour,* although it has also been called *selected tour* or *flexitour.*

Group Variable.   This variation applies to groups of employees constituting a department or an integral office unit. All members of this group must arrive and depart at the same time, based on the predetermined variable schedule. The department head is generally responsible for ensuring that these variable time arrangements are in accordance with overall production requirements.

Individual Variable.   In this variation, each individual employee chooses his schedule for the next accounting or preassigned period. Teams of employees may have to coordinate their chosen alternatives to accommodate interrelated work processes. The employees themselves must consider the level of interdependence of working conditions and arrive at the final schedule through negotiation and mutual consideration. In the public sector, the Office of Personnel Management terms this variation, *individual tour.* In most cases, the final arrangement requires approval by the supervisor involved in the particular situation.

Individual Flexday Model (Floating Day)

This variation allows each individual employee to choose his daily arrival hour within the flexible band specified by the organization. The employee does not have to receive supervisory approval ahead of time and is free to choose the starting hour of each separate day as long as he works no more than 8 hours. There are a few subvariations within this alternative.

Fixed Lunch Break.   The gliding working day (called *Gleitzeit* in Germany) allows an employee to choose a starting time within a flexband. Since the lunch break is fixed, this means that there is a single core time which starts at the end of the morning flexband. If the organization designates a specific time and length of the lunch break, the starting hour chosen by the employee for a particular day will determine the time when he finishes his workday.

In case of high task interdependency or a need for continuous coverage of a service or process, the employees involved in a team are responsible for the coordination of their times of arrival and departure. This arrangement can be voluntary, or a rotating schedule can be devised to solve the problem. Although such a task seems to necessitate a high level of interaction and cooperation, the threat of losing the privilege associated with this advantageous system helps employees to solve these problems with a minimum of difficulty or conflict.

VARIABLE LUNCH BREAK.

A more advanced level of flexibility allows the employee to decide the time and duration of the lunch break within certain limitations. Usually, a minimum period is prescribed by the organization.

Double Core Periods.   In order to further accommodate individual needs and desires, certain organizations or departments have provided two core time periods each day, allowing a third flexband in the middle of the day. Usually, firms provide a midday flexband of 2 hours, enabling an employee to take a lunch break which typically extends from a minimum of ½ hour to a maximum of 2 hours. This arrangement provides employees with the opportunity to join their families for lunch, go shopping, keep appointments, or participate in athletic activities. Employees may now attend to their own needs on their own time, without supervisory permission and without the guilt feelings associated with being a few minutes late or having to take time off the job. Management has decreased causes of pressure, anxiety, and stress, and has eliminated what is often an unpleasant atmosphere on the job by giving employees more control over their time off the job.

No Core Time.   A high level of flexibility may be provided by an organization which does not impose any core time constraints as long as the employee fulfills his obligation to work 8 hours daily. This variation may provide a maximum level of flexibility through a bandwidth extending to a full 24 hours. Although such a bandwidth would afford maximum flexibility for the individual employee who has to work 8 hours daily, the successful implementation of such a schedule would be difficult.

Overtime Compensation

The preceding discussion of the variations within an 8-hour working day was based on the assumption that carry-over of credit or debit hours from one day to another is unacceptable to management. The chief reason for this is that a debit of 1 hour in one day may not equal a credit granted on the next day. In other words, the ninth working hour in one day is appraised as more valuable to the employee (overtime compensation) than the eighth hour. Still, it is conceivable that management would agree to such an exchange and allow an employee to carry over credits or debits with the provision that the ninth hour is credited on a ratio basis, for example, 150 percent of the eighth hour, if the law permitted it.

VARIATIONS WITHIN A WORKING WEEK
(40 HOURS)

Under the present laws, many employees in the private sector in the United States who are entitled to overtime payments for any number of hours worked over 40 in 1 week receive a premium on their wage or salary. This provision enables a certain level of flexibility between days by allowing an employee to compensate by working fewer hours in one day for extra hours worked in another during the week. Therefore, finishing time is no longer related to starting time. The possibility of debit or credit hours carried over from one day to another provides a much higher level of flexibility and self-determination for the working individual. Like the 8-hour variations, the level of flexibility within the week can be different for various departments of the same organization. The levels of flexibility within the week are the same as those for the single day, with the exception of the carry-over option. Listed from least flexible to most flexible, these options include one core period daily with a fixed lunch, lunch break with a midday flexband, two core periods, and no core time. (See Figure 4-1.)

The maximum number of carry-over hours allowed from one day to another is designated by the organization and must be consistent with aspects of the flexitime system such as the width of the flexbands and the range of the bandwidth. The individual employee is responsible for keeping track of accounted hours (with the help of a form to fill out or a recording device) so that at the end of the week he will have worked the contracted hours required.

Day Off—Compressed Week

The organization may allow the employee a half day or even a full day off to use up accumulated credit hours. This means that the organization allows the employee to be absent during core time. This variation of flexitime is similar to the alternative work schedule known as the compressed week (i.e., 10 hours a day for 4 days). This schedule has been

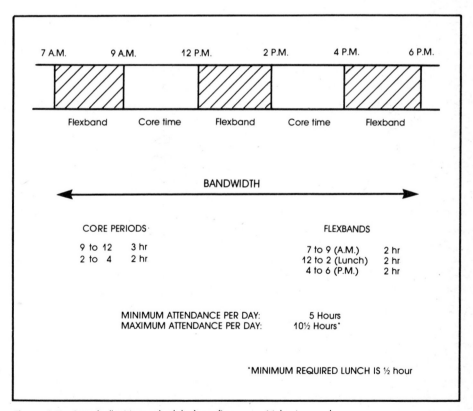

Figure 4–1 Sample flexitime schedule for a firm open 11 hours per day.

experimented with quite widely in the United States, where the intention was to provide an additional free day to employees, especially during weekdays when offices, shops, and medical services are open for business. The compressed workweek has been criticized on the grounds that the long work hours required on a regular basis cause strain and fatigue. It must be emphasized that if any employee chooses to work a compressed week under flexitime, it is his choice. Furthermore, the 4-day workweek, in which the day off is predetermined, lacks the flexibility of a schedule which allows the individual to choose the free day. Under flexitime, the employee may choose his day off, within certain restrictions, as well as the hours he wishes to put in to accumulate his 40 hours.

An organization which allows core time off may choose to limit the particular day an employee may opt to be absent by designating *core days.* Typical core days are Tuesday, Wednesday, and Thursday: employees *must* be present during core hours of these days.

Another way to limit core time off is to limit the number of absences during core time periods within a settlement period. For example, if there are two core time periods per day or ten per week, employees may be permitted to be absent for two out of the ten core periods. This would mean that 2 half days, or 1 full day may be taken during the settlement period.

Weekend Redefined

A highly flexible system allows employees to choose an alternative to the weekend, even to the extent of taking it during the middle of the week. Just as an organization may expand its bandwidth to include many hours each day (e.g., 6 A.M. to 8 P.M.), it may expand the discretionary time available to employees beyond 5 days, Monday through Friday, each week. In this case, employees would be able to choose to schedule their working days among any of the 6 or 7 days the facility is open. Employees may decide to schedule their "weekend" during the middle of the week, or contiguous to one of the traditional weekend days. For example, because facilities are often crowded on Saturday—entertainment places, zoos, beaches, tennis courts, department stores, and resorts are unapproachable—it might be appealing for the employee to schedule his weekend for Sunday and Monday. In smaller towns, one may find a necessary office or service closed for the entire weekend. Resorts may be congested and difficult to get to because of heavy traffic. A weekday off may offer great opportunities for individuals who are willing to consider Saturday as a regular working day (many department stores already do). In a system with maximum flexibility, the employee could conceivably take 3 days off in a sequence (assuming that core time can be taken off), and then even combine these days with the following Saturday and Sunday and benefit from a 5-day holiday combining two "weekends" into one. Of course, this means going a longer period without a day off. This option is possible only in organizations that have their facilities open continuously, 7 days per week.

A MONTH AS A SETTLEMENT PERIOD

The accounting period may coincide with the settlement period in some organizations, although this is not a prerequisite for the implementation of flexitime. The accounting period —the period from paycheck to paycheck—is usually 2 weeks or, occasionally, 1 month.

Under this variation, carry-over of credit and debit hours from one week to another is allowed within limits (usually between 5 and 15 hours can be banked). This arrangement is highly flexible and has been favorably accepted by many employees in Europe. If it is not against legal or contractual regulations, banking of hours within a preassigned limit from one month to another is permissible and even recommended.

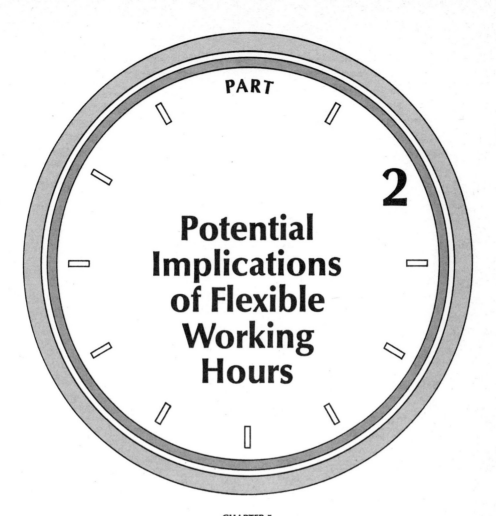

PART

2

Potential Implications of Flexible Working Hours

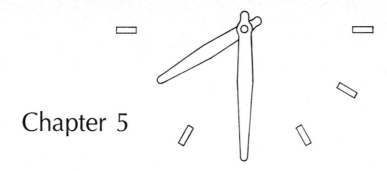

Chapter 5

Advantages and Disadvantages for Employees

ADVANTAGES

Introduction

When evaluating the impact of flexitime on the worker, one must remember that the quality of work life affects the individual's total life situation. Factors which influence the worker's quality of work life include the task, the physical work environment, the social environment within the work situation, the administrative system of the company, and the relationship between life on and off the job.[1] Flexitime can have a significant impact in each of these areas, resulting in change (improvement) in the quality of life, both on and off the job, for the worker.

A work environment increasingly dominated by technology has meant the acceptance of worker alienation and disorientation as the price paid for more jobs and higher wages. Socioeconomic norms have been evolving to resist these developments, however. Significant numbers of workers are protesting actively through their unions or other advocates, or passively via their work product and productivity levels. They are unwilling to work in a dehumanized setting where they are considered "a replaceable part."

This problem is not confined to the blue-collar worker. The time is approaching when disaffection with the nature of the job will be as widespread among white-collar workers as it has been among blue-collar workers. In order to promote productivity and efficiency, principles derived from scientific management, systems analysis, operations research, and other techniques traditionally applied in the industrial setting have been used to evaluate white-collar jobs. Computer technology and office automation have contributed to the problem by routinizing many types of white-collar jobs. The end result is that the atmosphere in many white-collar jobs resembles that of the assembly line.

Further advances in technology mean that routine activities are becoming automated, causing job insecurity and concern over job availability. Accelerating changes in technology mandate the development of flexible workers and organizations capable of adjusting to and accommodating change as a continuing part of working life.

Flexitime, while not a panacea for these concerns, can have a significant impact by improving the quality of life for both the blue- and white-collar worker. The impact of flexitime is felt in two broad areas: (1) improvement in the quality of work life derived from a degree of personal control over the work environment (which is increasingly out of the worker's control) and (2) an improvement in the quality of life outside work because of the ability to adjust one's work life to accommodate a personal life-style. Flexitime provides the employee with greater freedom because it allows him to determine his working schedule within certain limits, according to his personal needs. Not only is the employee granted the right to decide, but he is also given the privacy of not having to explain or account for his decision, so long as it remains within the bounds set by the company. This twofold freedom can help to offset the negative aspects of technological change described earlier. Specifically, flexitime can help the worker (and the organization) to deal with feelings of job alienation. Involvement in decision-making processes and in the teamwork which is necessary to coordinate flexible hours can make the worker feel that he is an active participant in the organization instead of an anonymous "replaceable part." The routinized aspects of certain jobs can also be reduced, as flexitime gives the worker some control over his time on the job and his schedule for the completion of tasks.

Work Environment

Bioclock.   It is now widely recognized that individuals vary in their psychological and physiological needs. Not only do the needs of the individual vary from other individuals, but these needs vary within the individual during the day. Most organizations, however, have either failed to recognize this aspect of the individual or chosen to ignore it. The result is that the organization places a higher priority on appropriate membership behaviors, that is, behaviors associated with attendance, than on actual performance. In other words, higher priority is placed on reporting to work, preferably on time, than on working efficiently and productively once there. The introduction of flexitime reverses these priorities: performance is emphasized over membership behavior. By defining a range of appropriate membership behavior, the organization allows the employee to choose the behavior—specifically, attendance patterns—which are most appropriate for him. A system of flexible working hours thus allows some degree of adjustment to variations in the individual's bioclock. The employee can adjust his work schedule to his own pace of life.

For instance, some employees prefer to sleep later in the mornings and may spend the time between 9 A.M. and 10 A.M. at work in a semisomnolent state; on the other hand, there are those employees who are up at the crack of dawn but may begin to fade by 4 P.M. Under flexitime, both can arrange their workday to better conform to their own biological clock. They are more likely to work effectively during the hours they are present if they have some control over deciding what these hours are. Flexitime also means that if an employee is out particularly late at night, or is tired, he can come in later in the morning and proceed to work effectively and efficiently from the moment he arrives. Under a nonflexible system (or a less flexible system), the same employee would either arrive on time and work at less than top efficiency, or would be tardy or absent.

Because the employee can choose the working hours which coincide with his efficiency cycle, he will be more alert, and take greater interest in his work. When the employee arrives at work, he is ready to begin. As a result of this and other factors, work climate can improve because workers feel healthier, more energetic, and better able to contribute more to their job.

Transportation. When organizations define the workday for their employees, they do not include travel time to and from the work place as part of the workday. This time is considered part of the employee's free time. The employee may choose to live a great distance from work, traveling a long way each day in order to have the opportunity to benefit from suburban life. (A recent newspaper article reported that 1.3 million workers travel 50 miles or more to work each day.) Or, he may prefer to live near his place of work. The other major aspect of time spent traveling is the method of transportation utilized. Public transportation can be faster or slower depending on its convenience to home and work, and the level of traffic congestion along the route.

There are several ways in which the implementation of flexitime improves the transportation situation for the worker. Employees traveling on public transportation may be able to schedule their traveling at off-peak hours, avoiding crowding and realizing the savings of off-peak ticket prices. Further, the employee may be able to schedule better connections, reducing waiting times for trains or buses. Those traveling by car at off-peak hours avoid traffic delays and reduce associated pressure and tension. Traveling is safer during less congested periods of the day, and can take significantly less time. It may become possible for the worker to form car pools with neighbors or co-workers who previously worked on different schedules. Cost savings can be quite significant if it means that a family can now function with one car instead of two. Finally, traveling—especially driving—can be arranged to avoid extreme and dangerous weather conditions.

All of this can mean a significant improvement in the quality of free time for the worker. By minimizing the unproductive time associated with commuting, the employee has more free time to spend as he wishes outside the work environment. He may be better able to schedule his work hours around the needs of his family—for example, enjoy breakfast with his children, drop them off at school, or give his wife a ride to work. The overall result is an improvement in the quality and quantity of time spent *outside* work.

Tardiness. Tardiness has been a continual and irksome problem faced by many organizations. For workers, the pressure to be on time is intensified by the possibility of disciplinary action by the firm, such as a note on the employee's personnel record, a warning from management, or even docked pay or reduced time off. Such actions are often associated with embarrassment and even shame for the employee. This, combined with the responsibility which most employees feel toward fulfilling their job, means that being late to work can be a guilt-producing, anxiety-filled experience. This guilt is reinforced by the demoralizing experience of having to account for one's whereabouts to the supervisor.

Within the organization, the cycle of tardiness, possible disciplinary action, and guilt are, in a sense, a waste of time and energy which could be devoted to productive activity.

Tardiness or membership behavior is not related to on-the-job productivity but to attendance at work. Productivity is affected only indirectly, as less time is actually spent on the job when the employee is late to work. It is a misplacement of goals for both the organization and the individual to focus such energies on membership behavior rather than on task completion. But too often, it seems, organizations and individuals place greater emphasis on attendance and other associated behaviors.

Flexitime eliminates the concepts of tardiness and punctuality. Because the workday for an employee starts when he arrives, the missed train or the unexpected traffic jam no longer means tardiness. Because of the elimination of the need for controls for punctuality, the stress caused by a need to reach work on time or by fear of being late for an appointment or engagement outside work is removed.

However, there remains one form of tardiness which may occasionally be a problem to the organization. This problem may arise when an employee arrives for work during the core time. The organization must decide the seriousness of this offense and clearly define possible disciplinary action to employees. One suggestion is to require employees to make up this time on a double time basis. For example, if the employee arrives 15 minutes after core time has begun, he would be required to work ½ hour extra to make up for this time. Note that the shorter the core time period, the less likely it is that this would be a problem.

With the virtual elimination of tardiness, the quality of life for the employee is improved in several ways. First, the employee is given the opportunity to decide his own hours, eliminating the unpleasant necessity of having to explain his lateness. Second, the number of stress situations with which the employee must deal are reduced. Third, the guilt and embarrassment associated with tardiness are eliminated. Finally, in the case of those workers who would be docked pay for tardiness, flexitime can mean no more reductions in wages.

For the organization, the reduction in tardiness has significant benefits as well. The supervisor is relieved from the burden of having to monitor the arrival times of employees and deal with offenders. Relations within the work group can be improved because the friction between those who are punctual and those who are chronic offenders is eliminated. Finally, both the organization and the worker are able to refocus their efforts on the appropriate goal—the completion of the task—instead of expending emotional and economic resources reinforcing appropriate membership behavior.

Nonpaid Overtime for Exempt Employees.   Many management and upper-level employees work long hours for which no overtime is credited or received. In the past, this has been expected of management, and compensated for by the status of being a member of management. Further, company policy usually dictated that staying late in the evening was no excuse for being late to work the next morning.

At the very least, with the implementation of flexitime, the additional hours worked by management employees are recorded and reported to the personnel department. These employees would, therefore, be credited with the additional time worked. Further, because exempt employees are subject to the same time-recording system as nonexempt employees, extra time worked is measured, and commensurate time off may be taken later (up to certain limits and as long as banking is allowed) instead of being donated to the firm. This does *not* necessarily mean that the time off is granted at overtime rates, however (see discussion of overtime in Chapter 18).

Work Performance

Planning and Teamwork.   The implementation of flexitime can have a direct impact on work performance, primarily because of the demands it makes on the employees in an organization. A major demand is made in terms of planning and teamwork, particularly in service organizations and organizations in which the tasks performed are continuous processes.

In the case of service organizations, employees must be available to deal with clients throughout a defined period of the day, which is usually longer than the core time. This requires that employees coordinate their schedules in order to ensure complete coverage. Planning can be imposed by the organization or can originate from the workers themselves. If planning is imposed by the organization, flexibility available to the employees is reduced. In order to minimize this disadvantage, the organization should attempt to limit its imposition of control to the minimal level. For example, it might be possible to rotate responsibility for coverage during early morning hours on a daily or weekly basis. The employee assigned to this coverage would lose his flexibility for this period, while other employees in the unit would be free to utilize the flexitime privilege as they desire. It is preferable, however, to give employees the opportunity to plan required scheduling themselves. This additional responsibility and opportunity for decision making reinforces the concept behind flexitime —the emphasis on the individual within the organization. Furthermore, it requires the work group to develop the cooperation, teamwork, and group problem-solving facility necessary to be able to deal with this new responsibility. The work group will be motivated to develop these skills in order to maintain these newly acquired freedoms and avoid the imposition of management control. In many cases, the problem of scheduling may be easily solved if one worker plans to arrive at an early hour or leave late each day under flexitime. In situations where maintaining coverage means more of an inconvenience for employees, the supervisor should be aware of group interaction and be alert to the possibility of one employee dominating others, or of another employee being taken advantage of. If planning is successfully handled by the work group without intervention from management, the skills acquired by the group in decision making and problem solving can be expected to have an impact in other job areas. A significant improvement in the quality of work life can result for the employee as he exercises his new rights. Moreover, the organization benefits as efficiency and productivity improve. At one firm, studies showed that morale had improved because of the sense of team spirit which developed; employees felt that they belonged to an identifiable group.[2]

Flexitime is more difficult to implement in continuous process operations such as assembly lines, and consequently planning and teamwork become even more critical. In fact, these aspects become the main prerequisite for successful implementation. If the system is successful, employees can experience benefits similar to those described for a service organization.

Efficiency and Task Completion.   Research has shown that many individuals will make strong efforts to complete tasks which they have begun, and that the act of completion itself is a rewarding experience to many employees. Through flexitime, the organization can play a major role in facilitating this reward by creating conditions in which the individual is able to experience the satisfaction of completing a task. Having experienced this type of reward, the employees should be motivated to repeat the experience, knowing that he will be credited not only with hours worked, but also with the completion of the project.

Flexitime helps to improve the quality of working life by making the experience of task completion more available to the employee, if not actually encouraging it. Under flexitime, it is possible to credit the employee for extra hours worked by *employee choice* in a day. (Overtime premiums would not apply if it were the employee's decision to work more than the usual number of hours.)

Workers would not have to stop in the middle of a job because it is quitting time, put equipment away and clean up the work site, and then waste precious time in the morning setting up the task and getting under way again. This advantage applies to both blue- and white-collar workers—a manager can finish a report, a secretary can finish a typing assignment, or an assembly line can finish a batch of goods.

Increased Job Knowledge.   As a corollary of the increased planning and teamwork required when implementing flexitime, many workers have significantly increased their job knowledge relating to their own tasks as well as the tasks of others. In order to maximize flexibility, many employees agree to cover for one another, both horizontally and vertically within the organization. They may be required to accept additional responsibility when peers or superiors are absent. In order to do this, employees must be willing and able to exchange job functions and roles. As a result, employees develop skills and abilities which would otherwise be denied them. Not only is advancement opportunity improved, but the boredom and staleness associated with repetitive tasks are reduced as well.

Furthermore, this type of activity encourages the members of a work group to utilize their group decision-making skills, requires cooperation, and reinforces teamwork. Often, job knowledge requirements have opened previously nonexistent communication channels among workers. Some organizations have been cognizant of this phenomenon and have encouraged it through formal training programs. However, it is recommended that management monitor this type of activity carefully in order to ensure that unqualified personnel are not accepting positions of responsibility.

According to one company, "the program has forced us to develop people who have knowledge of more than one job. Therefore, job knowledge has increased dramatically".[3] Increased job knowledge for employees can result in higher ratings (rated skill levels), which makes them eligible to bid on more highly rated jobs in a union environment. In both union and nonunion environments, the employee can demand better wages based on his increased job knowledge and the resulting increased value to the company.

Home-Work Relationship

Family, Social, and Recreation Activities.   Flexitime often effects tremendous change in an individual's family and social life by effectively increasing the amount of leisure time available through a more convenient or appropriate schedule. Increased control over when leisure time is available can have a significant impact on the structure of family life. Many of the traditional family roles—the husband as breadwinner, the wife as housekeeper (or homemaker) and babysitter—have been reinforced by rigid schedules of working hours. In a typical family, the husband leaves early in the morning, is gone all day, and arrives home so late that he has little opportunity to interact with his children. The wife assumes the responsibility of delivering the children to school, picking them up, performing household chores, and cooking the evening meal. Flexitime provides the opportunity for the husband to participate in these activities. For example, he might leave later in the morning in order to have breakfast with his children and drive them to school, he might schedule a longer midday break in order to go home for lunch, or he might leave work early in the day in order to be able to spend more meaningful time with his family. For the wife, benefits include a husband who is more active in family life and able to share some of the responsibilities previously delegated to her, assuming, of course, that he chooses to do so! (See Chapter 16.)

If both husband and wife are employed, they can adjust their starting and finishing times to one another or to their children's school schedules. They can coordinate their nonwork time to maximize efficiency in performing required household chores. In cases where parents must take time off from work to attend to the needs of their children—e.g., doctor's appointments, parent-teacher meetings, school functions—flexitime can help by giving the parent the opportunity to participate in these activities without having to lose time at work.

Because the employee has choice concerning his leisure time, a host of new possibilities can be considered. For example, recreational areas can be utilized during nonpeak or daylight hours, and social activities and hobbies which were previously impossible to consider become feasible.

When we described the variations possible in a flexible working hours system, we mentioned the concepts of core time and the floating weekend. Core time off means that the employee may take half or full days off from work. The implications for leisure time are numerous. Perhaps most important, the employee may create large blocks of time for hobbies, social clubs, community activities, and sports. Or this time may be combined with the weekend for early getaways or late returns, extending weekends into minivacations. The idea of the floating weekend may mean grouping two weekends together for a longer vacation, and utilizing recreational facilities or resorts during off-peak periods. In addition to increased enjoyment of facilities which are not overcrowded (e.g., seaside resorts), the employee may realize cost savings because of midweek reduced rates at resorts (see Chapter 7 for further discussion).

Shopping and Appointments.   Flexitime provides the opportunity for individuals to shop, do errands, and have doctors' appointments within the context of a normal workday. This can be a major advantage to employees who have had to use vacation days or personal time off (and, in some cases, lose wages for time away from the job) to conduct this type of activity. This can be a particular advantage to working couples with children who require this type of attention.

Education.   Educational opportunities may arise as flexible scheduling results in access to courses previously unavailable to employees because of fixed work hours. Employees may be able to attend classes during their lunch hour, early in the morning, or late in the afternoon, depending upon core hours. If the organization allows core time off, educational activities could be pursued at any time during the day. Organizations may wish to encourage continued education in fields which would help the employee perform his job more effectively by paying for all or a portion of the tuition. As a result, both employees and the organization will be enriched as employees gain additional knowledge and skills.

DISADVANTAGES

Economic

Possibility of Reduction in Overtime Earnings.   Many firms implementing FWH have experienced reductions in the number of hours of overtime worked by nonexempt (nonmanagement) employees. Although a benefit to the firm, this can represent a decrease in income for the employee. This can, in fact, become a serious problem for the worker if the overtime was regularly scheduled and budgeted as a relied-upon source of income.

A major concern of employees and many unions has been that a reduction in overtime is likely to occur because of management-imposed pressures on the worker to schedule his time according to the needs of the firm. This pressure may be overt, in terms of limiting the worker's choice of hours over and above those embodied in the formal flexitime agreement, or they may be more subtle. The employer might indicate the schedule the employee should "volunteer" to work, threatening him with sanctions, either directly or by implication, if he should "choose" otherwise. For example, employees could be made to feel that pay raises and promotions would be determined by being available at straight time pay when management dictates. The decision still remains with the employee, but the implications of the decision are far more significant. Regardless of whether the situation is perceived as coercion, employees will feel resentment toward the system and its probability of success will be diminished.

Even under a flexible working hours system, there can be legitimate needs for overtime —e.g., during periods of heavy work loads, seasonal trends, backlogs of work. Overtime rules must be carefully defined by the firm in order to avoid disadvantageous results for the employee.

Employees Not Included in Economic Benefits Realized by the Firm.   In addition to the problems created for workers by the reduction in income resulting from reduced overtime hours, a source of controversy between labor and management has been the redistribution of benefits resulting from flexitime. Many firms have realized savings through productivity rises and better use of capital assets with the implementation of flexitime (see Chapter 6). Workers, and especially labor unions, have questioned the rationale for permitting management to retain all residual benefits from the introduction of the system. In their view, insofar as higher productivity results from a more intensive use of labor, at least part of the resulting gain should be distributed to the workers in the form of higher earnings, bonuses, profit sharing, or improved benefits such as increased paid vacation or improved medical insurance.

Loss of Personal Absence Privileges.   In many firms, employees are routinely granted time off with pay for personal needs, such as doctors' appointments, which cannot be scheduled during nonbusiness hours. This paid time off can accumulate significantly during the year, depending upon the leniency of the firm. It thus represents an economic commodity to the employee.

One of the chief advantages to the firm, when implementing flexitime, is the reduction of paid personal time off. Concomitantly, it can also be viewed as a disadvantage to employees. Under flexitime, the employee is allowed to use the flexbands for personal time off, but must ensure that these hours are made up during other flexbands. Time away from the job is no longer absorbed by the company as "unproductive" or "lost" time. Since the company is no longer the benefactor under flexitime, the employee must work a predefined number of hours (excluding banking) during the settlement period, regardless of appointments, personal business, or problems.

In contrast, however, many employers permit employees to take personal time off, but dock their pay for the hours not worked. These employees may well see flexitime as an advantage which gives them the opportunity to take occasional time off without having to sacrifice their income level.

Scheduling

Since the total work force is available only during core time, problems with scheduling are inherent in flexitime and can affect communication, supervision, and task performance, especially if tasks are highly interdependent. Firms which provide services to companies are particularly susceptible to these types of problems. Placing limits on participation or level of flexibility seems to be the most feasible solution to the problem.

Exclusion of Workers from Participation.   Certain types of employees within firms, because they provide services to other employees, must be excluded from participation in flexitime or severely limited in their degree of participation. Examples of such positions are switchboard operators, receptionists, security guards, cafeteria and elevator personnel, and any others who must be available to provide services during the entire bandwidth of the day. (Often, because of the increased bandwidth, additional shifts are required for these jobs.)

The position of these employees in relation to those who are enjoying the advantages of flexitime is diminished. This can aggravate an already existing problem of perceived inferior status by these types of employees.

Scheduling in Cases of High Task Interdependence.   Flexitime is most effective when individual workers are responsible for tasks which can be completed independently of other tasks and do not require the participation of other workers. However, jobs in factories are often closely linked and highly interdependent: the tasks of each worker are dependent upon work from other members of the group. This problem typically exists in an environment such as an assembly line, where the task represents a process and the group is a team or a shift.

In such situations, the core time corresponds closely to the bandwidth, and the scope of individual flexible working hours is significantly reduced. To alleviate this problem, many companies have allowed teams to choose common flexible start and finish times. Usually such schedules are selected for a specified period of time (e.g., a settlement period), and may sometimes have to be coordinated with other work groups. Any deviation by an individual would have to be approved by the supervisor or co-workers, as in a nonflexible system.

For the most part, such arrangements have worked well, although they can become a possible source of friction within the group or team. For example, weaker members of the group may too frequently be required to adjust their schedules to accommodate the desires of stronger members of the group. Management should carefully monitor this type of activity, and, if necessary, establish guidelines so that no member of the group can take advantage of another. Seniority might be a basis for these guidelines, or a system of rotation might be established.

Time Recording

The reintroduction of the time-recording device (e.g., the punch clock) is considered by some employees to be a disadvantage of flexitime. Time-recording devices have often been regarded as a means of differentiating the status of employees (specifically, between management and nonmanagement). In addition, time recording has been viewed as a technique for controlling tardiness and absence, frequently for punitive purposes. Workers were docked pay, reprimanded, or put on probation if they punched in late.

However, the recording of time is a necessary prerequisite of the freedom of the individual to distribute his time. Further, it is indiscriminate in the sense that all employees, management and nonmanagement, must use the device. There is no status differentiation involved. Once this distinction is realized, the objections to mechanical recording of time are usually dropped and the reintroduction of time-recording devices no longer considered disadvantageous (see Chapter 19).

Need for Structure

Many individuals depend heavily upon the organized structure imposed by a full and consistent work schedule with hours defined by an outside source (the organization). This structure is important to their psychological well-being. Long periods of unprogrammed time possible under certain flexitime arrangements and the recurrent requirement to choose alternatives may be unsettling.

For certain people whose jobs are the only interesting and purposeful activity in which they are engaged or for those who have unhappy family lives, the opportunity to schedule their own time and to increase leisure or personal time is undesirable. When given more time off the job, their frustrations, conflicts, and boredom increase. This may take the form of aggressive or antisocial behavior directed at the organization.

NOTES

1. Davis, L.E., and Cherns, A.B. *The Quality of Working Life,* New York: The Free Press, 1975.
2. The Conference Board, Inc. The Altered Work Week, A Symposium Held in Ottawa, November, 1973. New York: 1974.
3. Ibid., p. 41.

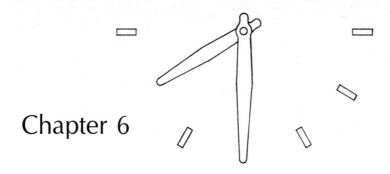

Chapter 6

Advantages and Disadvantages for the Employer

ADVANTAGES

Introduction

The advantages derived from the implementation of flexitime described so far are those accruing to the individual. Many of these changes, when aggregated to represent all the employees of the firm, become significant advantages accruing to the firm as well. For example, improvements in areas such as morale and motivation may lead to very real improvements in productivity and performance, which can ultimately lead to reduced costs. In addition, there are ways in which flexitime can have a direct economic impact on the firm through better use of capital assets.

The following section describes the potential advantages to management resulting from the implementation of FWH in four areas: organizational climate, improved membership behavior (if there is absenteeism and tardiness), improved performance, and decreased capital costs.

Organizational Climate

Working Climate. Through the implementation of flexitime, many firms have experienced a significant improvement in the climate of the organization. By climate, those intangible elements of the work environment are meant which help to set the general mood of employees in the work area. These elements affect the relationships among employees, the relationships between employees and supervisors, and the attitudes of employees toward their work.

Flexitime gives supervisors increased opportunities for humanistic management. In fact, if the system is to be successful, more humanistic management is required because of the degree of self-determination which employees are allowed. Of the few reported failures of flexitime experiments, most have resulted from situations where uncooperative, authoritarian supervisors have been unwilling to attempt to alter their supervisory style to accommodate the new system.

One company reported the following:

Most firms have reported that the trust and increased responsibility placed in their employees have been more than repaid in terms of an improved relationship between individuals and their bosses. Employees are more open minded, attitudes towards changes in the organization and to procedures improve, and there is a marked increase in cooperation. The employee feeling that he is a nine to five "drone" is reduced and replaced with a sense that he is a responsible human being with the opportunity to make decisions which affect his working life.

Another company reported the following:

With respect to interpersonal relations, we feel that the broader involvement in planning on the part of the employees, coupled with an increase in their responsibility, supports the conclusions reached in an attitude survey we did recently in which 25% of those involved claimed somewhat better relationships had developed with their supervisors. Also, 38% claimed improved relationships with other employees.

Employee commitment to the task is increased, resulting in attitude reorientation away from the clock toward the task at hand. The following comments of a manager from a case study reinforce this point:

I think there is more emphasis on the work "per se" under flexitime. Our department's productivity is at least as good as before and in some instances better. As an individual employee, I am very much in favor of flexitime. My people appear to be much happier under flexitime. When the work load has been heavy over the past 2 months, they stayed to try to keep work flowing quite evenly.

Another way in which flexitime can improve the organizational climate is through the democratic application of the system. Under a fixed system of working hours, there are usually some groups, mainly white-collar employees or managerial who are allowed to be a bit freer in their arrival and departure times. Many management employees feel, for instance, that a perquisite of membership in management is the right to arrive a few minutes late each day. With the introduction of flexitime, such privileges disappear for individuals or groups—or rather, *all* groups have this privilege, assuming that flexitime is implemented for management as well as nonmanagement.

Finally, flexitime improves the organizational climate by allowing employees to adjust their working hours to suit their efficiency cycles or bioclock. While this was discussed earlier, it should be noted here that if employees are allowed to choose their hours to fit their physiological temperament, they will be more alert, more cheerful, and, in general, in a better frame of mind to perform effectively and to interact positively with their fellow workers.

Improved Communications and Management Skills.   Many firms implementing flexitime have experienced a significant improvement in communication patterns within the organization. Under flexitime, the staggered schedules within a department or work group place a strain on both horizontal and vertical channels. Unless more efficient and extensive patterns of communication are developed within the work group, the success of the flexitime system will be jeopardized.

For example, temporary absences due to differences in schedules force managers to give employees sufficient instruction to perform for a minimal amount of time independently. By the same token, employees must communicate their plans to each other, particularly if their jobs require cooperation or teamwork. An employee must ensure that teammates are aware of his proposed schedule and have sufficient information on the job at hand to be able to continue in his absence. What emerges from this increased communication is a heightened sense of cooperation and team spirit, where one person can rely on another to act as his "deputy." Increased willingness to cover for one another means more overall flexibility. Employees are ready and able to perform the jobs of other employees when necessary.

A corollary of this improvement in communication is an improvement in management skills. Because the flexitime schedule may mean that the manager is absent during part of the day when employees are working, the manager must plan daily work assignments and projects, and communicate them to his employees in such a way that they can perform effectively when he is absent.

The results from one firm bear out this hypothesis· 22 percent of the supervisors felt that their planning, organizing, and management skills had improved as a result of flexitime. However, 6 percent of the supervisors felt that their skills had decreased. This might be explained by resistance of these supervisors to the implementation of flexitime.

Such enforced planning can lead to greater efficiency and can have an impact beyond day-to-day scheduling of work. One company reported the following:

> For a number of years, we had plans of both a long term and a short term nature which we found very difficult to formulate and implement all the way throughout operations, especially at the clerical levels. We find that now, because all employees are involved in what a specified department does, the planning process and implementation has substantially improved.

We may infer from this statement that employees in this firm experienced increased job knowledge and job responsibility as well as improved communication. Improved communication and a high level of cooperation were the groundwork necessary for these additional benefits to be realized by the employee and the firm.

Improved Recruiting and Reduced Turnover.   Flexitime can have a positive impact on organizational climate through improvements in recruiting and reductions in turnover. Because of the appeal of flexitime, and the fact that relatively few organizations offer this benefit, those organizations under flexitime who have actively recruited employees have found that responses have significantly increased.

The stringent Equal Employment Opportunity requirements imposed by the government have made the recruiting of minorities and women a particular problem for certain firms. Flexitime has been a significant advantage for these firms because of its ability to attract staff in a tight labor market. A major Swiss company reported that 30 to 40 percent of all job applicants applied principally because of flexible working hours. Prior to the introduction of FWH, this firm had difficulties recruiting new personnel.

The increase in applicants for positions has a positive side effect which should be mentioned. The applicant may have selected the organization because of the opportunity for flexible working hours. If the applicant is hired, his level of identification with the firm will be high, improving the organizational climate.

The fact that employees have selected the firm because of the opportunity for flexible working hours implies that they will not be as hasty to leave the firm as they might otherwise be. Many firms have experienced a reduction in labor turnover because, once accustomed to flexitime, the employee is unlikely to be attracted to a firm which does not offer this level of flexibility. Further, events which in the past might have led to turnover may now be accommodated through flexitime. For example, if an employee's car pool is disbanded, in a nonflexible system the employee might not have other alternatives for transportation to work. Flexitime, however, might allow the employee to join another car pool leaving at a slightly different time.

These ideas have been confirmed by many companies under FWH. For example, a German insurance company employing 1,300 people realized a 10 percent decrease in personnel fluctuation in 1972, the first year of FWH. Another firm, after introducing flexitime in 1967, experienced a drop in the turnover rate from 12.9 to 4 percent in 1968. In addition to the savings in recruiting which can result from such trends, savings in personnel costs and training can be significant. There are additional intangible benefits, such as the increase in experience and expertise of the work force in general, as employees remain longer with the company.

Improved Membership Behavior

Reduced Tardiness and Absenteeism.   Many firms have silently tolerated occasional and even frequent tardiness due to late train arrivals, traffic jams, or other situations affecting employees' arrival at work. Often, if employees arrive during a certain grace period, they are paid for the time in which they are tardy without having such time away from the job charged to leave credits, personal time off, or vacation time. This usually amounts to between 12 and 20 minutes of tardiness time every accounting period. Needless to say, such a system was not designed to motivate employees to arrive at work on time. Further, considerable costs could accrue to the firm over a period of time because potential output is not fully realized. These "lost hours" of output may be made up by employees outside the normal hours of work at overtime rates of pay.

Within the flexitime system, tardiness is virtually eliminated, since an employee's day begins when he arrives. The only way in which an employee might be late is if he arrives at work during the core time instead of during the flexbands.

Reports from the field have substantiated these claims of reduced or eliminated tardiness. One firm attributed the decrease in lateness to "the basic freedom employees have to choose working hours and days off to accommodate personal situations."[1] Another firm reported that the instances of employees arriving late or leaving early decreased by over 50 percent during the test period, while the average hourly loss due to late arrivals and early departures decreased by over 80 percent.[2]

In addition to a significant reduction in tardiness, most firms experienced decreased absenteeism after flexitime was introduced. Several reasons have been postulated to explain this trend. First, it seems likely that employees who might have called in sick under an inflexible system will sleep later and come in later during the morning under flexitime. Such a procedure would constitute a mark against the employee's personnel record under inflexible hours, but is of no consequence under flexitime. In a similar vein, employees who call in sick or take a day off for personal or family business can often come to work, taking off only the time required. Finally, there have been instances where employees who would have been late for work in the morning have preferred to call in sick rather than arrive late. Because the starting time is no longer rigidly fixed, such misuses of sick leave are no longer necessary. A German manufacturing firm reported a 50 percent reduction in days lost due to illness and personal reasons.

In addition to the effects of flexitime on short-term absences (1 day) described above, many firms have been surprised to find an impact on longer absences (longer than 1 day) usually attributed to sickness. For example, one American employer reported an 18 percent drop in long-term absenteeism for a group of 233 employees.[3]

One explanation for these types of reductions in absenteeism (long- and short-term) is that, under inflexible systems, employees are reinforced in certain situations for *not* coming to work. For instance, there may be more severe penalties for tardiness than for sickness —for example, docked pay, warnings, and suspensions—encouraging employees to call in sick rather than be late for work. For the employee who is genuinely ill, concerns over penalties for being tardy if he does make an effort to come to work are no longer a consideration.

Improved Work Performance

Increased Productivity. Although there have been few controlled studies measuring changes in productivity resulting from the implementation of FWH, there are enough formal and informal reports to support the idea that flexitime can lead to an increase in productivity. In general, firms have reported that employees are more willing to make an extra effort where circumstances demand than they were prior to the introduction of flexitime.

A research team in Europe (IMEDE) set out to accurately measure changes in productivity. By its definition, the input of labor and personnel had to be directly related to a measurable and quantifiable output in terms of quantity produced. This meant that productivity measures were limited to production settings. Working within these limitations, they reported on productivity changes at four companies before and after the introduction of flexitime. A Swiss watch manufacturer employing 1,200 people reported an increase in productivity of more than 4 percent. Another watch manufacturer had experienced an 8 to 10 percent increase in productivity each year for 3 years prior to introducing flexitime. After the introduction of flexitime, overall productivity rose by an impressive 15 percent. Company officials believed that the additional 5 to 7 percent increase was due to flexible working hours. The same company also pointed out that not all departments succeeded with a productivity gain. Two departments were led by supervisors who did not want to adapt to the new system, and who continued to instruct their subordinates as to what time they were to arrive and leave. The productivity of these units dropped by 25 percent. It must be noted, however, that since the introduction of an improvement can often be a motivating factor by itself, the positive effects of flexitime may decline somewhat in the long run.

Another aspect of increased productivity is the increase in responsibility toward work. This is represented by a shift in attitude: employees come to work to do a job, a complete task, rather than to work 7½ hours per day. Jobs in hand tend to be finished, since the employee knows he will be credited for any extra time worked.

Because employees arrive at different times during the morning, most firms have experienced quicker starts. The casual gossip at the beginning and end of each day tends to be reduced because of the random manner of arrival. Each employee quietly settles down to work when he arrives. Further, because the employee is scheduling his time according to his bioclock, when he arrives, he is ready to begin work.

Finally, the flexbands can provide a quiet time for many employees when they can accomplish much without disruptions from telephones, fellow employees, or customers. Many employees arrive at the earliest possible time or work till late for precisely this reason.

Decreased Overtime.   Improved productivity under flexitime is partly due to the fact that employees are more likely to be available during work-load peaks and troughs. Because of this, many firms experienced significant decreased overtime costs after flexitime was introduced. This has been controversial, and a source of contention with labor unions because it may mean reduced income for many employees who have come to expect overtime pay on a regular basis (see Chapter 5). The benefits to the firm, however, cannot be overlooked.

Reports from firms which have introduced flexitime indicate varied but significant reductions in overtime worked. One pioneer of the flexible hours system claims to have reduced overtime by 50 percent for the firm's 2,000 employees. A chemical firm in Germany with more than 1,000 employees realized a reduction of 70 percent in overtime.[4]

In a research report conducted at IMEDE in 1974, Elbing and Gordon cited one of the most complete studies on changes in overtime conducted in a large firm in Canada. The researchers compared not only the total amount of overtime premiums paid, but also the total number of overtime instances. In 1973, the ratio of overtime instances to the total number of employees was 17 percent. This figure was reduced to 8 percent in 1974, with the introduction of flexitime. Moreover, the total amount of overtime payment was reduced by 33 percent from 1973 to 1974.

There are two reasons why firms may experience decreases in overtime. (See Chapter 5 for further discussion.) First, a flexible hours system allows the worker to schedule work time not only around his personal needs but around work demands as well. Studies have shown that employees will voluntarily schedule work periods to coincide with work-load peaks. In cases where this happens a better overall matching of work time to work load may result in a reduced need for overtime and a consequent reduction in overtime payments. This implies that the worker is willing—up to a point—to schedule his time in order to experience certain intrinsic and extrinsic rewards such as the satisfaction of completing a task and gaining recognition for that task. There are, nevertheless, other variables which will affect the individual's willingness to schedule his time by this criterion—especially the possible intrusion of the schedule on the employee's personal time. If the employee does not experience any reinforcement for scheduling his time based on work demands, it is unlikely that he will be willing to continue doing so, because he will have other more rewarding criteria to use as a basis for scheduling.

Second, a firm may also experience reductions in overtime simply because employees are available throughout a longer period during the day. For example, a memo is handed to secretarial staff at 4 P.M. which must be completed and sent out by 9 A.M. the following morning. Under a nonflexible system, overtime would be necessary to complete the memo that afternoon. Under the flexible hours system, the memo could be assigned to a secretary who routinely works from, say, 10 A.M. until 6 P.M., eliminating the need for overtime.

Other data indicate that decreases in overtime tend to vary, based on the type of work environment. Specifically, one study indicated that overtime decreases were consistently higher in administrative environments than in production environments. A study in an Austrian firm compared the amount of overtime worked by 1,600 employees before and after the introduction of flexitime. For blue-collar workers, the reduction in overtime was 10.9 percent, whereas for white-collar workers a 16.1 percent reduction was realized. Similar results were reported by a Swiss watch company, where overtime dropped by 25 percent in the production department and 50 percent in administrative departments.

There are two possible explanations for this phenomenon. The first, and simplest, is that flexitime is more difficult to implement and usually more limited in scope in a production environment. The studies mentioned above do not indicate whether both departments had the same level of flexibility available to them. A second possibility is related to the nature of blue-collar workers' jobs. If the work is repetitive and inflexible by nature, improvements resulting from the implementation of flexitime are more limited than in white-collar jobs, where a greater degree of self-determination is possible. On the other hand, flexitime might be one of the very few improvements possible in blue-collar jobs.

Service to Customers.   A tangible and immediately realized benefit of the introduction of flexitime is increased service to an organization's customers. Because the bandwidth has increased, in some cases by up to 3 or 4 hours, service-oriented organizations can increase their responsiveness and availability to their clients. Moreover, this improvement is achieved without having to introduce extra shifts or hire part-time personnel.

Service organizations which plan to extend their service hours when they implement flexitime should be sure that early and late hours are adequately covered by personnel. This may take no extra scheduling if the work force is sufficiently large. If this is not the case, however, some sort of rotating schedule which maintains as much flexibility as possible may be necessary.

Utilization of Equipment and Decreased Capital Costs

Many firms have realized cost savings through the introduction of flexitime by fuller utilization of their plant and equipment. Improved efficiency is achieved by extending the available hours over which the fixed assets of the company are utilized in a productive capacity. However, the opportunity to increase the efficient use of capital resources can only be fully realized if the pattern of employees' starting and finishing times is spread evenly over the entire bandwidth. If this is the case, it may even be possible to eliminate some equipment because of decreased demand during peak usage periods of the day. A Swiss machinery producer with 30,000 employees reduced its annual costs for social installations such as the canteen, showers, and recreational and athletic facilities by 30 percent because these installations had lower peak usage after the introduction of flexitime. Also, employees could plan ahead for their usage of all these facilities.

DISADVANTAGES

Costs

One of the chief considerations when implementing flexitime is the cost of the system. These costs include initial capital investment and long-term overhead costs. There are trade-offs to be made between these aspects—for example, higher initial investment in the system can mean lower administrative costs in the long run.

Implementation Costs.   When an organization decides to investigate the possibility of implementing flexitime, there are certain initial costs which must be considered. For a proper investigation, a team or steering committee should be appointed whose responsibility it is to gather appropriate information and to create a proposal for the implementation of the system. The size of the committee will vary, depending upon the size of the firm—it may even be a committee of one. The salaries of these employees should be included as part of the initial study costs, especially if their time is devoted exclusively to this project, as it should be (for further discussion, see Chapter 17).

Additional costs may include travel, the costs of testing certain equipment, secretarial help, and use of other organizational resources. Finally, costs may be incurred when a test site is chosen and a small group of employees selected for the initial pilot study. At this stage, most companies prefer to use a manual recording system for recording hours worked. Again, these costs must be included.

Once the committee has completed its investigation, submitted a proposal, and had it approved, the company is ready to invest in the time-recording equipment required for flexible working hours, unless the company has decided to use a manual self-reporting recording system. (A complete description of time recording systems is included in Chapter 19.) In general, the more advanced the recording system, the higher the initial investment costs but the lower the long-term administrative costs. A computerized system is the most expensive to implement, but it can actually reduce existing administrative costs through the automation of functions currently performed manually. The decision makers must also keep in mind that record keeping must become more elaborate and therefore more expensive as the number of options and possibilities under flexitime are increased. For example, a flexitime system allowing banking would require a more sophisticated record-keeping system than a system without banking.

Even the most sophisticated time-recording systems will incur some administrative costs. Errors in time recording (e.g., the employee forgets to shut off his meter and remove his key when he leaves for the day), absence from the office on company business, and other contingencies may require special handling. This may mean additional costs, depending upon the extent to which the FWH system can be integrated into existing procedures.

The organization may take one of two approaches to the administrative handling of flexitime: it may allow employees to be responsible for their own manual calculations and reporting, or it may assign the personnel department or accounting department to these tasks. This decision depends on the style of organization and the type of time-recording system used. If the time-recording system is a manual one, it makes more sense for employees to do their own accounting, especially since this is consistent with the responsibility already entrusted to the individual to report his hours accurately. In a computerized system where summary reports are generated, it is more logical to centralize paperwork. In either case, these costs must be included in the costs of flexitime to the organization. Further, they must be weighed against the initial investment in recording equipment in order to arrive at a cost-effective decision.

Overhead Costs.   Because of the extended bandwidth, many firms have found that when they institute flexitime they must extend the hours of availability of their plants and facilities. Depending on the length of the bandwidth, open hours may be extended during the normal working week by as much as 25 to 50 percent. As a result, FWH will increase the cumulative costs of the firm's facilities.

Perhaps the most obvious of these additional costs are those due to increases in heat, light, and power resulting from the provision of services at the extremities of the bandwidth. For example, where a building was formerly open between 8 A.M. and 6 P.M., it may now be open from 6 A.M. until 8 P.M.—an increase of 4 hours per day. Moreover, additional services such as cafeteria facilities, security personnel, and elevator and switchboard operators may be required.

The organization must also consider the safety of its employees when implementing FWH. Maintenance of security is more difficult when employees arrive and leave over a much wider period. Also, since employees are more likely to be working alone at the extremities of the bandwidth, there may be security problems, such as access to confidential information, possibility of theft, and the safety of the employees themselves. These possibilities may require enlarging the security staff of the organization.

Organizational Problems

Coordination and Communications Planning.   The successful implementation of flexitime requires, and is often responsible for creating, channels of communication within the organization. If communication problems existed before the implementation of flexitime, FWH can aggravate these problems. If workers are unwilling or unable to communicate their schedules to other workers, the results can be a lack of work, idleness, standstills, and general friction among workers. This is particularly true in environments where teamwork is required. If these communication problems are not resolved, they may jeopardize the implementation of flexitime, and from a more general perspective, disrupt the smooth functioning of the organization itself.

Another aspect of communications may be influenced by the implementation of flexitime. Internal and external communications may deteriorate since the time that all company personnel are available is reduced to core time. Most organizations have not found this to be the case, however. Internally, employees make an effort to schedule meetings during core time and work independently during the flexbands. In dealing with external communications, most service organizations establish some type of minimum schedule in order to ensure that there are full services available to customers for the full day. In some cases, this has meant extending service hours.

In jobs which are highly interdependent, such as on assembly lines or in certain clerical positions where the output of one person is the input of another, flexitime can create problems at points of interface if not implemented properly. Again, adequate systems design and communication must be established among workers so that teams can plan and coordinate their schedules. This may require careful supervision at first to ensure that workers are cooperating to the necessary degree.

Another possibility in continuous process environments is a larger in-process inventory. Workers would be more independent from one another if each worker had enough inventory as input to keep him busy until his teammate arrived. Again, this may require careful planning and supervision to maintain appropriate inventory levels.

Some supervisors have complained that FWH places an increased burden on them. The company, or the individual supervisor, may feel that supervisory coverage is required for the entire bandwidth, effectively reducing the level of flexibility allowed the supervisor by extending his hours. One manager expressed the following concerns:

> First line supervisors . . . absorb the scheduling problems associated with these systems, which is clearly added work and compounds the problems of work flow. . . . And additionally, these exempt employees probably feel as though they have to be on the job when the first worker appears and until the last leaves. If these first line supervisors are feeling put upon by this groovy new concept, then all subordinates will probably pay the price.[5]

However, the supervisor may be unavailable to employees during parts of the flexband if the supervisor exercises his right to FWH (as he should). This places demands on the supervisor to plan and communicate with the employees so that they are able to function in his absence. Many organizations have reported improved supervision as a result of this aspect of flexitime. Supervisors must be willing, however, to delegate responsibility to their subordinates—a new and difficult concept for many first liners.

Misuse of Flexitime.   One aspect of flexitime which concerns many firms is the possibility of employees attempting to cheat the system. It must be emphasized that by choosing to implement flexitime, the organization is making the commitment to trust its employees. FWH demands a mutual sense of responsibility and trust between the employee and the organization. This mutual trust and responsibility can be jeopardized if an employee should attempt to cheat on his hours. Further, the firm could suffer significant financial loss if cheating were to occur on a broad scale.

We have heard of no cases where extensive cheating became a problem. Most firms have been pleased to report that the few instances have been reported by fellow employees. Cheating the system jeopardizes the privileges of all employees. Further, it creates an atmosphere which is not conducive to cooperation and communication. As a result, employees themselves discourage this type of behavior.

Availability of Flexitime to All Employees.   We have mentioned earlier that it may be difficult to make flexitime available for certain types of employees within an organization, specifically, those employees who provide services to the organization such as security personnel, maintenance personnel, switchboard operators, receptionists, and cafeteria employees. The implementation of flexitime for other employees may aggravate the problem of perceived inferior status for these workers since they are unable to participate in the system.

It is recommended that the firm attempt to implement flexible scheduling for these employees even if on a more limited basis. An alternative which has been considered by some firms is wage differential for those employees unable to participate in FWH. Of course, this may pose problems with workers who are eligible to participate in flexitime but who would prefer to earn additional money. Further, if workers are unionized, extensive negotiations may be required.

NOTES

1. The Conference Board, Inc. The Altered Work Week, A Symposium Held in Ottawa, November, 1973. New York: 1974, 42.

2. Elbing, A.O., Gadon, H. and Gordon, J.R., Flexible working hours: it's about time. *Harvard Business Review,* January/February 1974, 18–33.

3. Ibid.

4. Ibid.

5. Zalusky, J.L. Alternative work schedules: a labor perspective. Paper presented to the National Conference on Alternative Work Schedules, March 1977. Also cited in *The Journal of the College and University Personnel Association,* 1977, *28,* 30, 55.

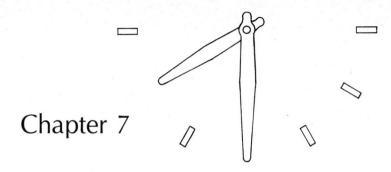

Chapter 7

Advantages and Disadvantages for Society

FLEXITIME AND THE ECONOMY

The implications of flexitime for society are significant, particularly in terms of its potential impact on the economy. There are two aspects of the economy which could be influenced by the introduction of flexitime: the national productivity level and the unemployment rate. One must keep in mind throughout the following discussion that these effects are possibilities only—flexitime has not yet been implemented on a large enough scale to verify these theories.

Productivity

Although there is some evidence that flexitime increases productivity, it is not sufficient to allow us to generalize at this point. However, there is a large body of theory which, when applied to flexitime, suggests that such an increase is not unrealistic.

The implications of an increase in productivity are unclear. On the one hand, increases in output are possible *without* an accompanying increase in capital costs. The more efficient use of capital (property, plant, and equipment) implies a decrease in costs which could be passed on to the consumer and result in increased demand for goods.

On the other hand, the impact on the individual must be carefully evaluated. Increased productivity by employees implies an eventual increase in wage rates (as the economy returns to an equilibrium point), which can be considered a benefit. But the cause of the increase in productivity is unclear. Does the worker actually work harder under flexitime? Or is the more efficient utilization and management of time the chief reason for any changes in this area? If the former is true, the worker has some justification for demanding a higher wage rate or a shorter workday. Adjustments of this type would tend to offset any increase in productivity. In reality, however, any increases in productivity are the result of a combination of the factors mentioned above.

An additional economic benefit of FWH should be mentioned. A significant decrease in staff turnover, resulting from the implementation of flexitime, can mean a more productive economy. Not only are savings accrued through reduced recruiting and training costs, but the work force as a whole can be characterized as more experienced because of the tendency to remain in a job longer.

The Unemployment Rate

A well-documented trend over the last 15 years has been the growing number of women joining the labor force. In fact, economists have gone so far as to partially attribute the high unemployment rates of past years to the entrance of women and youth into the job market. These groups then seek jobs of a special nature. For example, women with families might seek employment which would allow them to be at home when the children arrive from school; students might typically seek jobs which would fit in with their studies or class schedules. For both groups, jobs which allow some degree of flexibility in scheduling would be highly desirable.

FWH encourages this secondary labor force of women, students, and even older people to enter the labor market by providing the opportunity for these potential workers to meet financial, social, and intrinsic needs through employment while they fulfill their other responsibilities. Women with families may be able to return to work at an earlier period in the family cycle if they so desire. Those workers under financial stress may be able to arrange hours in such a way that they can take a second job. (In a plant in Ohio where flexitime was implemented, the rate of moonlighting increased from 10 percent to 20 to 25 percent.) Further, because these workers in many cases are secondary wage earners, working on a part-time or temporary basis, they may be willing to accept the more monotonous types of jobs which would be objectionable to a primary wage earner. Many secondary wage earners (often women with children) may view their jobs in strictly financial terms—they may not value the intrinsic rewards of working because of an orientation to areas outside work as a source of real fulfillment.

Economists have expressed concern that these new entrants to the labor market and second-job holders may cause an increase in the labor supply, raising the unemployment rate. Furthermore, these new entrants may displace primary wage earners in certain situations where the two groups are competing for the same job. Because the new entrants are primarily secondary wage earners, they may be willing to work for less in order to obtain employment. The end result is not only an increase in the unemployment rate, but a shift in the composition of the work force. However, any such changes are likely to be confined to the unskilled or semiskilled sectors of the work force. Also, one must keep in mind the benefits accruing to those entrants to the work force who are able to work only because of a flexitime schedule.

A counterbalance to the increase in the labor supply involves the impact of flexitime on nonwork activities. With FWH, workers will be able to schedule leisure time to their best advantage. Free time to engage in recreational activities and leisure pursuits may create additional demands for these goods and services. New job markets will arise to service this demand for expanded recreational and leisure industries, and this may help the economy to absorb some of the new entrants to the labor force.

The preceding discussion has focused upon the idea that flexitime contributes to the trend toward increased unemployment witnessed over the past two decades through the additional incentive offered to traditionally nonworking subgroups such as women and youth to join the job market. This may be somewhat offset by the expansion of leisure and recreational industries. There is another aspect of FWH, however, which can have an effect on unemployment rates. When signs of slack appear in the economy, companies on flexible schedules may be able to persuade their employees to work on a reduced schedule (e.g., core hours only), in order to avoid having to lay off employees. Special inducements could be offered for workers to make use of free time for educational programs, special training to expand job knowledge, or community activities. If the shift were considered permanent, training programs could be devised to facilitate transitions to employment of a different kind or at another location.

During periods of increased economic activity, employees may be willing to work additional hours, crediting their account for time off later. FWH provides the potential for facilitating adjustment to a moderate rate of growth or shrinkage in the job market, particularly if this change is of a local or temporary nature. It is important to note that although flexitime may function as a stabilizer, helping to smooth fluctuations in production and employment, its effectiveness is short-term only. While it may help industry to cope with seasonal variations, long-term slumps or increases in economic activity must be dealt with through other measures.

ENERGY COSTS AND SAVINGS

There are two aspects to changes in energy consumption resulting from flexitime. First, overhead costs at a firm may increase because of the need to keep the work place open for an extended day. These overhead costs can include light, heat, and services such as maintenance, elevators, cafeteria, and the switchboard. However, fixed costs allocated per finished good may be reduced as a result of the more effective use of property, plant, and equipment. The extended workday implies the extended availability of specialized equipment. If the work process can be scheduled so that any such equipment is utilized throughout the bandwidth, there may be more efficient use of such equipment and a possible decrease in overhead costs.

It is difficult to determine whether or not these countereffects would balance out. The results may be different for each organization implementing flexitime, and should be carefully monitored during the implementation stage.

Another, and perhaps more significant, impact of flexitime on energy consumption concerns travel to and from work. Although already discussed in terms of advantages to the individual, the point is worth reiterating. Because employees have a degree of choice in their travel time, they have the flexibility to be able to form car pools, travel at off-peak hours, and utilize public transportation. By avoiding peak hours, employees avoid bottlenecks in elevators, crowded parking lots, and traffic jams. As peak load demand for public transportation is more evenly distributed over a greater period of time, employees may be attracted to this mode of traveling. Increased ridership could lead to improved facilities, not to mention a decrease in highway congestion because fewer people drive their own cars.

The more efficient use of public and private transportation can mean a general reduction not only in energy consumption but also in the amount of pollution from carbon monoxide car emissions.

HUMAN RESOURCES

Recreational Facilities

Just as commuter traffic is concentrated on Mondays through Fridays during certain hours, the peak loads on recreational facilities occur on weekends. The freedom of the worker on a FWH system to leave a little early or arrive late may enable him to schedule recreational activities during the week. For example, he may fit in golf or tennis during the late afternoon while it is still light, or arrive late at work in the morning after an evening of bowling or an early morning tennis game. Thus, FWH may allow the worker to schedule recreational activities during the week when facilities are more accessible (and less expensive), in place of, or in addition to, weekend recreation. This benefit is especially appealing at a time when physical activities and health culture are given high priority by many individuals.

Carried to the furthest degree, staggering leisure time could mean flexible weekends, allowing access to less crowded facilities and uncongested travel routes to those facilities. Taking a midweek "weekend" would not only make the use of special facilities more pleasant and less difficult for the individual, but it implies better utilization of the resource itself. Those who object to time off which does not coincide with that of friends or family may wish to retain Saturday and Sunday for their time off. Those willing to be more flexible, however, may reap significant advantages from the flexible weekend concept.

Adult Education

Advances in technology require periodic retraining or additional education for many employees—from technicians to professionals. The opportunity to increase skills or knowledge allows the individual to increase his value to the employer and his marketability in the job market place. Alternatively, an individual may wish to explore certain areas of interest which have no relation to his job, or to pursue a change in career by obtaining the required education.

Flexitime may allow employees to take advantage of some of these educational programs which were previously unavailable. For example, if there are two core periods during the day (a flexible lunch hour), a worker may be able to schedule some type of educational activity during the middle of the day. If there is sufficient flexibility, employees may be able to attend daytime programs; they may no longer be restricted to evening programs.

Carried a step further, FWH may encourage the expansion of adult education offered by local institutions, including vocational and technical programs. Further, it may encourage employers to offer educational and job-oriented training courses.

Reduced Stress

In our discussion of individual advantages, we described one of the benefits of FWH as reduced stress. This benefit has implications for society which must be considered as well.

The first of these is a contribution to a decrease in accidents, because when there is no longer any necessity to be on time, the pressure of rushing to work is diminished. This pressure often causes emotional and physical stress, leading to careless driving, increased risk taking, and excessive speed—all of which add up to a high rate of accidents.

Moreover, as a result of reduced stress and a reduced rate of accidents, the social costs of emergency services and medical care may be diminished. Granted, the accident rate must be significantly reduced for this to occur, but reduced stress can certainly mean a healthier population and reduced medical costs.

IMPACT ON THE FAMILY

From a societal point of view, FWH can have a major impact on family life. Changing societal values have made it acceptable for women with families to work. Working couples with children faced with scheduling problems have created a tremendous demand for day-care facilities. The so-called latch key child has also been a by-product of this problem. A potential solution for these scheduling dilemmas is the staggering of working hours made possible by flexitime. If the daily work schedule can vary by as much as $3\frac{1}{2}$ to 4 hours, then it can be possible for a parent to be present both when the child leaves for school and when he arrives home—even if both parents must commute and work a full day. One researcher in Switzerland went so far as to claim that the incidence of school failures was lower in those families whose parents worked under FWH systems.

As was mentioned in the section on economic benefits, flexitime encourages women with families to enter the work force who might not otherwise consider it, or who would put it off to a later date. Not only does FWH allow the wife to juggle work and family responsibilities, it allows the husbands to participate in family activities and responsibilities to a greater degree. The degree of change in family life may vary from simply a father who is more visible to his children to parents who truly share full responsibility for the care of the children (see Chapter 16).

SERVICE INDUSTRIES

There are two aspects to the implementation of FWH in service industries: the impact on workers within the service industry and the impact on customers of the service. Briefly, the worker may find his situation improved when the workday is extended by flexitime because peak loads are diminished, unless he is held (or feels) responsible for the entire bandwidth, or unless customers are restricted to contact with the organization during core time only.

Customers may be affected positively or negatively by the impact of FWH depending upon the way in which the system is implemented by the firm. On the negative side, there may be restrictions on times when delivery or collection of goods is possible. Further, contact with the public may be restricted to core time only.

On the more positive side, increased hours of contact may be possible since the bandwidth is greater than the original fixed working day. This requires a staff large enough to ensure that the entire bandwidth is covered by coordination among the department members. This can help to distribute peak contact load by spreading customer contacts over a longer period of time.

Because services are available for the entire bandwidth, customers who work but must take care of personal business can schedule it around their work hours, eliminating the need to take time off. It would be particularly helpful if flexitime were operating in such services as government agencies, motor vehicle departments, and repair trades.

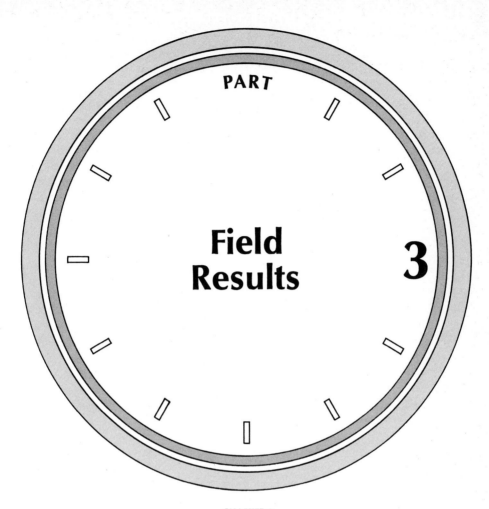

PART

Field Results

3

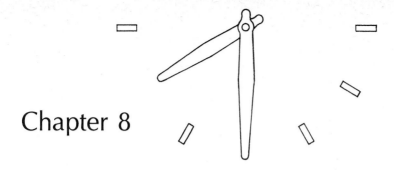

Chapter 8

The European Experience

INTRODUCTION

Notwithstanding the efforts of the many proponents of employee individuation, the actual reason for the invention of flexitime in Europe was a practical organizational need created by the external environment. A serious problem arose in the Ottobrunn Research and Development plant of the German Messerschmitt-Bolkow-Blohm aerospace company in 1967 because of traffic congestion on the local routes connecting the major highways to the plant. A personnel manager implemented the concept of flexible working hours to alleviate this problem.*

Other benefits resulting from this system were soon discovered, and the concept spread quickly throughout West Germany, where approximately 30 percent of the labor force is on some form of flexible working hours (FWH). The concept has been widely adopted in many other European countries by now, including Switzerland (40 percent of labor force), France, Austria, England, the Scandinavian countries, and to a lesser extent, Ireland, Italy, Spain, Portugal, the Benelux countries, and even the Soviet Union and Poland. In other parts of the world, especially in Japan and Australia, there are reports of increased experimentation with the system.

The period between 1970 and 1973 was the time of rapid implementation of the concept in Western Europe. A few factors common to most of the countries mentioned explain this phenomenon.

1.   In the early 1970s, the unemployment level in most of Western Europe was extremely low (2 to 4 percent, compared to 7 percent in the United States). A shortage of labor and the desire by employers to attract new workers, as well as to retain existing employees, was a major impetus in adopting alternative work patterns. Employers felt that schemes such as flexitime would make a firm more desirable to employees, giving it a competitive edge in recruiting and in limiting turnover. For example, in Germany and Switzerland, where the

*The credit for the original concept is given to Mrs. Christel Kaemmerer of Königswinter.

shortage of skilled and salaried employees was acute, women became a particular target of recruiting efforts. Flexitime fulfilled employer expectations by helping to attract this group of employees.

2. The compressed workweek could not be considered a viable alternative to flexitime, since in most European countries weekly working hours extend beyond 40 hours per week. Compressing more than 40 hours into 4 days would result in extremely long working days. For example, in Switzerland the working day is 45 hours by legislation, but can be 42 to 44 hours through collective bargaining. In this situation, a 44-hour week would mean 4 days of 11 hours each. When commuting time is added, the length of the working day becomes prohibitive.

3. There was less legislation restricting full utilization of the flexitime concept than there has been in the United States.

The daily bandwidth in most European countries allows considerable variation in working hours and a carry-over from one day to another (e.g., in Switzerland, the bandwidth is 10½ hours; in France, 10 hours; in other countries, 12 hours). In addition, a carry-over from week to week is not restricted by legislation. Furthermore, carry-over from one month to the next (a month is the usual accounting period in Europe) has often been approved by local unions, sometimes overruling objections at the national level. Overtime restrictions, therefore, did not limit the implementation of highly flexible models the way they have in the United States. Thus, European firms were able to include the banking of hours as a routine feature of the flexitime system. Most flexitime arrangements which include banking typically allow ranges of carry-over from 10 to 20 hours per month. Furthermore, most companies allow half or even full days off for hours accumulated during the flexbands. This policy allowed employees to extend weekends and holidays, making a compressed week an occasional possibility for the individual employee.

Although the original adoption of flexitime was a result of practical organizational needs, the commitment of management in Europe to the philosophy of individualization and self-determination has made its contribution, too. This commitment corresponds to the view that society has a responsibility to grant the individual maximum freedom of decision in a world dominated by technology and time constraints. Throughout Western Europe, organized labor is directly involved in national politics and has promoted legislation which grants employees a higher level of participation in organizational policy making. Governments are actively involved in promoting legislation reflecting a concern for the quality of work life. For example, Germany, Sweden, and Yugoslavia have created regulations for labor-management codetermination through the participation of labor representatives in corporate boards of directors or through the system of Works Councils.

Assisting the spread of flexitime is the fact that multinational corporations transfer managerial practices to subsidiaries in other countries (e.g., Nestlé, Inc., introduced flexitime into the Benelux countries).

Companies employing the flexitime system vary in the type of product or service offered. They include chemical and pharmaceutical production, advertising, the research and development laboratories of a glass manufacturer, furniture manufacturing, insurance companies, factories, banks, transportation, government offices, hospitals, union-owned companies, the army, metals and engineering industry, textiles, food, commerce, public departments, airline administrative offices, local government authorities dealing with land drainage, flood prevention, defense works, pollution prevention, and fisheries, a grocery chain, accounting and data processing departments, administrative and engineering offices, a bakery, a city street-cleaning agency, research institutes, and electric power plants.

The number of employees working under flexitime systems ranges from approximately 100 in a German assembly factory to 6,500 in a Swiss chemical and pharmaceutical company. Most workers involved in flexible scheduling are white-collar and salaried employees, since implementation is easiest at this level. Production management has felt that flexitime has limited potential for success in a blue-collar environment. Although experimentation has shown that individual work stations as well as team production units can work under flexible hours in this environment, the introduction of flexitime on the assembly line is still seen as difficult. However, the prognosis is more favorable for production of small items where work-in-process inventory can be easily accommodated. As verification of these limitations, while 40 percent of the labor force in Switzerland and 30 percent in Germany are on flexitime, only 10 percent and 3 percent, respectively, are blue-collar workers. Over 20 percent of the work force in France and 10 percent in Britain are on flexitime, yet the ratio of white- to blue-collar workers in France and Britain is 10 to 1. Scandinavian countries have slightly better statistics in this area.[1]

Over the years, the concept of flexible working hours has spread at an incredible rate. Starting with a single German company in 1967, a wide variety of working establishments in over a dozen European countries have successfully adopted and expanded the system to suit their particular needs.

GERMANY

A German delegate at the Eleventh Anglo-German Personnel Management meeting of the European Association for Personnel Management gave his explanation for the widespread acceptance of flexitime in the West German work force (over 30 percent). He stated that "there are two main arguments. First, a mutual problem—bad traffic congestion . . . the second is that we live in a democracy and, therefore, an employee should, within reasonable limits, be given a choice in his hours of work." Many organizations have also used flexitime as an attraction to recruit workers for vacant positions in white-collar jobs and service areas where employees are in contact with the public.

As mentioned earlier, flexitime (called *Gleitende Arbeitszeit* in German) originated in the German aerospace company of Messerschmitt-Bolkow-Blohm, in 1967, as a response to the intense traffic congestion caused by the simultaneous arrival and departure of thousands of employees. The system was implemented for 6,000 white-collar workers out of the 20,000 members of the work force.[2] The workweek consists of 40 hours. Under the flexible working hours schedule, workers may arrive between 7 and 8 A.M. and leave between 4 and 6 P.M., except on Friday, when quitting time varies between 1:30 and 4 P.M. A 45-minute lunch break has been fixed by the organization. The company allows two half days to be taken off during core time within the settlement period, but no full days off are permitted. The settlement period is 1 month and balances may be carried forward to the next month.

Employees may carry over up to 10 credit or debit hours per settlement period, although the average has been about 4 credit hours.

Workers felt that the introduction of flexitime resulted in: better working conditions (65 percent); a better balance between work and private lives (31 percent); easier traveling conditions (23 percent); avoidance of the morning rush hour (6 percent); more freedom (12 percent); and improved coordination between work rhythm and work load (6 percent). Only a small percentage felt that flexitime resulted in less time for communication. The company itself has also found the system to be advantageous. There is an estimated $40,000 a month saving due to increased productivity and lower absenteeism. Fewer recruiting problems and travel difficulties have been encountered. Thus, the advantages which the workers view as an integral part of flexitime are reflected in the financial reports of the company.

Another German firm, Lufthansa's Cologne office, claims that flexitime eliminated 1-day absences due to sickness, and that efficiency markedly increased. Other companies in Germany report that working conditions have improved without any increase in administrative costs and that accounting procedures were simplified (Boehringer Mannheim GmbH).[3] According to a survey conducted in 1973 by the Deutsche Gesellschaft für Personal führung (German Personnel Management Association) to which 30 companies replied, 24 reported improvement in working atmosphere; 25, reduction of paid absences; 23, self-adjustment of work time to work load; 15, reduction of overtime; 17, increased individual productivity; 19, improved recruitment success; and 6, reduced personnel turnover.

Both employees and management have reported extremely positive attitudes toward flexitime, although the latter has expressed some critical comments. Employees in one German company are pleased at being able to arrive at work at a later hour; 96 percent at another firm claim to like the system; a majority of those at yet another company insist upon the use of flexitime. Concerning the use of time clocks, the employees at one plant feel no resentment or sense of oppression at having to clock in; as a matter of fact, a large majority seems to prefer the installation of time clock apparatus as opposed to manual recording systems. However, the type of recording apparatus utilized is the cumulative recorder, not the traditional punch clock.

A typical example of the implementation process was described by Wade. The management of a German company, J. Walter Thompson, worked with the Works Council (Betriebs-rat), a legally constituted body of employee representatives who are not necessarily trade union members, in order to assess the feasibility of flexitime. Employees were asked to vote on the flexitime question after the Betriebsrat and management had agreed upon an acceptable plan. Employees were given the basic scheme and were surveyed on the acceptability of the time clock that was planned for use. When flexitime was voted in by employees, management set up the necessary rules. In addition, some new ideas contributed by management, the Works Council, and employees were incorporated into the original design, including the elimination of the plans for the clocks.

In 1973, it was estimated that 3,000 companies in Germany employed some variation of the FWH system, and that about 10 percent of the labor force was either working under an FWH system or committed to implementing it.[4] At that time researchers also reported that companies on flexitime were not confined to large offices like the Deutsche Lloyd Insurance Company in Berlin, Hanover, and Munich. Factories, banks, pharmaceutical companies, transportation, various governmental offices, hospitals, a union-owned company, and the army are all examples of industries in which flexitime has been adopted. Affiliates of multinational companies like IBM Germany and Grace GmbH. have also installed the system. In Germany, flexitime has crossed both industry lines and size barriers and is now in evidence in almost every line of work. It was estimated that by 1977, some form of flexible working hours was in operation in a *third* of all German companies, covering 3 million workers, or close to 30 percent of the labor force.

SWITZERLAND

Reports in the German-speaking press of the initial success of flexible working hours soon brought the system to the attention of Austrian and Swiss organizations. Elbing, Gadon, and Gordon reported in 1973 that a study by the Swiss Employers Association estimated that 30 percent of the labor force in Switzerland was on flexible hours. Its rapid acceptance there was largely because of the shortage of labor and the necessity to design working hours which were attractive to women and part-time employees.

Many companies in Switzerland are attempting to create a more democratic industrial society. All workers are paid on a monthly basis, informal dress is encouraged, and the use of titles is decreasing. Flexitime, through its support of individual freedom of choice, has proven to be an important manifestation of this classless philosophy. It is in Switzerland that the practice of flexitime is most widespread. Over 40 percent of the workers in Switzerland are estimated to be using the system, and as many as 70 percent are on flexitime in the Zurich-Winterthur industrial and commercial area. The organizations involved include metals and engineering industries, textiles, chemicals, commerce, food, banking, insurance, and public departments.

A Swiss organization which has received wide exposure for its relatively early implementation of flexitime is Sandoz Products Ltd., a chemical and pharmaceutical firm.[5] A test scheme was introduced in 1970 which involved approximately 500 individuals. Since the reactions of these employees were almost uniformly positive, the program was introduced to 2,500 workers in July 1971, and by 1973 the system had been extended to include 6,500 employees. The workweek is 43 hours long, which means that the average day is 8 hours and 35 minutes. The bandwidth stretches from 7 A.M. to 7 P.M., with core times between 9 A.M. and 12 noon and 2 P.M. and 3 P.M. The minimum lunch break is 45 minutes. A carry-over of 10 debit or credit hours in 1 month is permitted. Hours worked are tracked by the honor system—each employee is responsible for completing his own time sheet, which is then inspected by his immediate supervisor.

Sandoz officials claim that the majority of workers have remained on the schedules which were in effect before the introduction of flexitime. Other employees, however, immediately varied their schedule to some degree and then remained on that schedule as a fixed timetable. The knowledge that this variance was possible seemed to be psychologically important, although employees who varied their schedule did so only once. Two basic reasons for initial consideration of a flexible working hours system at Sandoz were traffic congestion and a high rate of labor turnover. The former problem was significantly improved by flexitime, since workers now arrived and departed at different times. In terms of turnover, in 1970 the Sandoz rate of reduction was 14.6 percent, which was further reduced to 12.4

percent after the large-scale introduction of the system. This is less than half the national average. The company claims that this achievement can be credited to the flexitime system.

However, in spite of the positive organizational and environmental benefits achieved, Wade reports that reactions to flexitime varied within the ranks of this organization. Workers at lower levels were very much in favor of the new schedule and felt that it afforded them a greater degree of individual equality. In contrast, management, especially first-line supervisors, expressed a greater amount of skepticism, objecting to the fact that factory workers experienced an unnecessary level of flexibility in their work situations. Middle managers also objected to the loss of some control over white-collar clerical employees—specifically secretaries—and found that they were forced to organize their tasks around a secretary's availability. In most cases, this problem was alleviated by additional cooperation to accommodate each other's schedules.

FRANCE

The reasons for the adoption of flexitime *(horaire variable)* in France are similar to those expressed by West German firms. They include the alleviation of traveling difficulties; the recruiting advantage; the reduction of overcrowding at main entrances, parking lots, and elevators; and the reduction of short-term absences.

In 1974 it was estimated that 200 companies employing 50,000 workers were using flexitime. By now, however, it is estimated that approximately 1 million of France's labor force, employed in 2,000 organizations, are on some form of flexitime. In most cases, management initiated the introduction of flexitime; however, it took some time before workers were willing to accept the concept. They were skeptical of flexitime as a management innovation. In spite of employee reluctance, however, no decrease in output or production was found in any instance, and absenteeism was diminished in most cases.

In the early 1970s, legislation in France, established to protect workers, required that all employees in a particular organization work a similar number of hours. This legislation prevented large variations in the number of hours worked daily, thus restricting the implementation of flexible working systems and preventing banking of hours. However, a 1973 act which was substantiated in 1975 by a government circular waived the above provision. Significant variations of daily hours are now allowed and carry-over from one week to the next is set at 5 hours. Although employees should receive overtime pay for hours exceeding 40 per week, by agreement between employees and management banking of up to 5 hours is allowed when these hours are accumulated in one week and taken as credit the next week. It is recommended, however, that daily working hours be limited to 10 and weekly hours to 45. In France, however, as in its neighboring countries, workers are most interested in extending vacations and weekends, a trend most unions support. This focus diverts attention away from the adoption of flexitime.

There is one experiment, widely cited, which seems representative of the French experience. Staff members of the accounts and data processing departments of Bergerat-Monnoyearur were involved in a flexitime experiment. No part-time employees nor those performing specific service tasks, e.g., switchboard operators, were included. The bandwidth was from 8 A.M. to 7 P.M. with core times from 9:15 A.M. to 3:30 P.M., and a fixed lunch break assigned from 12:30 to 1:15 P.M. Hengstler cumulative time recorders were used by all employees. The settlement period was 1 month, and a carry over of 10 debit or credit hours was permitted.[6]

The organization found flexitime to be extremely beneficial for employees as well as for the organization. Employees seemed more relaxed, more cooperative, and experienced an increase in morale and individual responsibility. Absenteeism, one of the original reasons for the introduction of flexitime, was reduced by 60 to 75 percent. Thus, flexitime helped the organization to accomplish its objective—reduced absenteeism—through the provision of benefits to the worker. Consistent with this (and a requirement for the success of the system by the firm's criteria), employee reaction was very positive toward flexitime. Similar results were obtained in a survey carried out at Sommer S.A. and at Biscuiterie Nantaise. Sommer S.A. reports 74 percent of employees are regular users of *horaires souples,* and roughly 85 percent at B.N. Satisfaction is high, and the employees list the advantages of flexitime as follows: 90 percent report advantages in terms of transportation, 88 percent report positive effects on personal life, 74 percent report positive effects on family, and 74 percent feel that their organization of work has improved.

ENGLAND

Although only approximately 10 percent of the British work force is currently on flexitime, the Department of Manpower in England claims that flexible working hours could feasibly become a feature of employment for up to 50 percent of all employees.[7] The amount of flexibility enjoyed by British firms on flexitime varies a great deal from one company to the next. Flexbands range from 15 minutes in the most restrictive cases to 3 hours under very flexible systems. The amount of debit or credit hours which can be carried forward varies as well, although most firms allow only a few hours of banking. The settlement period in England is usually 1 month, coinciding with the accounting period (the period between paychecks) of most firms. Sixty percent of the companies on flexitime schedules utilize specially developed time-recording equipment. Most of the others use existing, modified time clocks, and some are even trying the honor system via time sheets.

The British Institute of Personnel Management has reported results of periodic surveys of its members and concluded that flexitime is enthusiastically approved by management and workers alike. These findings are confirmed by studies which reported that most of the employees under flexitime seem to react positively to the system and do not want to return to the routine of their original fixed hours scheduling.[8]

The positions that unions in England have taken on flexitime are not consistent. While union leaders at the national level have voiced opposition to flexitime more strongly than in other European countries, the local unions have supported the system. This support, at times, has been an outright rejection of the national union leadership. Recently, union leaders have undertaken a reevaluation of the implications of flexible working hours system, although no official statement has yet been issued.

The Legal and General Assurance Society is an insurance company which introduced flexitime in 1972.[9] Over 230 individuals were involved in the system. Employees were contracted to work 35 hours per week, and the working day extended from 8:30 A.M. to

6 P.M., with 10 A.M. to 4 P.M. as the core period. Employees were allowed to use credit hours to take a full day or two half days off each month, and 7 hours of debit or credit time could be carried forward monthly.

Seventy-six percent of the workers felt "very favorably" toward flexitime, and eighteen percent felt "favorably" toward it. Specifically, they enjoyed the freedom to choose starting and finishing times and the ability to build up credit hours. Seventy percent were indifferent to the newly installed cumulative time-keeping equipment. The company found that once employees selected their new schedule from the range possible under the flexitime system, they tended to stay with this schedule and did not make further use of the flexibility available. Employees reported that the system provided a better environment for the accomplishment of work-related activities. Improvements were observed in performance, use of skills, participation in group planning, and trust exhibited by management, while stress and fatigue among workers were reported to have decreased.

The reactions of the supervisors and managers are comparable to those of the workers described above. Of the 94 managers and supervisors involved, 70 percent felt very favorably toward flexitime, and nearly 85 percent experienced a greater degree of personal freedom. Nevertheless, the majority of these individuals also felt that flexitime has no effect on absenteeism, overtime, or on the quality of work performed by their employees. Only 22 percent felt that there has been a marginal or significant increase in productivity.

Thus, the experience at the Legal and General Assurance Society is somewhat mixed. While workers indicated overwhelming support for the system, managers and supervisors had more mixed feelings.

Another English company, the Essex River Authority, has realized improvements in productivity, absenteeism, tardiness, and short-term sickness absences, and a decrease in traffic congestion.[10]

The Schreiber Wood Industries, a furniture manufacturing company that has implemented flexitime, has realized a much higher profit and found that employees do not seem to want to return to the routineness of their fixed schedules. Workers felt that the ability to finish a task before leaving work was an important aspect of flexitime. Further, they reported a better balance between working and private lives. Avoiding rush hour traffic was also considered a benefit. In this company, consistent with its policy of dealing with employees on a trust basis, an honor system was the only form of time recording used. The company delegated the control function to its employees through a work-force, or shop-floor, committee of employees. This committee examined absenteeism among fellow workers in order to limit malingering. Thus, flexitime is one aspect of an overall management philosophy which grants as much autonomy as possible to the work force. Within this context, it is not surprising that managers reported a reduction in turnover and a greater sense of worker responsibility.

Employees in another firm, Allen and Hanburys Ltd., were given a questionnaire concerning their attitudes toward flexible working hours. One hundred percent accepted the concept of flexitime and two-thirds claimed that working conditions were improved with the system. Those who felt that conditions had worsened since the implementation of the plan did not disagree with the system, but felt that certain restrictions had been placed upon them through the need for extensive teamwork.

Other research conducted in England has shown that English organizations tend to be consistent in their opinions of flexitime and its effects. In one company, Pilkington Brothers Ltd., 100 percent of the employees were in favor of flexitime, 80 percent felt that it increased morale, and 52 percent felt that it increased responsible attitudes among the staff. In two other firms, Wiggins Teape and Pakcel Converters Ltd., approximately 98 percent of the employees in each voted for the introduction of such a scheme. At Pakcel Converters, 74 percent of employees felt the plan to be advantageous to the workers.[11] In a poll of 700 British employees, the *Department of Employment Gazette* found that neither workers nor management had any complaints concerning flexitime. Only 1 out of 5 found the time clock system irritating, an echo of previous findings.

Another study reported that female employees in local government council offices felt that flexible working hours were advantageous with respect to travel, domestic arrangements, and shopping, and that they were now able to adjust their work times to the work load.[12] Management, in general, was worried about sufficient coverage at the extreme ends of the flexitime bandwidth, yet most seemed enthusiastic or satisfied with the system.[13] They also felt that flexible work hours heightened the ability to plan work well. Moreover, in reappraising attitudes toward time-keeping mechanisms, it was found that attitudes which were originally negative became more positive as employees experienced the benefits of the information provided by the cumulative recorders.

SCANDINAVIA

The experience of flexible working hours in the Scandinavian countries was summarized in 1973 by Elbing, Gadon and, Gordon:

> Complicated nation-wide labor contracts in Scandinavia tended to slow the introduction of flexible hours or "flextid". National unions resisted. Interest by local unions, however, has resulted in pressure to change the attitudes of the national unions.

These researchers go on to describe one progressive Stockholm firm in which management agreed to the local union's request for flexible hours. When the national union refused to agree to a contract modification, however, the local union threatened to buy time on television to condemn the national union for its stand against the interests of its local branch. Following this action, the system was implemented. By now, numerous additional companies are using flexible hours in Sweden and Denmark, and sporadic experiments are reported in Finland and Norway.

Recently, Mr. Tony Anderson of the Swedish Association for Personnel Administration reported that a great number of companies are using flexitime in industry and in the service sector, especially in big cities, although no accurate statistics are available to date. However, although flexitime does seem to be gaining popularity in Sweden, there seem to be social and environmental constraints which are limiting its implementation. Betsy Fryman describes two possible reasons:

> One reason, perhaps, is that country's extensive system of municipal childcare facilities, easing the burden on working mothers of taking children long distances to baby-sitters and nurseries, and picking them up at some fixed hour later on. Another factor is the short period of daylight

in the winter. Even with flexibility, the Swedish worker would have little or no daylight at the end of the day to enjoy recreational opportunities much of the year.[14]

In general, the well-known trends toward liberal work legislation in Sweden further reduce the level of priority assigned to flexitime. For example, by law, every worker receives at least 5 weeks vacation per year. Parenthood benefits provide *either* parent with leave following the birth of a child, allowing them to share the 7 months of permitted time off, and *either* parent has the right to take a leave if a child becomes sick. The opportunity for sabbaticals is increasing, and focus on the retired employee through part-time work availability is becoming more widespread. Still, it is impressive that in spite of its low priority, flexitime is spreading rapidly.

OTHER COUNTRIES

Because of the geographical proximity of European countries and the interdependence of their economies, flexitime has penetrated all borders, though little research or documentation is available outside the countries already described.

In Italy, *L'orario flessibile* was implemented at Fiat, and 25,000 employees, mainly administrative and technical staff, are enjoying a relatively restricted form of flexitime. Elbing, Gadon, and Gordon[15] reported that at IBP, 99 percent of the employees were in favor of the system and 90 percent use it, "with young people coming early and leaving early, middle-aged employees extending their lunch hours and mothers arriving later in the morning." Other companies using the system are Perugina, Dalmino-Bergamo, Italsider-Genoa, and a variety of firms in Milan. Since this report, little new information is available.

In 1978, Rene Cordeire, the executive secretary of the Portugese Personnel Management Association, reported that there are various companies employing *Horario flexibile,* but no statistics are available as yet. The report from Spain is similar although flexitime seems more common and has support from the Civil Service Authority.

Stover reported experimentation at the Albert Heyn company in the Netherlands with positive results reported by both management and employees. Nestlé has been an early user in many of its subsidiaries including the one in Holland. There are some reports of sporadic usage of flexitime from Belgium (Meisser, Electronic General) and Luxemburg (F.A. Mersch).

Israel has also shown interest in the system. Because of the central role of the National Labor Federation in negotiation and contract signing, regulations for work arrangements are uniform, although they allow limited freedom to the local union to agree on any variations in working hours and overtime regulations. In spite of these limitations, flexitime has come to the attention of both the employers and the labor movement.[16] For example, two insurance companies have implemented flexitime on an experimental basis, one university administration is experimenting with a limited version, and an extensive 6-month trial has been initiated by the Civil Service Commission for 400 employees in 5 offices.[17] Interest in the system is growing, as evidenced by the numerous seminars on the topic conducted by the Israeli Management Association. Further, in 1976 the National Labor Federation formed a committee to investigate the appropriateness of the system for a variety of professions in the work force. Although interest is growing, other working conditions receive priority:

sudden economic fluctuations demand continuous negotiations on salary and fringe-benefits issues; the common practice of 6 working days weekly is challenged by various organizations; and the summer working hours which allow employees a longer free afternoon (by starting earlier in the morning and/or skipping lunch) has been a common practice in a variety of organizations. The compressed workweek (and reduced weekly hours) has been adopted by a few private companies representing a trend similar to that expressed by the interest in flexitime.

Poland and the Soviet Union have recently shown interest in flexitime. Various industries in Estonia, in the Soviet Union, have established flexible working hour schedules.[18] Employees must work 41 hours per week. Anything over that amount is placed in a time bank. The employee may only draw 85 percent of the time he contributes. The remaining 15 percent is put into a general fund and is used by supervisors to reward deserving workers. In a survey of the employees, nearly 70 percent felt that the value of time had increased for them, almost 70 percent felt that they were able to devote more time to child-rearing activities and almost 65 percent planned their leisure time more effectively. Over half of the employees involved felt less tension on the job site and improved relations with their superiors. Employees also felt that flexitime eliminated the fear of being late. Estonian management is enthusiastic about the system because of its ability to recapture time lost through lateness or absenteeism and because of the decrease of overtime remunerations.

SUMMARY

Over 5 million people were involved in some sort of flexible working hours schedule in Europe in 1976, demonstrating that flexitime can be applied to any organization with a favorable climate if technological factors do not restrict its use.[19] A company does not have to alter existing work structures, and no special type of social organization is needed. The considerations for the successful implementation and maintenance of the system include production control, an administrative system, the specification of the role of the work council, and receptive employee and managerial attitudes.

The importance of this last factor, a receptive attitude, cannot be underestimated. In general, employees (at any level) tend to be receptive when they have been included in the planning, design, and implementation phases. It is in this area that work legislation and practices in Europe have created an environment particularly suited to the adoption of flexitime. Specifically, the Works Councils in England, the *Betriebsrat* in Germany, and the level of union involvement in other countries have required a high level of interaction with employees (or employee representatives) in the planning of such systems. This level of inclusion is reflected in the success rate of flexitime systems throughout Europe, and its phenomenal rate of adoption since 1967 when it was first introduced.

Time-Recording Systems

Various time-recording systems are currently in use throughout Europe and others are still in experimental stages. In general, the concern is to provide the greatest degree of freedom while maintaining a minimal amount of management control. Common throughout Europe —especially in England, France, Germany, and Switzerland—are the electromechanical instruments which show only the daily cumulative total of hours worked, and not starting or finishing times.

In Britain, for example, 60 percent of the companies using a flexitime system have specially developed equipment for time-recording purposes. Others are using existing, modified time clocks. One company (Pilkington Brothers Ltd.) utilizes a clock and card system in which the cards are sent to the computer department of the firm every week and a printout is created which shows credits and debits, sick leave, holidays taken, etc. Still others use a manual system, which the employee is on his honor to complete, although a supervisor's signature is usually obtained on a periodic basis.

One German company (Messerschmidt) uses a time clock from which punched cards are fed into a computer every 10 days. Another German firm (Lufthansa's Cologne office) uses a sophisticated time clock which graphically records starting and finishing times on a special identity card.

In general, Europe is more sophisticated in its use of time-recording mechanisms for flexitime than the United States. The most obvious explanation is that organizations in Europe have been experimenting with flexible working hours for a longer period of time. Indeed, all of the cumulative time-recording mechanisms designed specially for flexitime which are sold in North America are manufactured in Europe.

Level of Utilization of System by Employees

The level of utilization of flexitime varied from company to company and country to country. In most of the countries described, the credit-debit system was enjoyed by a majority of workers. In two British government offices, 68 percent of the employees had built up enough credit hours to take one-half to a full day off per month and 50 percent of these employees did this regularly. Less than 5 percent had built up debits, and this seemed to be a pattern which was avoided by most workers. In another English firm, 30 percent of the employees felt that a desirable aspect of the work situation was the ability to accumulate credit hours and to be able to take a half or a full day off. (Note that this implies core time off as a part of the flexitime system implemented by these firms.) In an organization in Germany, most of the employees involved had approximately 4 hours credit per month and few had built up any debit hours.

In terms of use of the *variability* offered by flexitime, it was found that most European employees, like their American counterparts, tend to plan their workday within the range available according to their needs and to vary little from this schedule. Those workers that do change their schedules do so soon after the implementation of FWH, although a few changes occur later on as the employees become more experienced with the plan. In general, it was established that employees' arrival and departure times are *earlier* than before flexitime implementation and vary little from week to week. The determinants of an employee's schedule are usually the avoidance of peak traveling hours, the coordination of travel time with other employees, and habit—older employees, for example, tended to remain on the schedule which they had observed before the implementation of flexible working hours. In some cases, it was observed that there was only slight use of the plan at first, but gradual adaptation led to greater utilization of flexitime after several months. Although workers did not vary their schedule significantly from day to day, they felt a sense of freedom with the knowledge that they were able, if they desired, to vary their hours at any time. Young people tended to arrive and leave work earlier while middle-aged people extended their lunch hour periods. Mothers arrived later in the morning than young people and, therefore, left later in the evening.

In summary, although many employees adhered to a relatively fixed schedule while on flexitime, two kinds of benefits resulted in overall positive attitudes: first, the psychological aspects of control, freedom, and responsibility; and second, the more substantive benefits of better home-work coordination and ease of transportation.

NOTES

1. Keppler, B. European industries. In Robison, D. *Alternative work patterns—Changing approaches to work scheduling.* Report, of a Conference cosponsored by the National Center for Productivity and Quality of Working Life and the Work in America Institute, Inc. New York, 1976.

2. Bolton, J. H. *Flexible working hours.* London: Angar Publications Ltd., 1971.

    Wade, M. *Flexible working hours in practice.* New York: Halsted Press, 1973.

3. Stover, R. Personnel management innovations in Europe. *Personnel Journal,* February 1972 *51,* 113–115.

    Wade, M. op. cit.

4. Elbing, A. O., Gadon, H., and Gordon, J. R. M. Flexible working hours: It's about time. *Harvard Business Review,* January-February 1974, pp. 18–33.

    ———Time for a human time-table. *European Business,* Autumn 1973, pp. 46–54.

5. Willatt, N. Flextime at Sandoz. *European Business,* Autumn 1973, pp. 56–61.

6. *Flexible working hours.* London: Institute of Personnel Management, 1972.

7. Caulkin, S. The flexible working age. *Management Today,* March 1976, pp. 81–85.

8. Wade, op. cit.

9. Evans, M. G. *A longitudinal analysis of the impact of flexible working hours.* Faculty of Management Studies, University of Toronto, undated.

    ———. Notes on the impact of flextime in a large insurance company. I. Reactions of non-supervisory employees. *Occupational Psychology,* 1973, *47,* 237–240.

    Partridge, B. E. Notes on the impact of flextime in a large insurance company. II. Reactions of supervisors and managers. *Occupational Psychology,* 1973, *47,* 241–242.

10. Summers, D. *Flexible working hours—A Case study.* London: Institute of Personnel Management, 1972.

11. Wade, op. cit.

12. Bartlett, J. B. Attitudes to the changing week. *Personnel Management,* 1973, *5,* 36–38.

13. Baum, S. J. and Young, W. McEwan. *A practical guide to flexible working hours.* New Jersey: Noyes Data Corp., 1973.

14. Miller, J. *Innovations in working patterns.* Washington, D.C.: U.S. Trade Union Seminar on Alternative Work Patterns in Europe, 1978, 7.

15. Elbing, A. O., Gadon, H., and Gordon, J. R. Time for a human time-table. *European Business Review,* Autumn 1973, *39,* 46–54.

16. Ronen, S. Flexitime as a planned organizational change—The Israeli experience. *The Israel Review of Business Economics,* 1976, *2,* 1, 5–18.

17. Barkai, J. *Flexible working hours as a planned organizational change and its effects on different organizational variables.* Unpublished Dissertation, Faculty of Management, The Leon Racanati Graduate School of Business Administration, Tel Aviv University, November 1976.

18. Shipler, David K. Soviet experiment in flexible work hours said to be succeeding. *The New York Times,* March 20, 1978.

19. Stein, B., Cohen, A., and Gadon, H. Flexitime—work when you want to. *Psychology Today,* June 1976.

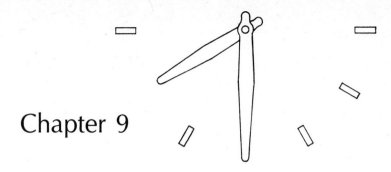

Chapter 9

The Public Sector: A Case Study Office of Personnel Management

INTRODUCTION

Relevance of the Case Study

A case study describing the implementation of flexitime within a large organization of the federal bureaucracy such as the Office of Personnel Management (OPM), can be examined on several levels, ranging from micro to macro:

1. The implementation and results of flexitime within specific bureaus or regional offices (which represent reasonably sized organizations themselves).

2. The subsequent implementation of flexitime throughout all headquarters' offices of the organization.

3. The role of the organization in implementing flexitime throughout the federal government. This role is unique for the Office of Personnel Management—and will be discussed in further detail.

The focus of this case study will be on the second level: the implementation of flexitime throughout all OPM headquarters. What is described here is the chain of events leading to flexitime implementation, although the OPM itself has pointed out that the sequence of events was not necessarily part of a master plan. The three bureaus that first implemented flexitime did so on their own. A management decision was then made that no further flexitime experiments could take place until a thorough study had been made of the existing systems and a recommendation made whether or not to have one uniform program throughout the central office.

Despite the fact that the initial introduction of flexitime into the OPM was not planned, a description of this methodology may be helpful for large organizations in the public and private sectors considering flexitime installation. The OPM provides a description of a

methodology for breaking an organization into units small enough to be the focus of evaluation for a new system, and for forming a group to study results obtained and to make
recommendations regarding their applicability for the rest of the organization.

For those employed in the public sector, this case may help to provide information on
dealing specifically with the federal government—a bureaucracy with limited flexibility. In
this sector, flexibility is limited not only by the many levels in the reporting structure of the
bureaucracy and by union-imposed restrictions but also by federal laws and regulations
governing personnel policies, which may make it difficult to implement new policies and
procedures.

Of course, the private sector is not free from those types of problems either, and we
therefore feel that a case study of the Office of Personnel Management can also be quite
helpful for those in private industry considering flexitime. In particular, those organizations
whose nonexempt employees are unionized may find this study relevant.

Background and Organization

The Office of Personnel Management is a complex organization, with its central office
located in the metropolitan Washington, D.C. area, and 10 regional offices providing decen-
tralized operations in the field. Figure 9-1 is a simplified organization chart of the OPM. The
central office is made up of many bureaus and staff offices reporting to the Office of the
Executive Director. The basic purpose of the OPM is to provide policy leadership in the area
of personnel management and to administer a merit system of recruiting, examining, training,
and promoting throughout the federal government. In general, the Office of Personnel
Management provides certificates containing the names of qualified people for government
agencies, and an array of other personnel services to applicants, employees, and retirees;
it is the central personnel agency of the executive branch of the government.

Because of the OPM's key role in administering laws and regulations pertaining to
working hours for federal agencies, the flexible work hours concept came to its attention
in 1973 when the Social Security Administration requested advice as to whether such a
system was permissible under the personnel laws and regulations applicable to federal
employees. The Bureau of Policies and Standards, which has overall program responsibility
for flexitime policies in the federal government, determined that the rigid scheduling requirements for federal employees precluded use of compressed work schedules which allow
banking and borrowing of hours from day to day. However, such laws did not preclude
flexible schedules which would allow employees to vary their starting and quitting times
within the 8-hour day and 40-hour week. Since flexible schedules had been used in Europe
and in the private sector in the United States with beneficial results for both employees and
their organizations, the Office of Personnel Management decided to actively inform federal
agencies of flexitime's advantages and disadvantages and the degrees of flexibility available
under current law. At the same time, it was decided that the OPM, as the central personnel
agency, should propose legislation to Congress which would amend the overtime pay laws

*Prior to January 1979 the Office of Personnel Management was called the Civil Service Commission
(CSC). For constructive comments and helpful suggestions on an earlier draft of this chapter, the author
is grateful to the following officers of the Office of Personnel Management: John J. Burns, Chief of Policy
and Program Development, Personnel and Labor Relations Division; Barbara Fiss, Program Manager;
and Thomas Cowley, Bureau of Policies and Standards.

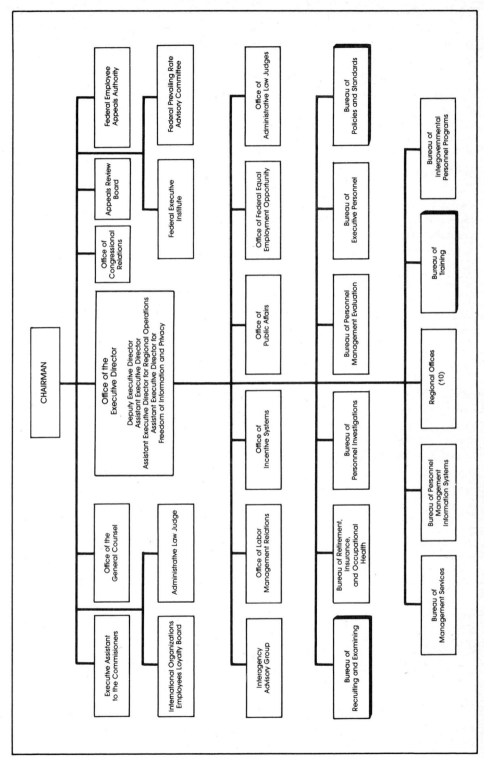

Figure 9–1 Organizational chart, Office of Personnel Management.

and the laws pertaining to scheduling requirements for federal employees in order to give agencies and employees an opportunity to test all forms of flexible and compressed work schedules. This legislation is discussed in greater detail in Chapter 18.

Because the bureaus and regional offices within the OPM tend to function somewhat autonomously, it is possible to implement certain policies and procedures within these organizational components, independently of the rest of the organization. In light of the great interest in flexitime within the OPM, several bureaus made independent decisions to test the concept: the Bureau of Policies and Standards, the Bureau of Training, and the Bureau of Recruiting and Examining were the first components within the OPM to implement flexitime.

Because the great potential of this system was observed in these bureaus and favorable reports were received from other federal agencies that had implemented flexitime, a task force was formed to investigate the possibility of implementing flexitime for all Office of Personnel Management employees throughout the metropolitan District of Columbia area. Since the OPM acts as the central personnel agency for the executive branch, implementation of flexitime within the OPM could well serve as a model and facilitate adoption of flexitime schedules in other agencies of the federal government. While flexitime was first instituted on a micro level—individual offices and bureaus of the government—it has the potential for adoption on a macro level, and the OPM represents the vehicle for this possible transition.

The discussion of FWH in the federal government begins by describing the feasibility study and pilot project completed in a single bureau of the OPM, the Bureau of Policies and Standards (BPS). The activities of the BPS became a major source of information when the OPM decided to investigate the feasibility of implementing flexitime throughout its central office. A task force was formed which, instead of conducting new feasibility surveys, collected information already available in the BPS concerning flexitime experiments and information on experiments conducted by other departments or bureaus within the OPM and other federal agencies. This process of information gathering is illustrated in Figure 9-2.

Following the brief description of activities in the BPS, a detailed report and analysis of the task force methodology, conclusions, and recommendations is presented. Then, in the next chapter, a broad picture of the position of flexitime within the federal government is given.

Much of the information presented here is taken from the report produced by the task force, especially from its results, conclusions, and recommendations. The other major source of information is the CSC *Personnel Manual Letter,* No. 610-1, which sets forth the policies used for introducing flexitime throughout the central office. The degree and amount of information investigated by the task force was extensive. Much of this information is presented here, not because of its general interest value, but because it provides the reader with an idea of the full extent of the aspects of organizational and personal life affected by flexitime. The presentation of this information may help the reader to successfully implement flexitime in his own organization, incorporating details which might have otherwise been overlooked.

Legal and Contractual Constraints

Before continuing, it is important to reiterate the environment within which the Office of Personnel Management operates. Specifically, this encompasses the federal laws establish-

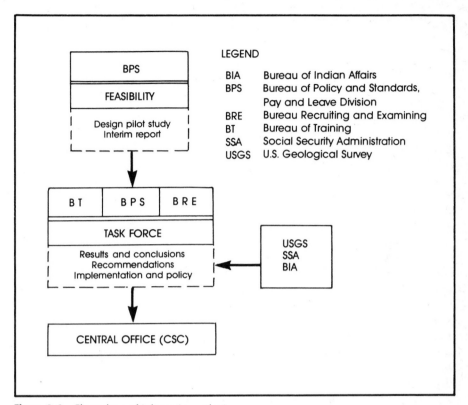

Figure 9–2   Chronology of information gathering.

ing the guidelines for hours of employment and any constraints imposed by labor unions. These laws were originally established to protect employees by ensuring, for example, that they are not forced to work more than a certain number of hours without being paid overtime and do not have to work a split shift. Unfortunately, these laws now constrain the level of flexibility of working hours which can be considered.* This problem poses questions concerning the validity of such laws in today's work environment.

The laws which apply to federal government employees state the following:

1.   Employees scheduled to work anytime between 6 P.M. and 6 A.M. must receive night differential pay.

2.   Working hours for full-time employees must be scheduled at least 1 week in advance and working hours are to be the same each day.

3.   Breaks in the working day (including lunch) exceeding 1 hour in length may not be scheduled by an agency.

---

*On September 29, 1978, President Carter signed the Federal Employees Flexible and Compressed Work Schedules Act of 1978, permitting federal agencies to experiment with flexible working schedules for 3 years, *notwithstanding* legal restrictions. See Chapter 18 for a discussion of this act.

4. No employee may work over 40 hours in 1 week or 8 hours in 1 day without receiving overtime pay.

5. The 40-hour work period must be performed in a period of not more than 6 of any 7 consecutive days.

An important aspect of these restrictions is the fact that there is no option of employee choice. Even if the employee wished to work outside the limits of these guidelines, legally he could not do so. This factor constrains the implementation of a flexible working hours schedule to an 8-hour day, worked between the hours of 6 A.M. and 6 P.M., with a lunch break generally consisting of ½ hour, for a total working day of 8½ hours.

INITIATING A FEASIBILITY STUDY AND PILOT STUDY

The Bureau of Policies and Standards (BPS) was a logical choice for an initial investigation of flexitime at the OPM, as the Bureau is responsible for governmental policies relating to hours of work. In February 1975 the director of the BPS authorized the formation of a study group to determine the feasibility of implementing flexitime, and if deemed feasible, to conduct a pilot study.

In conducting a feasibility study, the group submitted questionnaires to all 229 BPS employees in order to determine interest in flexitime. While awaiting the survey results, committee members investigated the possibility of implementation problems within each division of the Bureau. Their reports indicated a high degree of interest in the system, and no division within the BPS indicated an inability to introduce flexitime. In addition to the survey, subcommittees were formed to investigate subject areas relevant to flexitime implementation. These subject areas included time accounting systems, building and services, an analysis of the survey results, and the creation of an employee handbook.

The survey results, when they came in, indicated that the chances for a successful implementation of flexitime at BPS were excellent. Of 194 employees responding, 67.5 percent indicated that flexitime was either important or very important to them. Roughly 50 percent of the employees indicated that they would arrive between 6 and 8 A.M., and 50 percent between 8 and 9:30 A.M. In fact, the preferences for a flexitime model indicated by each division were similar enough to allow the committee to arrive at a single, general model feasible for use throughout the entire Bureau.

The positive results obtained in the feasibility study led the committee to the second of its objectives: to define criteria with which to evaluate the test, and to supervise its implementation. All BPS employees were included in the experiment. Ground rules, including the model itself, were derived through the survey results. The study group planned to conduct observations prior to the initiation of flexitime in order to provide a baseline for the evaluation of changes. Feedback on the effects of flexitime was to be provided through objective information and observations at three, six, and twelve months. The focus of information and observations would concentrate on two areas: Bureau effectiveness and employee satisfaction.

A major emphasis of the study group was the importance of an orientation program for both supervisors and employees concerning the program. Meetings were scheduled for each of these groups in order to introduce it to the concept. The objectives of the supervisors' meeting were to prepare them for changes in responsibilities resulting from the program, to enable them to be authoritative sources of information for their employees, and to allow a sharing of views, experiences, and potential problems. In addition, supervisors were instructed on methods to be used in providing continuing feedback on the experiment.

The objectives of employee orientation included acquainting employees with the specifics of the program and preparing them for carrying out their responsibilities under the system.

The committee decided to prepare a handbook explaining flexitime to supervisors and employees in order to provide a clear understanding of the extent and limitations of the system. Such a handbook, it was felt, would help to avoid later misunderstandings and labor relations problems, and was therefore an important element in flexitime implementation. In addition to their directives for implementing an experimental study, the BPS study group produced a detailed proposal for the evaluation of flexitime in the Bureau, including a proposed methodology, a list of variables to be measured, and guidelines on data collection. The guidelines set forth by the BPS in their feasibility report and experimental study provided much of the information used by the OPM task force in its evaluation of the possibility of flexitime for its entire central office. Moreover, these guidelines produced by the BPS were offered as the model by the OPM for other agencies and bureaus to follow as they undertook steps to implement flexitime.

INITIATING AN EVALUATION OF EXISTING FLEXITIME EXPERIMENTS

Interest and Decision to Investigate Appropriateness

As discussed above, the Bureau of Policies and Standards conducted a study in the early part of 1975 to determine the feasibility of implementing a flexitime experiment within the Bureau. As a result of this study, the BPS decided to engage in a flexitime experiment beginning in July 1975.

In the meantime, and quite independently from what was happening in BPS, two other bureaus, the Bureau of Training (BT) and the Bureau of Recruiting and Examining (BRE), implemented their own versions of flexitime within their respective bureaus. BT began its experiment in January 1975, and BRE in September 1975. All of this interest in flexitime can be traced to the OPM's leadership role in personnel management in the federal government. The fact that BPS was looking at the concept of flexitime to determine whether any changes should be proposed to Congress regarding hours of duty for federal employees was well known to the Commission management at the bureau level. These bureaus, on the basis of their delegated authority for fixing hours of duty for their employees, decided to conduct their own experiments in flexitime.

When the OPM's director of personnel and labor relations reviewed what was happening in the three bureaus, he realized that each of the three had implemented a different version of flexitime and that there was no uniformity in their proposed evaluation methodology. In addition, discussions with union officials had revealed that there was a good deal of union interest in extending flexitime, on an experimental basis, throughout the OPM's central office. As a result, he recommended to top management that a task force be formed to investigate the possibility of having one uniform experiment for all central office organizations. Top management approved this recommendation and ordered that a task force be formed.

Task Force Purpose and Objectives

The purpose and objectives of the task force, as stated in the action plan portion of the Task Force Report, were to undertake a "comprehensive review of central office flexitime experiments currently taking place and recommend the Commission's future course of action." Specifically, the task force set out to evaluate ongoing flexitime experiments both within the Office of Personnel Management and in other agencies, to assess their effect on the work force, operations, productivity, and services, and to make recommendations to top management concerning how the OPM should proceed with respect to its own implementation of flexitime.

Task Force Formation and Composition

The task force on flexitime was formed in October 1975 under the auspices of the deputy executive director of the OPM. Membership included representatives from each central office bureau as well as the larger staff offices. The recognized union, Local 32 of the American Federation of Government Employees, was also represented on the task force. The chairman was a member of the Personnel and Labor Relations Division of the CSC. The makeup of the task force was an attempt to ensure that information was received from each major central office organization, and that employees were appropriately and fairly represented by their union. This commitment to union participation was evident throughout the task force report in its areas of investigation as well as in its recommendations.

TASK FORCE PROCESS

Information Gathering and Method of Operation

The chief sources of information for the task force in its search for data were the three central office bureaus, the Bureau of Training (BT), the Bureau of Recruiting and Examining (BRE), and the Bureau of Policy and Standards (BPS). In the first two bureaus, this information included an analysis of the flexitime evaluations completed by their own management officials. BPS had not yet completed a formal review. (These three bureaus had implemented flexitime between January and September 1975).

In addition, the results of flexitime experiments in five commission regions (Boston, Chicago, Dallas, San Francisco, and Seattle), other federal agencies, state and local governments, industry, and foreign governments were evaluated. More specifically, management and union officials were contacted at the Social Security Administration in Baltimore and the U.S. Geological Survey in Reston (no union) to obtain information concerning the impact of flexitime on the operation of the agency and on labor relations.

In order to gather the necessary information, the task force relied upon several methods. From those bureaus currently engaged in flexitime experiments, the task force obtained special reports, as well as reviewing any existing data on productivity, leave taking, overtime, or any other statistical indicators which might describe the impact of flexitime. In addition, special studies were undertaken by the task force itself in areas where no data were available, or where it was felt that flexitime might have an impact if implemented throughout the OPM beyond that which was experienced in smaller applications. For example, implementation on a large scale might affect public parking availability for those who arrive later in the morning.

Scope of Coverage

In determining the scope of coverage of their report, the task force reviewed ongoing flexitime experiments and their generalizability to other OPM offices.

In order to conduct their study, the task force established four committees: mission effectiveness, employees and supervisors, facilities and transportation, and labor relations. The areas of investigation are outlined in Figure 9-3.

RESULTS AND CONCLUSIONS

Mission Effectiveness

In general, supervisors and managers in those bureaus undergoing flexitime experiments felt that there was an increase in productivity, although specific evidence was difficult to document because of difficulties in measurement. The Bureau of Training (BT) and the Bureau of Policy and Standards (BPS) had not made an attempt to measure the impact of flexitime on productivity because of the nature of their work. At the very least, however, management did feel that there was an increase in productivity resulting from improved morale.

The productivity measures taken by the Bureau of Recruiting and Examining (BRE) indicated favorable results. However, the task force was reluctant to attribute these results to flexitime, because of other concurrent factors which could have influenced productivity, such as changes in work-load volume and mix, changes in staff, and changes in measurement procedures. In spite of these problems in measurement, however, most managers and employees felt that there was an increase in productivity. As proof of this change, they pointed to a significant reduction in tardiness and to the more efficient use of hours at the beginning and end of the workday.

The committee also contacted agencies in other branches of the government experimenting with flexitime in order to gain information on their experiences. Of 8 agencies that had information on productivity, only 2 could report a measured increase (for specific information, see Chapter 10). In general, the task force found it difficult to obtain clear evidence of increased productivity because of the difficulties of measuring productivity per se, the unavailability of control data, and the problem of isolating the impact of flexitime as a sole causative agent.

None of the three internal OPM bureaus had conducted systematic studies to determine the actual degree of reduction in tardiness. However, most offices did feel that this problem

The scope of coverage will relate to (a) a review of experiments currently underway, and (b) whether current experimentation should be extended to other Commission offices. Each of the following areas will be examined in relation to (a) and (b) above:

Impact on service to the public, and other agencies.

Impact on employees, productivity, leave, and overtime.

Problems of supervision, including:
- accountability
- assigning and reviewing work
- coordination with other offices and agencies
- communications
- planning
- continuity of operations
- coping with work emergencies.

Impact of hazardous weather conditions and other such emergencies.

Impact on traffic and transportation.

Impact on labor relations.

Impact on building conditions, including:
- security conditions
- health unit coverage
- air conditioning, heating, lighting
- parking.

General items of concern, including:
- whether there should be a common core time for all central office organizations
- if present exeperiments are extended, whether all central office organizations should be
  required to participate uniformly in the extension, or
  whether experiments should continue to be handled on a bureau-by-bureau basis
- whether all bureaus and staff offices should be required to participate: if not, who should make the decision whether or not to participate
- what advance planning must be done prior to implementing an experiment
- whether there should be an attitude survey on flexitime
- who should be authorized to curtail or cancel experiments.

Figure 9–3 Scope of task force coverage.

had been virtually eliminated. The internal bureaus did report a significant decrease in use of short-term leave (1 to 2 hours). Employees were now able to incorporate matters such as doctors' appointments, personal business, and unexpected transportation problems into the flexband portions of the day.

Outside of the OPM the task force found impressive results in this area. The District of Columbia Department of Human Resources reported a 68 percent decrease in the amount of sick leave used and the U.S. Army Tank Automotive Command reported a 29 percent reduction in sick leave.

The only organization reporting usable data on overtime was the Social Security Administration, another agency outside of the OPM. They reported a 63.3 percent decrease in overtime usage during the flexitime experiment, while the same amount of work was produced. Although the data on overtime was sparse, the task force did feel that the potential for reducing overtime was great, not only because the increased flexibility of work hours enabled employees to work later in the evenings but also because there was a possibility of increased productivity.

The task force found that all OPM bureaus and regions on flexitime felt that flexitime had resulted in an improvement in service to the public and to other agencies. The most noticeable increase in service was in the early morning, especially before 8:15 A.M. One bureau did report that it had to make an effort to ensure that adequate service was provided during 'normal' hours (8:15 A.M. to 4:45 P.M.). The task force felt that potential existed for extending service, particularly telephone service to other time zones, which was usually difficult to coordinate.

There was not enough information available to be able to measure the impact of flexitime on reducing turnover. The BRE reported that they found flexitime to be an effective recruiting device, however.

In reviewing the results reported by the three bureaus within the OPM, the task force was faced with the problem of little solid evaluative data, which made it difficult to judge the effectiveness of the flexitime experiments. From the evidence reported here, it is clear that the task force often based its conclusions on the opinions, observations, and perceptions of those involved in the experiments. This problem is reflected in the Task Force Report and CSC *Personnel Manual Letter,* and in the directives requiring regular measurements and reporting of results from participating bureaus and agencies.

Employee and Supervisory Impact

In their attempt to determine the impact of flexitime on employee responsibilities and duties, the task force reviewed results obtained by other federal agencies outside the OPM and by state and local governments, as well as those obtained by the three OPM central office bureaus then using flexitime—BT, BRE and BPS.

Most of the data reported by outside organizations was obtained through interviews and questionnaires. The favorable nature of these reports is supported by the fact that most of the organizations that had started flexitime on an experimental basis had, after a period, extended its coverage throughout the organization.

The reports from the bureaus within the OPM were similar. Although there was little hard data, employee and supervisory perceptions about flexitime were positive. In general, the bureaus indicated that flexitime had had no adverse effect on employees' ability to carry out duties and responsibilities.

All organizations reported a marked increase in employee morale due to flexitime. Employees reported that they enjoyed the additional flexibility and autonomy at work, and the control in scheduling their personal lives. It should be noted, however, that as with all innovations, the novelty effect tends to wear off. For example, a field office of the Bureau of Indian Affairs, where flexitime had been in use for 2 years, reported that "in time, employees look upon flexitime as a right rather than a privilege." However, there has not been any evidence which points to a decrease in the impact of flexitime over time.

The task force found that most employees, even though they have flexible hours available, tend to establish regular arrival and departure times, with little day to day variation. This may be explained in part by the fixed transportation arrangements individual establish, which decreases the degree of possible day-to-day variation. When this happened, some organizations observed a tendency to revert to taking short-term sick leave and annual leave rather than disrupt the regular schedule. For example, an employee deviating from his normal arrival time may wish to take a small amount of leave—a privilege permitted whether or not flexitime is being used in the organization—in order to avoid having to work late to make up time lost in the morning and thus disrupting his means of transportation home. Consequently, the long-term reductions in tardiness and sick leave were not as significant as originally experienced.

The task force reported that employees on flexitime had no serious problems attributable to individual time management, working relationships, the lack of continuous supervision, or the assumption of the responsibility necessary to make flexitime work. Employees reported enjoying the aspect of flexitime which allowed them to set their own work schedules and manage their own assignments much of the time. Most supervisors and employees felt that employees could handle the additional responsibility delegated to them under the new system.

Office of Personnel Management employees did not report problems with working relationships on account of flexitime. In smaller offices where flexitime use was necessarily limited, potential problems in ensuring adequate coverage were avoided by spirited cooperation and understanding, and equitable solutions were found.

Problems in the Commission due to lack of supervision were largely avoided as well. Supervisors and employees made arrangements so that those employees working during unsupervised hours received work assignments ahead of time. The task force explained that a decrease in employee productivity was not experienced during unsupervised periods because most employees customarily worked without continuous supervision or guidance. A potential problem was the supervision of employees new to a work area. The task force reported that in those cases supervisors and employees had cooperated in planning and making arrangements so that the new employee was fully occupied and productive throughout his working day.

In terms of individual responsibility, the task force reported that Commission employees showed "a laudable measure of individual responsibility by engaging in fully productive work when supervision was absent" (*Task Force Report,* p. 8). These results were attributed to peer pressure to maintain the productivity level as a justification for management's "vote of confidence"—the implementation of flexitime—and in order not to jeopardize the privilege. The few individuals who did not live up to these standards tended to be those who had been sources of problems before the introduction of flexitime.

Impact on Supervisors.   The task force reported that the Office of Personnel Management bureaus (BPS, BT, and BRE) then using flexitime had an initial experience similar to other organizations in terms of impact on supervisors. Early difficulties were experienced during the shakedown period, but once the adjustment period had passed, supervisors generally became enthusiastic supporters of the program.

Commission supervisors did not experience any major difficulties with respect to the coordination of work with other offices and agencies. Other offices quickly learned to adjust their hours to coordinate with the core hours of the offices involved.

Some supervisors did at first have problems communicating with their employees, particularly in groups. Most supervisors now schedule any type of meeting during core hours to ensure the availability of all members of the work group.

Providing for continuity of operations, particularly where one operation is dependent upon the completion of a previous one, required additional planning and scheduling in advance of various work loads in order to maintain full productivity. Again, after the initial period of adjustment, this was not a problem in most cases. Along the same lines, coping with work emergencies did not emerge as a problem under flexitime as long as adequate coverage was maintained.

The handling of flexitime abuses did not vary significantly from the method of handling time and attendance abuses prior to flexitime. Ultimately, the supervisor has the right to withdraw the flexitime privilege if the seriousness of the violation(s) warrant. By the same token, the employee may seek recourse through the grievance procedure if he feels the punishment was unwarranted or excessive.

Facilities and Transportation

In order to obtain information on this subject, the task force developed a questionnaire and administered it to BPS, BRE, and BT employees. Approximately 65 percent of the employees responded—a total of 633 returned the questionnaires. The conclusions drawn from one part of the questionnaire were as follows:

1. The number of employees driving alone to work had decreased by 28 percent.

2. Employees in OPM car pools increased slightly.

3. Employees "dropped off" at their offices increased significantly—by 84.4 percent.

4. Of those who changed their mode of transportation because of the implementation of flexitime, 83 percent considered the change favorable.

5. The majority of employees saved travel time both from home to work and from work to home under flexitime, and 23.5 percent saved 31 minutes or more in travel time.

One may conclude from these results that employees experienced greater flexibility in their transportation arrangements. The possibility also exists for a significant time savings, with all its commensurate benefits (reduced energy consumption, more time with the family, etc.). The task force felt that these benefits would increase proportionately as more offices implemented flexitime.

The task force found from their questionnaire results that most employees prefer to report to work before 8 A.M. This phenomenon might be explained by a desire to avoid the traffic congestion typical of the later morning, a desire to spend more time in the evening with the family, or an ability to schedule transportation arrangements, such as car pools, or dropping children off at school on the way to work.

Because the implementation of flexitime in individual bureaus within the OPM would not have a significant impact on facilities and transportation, little relevant information was available on this subject. Consequently, the task force conducted its own investigation to determine the impact of flexitime. A survey was conducted on government and commercial parking facilities available to OPM employees. The task force reported that parking should pose no problem if the entire central office were to go on flexitime. The exception might be those employees arriving later than 8:30 A.M., since commercial lots may be full by that hour.

With respect to heating, ventilation, and air conditioning, federal regulations state that "the levels of service are based on the effort required to service a 5-day one shift operation providing adequate start up services before the occupant agency starts work and shutdown services after the occupant agency ceases work, even though the working hours of the occupant agency may be staggered or a system of flexible employee hours has been instituted." The task force measured the temperatures in buildings in which flexitime was implemented during the early morning (6 A.M.) and late afternoon and found that the temperature was within the range specified by the regulations. In the task force results the information was also included that in one particular building it cost $88.45 per hour for heating and $128 per hour for cooling. Based on these costs and the variations in temperature within the allowable range, it was decided not to change the schedules for heating and air conditioning. Although some discomfort was noted during the early and late hours in one building, it did not seem to have adversely affected scheduling of arrivals and departures.

Pedestrian and vehicular traffic into buildings was examined and did not appear to be a source of problems. If anything, congestion seemed to have been reduced. The task force noted that the opening and closing times of buildings would have to be extended to the duration of the flexband.

With respect to guard service, the task force reported that coverage in most buildings was adequate to ensure the same level of protection and safety during the full flexband as during a nonflexitime day.

A study of eating facilities and vending equipment indicated that adequate facilities were available if flexible hours were adopted. The task force did not mention any consideration of extending cafeteria hours to cover those who wanted to have breakfast, a late lunch, or an early dinner. This type of problem, frequently encountered by private industry, may be reduced in the federal government because of the limits placed on the amount of flexibility.

Because OPM employees are only a small percentage of the total federal employee population serviced by federal health units, it would be difficult to obtain additional coverage in this area. Therefore, the task force recommended that first aid training and first aid kits be made available to cover those periods when the health units are unavailable.

Several day care centers were contacted to determine if they would be willing to extend their hours to accommodate employees on flexitime. They responded as follows:

If a majority of parents are Commission employees, some would consider opening earlier and closing later.

If most or all federal agencies in Washington were to adopt flexitime, some would operate within the predominant flexitime schedules.

Several centers would not change current schedules.

Labor Relations

On the subject of union involvement, the task force emphasized that "the recognized union . . . has a right to be fully involved in the planning, implementation, and day-to-day activities concerning the impact of flexitime schedules for central office organizations" (*Task Force Report,* p. 16). The task force organizers supported this statement by including representatives of the local union on the task force itself. In general, the actions of the task force were consistent with the policy, stated in their conclusions, that management must deal with the union on any aspect that affects working conditions or personnel policy.

The union indicated to the task force its intention to raise flexitime as a bargaining issue in contract negotiations. The task force, however, felt that the issue was not suitable for negotiation because of the current experimental status of flexitime. The task force did concede that if flexitime progressed satisfactorily and the OPM decided to consider full implementation, the issue would then be negotiable.

The Task Force noted that the implementation of flexitime would not change the method of handling disputes between union and management. Again, the importance of consulting union representatives prior to any change of flexitime "policies, procedures and matters affecting working conditions" was emphasized.

Possible labor relations problems arising because of flexitime included the absence of a steward when the need arose, and the difficulty of scheduling meetings. In the first case, it was reported that absence of a steward during working hours had not caused difficulties. If the matter could not wait until a steward was available, the chief steward was contacted. In order to avoid problems with scheduling meetings, the task force requested supervisors to hold their meetings during core hours, so that all employees could attend.

The task force also contacted management and union officials outside the OPM—at the Social Security Administration in Baltimore and the U.S. Geological Survey in Reston (no union). Those organizations reported no major labor relations problems resulting from flexible schedules.

The union for the OPM, American Federation of Government Employees Local No. 32, indicated that if flexitime use were expanded, it would prefer extension throughout the entire central office rather than optional adoption for each bureau and staff office. However, the union did not object to variations in flexitime arrangements from bureau to bureau. The union specified that it must be involved in "the overall implementation policy, as well as the way [flexitime] is implemented in individual bureaus and staff offices" (*Task Force Report,* p. 17).

Other Considerations

If flexitime is extended to the entire central office, the task force recommended that uniform bandwidth, flexible hours and core time be implemented, although the union did not request uniformity. The reasons given were as follows:

Core hours should not differ too greatly from public hours in order to avoid problems of inadequate coverage and service to the public.

Core hours should be the same for all central office organizations in order to eliminate confusion and uncertainty in communication between bureaus and with the public.

In determining what the core hours and bandwidth should be, the task force considered two factors. First, core hours should extend late enough in the day to allow regional offices in different time zones to easily maintain contact with the central office. Second, the task force recommended curtailing the bandwidth by one hour (beginning at 7 A.M. rather than 6 A.M.) in order to comply with heating and air conditioning regulations without having to extend these services. This was not felt to be a major problem, since few employees arrived before 7 A.M. in reported studies.

The task force felt strongly that the vast majority of employees wished to go on flexitime, and it was concerned that if an individual bureau or staff group should decide not to adopt flexitime, employee morale might be negatively affected. With this in mind, the task force recommended that all central office organizations should be required to adopt flexitime. Exceptions should be made only in cases where operational considerations precluded implementation. Further, curtailment within an entire organization would have to be approved by the executive director, although the authority to curtail or terminate flexitime for individual employees could be delegated to supervisors. For instance, ensuring adequate office coverage during public hours may require decreased flexibility for some employees.

In spite of adverse employee reactions to personally recording arrival and departure times, the task force recommended a system of written accountability for the following reasons:

Without a system of accountability by means of individually reported times, any disciplinary action based on falsification of arrival or departure times would be next to impossible. Supervisors could not be expected to keep track of the comings and goings of all employees.

A written record is necessary to verify whether an employee subject to the Fair Labor Standards Act has worked more than 40 hours per week, so that the employee can receive overtime.

Supervisors are responsible for ensuring that employees work a full 8-hour day, each day. A written record allows verification of this rule.

In emergency situations such as dangerous weather conditions, a knowledge of the employee's regular arrival time will help to determine amount of excused absence.

Compensation for work-related injuries occurring during the early morning or late evening would require a record of duty.

While the task force emphasized the need for a system of written accountability, the majority felt that the system of recording need not be uniform for all offices.

The task force noted that flexitime may be applied to night shift employees as long as it will not interfere with shift operations or result in increased costs due to differential pay.

The question of whether it is necessary for a supervisor to be present during an entire bandwidth depends upon the need for constant supervision and the ability of workers to work unsupervised. There is, obviously, a great deal of variation, based upon the type of task and the individual employees involved. The task force concluded that when supervision is necessary, management has the obligation to provide it. This may mean curtailing flexitime for some employees in order to coordinate their schedule with the supervisor, or taking whatever measures are necessary to ensure full productivity. In general, however, the responsibility for this decision is delegated to supervisors. For the supervisors, this may mean curtailing their use of flexitime or extending their hours.

In order to determine the amount of leave excused for emergency situations such as hazardous weather conditions, the task force adopted the guidelines developed by BPS for use by federal agencies. The immediate supervisor should determine the reference point for excused time off and the amount of time for which the employee will be excused.

Based on policies developed by BPS for use in federal agencies, the task force advised that absences during care hours must be charged to regular leaves, such as annual leave, sick leave, or leave without pay. Employees may not make up time absent during core hours during the flexbands.

Employees must take a minimum ½-hour lunch break under the flexitime system. They may not work through lunch in order to leave 8 hours after arrival.

Although the three bureaus, BT, BRE, and BPS, conducted attitude surveys and consulted the local union before implementing flexitime, they did not develop hard data for use in evaluating the impact of flexitime on aspects of productivity such as leave and overtime usage, service, turnover, and reduction of backlog, in addition to the actual productivity measures. The task force emphasized that other bureaus and staff offices should develop means of evaluating the impact of flexitime on these areas. The advance planning package developed by the BPS, which includes a handbook for supervisors and employees, is recommended as a source of guidance.

The task force recommended that if flexitime is extended throughout the central office, it should be on an experimental basis. "The Commission's legislative proposal calls for a 3 year experimental period for the evaluation of flexitime within a representative sample of Executive branch organizations." On this basis, the OPM will continue to regard its own program as experimental.

RECOMMENDATIONS

The task force recommendations, presented in Figure 9-4, were, for the most part, derived directly from the results and conclusions. They focus upon the full implementation of flexitime throughout the central offices of the OPM located in the Washington, D.C. area, and specify who has the authority to disapprove implementation. These specifications reflect the task force's concern about the possible damage to employee morale in a situation of partial availability of flexible schedules, and about corresponding labor relations problems which could arise.

Other recommendations included specific details of the flexitime schedule—reflecting the conclusion that all central offices should be on the same schedule—and items of concern such as maintaining adequate coverage, expanding security guard service, unlocking stairwells during extended hours, and making available first aid kits and first aid training. A more general recommendation was the universal necessity for some form of a time-recording system to monitor individual arrival and departure times.

Finally, the task force emphasized the importance of advance planning, using the BPS model and the recommendations in the task force Report as a guide. The Personnel and Labor Relations Division was chosen as the focal point for implementation and evaluation. An 18-month experiment on flexitime was announced for the OPM with 6-month evaluation reports prepared by the Personnel and Labor Relations Division to be submitted to the executive director.

POLICIES AND GUIDELINES FOR FLEXITIME IMPLEMENTATION

Approval

After reviewing the findings reported by the task force and its recommendations, the executive director of the OPM agreed to implement flexitime in the central office on an experimental basis. As a result of the task force recommendations and their approval, a supplement to the CSC *Personnel Manual* was issued, announcing the experiment and describing the policies and guidelines for implementing flexitime for the 18-month experiment. These instructions to undertake the experiment were contained in the CSC *Personnel Manual*

On the basis of our findings and conclusions, the Task Force makes the following recommendations:

That all central office organizations located in the Washington, D.C., metropolitan area be given the opportunity to participate in flexitime, and that any decisions not to participate be based solely on operational considerations.

That the Executive Director make the final decision not to implement flexitime if, after consultation with managers, employees, and the union, a bureau director or head of staff office determines that his organization should not engage in flexitime.

That bureau directors and heads of staff offices be given the authority to disapprove any flexitime schedule that would result in increased costs, such as night differential or Sunday differential, unless such schedules are due to operational necessity.

That implementation be as soon as possible, after appropriate advance planning.

That a uniform bandwidth, flexible bands, and core hours be established as follows:

Operational hours	7:00 A.M. to 6:00 P.M.
Flexible hours	7:00 A.M. to 9:30 A.M.
	11:30 A.M. to 1:30 P.M.
	3:30 P.M. to 6:00 P.M.
Core hours	9:30 A.M. to 11:30 A.M.
	1:30 P.M. to 3:30 P.M.

That the central office "public" hours continue to be from 8:15 A.M. to 4:45 P.M. and that management ensure adequate office coverage during these hours.

That security guard service to FOB 9 be obtained between 5 and 6 P.M.

That stairwells in FOB 9 remain unlocked for the entire flexible bandwidth, i.e., from 7 A.M. to 6 P.M.

That first aid kits and first aid training be made available wherever employees are working beyond the hours of operation of health units.

That all organizations be required to have a system for recording employee arrival and departure times.

That each bureau and staff office be required to engage in advance planning using the BPS model as a guide, taking into consideration the conclusions contained in this report.

That the Personnel and Labor Relations Division serve as the focal point for flexitime implementation and evaluation, working closely with the BPS Project Officer on Flexitime, BPS Personnel Research and Development Center, and BPME Clearinghouse on Productivity.

That the Commission continue to engage in flexitime on an experimental basis for a period of 18 months, with 6-month evaluation reports by the Personnel and Labor Relations Division to the Executive Director.

Figure 9–4   List of recommendations made by the task force.

Letter No. 610-1, dated November 26, 1976, written by the Personnel and Labor Relations Division. It stated:

All central office employees will be authorized to work flexible schedules unless prohibited by operational or individual considerations. This letter provides the basic policies and procedures to be followed during that period.

The letter specified November 29, 1976, as the effective date for implementation. The following sections recapitulate portions of this personnel letter.

General Policy Decisions

Policy decisions for the 18-month flexitime experiment included the following:

1. All bureaus and staff offices should participate in the flexitime experiment, unless prohibited by operational considerations.

2. Public hours (i.e., 8:15 A.M.–4:45 P.M.) will remain unchanged. Each office must, therefore, ensure that adequate coverage is maintained during these periods.

3. Written records of arrival and departure times, maintained by individual employees, are mandatory.

4. Any absence during core hours must be charged to an authorized leave category.

5. Employees are required to take a lunch period so that they account for a full 8½ hours daily.

6. Heating, air conditioning, and ventilation coverage will not be increased during the experiment.

7. When leave time is granted due to emergencies such as hazardous weather conditions, the amount of time excused will be determined using the following criteria, developed by the BPS:

  a   Normal pattern of arrival. If the employee arrives within 5 to 10 minutes of the same time each day, this time should be used as a reference point.

  b   Predominant pattern of arrival. If one particular arrival time predominates (e.g., 4 out of 5 days), this time should become the reference point.

  c   Variable pattern of arrival. If no pattern of arrival can be discerned, the average of arrival times for the previous 10 days should be used as the reference point.

Delegation of Authority and Responsibility

The delegation of authority and responsibility reflects the policy of the Office of Personnel Management to encourage the greatest possible use of flexitime during the 18-month experiment as long as operations are not interrupted. The goal is to provide a true test of flexitime on which to base a final decision.

Authority.   The executive director retains the authority to disapprove flexitime for an entire bureau or staff office. This decision, however, should be based on the recommendation of the bureau director or head of staff involved.

  Bureau directors and heads of staff offices are delegated the following authorities:

1.   Authority to disapprove flexitime for segments of an organization. Such disapprovals can be made only for operational reasons. This authority may not be redelegated.

2.   Authority to disapprove flexitime for individual employees for operational reasons or because the employee requires continuous supervision. This authority may be redelegated.

3.   Authority to establish routine hours of duty between 6 A.M. and 6 P.M. in cases involving individual employees when administratively desirable. This authority may not be redelegated.

4.   Authority to disapprove any flexitime schedule that will result in increased costs to the OPM. This authority may not be redelegated.

Management representatives are responsible for ensuring that adequate personnel are available to carry out operations in a productive manner. These responsibilities include ensuring appropriate office coverage, providing for unforeseen emergencies, and ensuring adequate service to the public, other agencies, and other parts of the OPM. In fulfilling these responsibilities, management should use the following criteria:

1.   restrictions or denials in the use of flexitime will be imposed upon the *smallest work unit* or number of employees possible.

2.   restrictions or denials should be imposed only when alternative measures fail to resolve the conflict between the needs of the organization and the flexitime desires of affected employees.

3.   operational considerations will justify restrictions or denials only when employee participation adversely impacts upon work or service that cannot be effectively performed at a later time. (CSC *Personnel Manual Letter* No. 610-1, p. 4)

If an individual employee is denied the use of flexitime by management, he has the right to request a written explanation of the restriction or denial. Further, the employee may use the agency grievance procedure to plead his case. A decision will then be based upon the written document and the arguments provided by the employee. An individual employee does not have the authority to challenge the flexitime policy itself or the procedure established for the denial of flexitime.

Responsibility.   Bureau directors and heads of staff offices are responsible for administrating flexitime within their organizations, including developing an implementation plan, coordinating the plan with the flexitime representative, and advising employees and ensuring their full participation. Upper management is also responsible for ensuring that the plan does not interfere with mission accomplishment, and for providing a full evaluation of flexitime during the experimental period.

Supervisors are responsible for the day-to-day administration, particularly for maintaining full participation and equitable treatment of employees while ensuring adequate office coverage.

Employees using flexitime are responsible for accounting for a full 8-hour day and 40-hour week. Abuse will result in the cancellation of the privilege of working a flexible schedule and may result in appropriate disciplinary action in accordance with existing regulations.

The Personnel and Labor Relations Division is responsible for the overall evaluation of flexitime, including semiannual evaluation reports to the executive director. The exclusive representative (the union) will participate in these evaluations, and may submit separate reports to the executive director if its conclusions differ from those of the Personnel and Labor Relations Division.

The *Personnel Manual Letter* cautions that any modifications of the policy during the experimental period will be negotiated with the exclusive union representative, but that management retains the right to cancel flexitime at any time during the experimental period without negotiation.

Flexitime Model

The central office flexitime model is described in Figure 9-5 below. Because of legal and contractual constraints, no banking of hours is allowed from day to day or week to week.

In addition to the schedule depicted in the diagram, the following rules apply:

1 All employees must be present during the morning and afternoon core times.

2 Unless prohibited by operational considerations, employees may report at any time during the morning flexible band; thereafter, they must remain in a duty status for 8½ hours.

3 Employees must notify the immediate supervisor in advance of the intent to use flexitime during the midday flexible band; any time used in addition to the normal lunch period must be made up *the same day* during the morning or afternoon flexband.

Implementation Checklist

The *Personnel Manual Letter* emphasizes the importance of an implementation plan in each office for the flexitime experiment. The letter includes a list minimum items which should be addressed when considering implementation. This implementation checklist appears in the illustration in Figure 9-6.

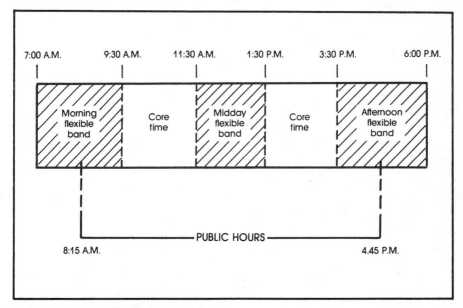

Figure 9–5 Central office flexitime model.

A. Organizational Participation

Call all parts of the organization participate fully in flexitime?
If not, can parts of the organizations participate on a partial basis?
Are there some parts of the organization that cannot participate at all?
Are there some key personnel who cannot participate?
Are all denials based solely on operational considerations?

B. Delegation of Authority

Will managers be delegated the authority to disapprove flexitime for individual employees?
If so, under what conditions?

C. Coverage During Public Hours

Are there parts of the organization that provide service to the public or other agencies?
If so, have provisions been made to ensure adequate office coverage during public hours, i.e., 8:15 A.M. to 4:45 P.M.

D. Sign-in, Sign-out

What sign-in, sign-out system will be used?
Have forms been cleared with the Reports and Forms Management Office, BMIS?

E. Supervision

Are there parts of the organization where a supervisor must be present during all working hours?
If so, have provisions for supervisory coverage been made?
Have supervisors been provided guidance on:
How to handle abuses?   Dealing with the Union?
Scheduling meetings and conferences?   Ensuring adequate office coverage?

F. Management and Supervisory Input

Have managers and supervisors been given the opportunity to express their ideas concerning flexitime?
Have these been considered?

G. Dealing with the Employee Union

Has the union been given an opportunity to comment on the proposed implementation plan?
Have their comments been considered?

H. Reports and Evaluation

During the experimental period, will reports and evaluations be required from subordinate managers?
If so, has an evaluation format been developed?

I. Flexitime Coordinator

Will a Flexitime Coordinator be appointed?
If so, what are his or her responsibilities?

J. Emergencies Arising Before and After Public Hours

Have provisions been made to deal with emergencies that may arise before and after public hours? (NOTE: the inside front cover and back cover of the Commission's telephone directory contains information on handling medical and other emergencies).

K. Advising Employees

Have all employees been advised of the organizational flexitime plan?

Figure 9–6 Checklist for development of bureau and staff office flexitime implementation plans.

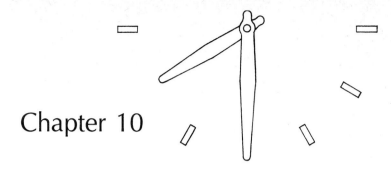

Chapter 10

The Public Sector: Field Results

INTRODUCTION

Having studied the elaborate implementation process at the Office of Personnel Management, the reader can better appreciate some of the problems, which are likely to be confronted in a large bureaucracy. In this chapter, some of the results found by agencies and bureaus throughout the public sector after the implementation of flexitime will be described.

At present, close to 200,000 federal employees in approximately 100 agencies and departments work under various flexible working hour schedules. Although there are large numbers of employees enjoying the FWH system, the level of flexitime use had been restricted. Legal constraints limited the level of flexibility to variations *within* the working day. Despite this limitation, flexitime programs were favorably received by employees and managers alike, improving both the quality of work life for the individual worker and the organizational effectiveness of the federal bureaucracy. At present, a 3-year experiment in increased flexibility is underway (see Chapter 18).

In order to justify the decision to implement flexitime, evaluative data on the results of existing flexitime programs, even if limited, should be available to decision makers. The information presented here represents a compilation of the behavioral and attitudinal data available to date within the federal government. The tables in this chapter provide data which were generated from experiments with flexible working hours in twenty-five separate government organizations. The data was extracted from individual agency reports made available by the Pay Policy Division of the Bureau of Policy and Standards, the Office of Personnel Management, * as well as from information acquired from agencies contacted directly. A guide to the tables that follow is provided here.

Table 10-1 *Organizational Effectiveness.* Table 10-1 includes all information describing the effects of flexitime on organizational effectiveness. This information was subdivided into three subtables.

*We wish to thank Ms. Barbara Fiss and Mr. Tom Cowley for their help and cooperation in making their data available and to all the agencies that provided additional information.

Table 10-1a contains all Productivity measures, including indicators of quality, quantity, and services.

Table 10-1b contains measures of the Work Environment. These are categorized as measures of Access to/Relations with Supervisors and Co-workers or measures of Control over Work Hours and Quiet Time.

Table 10-1c contains measures of COST relating to the implementation and use of flexible working hours.

Table 10-2   *Attitudes.* Table 10-2 contains measures of the Attitudes of organization members. This data was categorized into Morale/Job Satisfaction and Attitudes toward the Flexitime Program.

Table 10-3   *Membership.* Table 10-3 contains measures of Membership Behavior within the organization. The two categories used in this table are Leave Usage, which includes all forms of absenteeism, and Tardiness.

Table 10-4   *Time Management.* Table 10-4 presents data concerning personal Time Management. The data is subdivided into measures of Personal Time Usage and changes in Transportation.

Table 10-5   *Morning Arrival Distribution.* Table 10-5 presents the Patterns of Morning Arrivals in several organizations.

Table 10-6   *Summary Table.* An additional table has been compiled, summarizing the general trends indicated in Tables 10-1 to 10-5. In this table, the total number of organizations reporting data for a specific category is included, and a brief description of the direction of these findings is given. These findings are separated into two subcategories: objective data and survey data, as indicated in Tables 10-1 to 10-5.

The experiments conducted at each agency were not standardized; the criteria for evaluation were determined internally by each organization. Even those agencies reporting on the same dimensions or variables used varying criteria for measurement. With this in mind, only broad categories of information are reported here. Because the purpose is to indicate general trends, the measurements taken from agency reports have been grouped into these categories somewhat arbitrarily at times. However, the *original variable description* which was extracted from the agency report has been retained as part of each entry in the tables. Thus, the reader is cautioned to recall this methodology when comparing the results from these organizations.

Two types of findings are reported in these studies: objective data and survey results. In some cases, such as Attitudes (Table 10-2), the information source was strictly an opinion survey. In other tables, such as Organizational Effectiveness (Table 10-1), the types of results reported include both objective and survey data.

Survey data are indicated in the tables by the phrase "reported by [appropriate group]" —in other words, survey data represent a percentage of the population reporting a certain phenomenon. Such data vary widely in scope and methodology. Some reported results are the outcome of a large standardized employee survey, while other results are the outcome of a casual estimation of the opinions of a few workers or supervisors who were interviewed. Those results from organizations with the larger number of employees are usually the more formal survey results. (Number of employees=N.)

There is also a growing body of research to support the careful use of self-assessment as a predictor of job performance. This evidence is reviewed by Levine (1978), who supported the position that relevant, reliable, and accurate information about performance can be obtained by direct questions to employees. This information has been shown to be as reliable and in some cases more accurate than more indirect and unobtrusive measurement.

Objective data indicate a percentage change in the phenomenon itself (e.g., a percentage change in productivity). If an actual number is unavailable, we have indicated that the results are measured in the entry along with the direction of the finding. The results are separated into five basic categories, each compiled in a separate table.

ORGANIZATIONAL EFFECTIVENESS

The three subtables of Table 10-1 contain all measures that are concerned with how the organization functions in its environment. The data include changes in individual and group productivity, changes in the work environment, and changes in monetary costs to the organization.

Productivity

The productivity category reports all the measures which were defined in the agency studies and includes criteria such as quality of work, quantity produced, accuracy, efficiency, ability to meet schedules, and increases in interdepartmental or interorganizational communications, as reflected in the behavior of both exempt and nonexempt employees. Both objective and survey results are included in Table 10-1a and will be discussed separately in the following sections.

Objective data.   There were 17 measures of objective or measured data reported by 11 organizations, several organizations had more than 1 measure of productivity. Fifteen of the measures indicated favorable changes resulting from the flexitime experiment.

Most of these measures of productivity were attempts to quantify aspects of a specific job or task. For example, one agency measured the number of reports processed, the number of vouchers processed, and the amount of map production, and found increases in all areas. Another agency measured the amount of work processed and the amount of work backlog and found improvement in both areas. Other types of objective productivity measures used by individual agencies were varied and, at times, quite creative. They included successful contacts made on first telephone call, changes in overtime, compensatory time, or gratuitous time, work planning and coordination, service to other departments and customers, and time span for communication with other offices. It is interesting to note that all of these particular measures indicated favorable results.

In 2 of the 11 organizations, objective productivity measures were inconclusive. In one case, there was no change in the quantity of work processed, but there was a decrease in the error rate of the experimental group as compared to the control group. In the second

Table 10-1a Organizational Effectiveness: Productivity

Organization	Quality, Quantity, Services
Air University Maxwell Air Force Base (Alabama) $N = 100$	10% increase in successful contacts made on first call from outside Increase in ability to meet schedules reported by 48% of all employees, no change by 45%, decrease by 7% Increase in quality reported by 21% of employees, no change by 69%, decrease by 10% Increase in productivity reported by 26% of employees, no change by 61%, decrease by 13% Increase in quantity reported by 25% of employees, no change by 65%, decrease by 10%
Bureau of Alcohol, Tobacco, and Firearms Department of the Treasury (Washington, D.C.) $N = 25$	Increase in productivity reported by 32% of employees No change in productivity reported by supervisors Increase in quality reported by 50% of employees
Bureau of Data Processing Social Security Administration (Baltimore) $N = 350$	12% increase in productivity Increase in accuracy reported by 50% of employees Increase in quality reported by 52% of employees
Bureau of Health Insurance Social Security Administration (Atlanta) $N = 80$	Increase in employee productivity reported by 10% of supervisors Increase in employee productivity reported by 13% of employees Increase in organizational productivity reported by 16% of supervisors Increase in organizational productivity reported by 23% of employees Increase in time span for communication reported by 11% of supervisors Increase in time span for communication reported by 2% of employees
Bureau of Policy and Standards U.S. Office of Personnel Management (Washington, D.C.) $N = 240$	Productivity (measured)—inconclusive results Productivity (reported)—no change over time Slight increase in work planning and coordination Increase in service to others
Bureau of Recruiting and Examining U.S. Office of Personnel Management $N = 240$	No change or slight increase in productivity reported by supervisors Increase (measured) in service

Economic Research Service
U.S. Department of Agriculture
(Washington, D.C.)
N = 604

Increase in productivity reported by 39% of employees, decrease by 1%
Increase in unit productivity reported by 34% of managers, decrease by 7%

Environmental Protection Agency
(Washington, D.C.)
N = 1,720

Improvement in overall operations reported by 75% of supervisors
Increase in quantity and/or quality of work reported by 37% of employees

Library of Congress
(Washington, D.C.)
N = 150

7% increase in productivity in first quarter, 14% increase in second quarter

National Security Agency
Central Security Service
(Maryland)
N = 243

Increase reported by 51% of employees, no change by 48%, decrease by 1%

Naval Ship Engineering Systems
(Port Heuneme, California)
N = 1,700

Increase in productivity reported by 64% of employees, no change by 32%, decrease by 4%
Increase in quality reported by 55% of employees, no change by 40%, decrease by 5%
Increase in quantity reported by 57% of employees, no change by 39%, decrease by 4%

Navy Finance Center
(Cleveland, Ohio)
N = 64

Increase in employee productivity reported by 35% of supervisors, decrease by 3%
Increase in productivity reported by 56% of employees, no change by 44%

Navy Finance Office
(Long Beach, California)
N = 55

No change (measured) in quantity of work
Decrease (measured) in error rate

Office of Federal Records Center
General Services Administration
(Washington, D.C.)
N = 17

Increase in quantity reported

Table 10-1a Organizational Effectiveness: Productivity *(Continued)*

Organization	Quality, Quantity, Services
Region V, Department of Health, Education, and Welfare (Chicago) N = 211	Increase in productivity reported by 41% of nonsupervisors, no change by 62%, decrease by 8%
	Increase in productivity reported by 15% of supervisors, no change by 57%, decrease by 28%
	Increase in quantity reported by 21% of agency head, no change by 64%, decrease by 14%
	Increase in quality reported by 23% of agency heads, no change by 77%, decrease by 0%
U.S. Army Computer Systems Command (Fort Belvoir, Virginia) N = 82	Decrease (measured) in overtime, compensatory time, gratituitous time
	Increase in productivity reported by 65% of employees
	Increase in productivity reported by 31% of supervisors
U.S. Army Natick Laboratories (Massachusetts) N = 1,200	Increase in productivity reported by 100% of supervisors
U.S. Army Tank Automotive Command (Michigan) N = 400	2% increase in productivity
U.S. Office of Personnel Management (Seattle Region) N = 129	Increase (measured) in time span for communication with other offices
	Increase in productivity reported by employees
U.S. Geological Survey Department of the Interior (Reston, Virginia) N = 2,230	6% increase in reports processed
	14% increase in vouchers processed
	Increase in map production
	Increase in quality reported by 36% of nonsupervisors, no change by 63%, decrease by 1%
	Increase in quality reported by 38% of first-line supervisors, no change by 62%
	Increase in quality reported by 22% of upper level supervisors and managers, no change by 75%, decrease by 3%
	Increase in overall operations reported by 85% of all supervisors
	Increase in productivity reported by 27% of supervisors, decrease by 5%
U.S. Information Agency (Washington, D.C.) N = 33	5% increase in work processed
	16% decrease in work backlog

organization, productivity measures were inconclusive, but there were measured improvements in work planning and coordination, and service availability. The exact percentage results and the particular performance measurements in each organization are described in Table 10-1a.

Survey Data. Most of the survey questions dealt with perceived changes in productivity, quantity, or quality of work performed. Only two questions varied from this format: one question surveyed the ability to meet schedules and another measured changes in the time span for communications.

The results indicated the same ratio of positive to inconclusive or no change results as the hard data. Of 17 organizations reporting data, 14 were positive, 2 were inconclusive, and 1 reported no change. These 17 organizations addressed a total of 42 questions on productivity to their employees.

Of the 42 questions, 86 percent received a largely positive response, 2 percent negative, and 12 percent inconclusive. Findings were considered inconclusive when a majority reported no change, or the reported increase and decrease were close (within roughly 10 percent of each other). Of these questions, 25 were addressed to employees and 16 were addressed to supervisors (1 was nonspecific). Of the 25 employee questions, 92 percent received a largely positive response and 8 percent inconclusive. For the 16 supervisor questions, 81 percent received a largely positive response, 13 percent inconclusive, and 6 percent negative.

When reports of employees and supervisors were compared within the same organization, an important trend was revealed. In 6 out of the 7 organizations reporting such data, employees perceived greater improvements in productivity than supervisors (although the supervisors were consistently positive as well). This finding is consistent with the overall tabulation of employee versus supervisory responses described above—92 percent versus 81 percent reflected improvements.

In general, the employees perceived that flexitime influenced performance more positively than did their supervisors, although both groups perceived flexitime to have positive effects on productivity. Perhaps the most obvious interpretation of this difference is that an employee's favorable attitude toward flexitime influenced his report on performance. Employees may generalize or exaggerate the benefits because of their positive experience, and as an expression of their support for the program. On the positive side, distortion of this type represents evidence for employees' positive attitudes toward the program. For example, an employee may feel more productive for a variety of reasons: the communications level with peers and superiors may be higher, feedback from these groups may have increased, the employee may be enjoying a greater sense of autonomy, and he may actually be performing a greater range of job tasks. All of these would be contributing factors to the perception of increased productivity. On the negative side, it means that the data are somewhat suspect. However, there is little reason to suspect significant exaggeration about productivity, since most agencies made it clear to employees that the purpose of introducing flexitime was to improve the quality of work life, the overall organizational climate, and work-nonwork fit for the employees and their families. The organization was prepared to accept no change in productivity as a positive result.

Another possibility exists which may explain this phenomenon. It may be that supervisors' perceptions about flexitime's impact on productivity was less positive because their own attitudes toward flexitime itself were less favorable. The adjustment process necessary for first-line supervisors was described earlier, and it was pointed out that flexitime is often perceived as causing a decrease in autonomy and control for this group. These concerns may bias the supervisors' reports on productivity.

In spite of this problem, the evaluations of employees by supervisors must be given serious consideration because this type of report is often the source of effectiveness evaluations in organizations. An important part of a supervisor's job is to evaluate employee performance on a routine basis, whether subjective or objective measures are used. When one considers the positive tone of these reports, combined with the positive attitudes reflected in the employee reports and the favorable objective results, one can only conclude that the introduction of flexitime enhanced organizational effectiveness.

Work Environment

Work environment data included two categories of results: access to, and relations with, supervisors and co-workers; and control over work hours and quiet time—that is, times early or late in the day when few people are around and distractions are fewer. Most of this information, summarized in Table 10-1b, was the result of employee or supervisor opinion rather than objective data.

Access to, and Relations with, Supervisors and Co-workers.   Ten agencies measured aspects of accessibility and changes in relations between supervisors and employees, and employees with their co-workers. There were only two objective measures in this category: one agency reported an increase in the availability of division specialists, and another reported an increase in the availability of clerical support. The other agencies, in their questionnaires to employees, explored such variables as the perceptions of employees about their relationships with supervisors, their opportunity for decision making, employee access to, and satisfaction with, supervisors, supervisory skills, changes in degree and patterns of communication, work flow, difficulty in holding meetings, impact on working conditions, and employee perceptions of managerial style as measured by a Likert profile. Clearly, there is a wide variety in the variables which are grouped under this category.

Of the 10 agencies reporting these variables, 6 of the agencies indicated an overall improvement in work relationships, 3 reported no change, and 1 reported inconclusive results. In the latter case, the organization reported information obtained from employees, supervisors, and agency heads. While the supervisors and employees tended to report positive results or no change, the agency heads were more negative. It should also be noted that 2 organizations reported some supervisory problems (one reported a small decrease in supervisory skills), although their overall reports were positive.

This apparent disparity between upper level managers and supervisors, and employees is most easily explained as an adjustment problem with the flexitime system. Inadequate preparation for implementation, consideration of new work flows, and the necessity of changing work processes or scheduling may result in more negative evaluations at the upper management level. In general, it should be emphasized that the more effort the organization puts into the feasibility study and implementation steps (including training program for first line supervisors), the fewer problems are likely to arise later on. Most of the agencies involved were fairly thorough in their planning, with the result that any problems experienced were minor. The results show that while supervisory access and relations among workers and supervisors can be improved, problems can arise as well. The potential for such difficulties, their antecedents, and ways to overcome them are elaborated in Chapter 14.

Control over Work Hours and Quiet Time.   This subcategory of organizational effectiveness included questions on satisfaction with quiet time, the opportunity to work independently, scheduling problems, and telephone interruptions. Of the 7 agencies providing information, 6 reported an improvement and 1 reported no change. The "no change" organization only reported a lack of scheduling problems. It appears that the provision of control over work and time scheduling allows the employee to schedule greatly needed quiet time. This opportunity to work without interruptions can mean a more effective employee only if he is willing to take advantage of it.

Costs—Expenses and Savings

The cost category reflects all the aspects of flexitime implementation which increased or decreased cost that were mentioned in the agency reports. These include night differential expenses, plant operation, power consumption, maintenance, and overtime. Of the 11 organizations measuring costs, 9 provided objective information and 4 provided reports from supervisors and employees (2 agencies provided data in both categories). Table 10-1c summarizes this information. The information provided in this section should be considered only to the extent that it implies a trend. None of the organizations included here attempted an exhaustive study of the total expenses and savings accrued as a result of the flexitime system. The variables reported by these agencies were not chosen systematically; in particular, increases in costs were not adequately assessed. However, one variable, overtime, is well represented, enabling us to draw important conclusions.

Objective Data.   Of 11 measures of various aspects of costs within the organization, excluding overtime, 5 indicated cost savings, 3 indicated no change, 1 was inconclusive and 1 indicated a cost increase. The 3 organizations reporting no change in costs measured plant operating expenses, power consumption, and heating costs. This is interesting to note, as organizations are often concerned that flexitime will cause increased expenses in these areas. The organization reporting a cost increase experienced it as an increase in electrical consumption. Changes in overtime costs as a result of flexitime implementation were reported by 8 agencies. Of these, 4 reported a decrease in overtime costs, 2 reported no change, 1 was inconclusive, and 1 reported an increase. This increase was substantial— $7,400 per year paid to elevator mechanics for the additional maintenance necessary. This expense represents a problem that many organizations may have to face: the additional hours of the bandwidth may require additional service personnel on regularly scheduled overtime. For regular employees, however, the results show that overtime will stay the same or decrease under a flexitime system.

Survey Data.   Survey results on costs were reported by 4 organizations. Of these, 1 reported a saving in overtime costs, 1 reported no change in overtime costs, and 2 reported inconclusive results based on employee perceptions. However, because costs are relatively easy to quantify and perceptions are particularly subject to bias, objective results are more

Table 10-1b Organizational Effectiveness: Work Environment

Organization	Access to, and Relations with, Supervisors and Co-workers	Control over Work Hours and Quiet Time
Bureau of Alcohol, Tobacco, and Firearms Department of the Treasury (Washington, D.C.) N = 25	Most supervisors reported no problems with employee reactions 1.5 hours/day increase in availability of division specialists 1.25 hours/day increase in clerical support availability	
Bureau of Data Processing Social Security Administration (Baltimore) N = 350	No change in accessibility to supervisors reported by 89% of employees	Importance of determining hours was high for 75% of employees
Bureau of Policy and standards U.S. Office of Personnel Management (Washington, D.C.) N = 240	Increase in access to and satisfaction with supervisors reported by employees No change in relations with supervisors reported by employees No change in communications reported by employees	Increase in availability of quiet time reported by 12% more employees Increase in opportunity to work independently reported by 8% more employees Importance of control of work hours reported by 17% more employees
Bureau of Recruiting and Examining U.S. Office of Personnel Management (Washington, D.C.) N = 240		Increase in quiet time reported by employees Increase in effectiveness during quiet time reported by employees
Defense Mapping Agency Aerospace Center (St. Louis)	Improved relations with supervisors reported by 56% of employees, no change by 35%, decrease by 9% Increase in communications reported by 96% of employees, decrease by 4%	
Economic Research Service U.S. Department of Agriculture (Washington, D.C.) N = 604	Some work flow problems reported by 10% of employees No need to hold meetings outside of the core period reported by 84% of managers and 94% of supervisors	

132

Agency		
National Security Agency Central Security Service (Maryland) N = 243	Lack of supervisory problems reported by 93% of employees	Lack of scheduling problems reported by 98% of employees
Navy Finance Office (Long Beach, California) N = 55	No change in perception of managerial style (Likert profile)	
Region V, Department of Health, Education, and Welfare (Chicago) N = 211	Increase in difficulty of holding meetings reported by 36% of agency heads, no change by 64% Lack of supervisory problems reported by 29% of agency heads, minor problems by 57%, major problems by 14% No negative impact on working conditions reported by 95% of employees Improvement in-working conditions reported by 39% of supervisors, no change reported by 56%	Increase in quiet time reported by 70% of nonsupervisors Increase in quiet time reported by 59% of supervisors Improvement in the work environment reported by 64% of supervisors
U.S. Office of Personnel Management (Seattle Region) N = 129		Decrease in telephone interruptions during flexbands reported by employees
U.S. Geological Survey Department of the Interior (Reston, Virginia) N = 2,230	Increase in supervisory skill reported by 22% of supervisors, decrease reported by 6% Increase in employee decision-making responsibility reported by 65% of first-line supervisors Improvement in communications within each work area reported by 12%, decrease reported by 15% Improvement in communications with other government agencies and private industry reported by 9%, decrease reported by 9%	Employee benefit from quiet time reported by 73% of supervisors

Table 10-1c Organizational Effectiveness: Costs—Expenses and Savings

Organization	Energy, Overtime, and Maintenance
Bureau of Alcohol, Tobacco, and Firearms Department of the Treasury (Washington, D.C.) $N = 25$	Decrease in expenses reported by 47% of employees, no change by 45%, increase by 3%
Bureau of Data Processing Social Security Administration (Baltimore) $N = 350$	63% decrease in overtime use in comparable periods
Bureau of Policy and Standards U.S. Office of Personnel Management (Washington, D.C.) $N = 250$	No change (measured) in plant operation expenses Decrease (measured) in overtime use with confounding factors
Bureau of Recruiting and Examining U.S. Office of Personnel Management (Washington, D.C. $N = 240$	Decrease (measured) in overtime use, but decrease (measured) in work load
National Security Agency Central Security Service (Maryland) $N = 243$	Decrease (measured) in night differential expenses
Naval Ship Engineering Systems (Port Heuneme, California) $N = 1,700$	6% decrease in electricity consumption with confounding factors No change (measured) in heating costs

Navy Finance Center
(Cleveland, Ohio)
$N = 64$

Decrease in costs reported by 19% of supervisors; no change reported by 59%; increase reported by 22%

Navy Finance Office
(Long Beach, California)
$N = 55$

No change (measured) in overtime use

Region V, Department of Health, Education, and Welfare
(Chicago)
$N = 211$

Decrease in overtime use reported by 7% of agency heads, no change by 79%, increase by 14%

U.S. Geological Survey
Department of the Interior
(Reston, Virginia)
$N = 2,230$

Increase in overtime expenses for maintenance of $7,400/year
No change in power consumption
Small decrease in overtime use reported by 39% of first-line supervisors; substantial decrease reported by 23%; small increase reported by 15%
Increase in utilization of specialized equipment reported by 50% of the employees who worked with such equipment

135

desirable and reliable than survey data on this subject. Consequently, these data should be considered only in terms of the support or lack of support it lends to the objective results.

In evaluating the objective as well as subjective data on costs, one must keep in mind that the statistics reported here represent a *sample* of the possible areas of cost which may be affected under flexitime. No organization assessed the full impact of flexitime on costs, including, for example, costs of a time-recording system (whether manual or mechanical), and any administrative costs associated with it. A systematic study and analysis is necessary before any generalizations can be made in this area.

ATTITUDES

Table 10-2 presents changes in employee attitudes resulting from flexitime. These attitudes are grouped into two general categories: changes in attitudes toward the job, expressed as morale or job satisfaction, and attitudes toward the flexitime program itself. Because attitudes are perceptions by nature, all information in the table is recorded as opinion survey results.

Morale and Job Satisfaction

This category includes measures of the employee's own morale, how he perceives the morale of fellow workers, his feelings toward the organization itself, and different aspects of job satisfaction. Of the 17 organizations contributing information, all reported improvements in job attitudes. When the individual reports were examined, it was found that 21 of the 23 measurements taken in these 17 organizations were positive (5 organizations measured more than one aspect in this category). In one of the two nonpositive responses, 8 percent of the employees in one organization reported a decrease in morale. However, in the same organization 52 percent of the employees reported an increase in morale. Of those who reported a decrease, not all were on flexitime. This finding brings to our attention a problem which must be carefully considered during the feasibility stage. If a number of employees are, for task-related reasons, unable to participate in the FWH program, then management should expect a drop in morale and job satisfaction in that group. This relative deprivation can be minimized through careful education and explanation, but it will have to be considered a possible negative side effect in the overall evaluation of flexitime.

The second nonpositive response came from a group of supervisors who reported no change in satisfaction over a period of time. It would be most interesting to evaluate the changes in attitudes of supervisors in other organizations, because of the concerns expressed in this book about the adjustment of this group to flexitime. However, only one other statistic was available: in one organization, 79 percent of the supervisors reported an increase in morale. It is difficult to draw any conclusions based on these two discrepant findings, except perhaps to say that the impact on supervisors' attitudes is very much contingent upon the style of implementation, including the training and help they receive in coping with new demands placed on them.

Two of the reports on employee morale were the observations of supervisors. In one organization, 52 percent reported an increase and in another, 79 percent reported an increase in morale. These favorable reports reflect, indirectly, the favorable biases of supervi-

Table 10-2 Attitudes

Organization	Reported Morale or Job Satisfaction	Attitude Toward Flexitime Program
Air University Maxwell Air Force Base (Alabama) N = 100	Increase in individual morale reported by 52% of employees Increase in the morale of co-workers reported by 61% of employees Decrease in morale reported by 8% of employees (however, not all of these were on flexitime)	98% of employees felt flexitime should be continued
Bureau of Alcohol, Tobacco and Firearms Department of the Treasury (Washington, D.C.) N = 25	Increase in morale reported by 80% of employees, decrease by 0%	
Bureau of Data Processing Social Security Administration (Baltimore) N = 350	Increase in job satisfaction reported by 43% of employees Increase in morale reported by 63% of employees	80% of employees liked the mechanical recording system
Bureau of Government Financial Operations Department of the Treasury N = 627	Increase in morale reported by 87% of employees	100% of employees felt flexitime should be adopted permanently
Bureau of Health Insurance Social Security Administration (Atlanta) N = 80	Increase in individual morale reported by 11% of supervisors and 7% of workers Improvement in feelings toward the organization reported by 68% of supervisors and 61% of employees	No personal disadvantages reported by 95% of supervisors No personal disadvantages reported by 85% of workers 68% of supervisors and 80% of employees felt flexitime should be continued
Bureau of Policy and Standards U.S. Office of Personnel Management (Washington, D.C.) N = 240	Increase in satisfaction, immediate and sustained for nonsupervisors No change over time for supervisors	Increase in satisfaction with work hours by 52% to 88%, decrease in dissatisfaction with work hours by 19% to 4% 95% of employees felt flexitime should be continued

Table 10-2 Attitudes *(Continued)*

Organization	Reported Morale or Job Satisfaction	Attitude Toward Flexitime Program
Bureau of Recruiting and Examining	Increase in morale reported by employees	
U.S. Office of Personnel Management (Washington, D.C.) N = 240		
Defense Mapping Agency Aerospace Center (St. Louis)	Increase in morale reported by 72% of employees, no change by 20%, decrease by 8%	
Economic Research Service U.S. Department of Agriculture (Washington, D.C.) N = 604	Increase in job satisfaction reported by 62% of employees, decrease reported by 3%	85% of employees enjoyed flexitime; 6% disliked flexitime 76% of managers enjoyed flexitime; 11% disliked flexitime 88% of first-line supervisors enjoyed flexitime; 6% disliked flexitime 11% of employees found sign-in sheets highly objectionable; 28% found them inconvenient; 61% either liked it or were neutral
Environmental Protection Agency (Washington, D.C.) N = 1,720	Increase in job satisfaction reported by 48% of employees	87% of employees felt flexitime should be continued
Library of Congress (Washington, D.C.) N = 150		Reported as a benefit by staff
National Security Agency Central Security Service (Maryland) N = 243	Increase in morale reported by 55% of employees	

Organization	Morale	Flexitime findings
Naval Ship Engineering Systems (Port Hueneme, California) N = 1,700	Increase in morale reported by 89% of employees, no change by 9%, decrease by 2%	99% of employees and supervisors felt flexitime should be continued
Navy Finance Center (Cleveland, Ohio) N = 64	Increase in morale reported by 85% of employees; Increase in morale reported by 95% of managers and supervisors	
Navy Finance Office (Long Beach, California) N = 55		Reaction to flexitime inversely correlated to hierarchical level; at lower levels, highly positive response; at upper levels, responses were negative
Region V, Department of Health, Education, and Welfare (Chicago) N = 211	Increase in workers' morale reported by 51% of supervisors	92% of employees and 70% of supervisors felt flexitime should be adopted; 71% of agency heads felt flexitime should be adopted, 14% did not, and 14% were undecided
U.S. Army Computer Systems Command (Fort Belvoir, Virginia) N = 82	Increase in morale reported by 87% of employees	95% of employees felt flexitime should be continued
U.S. Army Natick Laboratories (Massachusetts) N = 1,200		100% of directors felt flexitime should be continued
U.S. Office of Personnel Management (Seattle Region) N = 129		44% of employees have changed their hours since flexitime: of these, 80% start earlier, 20% start later
U.S. Geological Survey Department of the Interior (Reston, Virginia) N = 2,230	Increase in morale in office reported by 79% of supervisors; High job satisfaction reported by 19% more employees	86% of all supervisors and 92% of all first-line supervisors reported flexitime a success; 95% of employees liked flexitime, 3% had no opinion, and 2% disliked the program
U.S. Information Agency (Washington, D.C.) N = 33	Increase in employee morale reported as the most important benefit	

sors. The supervisors themselves must be favorably disposed toward the system to report such positive results. Furthermore, these positive results can only improve the work environment, which would have the effect of further enhancing supervisory attitudes. Thus, supervisory and employee perceptions can interact and, under certain conditions, enhance each other.

Attitudes toward the Flexitime Program

Attitudes toward the flexitime program included such variables as the percentage of those who wish the program to continue, reactions to the time-recording system utilized, personal advantages and disadvantages, and satisfaction with flexitime or with the new work hours. Of the 15 organizations reporting results on these facets, 14 were extremely favorable and 1 was inconclusive. In 1 organization, the reaction to flexitime was associated with the hierarchical level of the employee: at lower levels, employees were extremely positive; at upper levels, responses were negative. This finding is consistent with the concerns expressed here for supervisors and managers during flexitime implementation. In particular, the manager's fear of loss of authority may be especially salient in a military organization. The concerns of managers and supervisors have been expressed in both attitudes toward the job and attitudes toward the flexitime program. The mixed nature of the findings indicates that while our concerns for this group are valid, problems can be avoided if appropriate training, orientation, and support is provided during the implementation process.

As for employees, the results are overwhelmingly positive: in addition to the favorable attitudes reported toward the program itself, substantial improvements were reported in job attitudes. When these perceptions are compared to the results described in Table 10-1a on productivity, there does seem to be some justification for the claim that these attitudes may very well contribute to improved organizational effectiveness.

Membership Behavior

Most of the membership behavior reported by organizations fell into two general categories: absenteeism and tardiness. Absenteeism includes all the forms of absence reported by the organizations, such as sick leave, short-term leave, and personal leave usage. No attempts were made to subcategorize absenteeism further, as the types of leave granted with and without pay and sick leave policy varied from organization to organization. In Table 10-3, results are recorded as they were reported by the organizations themselves.

Absenteeism

Objective Data.   Various aspects of absenteeism were measured by 12 organizations. The most frequently reported variables were sick leave usage and the more general leave usage. Some organizations specified short-term or annual leave use. There were 12 measures of sick leave from 10 organizations. In 10 of the 12, sick leave decreased, in 1 case there was no change, and in another, sick leave increased. (In the case of the increase, the organization noted that other factors were involved.) There were 14 measurements of changes in leave usage by 9 organizations. In the 8 out of the 9 which also reported on sick leave, we can

Table 10-3 Membership Behavior—Withdrawal

Organization	Absenteeism	Tardiness
Bureau of Alcohol, Tobacco, and Firearms Department of the Treasury (Washington, D.C.) $N = 25$	10 to 41% decrease in sick leave usage in 4 out of 5 branches	Eliminated Several branch offices report saving 1–2 staff hours per week because of decreased paperwork
Bureau of Data Processing Social Security Administration (Baltimore) $N = 350$	6 hours decrease/employee/quarter in annual leave usage 4.3 hours decrease/employee/quarter in leave usage without pay 2 hours decrease/employee/quarter in sick leave usage	
Bureau of Government Financial Operations Department of the Treasury $N = 627$	Increase in short-term leave, attributed to 3 employees only	
Bureau of Health Insurance Social Security Administration (Atlanta) $N = 80$	Decrease in personal leave usage reported by 16% of supervisors, and 23% of employees Decrease in organizationwide leave usage reported by 5% of supervisors, and 10% of employees	Decrease in tardiness reported by 11% of supervisors, and 24% of employees
Bureau of Policy and Standards U.S. Office of Personnel Management (Washington, D.C.) $N = 240$	No significant changes in leave usages	Decrease (measured) significant and substantial
Bureau of Recruiting and Examining U.S. Office of Personnel Management (Washington, D.C.) $N = 240$	Decrease in leave usage reported by supervisors	Eliminated

Table 10-3 Membership Behavior—Withdrawal *(Continued)*

Organization	Absenteeism	Tardiness
Economic Research Service U.S. Department of Agriculture (Washington, D.C.) $N = 604$	Decrease in use of annual leave reported by 36% of employees Decrease in use of sick leave reported by 29% of employees	37% of employees reported abuse of work schedule had decreased; 4% reported an increase 46% of managers reported abuse of work schedule had decreased; 9% reported an increase 42% of first-line supervisors reported abuse of work schedule had decreased; 4% reported an increase Before flexitime, 69% of employees were rarely late, 27% occasionally, and 4% frequently After flexitime, 96% were rarely late, 4% occasionally, and 0% frequently
Environmental Protection Agency (Washington, D.C.) $N = 1,720$	Decrease in personal use of leave reported by 37% of employees Decrease in use of sick leave reported by 23% of employees	Little or no abuse in time reported by 85% of supervisors
Library of Congress (Washington, D.C.) $N = 150$	43% decrease in sick leave usage	Eliminated, along with accompanying paperwork
National Security Agency Central Security Service (Maryland) $N = 243$	Decrease in sick leave usage reported by 81% of employees	Decrease in tardiness reported by 56% of employees
Navy Finance Center (Cleveland, Ohio) $N = 64$	9% decrease in leave usage in amounts of 3 hours or less 50% decrease in use of sick leave	Eliminated
Navy Finance Office (Long Beach, California) $N = 55$	No change (measured) in absenteeism	

Office of Federal Records Center General Services Administration (Washington, D.C.) N = 17	Decrease (measured) in use of short-term leave	Eliminated
U.S. Army Computer Systems Command (Fort Belvoir, Virginia) N = 82	No change (measured) in civilian annual leave usage 18% increase in military annual leave usage—factors other than flexitime were suspected of causing it 9% increase in civilian sick leave usage—other factors suspected 9% decrease in military sick leave usage	81% of supervisors reported no tardiness
U.S. Army Tank Automotive Command (Michigan) N = 400	Slight decrease in leave usage 29% decrease in sick leave	Decrease in tardiness to practically zero
U.S. Geological Survey Department of the Interior (Reston, Virginia) N = 2,230	2% decrease in annual leave usage 20% decrease in leave usage of 1 hour or less 9% decrease in leave usage of 2 hours or less 7% decrease in sick leave usage 16% decrease in sick leave usage of 1 hour or less 26% decrease in sick leave usage of 2 hours or less	Decrease in tardiness reported by 71% of supervisors, increase by 3%
U.S. Information Agency (Washington, D.C.) N = 33	No change (measured) in use of short-term and sick leave	Eliminated

assume that leave usage means absenteeism other than sick leave. The meaning of leave usage is unclear in the eighth organization. Of the 14 measures, 10 indicated a decrease in leave usage, 2 indicated no change, and 2 indicated an increase (in both cases, the organizations mentioned mitigating factors). When leave usage was examined further, it was found that 6 of the 14 measures specified short-term leave usage, and that in all but 1 case, short term leave had gone down. This finding plus the decrease in sick leave usage support the notion that flexitime alleviates the need for employees to call in sick when they have personal business to attend to, or when extra time off is required. (The organization reporting an increase in short-term leave attributed the problem to three delinquent employees.)

Subjective Data. Survey data on absenteeism were reported by 5 organizations. Of the 3 organizations that surveyed their employees on changes in sick leave, all 3 reported decreases. In 1 organization, 81 percent of the employees reported a decrease in sick leave usage. In 4 organizations, employees were queried on changes in leave usage or personal leave; in all of the 5 reports from these 4 organizations, employees indicated that they perceived a decrease.

Again, in this area objective data is more acceptable than survey results. However, these survey results do serve the purpose of confirming the objective data, and more important, of indicating that employee perceptions are accurate to the extent that they are consistent with the objective data.

Tardiness

There were 8 objective measures of tardiness reported by 8 organizations. All of the 8 seem to be straightforward measurements of tardiness under flexitime as compared to previous levels. In 6 of the 8 organizations, tardiness was eliminated; the remaining 2 reported substantial decreases.

When the subjective evaluations were examined, it was found that 7 organizations had used the survey technique, asking a total of 10 questions. Some of the aspects surveyed are noteworthy, as they include some of the beneficial side effects of decreased tardiness. For example, 1 organization reported a decrease in paperwork because it was no longer necessary to keep track of tardiness incidents for each employee; 2 reported a decrease in the abuse of time schedules. The remaining 4 survey items were straight measures of tardiness—all were decreases.

It is interesting to note that none of the organizations reported any problems with employee arrival *after* core time had begun. Perhaps this is reflective of employee arrival patterns—in almost all organizations surveyed, 80 to 90 percent of employees tended to arrive during the early portion of the morning flexband (see Table 10-5). In any case, from all indications there is strong evidence that tardiness is substantially decreased or even eliminated under flexitime.

TIME MANAGEMENT: PERSONAL TIME AND TRANSPORTATION

Table 10-4 describes some of the aspects of the employee's life outside the job which are affected by flexitime. The two categories which we have chosen to present here are (1) time for family, recreation, and control over personal life and (2) transportation.

Table 10-4 Time Management: Personal Time and Transportation

Organization	Time for Family, Recreation, and Control over Personal Life	Transportation
Air University Maxwell Air Force Base (Alabama) $N = 100$		3% increase in use of car pools
Bureau of Alcohol, Tobacco and Firearms Department of the Treasury (Washington, D.C.) $N = 25$	Improvement in ease of child care reported by 100% of those who had children	Improvement in ease of transportation reported by 84% of employees
Bureau of Data Processing Social Security Administration (Baltimore) $N = 350$	Increase in time available with family reported by 46% of employees Improvement in ease of child care reported by 82% of employees with these responsibilities Increase in control over work and personal life reported by 80% of employees	Improvement in ease of getting to work reported by 65% of employees
Bureau of Government Financial Operations Department of the Treasury $N = 627$	Increased participation in family, community, and social activities reported by 83% of employees Increased ability to schedule work hours around personal needs reported by 96% of employees	
Bureau of Health Insurance Social Security Administration (Atlanta) $N = 80$	Increase in ease of scheduling reported by 63% of supervisors and 85% of employees	Improvement in transportation reported by 58% of supervisors, and 56% of workers Improvement in ease of arranging car pools reported by 3% of employees
Bureau of Policy and Standards U.S. Office of Personnel Management (Washington, D.C.) $N = 240$	Increase of 51% in the number of employees reporting high satisfaction with work-nonwork fit to 84%	No change (measured) in mode of transportation 5% decrease in commuting time for employees who travel more than 1 hour to work

Table 10-4 Time Management: Personal Time and Transportation *(Continued)*

Organization	Time for Family, Recreation, and Control over Personal Life	Transportation
Bureau of Recruiting and Examining U.S. Office of Personnel Management (Washington, D.C.) $N = 240$		Decrease in transportation problems reported by employees
Defense Mapping Agency Aerospace Center (St. Louis)	Increase in individual freedom and leisure time reported by 81% of employees, no change by 14%, decrease by 5%	Increased ease of access to and from the facility reported by 85% of employees, no change by 8%, decrease by 7%
Economic Research Service U.S. Department of Agriculture (Washington, D.C.) $N = 604$		Decrease of up to 15 minutes in commuting time reported by 32% of employees; decrease of up to 30 minutes reported by 21%; 64% of employees reported that a car pool was the factor which determined their starting time
Environmental Protection Agency (Washington, D.C.) $N = 1,720$		Decrease in commuting time reported by 50% 4% decrease of employees driving to work alone 6% increase of employees in car pools
National Security Agency Central Security Service (Maryland) $N = 243$	4% utilized flexitime because of illness in family 2% utilized flexitime for shopping 13% utilized flexitime for medical reasons 6% utilized flexitime in order to care for children 14% utilized flexitime for recreation 10% utilized flexitime for education 25% utilized flexitime for other reasons	8% of employees utilized flexitime for transportation reasons
Navy Finance Center (Cleveland, Ohio) $N = 64$		147 employees using privately-owned vehicles reported a collective savings of 473 gallons of fuel per week

Table 10-4 Time Management: Personal Time and Transportation *(Continued)*

Organization	Time for Family, Recreation, and Control over Personal Life	Transportation
Region V, Department of Health, Education and Welfare (Chicago) $N = 211$	Improvement or no change in ease of child care reported by 100% of nonsupervisors Increase in ability to conduct personal business reported by 98% of nonsupervisors	Decrease in difficulty of getting to work reported by 73% of employees, no change by 26%, more difficulty by 1% Decrease in difficulty of getting to work reported by 26% of supervisors, increase by 49% (special problem with a rotating position)
U.S. Army Natick Laboratories (Massachusetts) $N = 1,200$		Reported that traffic congestion is eliminated
U.S. Office of Personnel Management (Seattle Region) $N = 129$		Decrease of 30 minutes/day in travel time reported by employees Employees reported being more relaxed upon arrival due to less traffic congestion
U.S. Geological Survey (Washington, D.C.) $N = 33$	Increase in time for family and children reported by 69% of employees Increase in time for recreation reported by over 50% of employees Increase in time for education reported by 43% of employees	Decreases in commuting time from 5 to 15 minutes reported by 54%, no change by 45%, increase by 1% of all employees Small decrease in gas use reported by 40%; large decrease reported by 12%; no change reported by 47%; increase reported by 1% of all employees

Time for Family, Recreation, and Control over Personal Life

This first category is quite broad, encompassing a number of facets of the employee's personal life, as well as the home-work fit. Examples of the types of aspects investigated include ease of child care, time available for family, control over work and personal life (through control over hours), community, educational, and social activities, satisfaction with work-nonwork fit, individual freedom and leisure time, and ability to conduct personal business. One organization reported that the reasons why employees chose to utilize flexitime included shopping, illness in the family, medical reasons, child care, recreation, and education. Because this category represents activities which occur *outside* the organization, it is strictly subjective in nature. Practically speaking, it would not be feasible for the organization to collect objective data in this area.

Opinions from the employees of 9 organizations were reported, and all were very favorable. Six questions covering various aspects of child care and family life were reported by the employees of 5 organizations. This does not include the organization mentioned above which reported child care as one of several reasons for flexitime use. All 5 of these organizations reported that employees experienced flexitime as beneficial for child care and family life. There were two ways in which this benefit was expressed. In some organizations, employees reported an increase in the amount of time available for family; employees of other organizations reported on ease of child care since flexitime implementation.

Another area mentioned by organizations under the category of personal time was the improved ability to schedule for leisure and educational activities. This aspect was singled out by 2 organizations: in the first, over 80 percent of employees reported an increase in leisure time; in the second, 50 percent reported more time for leisure and almost 45 percent reported more time for educational activities.

Aside from family life and recreation, the other most frequently measured aspect was home-work fit (although this variable was worded somewhat differently by various organizations). Some aspect of home-work fit was reported on by 5 organizations, and all were extremely positive. This is a particularly important variable as it includes connotations of autonomy and control. Through improved control over work hours, the employee is better able to fulfill his responsibilities at home and at work. The positive results expressed here lend support to the claims that it is in this area where some of the major benefits of flexitime can be experienced. It is also interesting to note the way this benefit is perceived: employees reported having extra time for certain activities under flexitime, although the number of hours worked had not decreased. Extra time is really a matter of control over existing time.

Thus, employees experienced benefits in three aspects of their personal life: family life and child care, home-work fit, and leisure activities. It is important to understand, however, that these really represent a single benefit—increased control over daily schedules where control is often perceived (and reported) as additional time. The way in which the employee chooses to make use of this added control reflects the area in which the benefit is experienced. Some employees may organize their schedules around day care facilities, others around recreational activities or educational opportunities. Whatever the case may be, the employee decides his priorities and chooses the area where he can maximize the benefits received through the best home-work fit possible. Improved home-work fit is, therefore, a general category of the possible benefits relating to the employee's personal life. From this perspective, flexitime serves as a link between the work environment and the employee's personal life which can help him to achieve a higher quality of life.

Transportation

The transportation section included information on the changes in the modes of transportation, the use of car pools, fuel consumption, and the amount of ease or difficulty required in getting to work that resulted from flexitime implementation. Objective data were reported by 3 organizations, although items measured were quite different: one reported an increase in the use of car pools, the other two reported slight decreases in commuting time for those employees traveling for more than 1 hour to get to work as well as gas savings. Of the 12 agencies reporting survey data, 11 reported positive and 1 reported inconclusive results. The most frequently asked questions involved some variation of ease in getting to and from work. Of the 9 organizations investigating this area, all reported that employees experienced an improvement in some aspect of their commuting. (In 1 organization, some supervisors reported increased difficulty in getting to work, but the organization qualified this report by describing it as a special problem of rotating supervisors.)

Small increases in the use of car pools were reported by 3 organizations, and a fourth reported that, for 64 percent of employees, the flexitime starting time was determined by the car pool schedule. These statistics are interesting when one considers that by joining a car pool the employee gives up the opportunity for flexibility on a day-to-day basis. Most organizations have found, however, that employees do tend to decide upon a schedule within the flexibility allowed and stay with it (see Table 10-5). Certainly, it is predictable that most individuals establish and live by schedules—whether based upon constraints from the outside or of their own choosing. In flexitime, one external constraint (work starting time) has been removed, and the individual is thus allowed to decide what other constraints or demands will determine his schedule. It should also be mentioned that the increased use of car pools results both in considerable savings for those who participate and in more efficient utilization of energy.

It is clear from these reports that employees were already beginning to realize benefits in terms of decreased commuting time and gas utilization, although flexitime schedules had been implemented on a very limited basis in their geographic areas of work. If flexitime were to be adopted on a widespread basis, especially in large cities, the benefits could become quite substantial.

MORNING ARRIVAL DISTRIBUTIONS

Table 10-5 presents a description of the arrival patterns of employees for 5 organizations on flexitime.In 3 of the 5, the morning flexband ranged from 7 to 9:30 A.M. In one, the flexband lasted from 6:30 to 9:30 A.M., and in the fifth, it ranged from 7:30 to 9:30 A.M. In 2 of the organizations there was a small population who varied from day to day, and who therefore could not be assigned to a specific arrival time.

When these arrival patterns are evaluated, it is clear that the tendency is for employees

Table 10-5 Morning Arrival Distribution

Arriving by:	Geological Survey Dept. of the Interior Reston, Va. N=1,773 Employees (1 Year Evaluation)		Navy Finance Center Cleveland, Ohio N=1,781 Arrivals (Average over 4 Months)		Environmental Protection Agency Washington, D.C. N=1,540 Employees (3-Month Evaluation)		Defense Mapping Agency Aerospace Center St. Louis, Mo.		Region V Department of Health, Education, and Welfare Chicago, Ill.	
	%	Cumulative	%	Cumulative	%	Cumulative	%	Cumulative	%	Cumulative
6:30	—	—	—	—	—	—	41	41.0	—	—
7:00	26.5	26.5	21.6	21.6	11.8	11.8	40	81.0	—	—
7:30	31.3	57.8	18.3	39.9	28.4	40.2	10	91.0	31	31.0
8:00	22.4	80.2	20.9	60.8	41.9	82.1	5	96.0	26	57.0
8:30	9.0	89.2	24.5	85.3	9.9	92.0	2	98.0	31	88.0
9:00	3.6	92.8	9.3	94.6	5.5	97.5	2	100.0	12	100.0
9:30	—	92.8	5.3	99.9	2.1	98.6	—	100.0	—	100.0
Vary	7.1	99.9	—	99.9	0.5	100.1	—	100.0	—	100.0
Total		99.9*		99.9*		100.1		100.0		100.0

* Percentages may not total to 100% because of rounding.

to choose an earlier starting time when given the opportunity under flexitime. For example, the table shows that between 60 percent and 80 percent of employees arrived by 8 A.M. By 8:30 A.M., 90 percent of employees had arrived at work in most cases. Perhaps the most important inference one can draw from this finding is that most employees tend to establish relatively fixed patterns within the flexitime schedule. This was implied, as indicated in Table 10-4, by the increase in the popularity of car pools reported in some organizations after flexitime implementation.

Another interesting point concerns tardiness. When one examines this table, it is clear how organizations can claim that tardiness is virtually eliminated. In all 5 organizations, between 93 and 100 percent of employees had arrived by 9 A.M.—½ hour before the end of the flexband and the start of core time. Because virtually all employees have chosen an earlier workday (starting at 9 A.M. at the latest), arrivals past 9:30 A.M. would be very rare occurrences. In fact, none of the organizations studied have mentioned core time deviations as a problem, or have even set up procedures for dealing with them.

Many organizations, when considering flexitime, express concern that wild variations in schedule by individuals and groups will be a disruptive element. They fear breakdowns in communication, difficulties for supervisors in carrying out their responsibilities, and, in general, loss of control over employee behavior. The information presented in this table should help to alleviate those fears.

SUMMARY

Table 10-6 has been compiled to summarize the general trends indicated in Tables 10-1 to 10-4. Included in this summary table is the total number of organizations reporting data for a specific category (N = number of organizations), followed by a concise breakdown of the results. Findings have been divided into two subcategories: measured or objective data, and survey or opinion results. In some cases, the information source is strictly an opinion survey, as in the attitudes table (Table 10-2). Other categories, such as productivity, contain both measured and subjective information.

A quick review of the summary table shows that the results were overwhelmingly positive. In all categories, under both objective and survey measures, the results support the use of flexitime. It is not surprising that every one of the experiments included in this report resulted in an expanded, permanent flexitime program for the organization in question.

CONCLUSIONS

The data presented here were compiled from reports prepared by various bureaus and agencies of the federal government on the effects of flexitime on different organizational and employee variables; 25 such reports were available, although it is estimated that some 100 agencies have implemented some form of flexitime to date. Although the reader was cautioned about the inconsistent, and, in some cases, nonscientific, nature of the data, these findings must be given attention because they are so overwhelmingly and consistently positive. General conclusions which can be drawn from the data are:

Table 10-6 Summary

	10-1 Organizational Effectiveness				10-2 Attitudes		10-3 Membership Behavior (Withdrawal)		10-4 Time Management	
Subtable	10-1A Productivity	10-1B Work Environment		10-1C Costs						
Category		1 Access and Relations	2 Control of Hours and Quiet Time		1 Morale and Job Satisfaction	2 Attitude toward Flexitime	1 Absenteeism	2 Tardiness	1 Personal Time Usage	2 Transportation
Objective Data	$N=11$ 9 positive 2 inconclusive	$N=1$ 1 positive	N/A	$N=9$ 6 positive 2 negative 1 no change	N/A	N/A	$N=11$ 7 positive 1 negative 2 no change 1 inconclusive	$N=9$ 9 positive	N/A	$N=3$ 3 positive
Survey or Opinion Data	$N=17$ 14 positive 1 no change 2 inconclusive	$N=10$ 6 positive 3 no change 1 inconclusive	$N=7$ 6 positive 1 no change	$N=4$ 1 negative 1 no change 2 inconclusive	$N=17$ 17 positive	$N=15$ 14 positive 1 inconclusive	$N=6$ 6 positive	$N=5$ 5 positive	$N=9$ 9 positive	$N=12$ 11 positive 1 inconclusive

1.   The organization, as a unit, can improve its level of effectiveness through flexitime implementation. Objective data on productivity, and subjective data on performance, interpersonal relations, tardiness, and absenteeism support this conclusion.

2.   Individual employees have reported improved control over work scheduling and work processes, as well as an increase in uninterrupted work periods. These benefits contribute to improved organizational and individual effectiveness.

3.   Employees' attitudes toward their jobs and the work environment are improved.

4.   Employees experience an improvement in the interrelationship between work and personal life—specifically, in the impact of work on personal life. This includes more flexibility in allocating time for recreation and leisure, educational and community activities, as well as the opportunity to take a more active role in family life and child rearing.

5.   Flexitime has the potential to improve employees' commuting to and from work, and thus their state of relaxation upon arrival. However, the data as presented here are inconclusive. Additional studies are necessary to confirm this hypothesis.

Although the results are so positive, there are a few problems indicated in the data, which can, however, be avoided through rigorous planning and judicious implementation. Organizational change techniques should be utilized, especially for the training and preparation of first-line supervisors. Often this particular group is less receptive toward the concept, and thus needs special attention.

In general, *all* levels of employees are more receptive to a new concept if they have had the opportunity to be included during the planning stages and to contribute their ideas. Useful insights may be obtained which might be overlooked at higher levels of management. In the same context, it is important to design each flexitime installation around the demands of the immediate work environment. This may mean different flexitime designs within an organization, or even within a department.

Although these results are promising, the lack of uniformity in the data indicates the need for rigorous analysis. There is a critical need for the standardized controlled experimentation proposed here, so that more reliable results can be obtained.

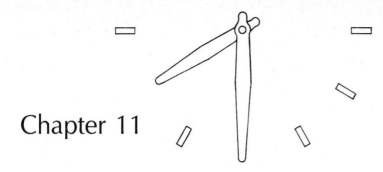

Chapter 11

The Private Sector: A Case Study SmithKline Corporation

SmithKline Corporation* was one of the earliest private organizations to implement flexitime on a wide scale in the United States. As a result, it provides an opportunity for an examination of both the short- and long-term impact of flexitime. An additional advantage to using SmithKline as the subject for a case study is the fact that there is a wealth of information already available on the company.[1] However, the following case study represents the first complete presentation of what happened at SmithKline.

The reader should find the description of the pilot study, the decision-making process, and the companywide implementation a helpful commentary on bringing about effective organizational change. The strategies adopted here represent a concern for companywide acceptance of flexible working systems—on all levels. This concern reflects the fact that flexitime was considered a benefit to the individual as well as to the organization.

BACKGROUND

SmithKline is a large and diversified firm manufacturing nationally distributed health products, headquartered in Philadelphia. As a major company, it offers an extensive product line and carries out a full range of business functions, including research and development, manufacturing, and marketing. Approximately 3,000 employees work in the company headquarters, including production workers, clerical staff, and management.

In 1972, SmithKline was operating under organizational and financial stress. Increased costs had eroded profits, there were limited new-product introductions, and the stock value was down. These pressures caused the management of the company to reemphasize the importance of increasing productivity levels. In translating this directive into action, the

*The author is grateful to Mr. Richard Hilles of SmithKline for his cooperative support and provision of the data and historical background for the case.

personnel department was faced with the dilemma of getting more work done with fewer people. Furthermore, any consideration of new benefits was constrained by cost factors.

An additional relevant factor was a change in the starting and quitting times at SmithKline. In an attempt to alleviate traffic congestion, the city of Philadelphia had asked the company to stagger its work schedule, along with other large organizations in the area. SmithKline complied, to the extent of deciding a new starting time for all employees, but there was no variation in starting times within the company. When the personnel department suggested extending the concept of staggered hours to different schedules for various departments, top level management rejected the proposal, expressing concerns about work scheduling and increased costs relating to building maintenance and power consumption.

It was within this environment that Richard Hilles, Organization Development Consultant working in the personnel department (referred to henceforth as "the consultant"), first came across the idea of flexitime in a journal article. His initial reaction was that the concept held real possibilities for SmithKline, but that the notion was precluded by top management's rejection of the staggered hours concept. Nevertheless, the consultant did discuss flexitime with the vice president of research and development, who was receptive to implementing the system in his department if top management could be convinced.

In the spring of 1972, an opportunity for a pilot study arose when the consultant was approached by a small branch (70 to 80 employees) of the R&D department in Upper Merion, a suburb of Philadelphia. These employees desired summer hours so that they could take advantage of recreational activities in the afternoons and evenings during the fine weather. The consultant met with three managers from this branch and suggested flexitime as a way to allow each employee to determine his own version of summer hours. The managers then discussed the idea with their employees, who were quite receptive. They stipulated, however, that such a system was not worthwhile unless it allowed a substantial degree of flexibility. The consultant then obtained the approval of the vice president of research and development (who had previously been supportive) to submit a proposal for a pilot study to the president and the operating committee. The proposal suggested that the Upper Merion branch become the subject of a pilot study which would evaluate the feasibility of flexitime on a companywide basis. A pilot study was necessary to test the flexitime system before implementing it on a large scale. Further, it was more likely that this approach would be accepted than an initial proposal for full scale implementation. The pilot study would allow upper management to take one step at a time, rather than having to make a major policy decision initially. The branch in Upper Merion was viewed as an appropriate subject for a pilot study for several reasons. First, the suburban location, removed from the company headquarters, eliminated the problems of selective implementation. The single branch could be put on the system, and the resentments, jealousies, and conflicts that would arise if one department was chosen from many at corporate headquarters could thus be avoided. Second, the Upper Merion office provided a full range of employee types—both in terms of salary and hierarchical levels. Finally, as a suburban branch, it tended to function somewhat independently and autonomously.

Approval for the pilot study was granted on each successive organizational level: the Upper Merion managers, the operating committee for the R&D department, the vice president of R&D, the companywide operating committee, and, finally, the president of Smith-Kline. In summary, this approval represents a fortuitous convergence of an employee request for summer hours and an idea looking for expression (flexitime). While the employees provided the impetus and the outlet for the expression of the idea, an intervention by the personnel department was necessary to place the idea within the context of organizational change, and thus to "sell" the idea to upper management.

Through an organization development (OD) approach, it was possible to view the potential impact of the intervention in terms of its broader organizational consequences as well as in terms of the possible benefits for the individual. While it took a grass roots movement to overcome organizational resistance created originally by the rejection of the staggered hours concept, the organization development strategy expedited the decision-making process.

CONSIDERATIONS FOR IMPLEMENTATION

It was felt that flexitime could be beneficial to the organization because of its positive impact on the individual. As a way of putting this philosophy into practice, flexitime was presented to the organization within the context of organization development, a practice very much in evidence at SmithKline. Flexitime was considered a structural intervention—that is, a substantive change in the environment—rather than a more traditional interpersonal intervention associated with OD.

As a structural intervention, flexible hours had the potential to affect aspects of work relationships and the quality of work life for employees at all levels. Specific areas affected by flexitime could include employee participation in supervisory activities, increased self-determination and autonomy, and team decision making. The consultant at SmithKline felt that such improvements in the quality of working life for the employee would lead to direct benefits to the organization through improved job knowledge, efficiency, productivity, and attendance.

In order to maximize these benefits, the consultant felt that it was important for employees to be involved in the implementation of the flexitime system at SmithKline. This decision reflects two important principles. First, in order to maximize the possible benefits to the employee, he must be included in the design and implementation process. To do otherwise would contradict the objectives of improving the quality of working life through increased participation and autonomy. In other words, the change *process* should be consistent with the objectives of the new system wrought by the change. Second, in the decision to implement flexitime from the bottom up, it was recognized that different departments might require different flexitime systems, based on work flow and task interdependence, as well as on varying legal and contractual limitations. Certainly the concept of "bottom up" implementation is negated if one system is implemented for the entire company.

Moreover, the concept of "bottom up" implementation makes good sense in terms of maximizing its acceptability to employees at all levels. At the lower levels, employees who feel that they have had a hand in the process may feel more of a commitment to making it work. Since the system includes their input, to have it fail reflects negatively on their contribution and on them. At the management level, inclusion in the design and implementation process forestalls rejection of the system based on objections that it does not consider their needs. (An earlier proposal at SmithKline for an extensive staggered hours program had been designed from the top and was ultimately rejected for just this reason.) Thus, the "bottom up" form of design and implementation was essential, not only in order to be consistent with the objectives of the flexitime system, but to improve its acceptability to employees and managers.

THE PILOT STUDY

Method

The pilot study was designed with the idea that a scientific study would be more valuable and reliable for evaluation than an anecdotal report. Also, it would have seemed somewhat inappropriate for a department such as R&D to participate in a report whose methodology was less than rigorous. The experimental design for the pilot study was based upon 3 units at the Upper Merion site: 2 units were experimental; the third was the control group which was not placed on flexitime. Comparisons would enable the researchers to measure changes due to flexitime. There were 15 supervisory and 58 nonsupervisory employees in the 3 units. Roughly one-third of the total were nonexempt, while the remainder were exempt. Within each of the 3 groups, however, was a full range of employees performing all sorts of jobs in all salary brackets. The study was concerned both about potential benefits accruing to the organization and about less tangible benefits for the individual derived from flexitime as a structural intervention. Consequently, both behavioral measurements and attitude surveys were collected. The behavioral measurements were used to indicate the impact on organizational functioning, whereas the attitudinal surveys indicated the more subjective impact on employees.

The extent of the program and the demands it would make on employees were carefully spelled out, as can be seen from this portion of a memo circulated to participants:

> The success or failure of the test will depend, in large measure, on the full cooperation of each employee. With the greater flexibility in individual schedules comes increased responsibility for arranging your work in a way which at least maintains and, preferably, improves current operating efficiency.
>
> I trust that, with your help, start up difficulties may be overcome quickly. The test may run as long as six months, although it could end earlier. After we obtain information on the advantages and disadvantages of flexible work hours, we will be able to decide if such a program should be established on a permanent basis. We will be asking for your reactions by means of periodic surveys.

The flexitime model used in the pilot study was developed through discussions between R&D supervisors and the consultant. The schedule included a 5-hour core period, from 9:15 A.M. to 3 P.M., excluding a 45-minute lunch period. The flexbands were from 7 to 9:15 A.M. and from 3 to 6 P.M., creating a possible 10¼-hour maximum workday (see Figure 11-1). However, nonexempt employees were limited to a maximum of 8 hours per day. Beyond this point, they must be paid overtime premiums. Within the standard 35-hour workweek, this means that nonexempt employees could not choose to work more than one 5-hour day per week without the company incurring overtime costs. (Otherwise, the number of hours to be made up would force the employee into an overtime situation; that is, more than 8 hours in one day would have to be worked.) Exempt employees were not subject to this

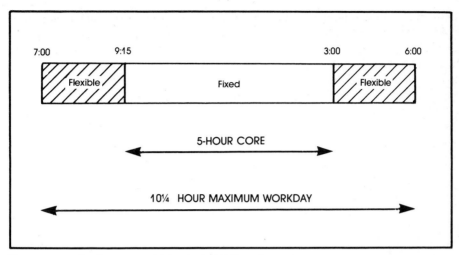

Figure 11–1   The flexitime model for the SmithKline pilot study.

limitation, and consequently were able to take advantage of the full 10¼-hour workday if they so desired. There were 4 additional aspects of the program itself which should be mentioned:

1.   The full use of flexitime in each department or work area was subject to the work requirements of the department and the approval of the immediate supervisor. On occasion, an employee could be asked to limit his use of flexitime in order to meet certain work demands.

2.   There was no flexibility either in the duration of the lunch period or the time it was taken.

3.   Hours worked in excess of 35 hours per week could not be banked.

4.   Because an accurate record of hours worked and arrival and departure times was necessary for data analysis, both exempt *and* nonexempt employees in the pilot study were asked to use a time clock.

Objective and attitudinal data were collected from different sources within the organization. Company records provided the objective data on behavioral changes such as absenteeism, cost of support services, number of sick days, and schedules of arrival and departure. The attitudinal, or subjective, data were obtained through questionnaires administered to participating employees. The questionnaires were administered three times: prior to implementation, at roughly 6 months, and 1 year after implementation. Two forms of questionnaires were used—one for employees and a supplement for supervisors. Supervisors answered both forms.

Questionnaire Results

In general, the evaluation of the 6-month questionnaire data indicated a nearly unanimous response in favor of flexitime by employees. Table 11-1 represents a summary of the differences between the experimental and control groups of employees after 6 months. Of the first 15 items on the questionnaire, only 1 was negative: employees did not care for the use of the time clock. Of the last 3 items, 16 through 18, which were expected to be negative, 2 changed in the direction expected: employees in the experimental groups felt that the quality of support services and communication about company activities had significantly declined since the implementation of flexitime.

Table 11-1   Employees Reporting—Effects of Flexitime 6 Months after Implementation

Items on Employee Form	In Comparison to the Control Group, the Experimental Groups Reported:
1. Degree of participation in decisions about work assignments	Significantly higher participation
2. Degree of difficulty in scheduling work requiring others	No change
3. Satisfaction with current work hours	Significantly higher satisfaction
4. Reaction to use of time clock	Less favorable reaction
5. Traffic congestion encountered to and from work	Significantly less congestion
6. Ability to handle personal business during the workday	Significantly greater ability to handle personal business
7. Impact of current work-hour policy on individual productivity	Significantly more favorable impact on productivity
8. Conflict with co-workers over scheduling work	Less conflict
9. Individual's flexibility to schedule work assignments	Significantly more flexibility
10. Desirability of respondent's department as a place to work	No change
11. Quality of communication about work assignments	No change
12. Conflict with supervisor about scheduling work	Less conflict with supervisor
13. Availability of others when help is needed	Greater availability
14. Ability to arrange meetings with others when necessary	Greater ability to schedule meetings
15. Inclination to work more than standard week	No change
16. Quality of communication about company activities of personal interest	Lower quality of communication
17. Availability of others for spur of the moment discussions or phone calls	Significantly greater availability of others
18. Quality of support services	Significantly lower quality of support services

SOURCE: Adapted with special permission from *The Journal of Applied Behavioral Science*, "A longitudinal study of flexitime effects: some consequences of an OD intervention," by Robert T. Golembiewski, Rick Hilles, and Munro S. Kaqno, 10: 4, pp. 516–517, 522, copyright 1974, NTL Institute.

When supervisors completed the same questionnaire from their perspective as employees, their reactions were practically identical. This group differed from employees only on items 10 and 13. They felt that their work place was more desirable than non-supervisory employees, perhaps reflecting a more favorable outlook based upon their higher status as supervisors. They also reported that others were less available when help was needed. This, again, may reflect their special vantage point as supervisors. On all other items, supervisors reported the same reactions to flexitime as employees, when reporting *as* employees.

When employees were surveyed again after 1 year on flexitime, there was little change in attitudes from those reflected on the 6-month questionnaire. Of the changes in attitudes from the pretest questionnaire to those at 12 months, 89 percent were in the hoped-for direction and remained consistent with the attitudes expressed at 6 months. It is interesting to note that while the 2 experimental groups on flexitime continued to express positive attitudes concerning the impact of flexitime, the attitudes of the control group, when measured on the same aspects, worsened somewhat. Although the actual reasons for this change are not clear, one possibility may be the fact that the group was left out of the special planning and benefits acquired by their fellow workers on the new system. In general, one might predict that any resentment would lead to a decline in morale, manifesting itself in aspects measured on the questionnaire.

The impact of the flexitime program on supervisors acting in their managerial role was measured by a supplement to the questionnaire. This supplement addressed itself to the effects supervisors had observed on employee performance and on their own effective functioning as supervisors. In this role, supervisors reported that the impact of flexitime was negligible; in general, the status quo was maintained as indicated in Table 11-2. There was no indication of a deterioration in the attitudes of supervisors toward the system, despite the concern by the implementors that their job would be made more difficult.

When the supervisors were again surveyed on the supplemental form after 1 year, there were positive changes from the reports at 6 months. Whereas attitudes reflected a "no change" condition after 6 months, they were consistently more positive after 1 year. This result can be interpreted in two ways. First, flexitime may have had a positive but delayed impact on this group. Second, it may have simply taken the supervisors a period of time to adjust to the new managerial style appropriate to flexitime.

Objective Data

Objective data were obtained from company records before and after implementation and compared to determine the effects of flexitime. When objective data were analyzed, the following was found:

1. Arrival and departure times stabilized for most workers. However, seasonal shifts were evident. Table 11-3 represents the distribution of employee arrivals and departures during the flexbands.

2. Although overtime was reduced by 75 percent, it is hard to determine the effect of flexitime, as this finding was contaminated by other policies designed to reduce overtime.

Table 11-2 Supervisors Reporting—Effects of Flexitime 6 Months after Implementation

Items on Managerial Form	In Comparison to the Control Group, the Experimental Groups Reported:
1. Productivity of your employees	Higher productivity
2. Morale of your employees	Higher morale
3. Quality of support services	Lower quality of services
4. Degree of conflict with employees over scheduling	Less conflict
5. Quality of communications about work assignments	No change
6. Flexibility to undertake projects or experiments	No change
7. Effort required to account for employees' time	Now more effort required
8. Problems with other supervisors regarding work hours	Fewer problems
9. Opportunities for employees to work independently	No change
10. Effort required to schedule work assignments	No change
11. Your employees' attitudes at work	More positive employee attitudes
12. Overall performance of your employees	Better overall performance

SOURCE: Adapted with special permission from *The Journal of Applied Behavioral Science*, "A longitudinal study of flexitime effects: some consequences of an OD intervention," by Robert T. Golembiewski, Rick Hilles, and Munro S. Kaqno, 10: pp. 576–517, 522, copyright 1974, NTL Institute.

3.   There was a 35 percent decrease in total paid absences for the full year in the experimental groups and an increase of 15 percent for the control group. However, the expected decrease in short-term absences (1 day or less) did not occur.

4.   The cost of support services was slightly less, in comparison with the previous year.

Conclusions on the Pilot Study

In general, the consultant concluded that flexitime in the pilot study had the predicted effects. Further, initially positive effects on employees tended to remain positive over time. For supervisors in their managerial role, the effects were no less positive, but took longer to manifest themselves. The implementors attributed their success with the system to the introduction, design, and implementation techniques used, as well as to the positive aspects of the system itself. Thus, they emphasized the importance of introducing flexitime within an OD context as a way of maximizing beneficial results. This is accomplished by encouraging employee responsibility and self-determination, while avoiding any accompanying decrease in the sense of commitment or ownership by supervisors and managers.

Table 11-3 Percentage Distributions of Time in and Time out, Approximately 10,000 Employee Workdays

Times In			Times Out		
Months 1–5		Months 6–10	Months 1–5		Months 6–10
6:45 A.M.	0.04%	0.02%	3:00 P.M.	1.3%	2.8%
7:00	0.3	0.9	3:15	7.2	11.1
7:15	1.7	2.6	3:30	5.5	6.7
7:30	6.4	7.3	3:45	3.9	4.7
7:45	3.2	5.1	4:00	5.1	6.1
8:00	4.5	7.5	4:15	6.4	7.7
8:15	12.0	15.0	4:30	15.1	14.1
8:30	21.0	23.2	4:45	20.8	17.7
8:45	25.3	18.2	5:00	12.8	9.8
9:00	16.6	11.7	5:15	8.1	6.8
9:15	6.9	6.7	5:30	5.1	4.8
9:30	1.9	1.7	5:45	3.7	3.0
9:45	0.1	0.1	6:00	2.3	3.2
10:00	0.1	0.1	6:15	1.1	0.9
			6:30	0.6	0.4
			6:45	0.4	0.05
			7:00	0.2	0.14
			7:15	0.3	0.05
			after 7:30 P.M.	0.3	0.2

EVALUATION AND APPROVAL FOR COMPANYWIDE IMPLEMENTATION

In February 1974, Mr. Hilles, the internal consultant, together with the vice president of the research and development department, presented the pilot study results to the president and the operating committee. In addition to a description of the pilot study and its findings, the following recommendations were made:

1. Managers at the corporate operating committee level must have greater latitude to establish work-hour programs which can enhance the effectiveness of their operating areas and, at the same time, recognize employee desires for greater flexibility. This recommendation may result in small differences in work hours among functional groups.

2. The corporate personnel department should continue to collaborate with operating managers in the design, integration, and implementation of work-hour modifications, in order to ensure compatibility of work schedules, both within and among different functional groups.

3. The flexitime program at Upper Merion should be made permanent.

Also included in the recommendations were brief descriptions of limited flexitime schedules which might be suitable in departments where full flexitime was not possible. These included staggered hours and flexibility within the working day.

The decision to implement flexitime was given additional support from the task force on the quality of work life at SmithKline. This group stipulated, however, that time clocks should not be used if flexitime were implemented, although they had been used in the pilot study. This recommendation is remarkable, considering the company's concern with the issue of increasing productivity (recall the president's directive) and the fact that the time clock represented the only means of determining employee attendance on an objective basis, insofar as decreased attendance would have an immediate and negative impact on productivity.

The decision was therefore made to implement flexitime on a companywide basis by the president and operating committee. Full implementation was to take place within 3 months of the decision.

COMPANYWIDE IMPLEMENTATION

Policy Decisions

As part of the decision to go ahead with flexitime, the consultant was appointed to organize, oversee, and direct companywide implementation. As a first step, the consultant made several policy decisions which were to be reflected throughout the implementation program. These initial decisions provided a framework upon which the program would be built. In making these initial policy decisions, the consultant had to be careful to maintain consistency with the goals and objectives of the flexitime program itself.

1. The first of these policy decisions was that there may be several versions of flexitime implemented at SmithKline. This reflects decisions made in the pilot study, where exempt and nonexempt employees exercised different levels of flexibility.

2. A corollary to this decision was the importance of "bottom up" systems design. Once the decision had been made that variations were necessary because of differing job demands, it seemed necessary to allow managers to design their own systems in response to the requirements in their departments. With this in mind, senior executives were advised that subordinate managers would develop flexitime systems appropriate for their individual organization units and their employees.

3. It was emphasized that *all* departments would implement some version of flexitime unless special job or employee requirements prevented it.

4. Some supervision from the personnel department and upper management was necessary in order to ensure that legal limitations were observed, to ascertain that managers consulted with employees and used the appropriate criteria in their design, and, finally, to oversee an evaluative study of all departments after a period of time.

Planning and Design

In order to implement these policies, two groups were created. The first group consisted of 23 work area representatives (ARs) from the various departments. These representatives were appointed by middle level managers to develop the appropriate flexitime programs for their areas, and to help in the data collection for the evaluation of the success or failure of the program. The second group, whose members were the consultant and a member from each main department, supervised the ARs, approved their programs, and acted as coordinators for the companywide implementation.

Three workshops were conducted by the consultant and his staff to introduce the ARs to the concept of flexitime, its variations, and the considerations they must make use of when designing a system for their areas. Each AR then developed a proposal, in consultation with the employees in his work area. Considerations were based on job requirements and scheduling demands. In addition to the actual flexitime scheme, each proposal was required to include implementation schedules, emphasizing the education of employees about the system. Further, the systems had to be contained within a maximum, predefined level of flexibility. This maximum level coincided with the system used in the pilot study—an employee might work a minimum of 5 or a maximum of 10¼ hours per day, within a 35-hour week. Core hours of 9:15 A.M. to 3:00 P.M. were observed. Each proposal was presented for review and, once approved, the AR was given authorization and responsibility for the programs in his area.

THE FLEXITIME PROGRAM

The flexitime program has now been extended to include some 2,150 employees in the corporate headquarters (out of about 3,000). However, approximately 40 percent are nonexempt, and because of federal wage and hours laws, their use of the system is limited. The systems themselves range from versions of staggered hours to the full level of flexitime allowed by management. Four examples of the different types of systems implemented are described below.

1. In the mailroom all nonexempt employees work a regular 40-hour week. Consequently, their starting time determines their quitting time.

2. Manufacturing office employees are, in the main, nonexempt and work 7¾ hours per day. Therefore, they can work only an additional 15 minutes per day before getting into overtime. Employees can determine when they will begin work in the period 7 to 9:15 A.M., but they can bank only 15 minutes per day to shorten one or more of the work days in the same week.

3. Nonexempt employees in the customer service unit work a 7-hour day and can bank up to an hour a day to shorten other work days in the same week. All employees must provide supervisors with advance notice of their arrival and departure times so that customer coverage can continue without interruption.

4. Employees in other areas of the firm—research and development, marketing (excluding field sales), corporate personnel, and so on—work a 7-hour day. Exempt employees can bank as many as 3¼ hours a day; nonexempt employees can bank 1 hour per day. Employees must use their banked hours in the week they are accumulated. All employees can determine when they will begin and finish work on specific days as long as they respect the core hours, but supervisors can require exceptions as needed.*

*Adapted from Golembiewski, R. T., and Hilles, R. J. Drug company workers like new schedules. *Monthly Labor Review,* February 1977.

Three groups of employees decided against using flexitime.

1. Manufacturing production, with some 650 employees, rejected the system as impractical. Representatives met with workers and discussed the possibility but rejected it because of the nature of the work flow. In an assembly line process such as this, each worker was too dependent upon others to permit flexitime.

2. The field sales force was the second group to reject flexitime. This group already had substantial control over its hours.

3. The security force was unable to implement a form of flexitime because of the rigid schedules necessary for full security coverage.

It should be noted that in keeping with the recommendation by the quality of work life task force, no time recording mechanisms were used. Employees at all levels, in all departments, are expected to report their hours on an *exception* basis. In other words, only variations in the standard 35-hour week are reported. Such exceptions may include overtime hours, absences, or vacation. If no exceptions are reported, the employee is paid for the standard workweek. (See Figure 11-2 for a sample of the time record sheet filled out by employees. For a more detailed description of this system of time recording, see Chapter 19.)

6-MONTH EVALUATION

In June 1975, a report was formulated, evaluating the effects of flexitime at SmithKline after 6 months of companywide operation under the system. As in the pilot study, evaluation was based on the attitudes of supervisors and employees obtained through questionnaires, and objective data from company records on changes in absenteeism, tardiness, and overtime. However, because of the major differences in types of jobs held by those who did not go on flexitime (manufacturing, field sales, and security) compared to those who did go on the system, no comparison group or time comparison was used when questionnaires were administered this time.

Method

Attitudinal data were collected by the ARs in their work areas. However, the decision to participate in the survey was the option of the AR. The ARs who did participate did not use any one pattern in polling nonsupervisory employees. They were requested to obtain a 10 percent sample on a random basis. However, the percentage sampled and degree of randomness varied because of variations in wage and skill levels within a work area, job demands, and employee availability. ARs were requested to obtain as many responses as possible from supervisors on the theory that supervisors would be particularly sensitive to problems with the program. About 30 percent of all supervisors were surveyed.

The result of this was a sample of 183 supervisors and 274 employees in 16 of the 23 work areas. This sample represented 20 percent of the employees on flexitime. The 7 work areas not participating in the study represented about 12 percent of the workers.

Questionnaire Results

Attitudinal results were reported for nonsupervisors and for supervisors. As in the pilot study, supervisors reported as both employees and managers.

Nonsupervisory Workers' Evaluation.   The reaction of this group was very positive: 83 percent wanted to continue under flexitime, while only 6 percent were in favor of returning to fixed hours. Benefits specified included reduced traffic congestion and additional time to attend to personal business. On the negative side, about 11 percent reported decreased availability of co-workers and support services. On the positive side, 43 percent reported

TIME RECORD					
Core Hours: _____ to _____					
DAY	DATE	TIME WORKED		TOTAL HOURS	
		START	STOP	DAILY	CUMULATIVE WEEKLY
M					
Tu					
W					
Th					
F					
Sa					
Su					
WEEKLY HOURS SUMMARY					
Regular hours		Overtime			Total hours
		Straight	1½	2	
Employee signature					
Supervisor signature for O.T.					
Advance vacation From: _____ To: _____			Absence reason		

Figure 11–2 Sample of a time record sheet used for exception reporting at SmithKline

that flexitime had helped to improve their productivity, while only 2 percent felt that there had been a reduction. These results are detailed in Table 11-4.

Supervisors' Evaluation.   In the survey, 183 supervisors were asked their reactions as supervisors as well as individual employees. Of supervisors reporting as employees, 81 percent were favorable, opposing a return to regular hours; 9 percent reported a desire to return to a fixed schedule. Thus, these attitudes were as favorable as those of employees reporting on the impact of flexitime. In their managerial role, this group responded favorably to flexitime on the whole. Concern, however, was expressed about flexibility in scheduling, employee coverage, and accounting for employees' time. On the more positive side, 85 percent of the supervisors felt there had been an improvement in employee morale, 45 percent reported an improvement in employee performance, and 32 percent felt flexitime had resulted in improved productivity.

Objective Results

Objective results studied were limited to trends in absenteeism and overtime.

Trends in Absenteeism.   Company records were examined to determine if the anticipated trend, a decrease in 1-day absence, occurred. The records of 50 exempt and 50 nonexempt employees were compared for two 5-month periods—one period before the implementation of flexitime had been put into effect, the other after. The comparison showed that while total sick days increased from 191 to 235 days, 1-day absences decreased from 78 to 67. Thus, the predicted decrease did occur and, furthermore, was particularly significant, since the overall trend in sick days increased.

Trends in Overtime.   A concern existed that overtime might increase under flexitime because additional staff support might be required if professionals worked unusual hours.

Table 11-4   Summary of Nonsupervisory Employees' Opinions about the Impact of Flexible Work Hours

	% Favorable	% About the Same	% Unfavorable
Opinion of SmithKline	93	7	0
Your productivity	72	27	1
Availability of other people	45	44	11
Traffic congestion	75	23	2
Ability to attend to personal business	82	16	2
Support services	45	44	11
Communications with others	46	50	4
Your performance	69	30	1
	Decrease 1–10%	No Impact	Increase 1–10%
Productivity	2	55	43
	Positive	Neutral	Negative
Your reaction to return to fixed work hours	6	11	83

However, a review of the overtime records indicated a decrease in overtime of 21 percent. The researchers qualify this finding because concurrent efforts were under way by the company to reduce overtime costs during this period. But they point out that the results were consistent with those identified in the pilot study.

Conclusions

The OD consultant concluded in his report that flexible work hours had resulted in very substantial and favorable attitudinal shifts among both employees and supervisors. Objective data were more difficult to summarize: absenteeism and overtime did not increase, and there is some evidence that they actually decreased. Moreover, there are indicators which imply that performance and productivity were improved. Based on these results, no alterations were made in the program, and it was recommended that the flexitime continue ''as a progressive example of SmithKline's employment practices.''

SUMMARY

The history of flexitime at SmithKline represents the well-planned and successful implementation of a system which had major impact on the great majority of employees at the corporate headquarters. As such, it is noteworthy not only because it bears witness to some of the possible benefits under flexitime but also because it describes a *change process* which is consistent with the goals and objectives of flexitime. It must be made clear that an ineffective change process can doom a new system to failure. SmithKline is an example of an extremely effective change process leading to an effective new system.

When considering the process of change, however, one cannot help wondering if the results obtained to date will remain consistent, or if the beneficial effects of flexitime will wear off. Some questions which might be considered are:

Will employees remain as positive in their assessment of flexitime, or will they take it for granted after a period of time? If this happens, will the improved productivity, communications, and personal relations reported by employees sink to their original levels?

Will the trends in decreased overtime and absenteeism continue?

Will supervisors, in their managerial roles, continue to view flexitime favorably, or will it become a burden? If employees slip in their attitudes, how will it affect the supervisors?

These questions are tantalizing, and one would hope that SmithKline, as one of the few organizations in a position to undertake a truly longitudinal study, might assume the responsibility of attempting to answer them.

NOTES

1. An interview with Mr. Richard Hilles, initiator and expeditor of the idea at SmithKline, supplemented internal documents provided by the company. The information obtained from Mr. Hilles provided the background and chronological thread, tying together the reported study results. Published materials included:

Golembiewski, R. T., Hilles, R., and Kagno, N. S. A longitudinal study of flexitime effects: Some consequences of an OD intervention. *The Journal of Applied Behavioral Science,* 1974, 503–532.

Golembiewski, R. T. Factor analysis of some flexitime effects: Attitudinal and behavioral consequences of a structural intervention. *Academy of Management Journal, 18,* September 1975, 500–509.

Golembiewski R. T., and Hilles, R. J. Drug company workers like new schedules. *Monthly Labor Review,* February 1977.

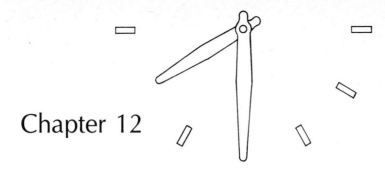

Chapter 12

The Private Sector: Field Results

ACCEPTANCE OF FLEXITIME IN THE UNITED STATES

The acceptance and implementation of flexible working schedules in the private sectors of United States industry has not been as rapid as one might predict, especially in view of its widespread adoption and popularity in Europe. This may be explained, in part, by the differing conditions in Europe which facilitated the acceptance of flexitime in the late 1960s and early 1970s.

Flexitime originated in Germany as a response to a massive traffic congestion problem; however, the system quickly gained popularity as additional benefits in areas besides traffic flow were identified. In particular, the Western European countries (especially Germany, Austria, France, and Switzerland) were concerned with the problem of high turnover of employees, a problem which was aggravated by a short supply of labor. The high level of employment in these countries allowed individual employees to "job shop" and to switch jobs easily when they found an organization which offered more in terms of salary, benefits, or convenience. From the organization's standpoint, it became more difficult to attract and hold employees. Within this context, management viewed flexitime as a special benefit which could help to overcome this problem and possibly attract additional candidates who had not previously considered employment. Candidates for jobs might choose an organization offering flexitime over a firm which did not, and, furthermore, might be less willing to leave a flexible schedule for an inflexible one. Thus, an organization had to consider offering the system in order to compete for desirable employees with those firms already on the system. The combined benefits of reduced traffic congestion and the competition to attract and keep employees contributed to the rapid adoption of flexitime in Europe.

In contrast, private sector organizations in the United States have not had similar incentives to consider seriously alternative work schedules. High unemployment has meant that employees are more easily replaced, in spite of the expenses incurred in turnover costs. The benefits from reduced traffic congestion alone are important reasons for considering flexitime, but apparently this has not been a sufficient impetus for most United States organizations. It may be that an effort by a single organization is considered futile in terms of its ability to improve the situation. The present level of traffic congestion and the concern over energy shortages may, however, provide an additional incentive to investigate alternative work schedules.

A second factor responsible for differences between Europe and America in the acceptance of flexitime is the variation in hours worked per week on the two continents. European workers have traditionally put in a longer working week than American workers. For example, 40 hours is usually the minimum, and 44 to 46 hours per week is not uncommon in Europe. In contrast, the typical employee in the United States works from 37½ to 40 hours per week, with a trend toward decreasing the weekly quota. These differences in the average workweek have influenced the type of alternative work schedule which has been considered. In the United States, where the trend has been to reduce the workweek, compressed schedules such as the 4-day, 9 to 10 hours per day workweek have been the focus of experimentation, in the hope, perhaps, of an eventual 4-day, 32-hour week. In Europe, a compressed workweek is less feasible because of the longer hours. For example, a 4-day, 44-hour workweek would mean an 11-hour workday, which would be excessive, especially when transportation time is added. For the Europeans, flexitime seems to be the most feasible alternative work schedule, in view of prevailing work conditions. In the United States, with an adequate labor supply and a focus on a shorter, compressed schedule, flexitime has taken longer to gain widespread acceptance.

Another aspect of flexitime which has impeded its acceptance in both Europe and the United States (although perhaps more so in the United States) is its effect on overtime. Flexitime has the potential to reduce overtime—primarily because the flexbands in the morning and afternoon extend organization hours, increasing the chance that personnel will be available for a longer time span during the day. Flexitime also has the potential to reduce the *need* for overtime work through improved work flow, conditions more conducive to the completion of tasks, reduced short-term absenteeism, and possibly even increased productivity. Some unions have objected to this reduction because they feel the worker has a "right" to a certain amount of overtime, and workers in certain types of jobs have come to depend upon overtime payments as part of their income.

Other important factors which limit the acceptance of flexitime on a widespread basis in the private sector are the laws and regulations governing work schedules, and the circumstances under which premium payments are required. In Europe, legislation regulating overtime payments are more relaxed than in the United States, allowing more variations in flexitime with respect to banking and carry-over. These restrictions are discussed fully in Chapter 18.

However slow the United States has been in considering flexitime, it is clear that the idea is gaining acceptance in the private sector at an accelerating rate. The current concern with organizational effectiveness, combined with the increased recognition of the importance of quality of working life, has created a climate conducive to the acceptance of alternative work schedules. Innovative managers, no longer restricted by traditional policies, are more willing to consider a flexible work schedule for their organization. Many others are awaiting results of experiments in other organizations before implementing the system in their work place.

The rate of acceptance by individual organizations has been encouraged by the support of federal, state, and municipal transportation agencies. For example, the Massachusetts Bay Transportation Authority (MBTA) and the Port Authority of New York and New Jersey have promoted variable work schedules for the business organizations in their areas. The MBTA is sponsoring, in conjunction with other groups, the Boston Variable Work Hours Project, which serves as a source of information and a coordination center for any Boston-based organization interested in variable work schedules. Conferences are held, during which information is presented and assistance provided. Because this is a joint venture between private business, public transportation agencies, and the public planning agencies, and because it has received full political support, it is of sufficient scope to offer the possibility for significant improvements in work life in the Boston area. A similar project was initiated by the Port Authority of New York and New Jersey for downtown Manhattan and is now also in progress for the midtown area. Other organizations across the country, such as New Ways to Work in Palo Alto, California, The National Council for Alternative Work Patterns, Inc., in Washington, D.C., The Baltimore New Directions for Women, and the Work in America Institute, in New York, are involved with the dissemination of information to the private sector.

At present, examples of flexible working schedules can be found in almost every type of organization in the private sector. The Hewlitt–Packard Company in Waltham, Massachusetts, and at several other sites in the United States, and the Westinghouse Electric Corporation in Pittsburgh have both been highly successful in implementing long-term programs for their manufacturing employees. Insurance companies, including Occidental Life Insurance Company of California and Metropolitan Life Insurance Company of New York, and utilities, including Pacific Telephone, Pacific Gas & Electric, and Mountain Bell, all have large flexitime programs. Banks such as The First Bank of Boston, the Export-Import Bank of the United States, and the Industrial National Bank of Providence, Rhode Island, use flexible schedules. Flexitime has been implemented by health care organizations, including Searle Diagnostics in Des Plaines, Illinois, and many divisions and regional offices of Blue Cross/Blue Shield. Professional organizations such as the American Psychological Association (APA) and the National Association of Social Workers (NASW), both in Washington, D.C., have also joined the movement. A list of companies with flexitime programs is available in the appendix.[1]

Although there are many examples of flexitime from many different industries, it is difficult to estimate exactly how many employees in organizations are currently using FWH because of its dynamic rate of acceptance. It is estimated that at least 1 million employees in the United States are on some form of flexible work schedules; however, over 200,000 of those are federal government employees and a large percentage of the remainder are accounted for by a few organizations in the private sector.[2] For example, Hewlitt-Packard and Control Data each have 20,000 employees on flexitime, and Metropolitan Life has 15,000.

A 1974 survey of 300 of the largest banking organizations in the United States (ranked by total deposits held) found, from 160 responses, that 10 percent of the banks had some form of formal flexitime program. Eighty-eight percent of these banks reported "positive or good results" from the program and the remaining twelve percent reported no change. No organization in the survey reported "poor" or "very poor" results from the program.[3]

In 1975, The Business & Professional Women's Foundation reported the results of a survey of 500 members of the American Society of Personnel Administration (ASPA) and

366 organizations outside of the society who were identified, from previous research, as users of some type of rearranged workweek.[4] Of the 354 responses obtained, 59 (17.7 percent) reported that they had implemented flexible working schedules for some or all of their employees. This number includes those using employee-chosen staggered hours, which can be considered the marginal or least flexible type of a flexitime program. Those using the more flexible systems—that is, systems allowing day to day flexibility—represent 14 percent of the total. Although it is difficult to make generalizations from these results because they are based on a subsample of known users, the survey does indicate that flexitime was gaining popularity in the United States prior to 1975.

More recently, in 1977, the Bureau of National Affairs (BNA) published the results of a survey in their Personnel Policies Forum. Responses represented a cross section of the business population by type and geographical location. A total of 12 percent of organizations reported some use of flexible schedules. However, this figure includes those organizations implementing flexitime for only a few employees. Only 2.4 percent of the organizations reported implementing flexitime for all or most of their employees.

In 1978, Nollen and Martin published Part I of an American Management Association (AMA) survey report on alternative work schedules. The research was based on a total of 805 returned questionnaires (28 percent of 2,889 samples).[5] A major finding of this survey was that an estimated 13 percent of all nongovernment organizations have some type of flexitime program for 50 or more employees. The authors also offer a projected national usage rate of 17 percent for 1979, based on the assumption that half of those who reported that they were planning to use flexitime would do so by the following year.

Since the dynamic state of flexitime in the private sector makes it difficult to generalize about its acceptance and effectiveness, it was felt that it would be helpful to present several short cases which, along with the more comprehensive case study on SmithKline, will enable the reader to get a feel for the types of programs used by various organizations. In addition, the specific results of the flexitime programs in these companies have been compiled and presented in tables similar to the results presented for the public sector (Chapter 10).

EXPERIMENTS WITH FLEXITIME IN VARIOUS ORGANIZATIONS

The systems described in the 11 case studies to follow represent all types of flexible schedules, from employee-chosen staggered hours to systems allowing banking and core time off. In several of these organizations only selected groups or departments are allowed to use flexitime—the system described does not necessarily apply for all employees of the organization.

Furthermore, many of the studies conducted by organizations included only a sample of the employees on the system rather than the entire population of flexitime employees.

Berol Corporation, International Headquarters

The Berol corporation is a manufacturer of writing supplies located in Danbury, Connecticut. The majority of employees on flexitime at Berol are managers, professionals, and clerical workers. The system has not been extended to manufacturing employees because of staffing requirements and job interdependence. In all, over 200 employees participate in the flex-itime experiment at three separate locations.[6]

The schedule used in this organization is unusual, in that during the summer there is no afternoon core time on Fridays, enabling employees to leave at the end of the morning core period if they wish. In order to ensure that total work hours are not reduced during the summer because of the reduced number of core periods, the remaining core times are slightly extended. Thus, the total core time remains 25 hours per week all year long. To add up to the required 40 hours per week, the employee must work a total of 15 flexband hours during the week in addition to the 25 core time hours required. The majority of employees do not seem to need the extra flexibility of one less core period during winter months because of limited daylight and school schedules. During this time of year, they prefer the later flexband hours for greater flexibility in the morning. It should be noted that during summer hours, some group scheduling is necessary to ensure that minimum coverage is maintained on Friday afternoons.

The effects of this program were assessed 2 months after the implementation, and the results are presented in the tables at the end of this chapter. The organization also attempted to assess long-term attitudinal effects by comparing those members who had been on flexitime to those not on the system at another location, but these results are difficult to interpret because of the lack of controls. One important finding was management's resistance to change until experience was gained with the new system. Berol is very satisfied with its program and perceives it as a low-cost, effective means of improving the quality of work life for its employees.

Control Data Corporation

In April 1972, Control Data Corporation adopted a flexible work schedule as an experiment in two of its operations at its corporate headquarters in Minnesota—the Microcircuit and Aerospace operations. Approximately 1,700 employees were involved in these experiments, including employees in production work as well as engineering, clerical, and support personnel.*

Management at Control Data spent about 1 month developing the program and educating employees as to the organization's goals and expectations regarding flexitime. Establishing specific schedules was the responsibility of the general manager of each division, who then delegated it further to the first-line supervisors. Management felt that the level of flexibility should be maximized for each employee as long as productivity did not suffer, and that the first-line supervisor was best equipped to make this decision.

Supervisors were required to work within overall guidelines, but the spirit of the experiment was to give employees as much flexibility as possible. Four basic types of schedules were used by the supervisors: (1) individual daily flexibility, used by 58 percent of employees, (2) employee-chosen (weekly) staggered hours, used by 36 percent of employees, (3) group-chosen (weekly) staggered hours, used by 2 percent of employees, (4) summer hours, used by 4 percent of employees.

Three years later, in April 1975, follow-up questionnaires were completed by 286 nonex-

*The author wishes to thank Michael Hopp of Control Data Corporation for his help and cooperation in obtaining relevant information.

empt employees and 100 managers chosen as a random sample of the 1,700 users of flexitime.[7] Estimates of productivity, turnover, absenteeism, and other measures were gathered, although no control group measures were taken. A summary of these questionnaire results is presented in the tables. Control Data feels the program was a success and now encourages all its subsidiary organizations to make use of flexible scheduling. However, the company does not *require* the use of flexitime in its various subsidiaries, as it believes that to be successful, the system must be wholeheartedly supported by the local organization implementing it. At present, an estimated 23,000 Control Data employees have flexitime available to them.

First National Bank of Boston

The First National Bank of Boston first experimented with flexitime in 1973. In this initial trial, 40 clerical workers were placed on flexible schedules. By 1977, well over 1,000 were using the system. Flexibility varies according to the work requirements of each unit, although the most common morning bandwidth is 7 to 9 A.M., with core periods ranging from 1 to 4 hours. Employees must work a total of 36¼ hours each week. The program was evaluated in the consumer finance department, where 93 percent of the 125 clerical personnel have altered their schedules since the introduction of flexitime in December 1974.[8] The results of an evaluation of this unit under a flexible schedule are presented in the tables.

Several of the conclusions reached in the evaluation were that productivity increased and the quality of work life improved in the consumer finance department. Customer service, turnover, and absenteeism were unaffected. In general, however, the organization is satisfied that it has helped to improve the quality of work life of its employees without interfering with organizational effectiveness.

John Hancock Mutual Life Insurance Company

In early 1972, the John Hancock Insurance Company in Boston began experimenting with rearranged workweeks. The focus of their effort was on the 4-day workweek, although they used flexible schedules as well. Initially no attempt was made to evaluate flexitime programs. In June 1977, a survey of 670 employees using flexitime was completed.[9] These employees represented a cross section of levels in the organization and were selected for the study because they made relatively frequent use of their flexible hours. Many other employees do not make extensive use of flexitime although it is available to them, because Hancock's regular business hours do not coincide with peak travel periods. The organization's work hours are ½ hour earlier than most organizations in the area, and by following these standard hours employees are able to miss the area's rush hours. The flexitime schedules in use vary from department to department, and depend on the requirement to have a manager approve changes in schedules, decide whether or not the lunch period is flexible, and set the length of the morning and afternoon flexbands. In general, the program has been successful; highlights of the survey results are included in the tables.

Hewlett-Packard Company

The Hewlett-Packard Company is a California-based electronics firm with offices and plants worldwide. The organization employs approximately 38,000 employees. Two-thirds of these are in manufacturing positions, almost 90 percent of whom use some form of flexible work schedules (over 22,000 employees). Information about this program has been obtained from several sources.[10]

Hewlett-Packard is committed to actively improving employee relations and working conditions. In keeping with this, the company first implemented flexitime at locations in Germany. At their United States locations where workers were requesting special summer schedules, the company responded by installing a flexitime schedule for the summer instead of an adjusted fixed schedule. This system was first implemented in 1972 at a plant in Waltham, Massachusetts. The program was well received by all and extended to the end of the year. With continued success through the winter months, the flexitime schedule was made permanent.

The schedule included a 6:30 A.M. to 5 P.M. bandwidth; 6:30 to 8:30 A.M. and 3 to 5 P.M. flexbands; and a core time extending from 8:30 A.M. to 3 P.M. with a mandatory ½-hour lunch break. It was also possible to request an extended lunch break, although prior approval from the supervisor was required.

Two aspects of the program at Hewlett-Packard make it an exceptional case: (1) no time-recording equipment is used—*all* employees, blue-collar as well as white-collar, are on the honor system; (2) the manufacturing operations run 24 hours a day on three shifts, and *all* are given some level of flexibility. Flexibility between shifts is achieved through buffers of work-in-process inventory between work stations. The schedules for the swing and graveyard shifts, however, are determined by the department managers, who are usually not as liberal as those on the day shift schedule.

In the planning and implementation of this program, management made four assumptions: (1) most employees would choose an early schedule; (2) most employees would establish a fairly regular pattern of arrivals and departures; (3) employees would enjoy flexitime and work at making the program successful; (4) the most significant impact of flexitime, in terms of job change, would be on first-line supervisors. The first two assumptions proved to be correct. As it turned out, 70 to 90 percent of the day shift was on the job by 6:30 A.M., and most employees did establish a regular pattern of arrival and departure times. In order to help effect the third assumption, education programs were conducted on the logistics of the system. The fourth assumption regarding the impact on first-line supervisors was also handled through educational and training programs. These programs concentrated on informing first line supervisors of their duties and responsibilities under flexitime and discussing potential problems or conflict issues. For example, it was emphasized that supervisors must understand that employees are expected to be able to work on their own for periods of time. Efforts were made to assure supervisors that they were not expected to extend their workday to the full bandwidth, and that flexitime does not represent a loss of authority. Management activity helped the supervisors to define their new roles as planners and coordinators.

This strategy yielded excellent results. When the program was implemented in Massachusetts, management was very pleased to find that problems were minimal and that when they did arise, solutions were achieved at the supervisor-worker level. The first-line supervisor problem was minimized, although not solved, by Hewlett-Packard. In an experimental survey, supervisors indicated that flexitime increased their work load in general, but that they were willing to handle the increased work because of the many benefits, both personal and organizational, which they had experienced. The results of a company survey of employees and supervisors are presented in the tables.

Hewlett-Packard's positive experience with flexitime is all the more impressive considering the difficulties of a successful application in a manufacturing situation. Two important reasons for Hewlett-Packard's success are: (1) the emphasis on accepting and confronting the potential problems which first-line supervisors may face; (2) the use of buffers, such as work-in-process inventory, between work stations in place of the inflexible assembly line. In a manufacturing situation, increased autonomy over work pace and flexitime are very closely related. As jobs are enlarged to more significant "whole" tasks, the establishment of buffers is possible, decreasing job interdependence. This enables the use of flexible schedules because one worker's performance is not entirely dependent on the presence of other workers. Flexible schedules have also been implemented at Hewlett-Packard plants in Palo Alto, California, Colorado Springs, Colorado, and Avondale, Pennsylvania.

Metropolitan Life Insurance Company

Metropolitan Life is one of the major flexitime users in New York City. A 4-month experiment at the home office in 1974 was highly successful.[11] This experiment reported improved attitudes and perceptions by approximately 400 clerical, professional, and supervisory employees. No loss of productivity was reported. Based on these positive results, the organization decided to implement the program, which now includes approximately 15,000 employees, companywide.

The basic flexitime model allowed employees to vary their starting times between 7:30 and 10 A.M. Quitting time was 7¾ hours after starting time. The exact schedule and the requirement for supervisory approval of the schedule chosen by the employee were decisions left up to each department.

In order to assess the program's effect on the company as a whole, an additional survey of managers and supervisors was undertaken in February 1976. The personnel department felt that employee reaction, assessed in prior evaluations, was so positive that there was no need to collect that information again. Their interest was in assessing the perceptions and reactions of supervisors and managers. The survey was based on responses from 884 managers and supervisors from the home office, head office, and other office locations.[12] From the survey results, it appeared that almost all supervisors and managers felt that the program was a success and should be continued, and that their jobs had not been affected substantially by the change. In terms of the impact of flexitime on employees, they reported an improvement in work group effectiveness and no changes in areas such as production, work flow, and service to policyholders. Also, supervisors and managers felt that morale and attitudes toward work had shown positive changes.

On the whole, the organization is quite satisfied with the system. Each office and department has tailored its own schedule to meet its special task requirements. Contributing to success is the use of flexibility in the implementation and design of the system as well as in the work schedule itself. Results from both the initial experiment and the management survey are included in the tables.

Occidental Life Insurance Company of California

In 1973, a major concern at Occidental Life of Los Angeles was maintaining the high caliber of its work force as reported by its personnel officer.[13] Faced with the disadvantages of being a downtown employer, it found it more difficult to attract and keep employees; traffic congestion and lack of public transportation seemed to be a particular problem. The firm first experimented with variable work schedules through the implementation of a summer hours program. Every Friday during the 4 summer months a break and a lunch period were eliminated, creating a 5½-hour workday. This allowed employees to get an early start on their weekend activities. Absences were reduced by 20 percent on these Fridays, presuma- bly because employees were reluctant to be charged with a full day's absence when they only had to work 5½ hours.

The successful use of this summer program led the organization to consider a permanent flexible work schedule. The company began a pilot program with about 700 employees from various clerical and technical areas. This program combined both gliding schedules (flex- itime) and employee-chosen staggered hours. In evaluating the program, Occidental found that work flow had been improved because people tended to adjust their schedules to meet situational and job demands. The firm was also pleased with the expanded periods of phone coverage, which facilitated dealings with offices in other time zones. In all, the system was considered a success.

As a result of the pilot program, flexitime was implemented on a companywide basis for more than 3,600 employees. Each operating area was allowed to design its own program within guidelines set by the company. The Occidental program now includes various types of schedules, such as gliding time, employee-chosen staggered hours, a flexible lunch period, and a shortened Friday schedule during the summer.

In terms of schedules for exempt salaried employees, roughly one-third of them are on flexitime schedules allowing daily flexibility; another third are on staggered hours; and the remaining third are on employee-chosen staggered hours. For nonexempt (hourly-paid) employees, a preset staggered hours schedule is most typical. About 63 percent are on this type of schedule; about 30 percent are on employee-chosen staggered hours, and the remaining 7 percent of these employees are actually on some form of flexitime.

The schedules are designed and monitored by each unit. In planning this rather complex program, emphasis was placed on creating maximum flexibility within the limits of depart- mental needs and restrictions defined by the organization. Attention was also given to the needs and problems of the first line supervisors. Meetings were held to train the supervisors and clarify their rights and responsibilities under flexitime. As can be seen in the results tables, the experience with flexitime was quite positive. Occidental is a strong supporter of flexible work schedules, and its representatives have participated in conferences to promote the concept.

J. C. Penney Company, Inc.

J. C. Penney, the large retail firm, has begun experimenting with alternative work schedules in the form of staggered work hours. During the first 6 months of 1978, approximately 1,100 nonunionized employees (or "associates," as J. C. Penney calls their employees) participated in a test program at their headquarters in New York City. Before and after the test, surveys were conducted to measure the effects of the program on employees and on organizational effectiveness.[14] However, the authors of the study caution that since the study coincided with the relocation to a new building, attitudes of employees toward the program and the company may be contaminated by other factors such as changes in transportation, a new cafeteria and the physical layout of the new work setting.

J. C. Penney calls its program "flexitime," although it is really an employee-chosen staggered hours system. Employees are allowed to choose their starting times, at 15-minute intervals, from the hours between 8 and 9:30 A.M. Departure times vary from 4 to 5:30 P.M. Since lunch is inflexible, departure time is determined by starting time. Employees choose their schedule for 6 months at a time, and are expected to honor this schedule during this period.

Both pre- and post-implementation surveys indicated very favorable attitudes toward this schedule. The post-implementation survey also indicated an increase in morale. Differences between management and nonmanagement responses were minimal. However, there were a few issues of concern expressed by department managers and supervisors, including the following:

1.   The issue of signing in and out provoked some controversy. The researchers explained that, prior to the test program, signing in and out was not required for a large percentage of employees. There was agreement that in future implementations, steps must be taken to make the importance of these procedures understood.

2.   Employees did not view the program as a true flexitime system, and requested further flexibility, at the discretion of each department.

3.   Some departments applied constraints to the employee choice of starting time in cases where such constraints were not really considered necessary by employees or the researchers. While the researchers admit that there are certain legitimate situations where limits are required, the reluctance of some department heads calls for attention and perhaps education, in order to demonstrate alternative work patterns which can be utilized under a more flexible work schedule. Further, it was emphasized that any department imposing limits should review and discuss constraints with associates.

The final recommendations of the report were to continue flexitime, and to expand it to other locations. Further, the report encouraged departments "to increase flexibility within the prescribed guidelines without impairing department coverage or productivity." J. C. Penney is a valuable example of a very large firm which has made the *first step* in considering alternate work schedules. The successful results obtained because of the careful planning and implementation of this first stage point the way toward increasing flexibility.

Pitney Bowes, Inc.

Pitney Bowes is a large organization involved in the manufacture and sale of mailing and copier systems equipment, with over 18,000 employees worldwide. The flexitime program discussed here is used by approximately 800 employees working mostly in financial and data entry areas in Stamford, Connecticut. This program was first implemented in 1974, as described in a corporate communication.[15]

Pitney Bowes considered and rejected the possibility of flexitime in its production and engineering functions because, as a government contractor, the firm is subject to the requirement that time and a half must be paid to all employees working in excess of 8 hours per day. Under a flexitime system, allowing fluctuation in the hours worked per day would become prohibitively expensive. In the finance and data entry areas, overtime payments are not required until the employee has worked more than 40 hours in one week, which thus allows fluctuations on a day to day basis. Flexitime was also considered and rejected in its branch office locations; it was felt that the system was unfeasible in a small office where a high level of job interdependence and heavy customer contact was typical.

The work schedule adopted allows for daily flexibility with banking of hours on a day to day basis. The accounting period is 1 week. Each department determined its own schedule within overall guidelines which were maximum bandwidth of 7 A.M. to 6 P.M., a maximum workday of 10½ hours, and core hours ranging from a minimum of 2 hours to a maximum of 3½ hours each day. It was emphasized that first priority in the scheduling decision should be the job requirements. The program began with a 3-month experiment, which included about 220 employees. During that period, time-recording equipment was tried, but received a mixed reception. Consistent with the overall policy of maximum flexibility and trust, the equipment was replaced by manual time-keeping procedures.

The organization devoted much time and effort to the training of employees and supervisors in the use of the system, with an emphasis on mutual employee-management trust and respect. Attempts were made to predict and avoid problem areas wherever possible. To maximize the acceptance and success of the system, first-line supervisors were active in developing the test program. After the 3-month experiment, the program was assessed and expanded.

Over a 3-year period, there has been only one case of reported abuse of the schedule. Management is very satisfied with the results, in terms of both the organizational benefits and the way employees have demonstrated maturity and responsibility in making maximum use of the system while maintaining responsiveness to organizational goals and objectives.

Sandoz, Inc.

Sandoz, Inc., instituted a flexible work schedule in its Colors and Chemicals Division in East Hanover, New Jersey, in July 1972. The original experimental group consisted of employees and supervisors at two buildings and was later expanded to include over 900 people at the East Hanover site.

The flexitime schedule consisted of a bandwidth from 7:30 A.M. to 6 P.M. and core periods from 9:30 A.M. to 12 noon and 2 to 4 P.M., with a minimum 1-hour lunch break which could be extended up to 2 hours. Employees were allowed to credit or debit up to 10 hours. While the average work week was 37½ hours, employees were allowed to work a maximum of 40 hours or a minimum of 22½ hours.

Two months into the experiment, surveys of the employees and supervisors were completed. Replies were received from 42 supervisors (response rate 82 percent) and 116 employees (response rate 65 percent).[16] As a result of the positive findings in the survey, the organization has judged the program a success and is expanding its use to other divisions.

State Street Bank & Trust Company

The flexitime experiences of the State Street Bank in Boston were described by two staff members, Mayoon and Schnicker, in a summary of a 2-month experiment which took place from January 27, 1975, to March 28, 1975.[17] This organization's first experience with variable schedules was with 3- and 4-day workweeks. They soon realized that this type of schedule was incompatible with their operations and decided to explore an alternative schedule in the form of flexitime. An experimental flexitime system for approximately 150 employees was then initiated.

It appears that in this case the program used was decided upon by management, with very little input from workers and supervisors. Volunteer departments were solicited and selected for the pilot study. The Flexitime Corporation provided time-accumulation equipment and information to the bank management. The program was installed with a bandwidth of 7:30 A.M. to 5:30 P.M., and a single core period between 11 A.M. and 2 P.M.

Prior to implementation, meetings were held with all participating workers to educate employees and gain their support. At the end of the 8-week period, questionnaires were completed by 128 of the participating employees.

The results of the trial period are presented in the tables along with results of measures (both objective and subjective) taken during an evaluation made 1 full year after the beginning of the experiment and 10 months after the initial trial. Under the current system, each department determines its own schedule within limits set by the organization.

The bank is a very satisfied user of flexitime, and the program is open to any employee groups who choose to take advantage of it. The management feels that flexitime is useful in recruiting and helps to keep turnover to a minimum.

RESULTS FROM THE CASE STUDIES

The tables presented here are the evaluations of the effects of the various flexitime programs on the 12 organizations from the private sector described in the ministudies, as well as the results from the comprehensive case study of SmithKline. Consistent with the format used in the chapter on the public sector, the findings are categorized into four subject areas, each represented by a separate table. These categories are organizational effectiveness, attitudes, membership behavior, and time management. In compiling the data, the original descriptions used by the organization in its reports have been preserved wherever possible. Findings were considered inconclusive when the majority of respondents reported no change, or the percent of employees reporting an improvement varied by 10 percent or less from employees reporting a decrease. An increase was reported when one-third or more of the respondents were positive, and negative responses were minimal. Two summaries of the data have also been compiled. Here is a brief description of each of the tables.

Table 12-1 *Organizational Effectiveness.* Table 12-1 includes all information describing the effects of flexitime on organizational effectiveness. This information was subdivided into three categories.

Category A contains all Productivity measures, including indicators of Quality, Quantity, and Services, *category B* contains measures of the Work Environment, and *category C* contains measures of Cost relating to the implementation and use of flexible working hours.

Table 12-2 *Attitudes.* Table 12-2 contains measures of the Attitudes of organization members. This data was categorized into Morale and Job Satisfaction and Attitudes toward the Flexitime Program.

Table 12-3 *Membership Behavior.* Table 12-3 contains measures of Membership Behavior within the organization. The two categories used in this table are Leave Usage, which includes all forms of absenteeism, and Tardiness.

Table 12-4 *Time Management.* Table 12-4 presents data concerning personal Time Management. The data is subdivided into categories of Personal Time Usage and changes in Transportation.

Table 12-5 *Summary Table of Measurements.* An additional table has been compiled summarizing the general trends indicated in Tables 12-1 to 12-4. Summary Table 12-5 describes the overall trends for each of the categories described in Table 12-1 to 12-4 in terms of the total measures available. Each measure was categorized as a positive finding, a negative finding, or no change resulting from the implementation of flexitime.

Table 12-6 *Summary Table by Organization.* This table is similar to summary Table 12-5, except that it describes the trends in terms of each *organization* described in the case studies instead of combining measures for all organizations.

Organizational Effectiveness

Quality, Quantity, and Services.   Each of the 12 organizations examined changes in quality or quantity of output and services, reporting a total of 36 separate criteria in these areas. As indicated in Table 12-1, 9 of the 36 measurements were objective—that is, based on actual measured changes in productivity; the remainder were surveys of employees and supervisors. The 9 objective measures, from 5 organizations, included criteria such as productivity changes compared to earlier data, supervisory ratings of work quality, ability to contact customers, usage of WATS telephone lines, and changes in efficiency ratings. Of the 9, 4 indicated improvements in quality, quantity, and services; for the remainder, results were inconclusive, or there was no apparent change in the criteria measured. One of the most impressive changes, reported by the First National Bank of Boston, was a 10 percent increase in productivity compared to the period 15 months earlier.

Of the 27 reports from employees and supervisors, 17 described perceived changes in aspects of productivity or performance. Other criteria included quality of work, efficiency, customer communications, services to policy holders, group effectiveness, and employee work habits. Of the 27, 19 were positive reports, 7 indicated no change, and 1 was negative. The negative report, from the John Hancock Life Insurance Company, described a concern of 30 percent of the managers that limited supervision resulting from flexitime increased inefficiency. The fact that the negative report was made by managers *only,* while the positive reports were made by managers *and* employees, seems to be typical of the problem we have seen before; that is, employee and managerial perspectives on flexitime can be quite different. Managers have expressed concern about the reduced control over employees which

Table 12-1 Organizational Effectiveness

Organization	Quality, Quantity, and Services	Work Environment	Costs
Berol Corporation N = 88 experimental N = 78 control	28% of employees reported a slight improvement in performance; 60% reported no change; 12% reported a slight decrease		Savings realized by reduction in absenteeism and personal leave allowances
Control Data Corporation—results from employees on various schedules 58% on FWH N = 286 nonexempt employees N = 100 managers	66% of the workers reported an increase in productivity; 11% reported a decrease; 23% reported no change 51% of managers reported an increase in productivity; 3% reported a decrease; 46% reported no change	41% of employees reported an improvement in departmental cooperation; 24% reported a decrease; 35% reported no change 49% of employees reported an improvement in inter-shift cooperation; 13% reported a decrease; 38% reported no change 14% of managers reported an improvement in their relationship with employees; 13% reported a decline; 73% reported no change 30% of employees reported an increase in the need for supervision; 46% reported no decrease; 24% reported no change	
First National Bank of Boston N = 125	Majority (50%+) of employees reported that their productivity increased Productivity increased 10% in comparison to the 15 months prior according to a hard measure Supervisor rating of work quality showed no change after flexitime		

184

John Hancock Life Insurance Co., Inc., Boston
N = 670

Contact with customers was facilitated by the extended day

95% of managers and employees felt that quality of work produced and ability to handle peak loads either increased or remained the same

90% of managers and employees felt productivity either increased or remained the same

30% of managers reported employee inefficiency increased because of limited supervision

68% of employees felt that supervisor availability was not changed

70% of managers felt that superior availability was not changed

Managers reported increased need for planning, organizing, and scheduling work

23% of new employees (hired in past 2 years) reported that flexitime was a factor in attracting them to the organization; 16% of employees with the organization for over 2 years reported that flexitime is a factor in retaining them

Hewlett-Packard
N = 200

60% of employees reported an increase in productivity; 3% reported a decrease; 37% reported no change

57% of employees reported an improvement in efficiency; 8% reported a decrease; 35% reported no change

25% of employees reported an improvement in customer communication; 20% reported a decline; 55% reported no effect

94% of supervisors reported there have been no problems meeting goals and objectives; 6% report some problems

95% of supervisors reported no problems scheduling overtime; 5% reported some problems

56% of supervisors reported that interfacing with other departments was no problem; 7% reported some problem; 5% reported difficulties

Table 12-1 Organizational Effectiveness *(Continued)*

Organization	Quality, Quantity, and Services	Work Environment	Costs
Metropolitan Life Insurance Company	50% from Study A reported that flexitime has a positive effect on service to policy holders; 44% reported no effect; 6% reported a negative effect	61% from Study A agreed that employees who come in early are able to work better because of fewer interruptions; 27% were neutral; 12% disagreed	7% from Study A reported that overtime had increased; 15% reported that it had decreased; 54% reported there was no change
Study A *N* = 884 supervisors and managers	40% from Study A reported flexitime increased production; 7% reported a reduction	47% from Study A agreed that employees who work later in the afternoon work better; 37% were neutral; 20% disagreed	Managers from Study B reported positive effects of flexitime on overtime
Study B *N* = 404 clerical, professional and supervisory employees	76% from Study A disagreed that flexitime had caused work to slow down; 5% agreed; 18% were neutral	74% from Study A agreed that employees work satisfactorily without supervisor; 15% were neutral; 11% disagreed	
	57% from Study A reported that flexitime had a favorable effect on work group effectiveness; 38% reported no change; 5% reported an unfavorable effect	Managers from Study B reported positive gains in employee time handling	
	No significant changes in productivity in Study B—objective measures	23% from Study A reported that job was less difficult under flexitime; 22% felt it was more difficult; and 55% reported no change	
	Managers in Study B reported positive gains in productivity and employee work habits		
Occidental Life Insurance Company *N* = 700	No change in productivity Small improvement in services	More efficient work start-up reported 61% of employees reported internal communications were not

J. C. Penney, New York $N = 613$	26% of employees felt that flexitime improved phone coverage; 19% felt it worsened 62% of employees felt that productivity during unsupervised periods had not changed 44% of employees felt flexitime contributed to work efficiency; 55% saw no effect; 1% felt flexitime detracted from efficiency	27% of employees felt flexitime contributed to having good relationships with co-workers; 69% felt no change 24% of employees felt flexitime contributed to having good relationships with their supervisor; 72% felt no change 13% of employees felt flexitime contributed to availability of employees in the company; 73% felt no change	changed; 32% reported that internal communications worsened No problem or improvement reported in external communications Increase reported in available quiet time
Pitney Bowes $N = 220$	No conclusive indicators Some departments reported efficiency increased during peak work periods Better usage of WATS line	Improved cross training 44% of supervisors reported employees more responsible toward their work load and better able to manage their own work 66% of employees reported improved relations with their supervisors Supervisors reported an improvement in their own work planning	Introductory costs small in terms of dollars, but high in terms of time taken by those involved in implementation process

Table 12-1 Organizational Effectiveness *(Continued)*

Organization	Quality, Quantity, and Services	Work Environment	Costs
Sandoz, Inc., East Hanover, NJ N = 42 supervisors N = 116 employees	38% of supervisors felt that employee work output increased; 62% felt no change 36% of employees felt productivity improved; 63% felt no change; 1% felt it was worse	35% of employees felt that work load coordination improved; 61% felt no change; 4% felt it was worse 94% of employees felt that coordination with their supervisor was satisfactory under flexitime; 1% felt it was unsatisfactory; 5% had no opinion 50% of supervisors felt no change in ease of scheduling; 29% felt scheduling was easier; 21% felt scheduling was harder 70% of supervisors felt no change in their roles; 12% felt a positive change in their role; 18% felt a negative change 91% of supervisors felt no loss of control over their work section; 9% would like more control over the use of flexible periods by employees	21% decrease in overtime (other organizational efforts to reduce overtime costs may have influenced this finding)
SmithKline N = 183 supervisors N = 274 employees	72% of employees reported that their productivity had improved; 27% reported no change; and 1% reported an unfavorable impact 69% of employees reported that their performance had improved; 30% reported no change; and 1% reported an unfavorable impact	45% of employees reported flexitime had a favorable impact on the availability of others; 44% reported no effect; 11% reported an unfavorable impact 46% of employees reported improved communications with others; 50% reported no change	

188

State Street Bank
$N = 128$

45% of supervisors reported an improvement in employee performance

32% of supervisors reported flexitime had resulted in improved productivity

47% of employees reported that they were more productive under flexitime at 2 months

No change in efficiency ratings from 1974 to 1975

42% of employees reported that they receive extra cross-training

Turnover in flexitime departments dropped by at least half in 3 or 4 departments

30% of employees reported flexitime a factor in their continued employment

55% of new employees reported flexitime was a factor in their decision to accept employment

Cost of purchase of time accumulating equipment $60/employee—expected to pay for itself in 1 year

Overtime payments in the Trust Operations Department dropped from $25,208 in 1974 to $7,616 in 1975 (80 employees involved)

flexitime implies. The organization must take active steps to alleviate these concerns and to help the manager decrease his dependence on constant monitoring as a means of maintaining productivity in the work unit.

In general, although there was a slight indication of change in productivity in the objective measures, employee and supervisory perceptions of its effects were consistently positive.

Work Environment.   In 10 organizations, a total of 37 measurements of changes in the work environment were reported. As shown in Table 12-1, 18 of the 37 were positive, and 16 indicated no change resulting from flexitime implementation; only 2 of the measurements were negative. In 2 organizations, employees reported that flexitime had been a factor in attracting them to the organization and retaining them, once employed. In terms of management-employee relations, the overall effect seems to have been unchanged. Six organizations reported various aspects of this relationship from the employee point of view, including the following: supervisory availability—68 percent of employees in one organization reported no change; coordination with the supervisor—94 percent of employees felt coordination was satisfactory in another firm; improved relations in general—2 organizations reported no change, 1 reported an improvement. From the supervisors' perspective, 44 percent of the supervisors in one report felt that employees were better able to manage their own workload. Supervisors in another measurement reported an increased need for planning and scheduling, while a different organization reported actual improvements in these areas. This reinforces the point that supervisors and managers must supplement or replace monitoring as a form of employee control, depending upon the level of flexibility allowed. Planning and scheduling are among the more effective means available to the supervisor to help decrease the reliance on monitoring.

One further change in the work environment should be noted: 4 organizations reported the impact of flexitime on aspects of cooperation, communication, and coordination. In all 4 reports, a high percentage, although not necessarily a majority of those surveyed, felt that the overall effect had been an improvement. The impact of flexitime on the areas of communication and cooperation may be moderated by variables such as work unit size, organization climate, and management style; however, these effects have yet to be explored.

Costs.   In 5 organizations, a total of 7 items in this area were reported. As shown in Table 12-1, 4 of these measures were concerned with reductions in overtime, 2 of which were based on organization records. Both of these objective measures indicated great reductions in overtime costs, although one organization did not attribute the total savings to the flexible schedule, as other factors also affected the reduction in overtime. Of the 2 subjective measures of overtime, 1 was positive while the other indicated no change. One organization realized a reduction in costs as a result of decreased absenteeism and personal leave usage.

Other measures of cost dealt with the expense of implementing the flexitime program itself. One organization reported that expenses in terms of dollars were low, although in terms of time invested for those involved in the implementation process, the cost was high. It is important to emphasize that the chances for success of a flexitime program (or any organizational change, for that matter) are directly related to the level of commitment and the amount of time the organization is willing to invest. The only major monetary expense should be on time-recording equipment, unless other organizational changes accompany the flexitime program.

In terms of compiling data, it is somewhat inconsistent to group together start-up costs, such as expenditures for time-recording equipment, with changes in expenses resulting from the use of the system itself, such as overtime costs. It is important to keep this differentiation in mind when evaluating the overall impact of costs on the organization. In summary Table 12-5, data on start-up costs from Table 12-1 have been omitted (2 measures) for this reason. There is a notable lack of data in this category—less than half of the 12 organizations reported cost information. Organizations attempting to implement a flexible schedule should record pre- and post-implementation data on expenses such as energy consumption, machine usage and down time, and support services, and on savings in areas such as overtime, employee absenteeism, and turnover in order to assess the program's real costs. Amortized start-up costs may be weighed against any anticipated savings in order to "sell" the flexitime concept to cost-conscious management.

Attitudes

Before describing the impact of flexitime on the attitudes of employees, it is important to note that because attitudes are a form of self-perception or personal evaluation of an object or situation, the concept of objective measures is inappropriate for this category. All measurements are subjective because they are reports of self-evaluations. This does not, however, make this category of data less valuable or reliable, since attitudes often predict behavior. For example, an employee whose attitudes toward his organization are unfavorable is more likely to be absent frequently, to be tardy, and, ultimately, to leave the organization. The measurements of attitudes are reported in Table 12-2.

Morale and Job Satisfaction.   In 10 of the 12 organizations, changes were reported in job satisfaction and morale after flexitime implementation for a total of 13 entries in this category. In 10 of the entries, the majority of employees reported improved attitudes, and in some organizations, employees were virtually unanimous in their reports of more positive attitudes. In the 3 remaining entries, no changes were reported—no organization reported decreases in morale or job satisfaction as a result of flexitime. While one must be cautious in attributing these improved attitudes entirely to the implementation of flexible working hours, the organizations reporting this data have described this as the major cause.

Attitudes towards Flexitime.   A total of 21 items on attitudes toward flexitime were reported by 11 organizations. All entires indicated overwhelming support for the flexible schedules. Types of questions regarding attitudes toward flexitime included desire to continue the program or make it permanent, problems monitoring the program, satisfaction with the use of flexitime, and feelings about returning to fixed hours.

As was expected, employee reactions to the program were consistently more positive than supervisory reactions, but in no case did a large percentage of supervisors indicate that they wished to discontinue the program. This reinforces the point that in many organizations, special training and educational programs are necessary in order to reduce the threatening aspects of flexitime for supervisors.

Membership Behavior (Withdrawal)

Absenteeism.   A total of 20 items related to absenteeism and various forms of leave usage were reported in 10 organizations. These findings are described in Table 12-3. There were 11 measures from 7 organizations based on objective measures of leave usage and absentee-

Table 12-2 Attitudes

Organization	Morale and Job Satisfaction	Attitudes toward Flexitime
Berol Corporation $N = 88$ experimental $N = 78$ control	A significantly greater number of employees on flexitime reported a higher general satisfaction level than those not on flexitime	37% of employees were very satisfied with flexitime; 52% of employees were satisfied; and 11% of employees were dissatisfied
Control Data Corporation—results from employees on various schedules 58% on FWH $N = 286$ nonexempt employees $N = 100$ managers	85% of employees reported improved morale; 5% reported a decline; 10% reported no change 65% of employees reported improved attitudes; 17% reported a decline; 18% report no change	
First National Bank of Boston $N = 125$		75% of workers liked flexitime; 22% had no opinion
John Hancock Life Insurance Co., Inc. $N = 670$	95% of employees reported job satisfaction increased or remained the same	35% of employees felt their original attitude toward flexitime had become more positive
Hewlett-Packard $N = 200$	96% of employees reported increased morale; 4% reported no change	76% of supervisors reported no problems monitoring the program; 22% reported some problems; and 2% saw no difficulties 95% of all surveyed reported the program successful; 2% reported it unsuccessful
Metropolitan Life Insurance Company Study A $N = 884$ supervisors and managers Study B $N = 404$ clerical, professional, and supervisory employees	92% from Study A reported flexitime had a positive impact on morale; 1% were negative; 7% reported no effect	86% from Study A were favorable toward flexitime; 6% were unfavorable; 2% were neutral 97% from Study A were satisfied with flexitime; 1% were dissatisfied; 2% were neutral Employees reported highly favorably on satisfaction with flexitime and work-related advantages in Study B

Company	Findings
Occidental Life Insurance Company $N = 700$	14% of all employees were very satisfied with the program; 76% of all employees were satisfied; 2% were dissatisfied; and 8% had no comment
J. C. Penney $N = 613$	88% of employees felt that most employees felt good about use of flexitime; 1% did not think most employees liked flexitime 60% of employees felt flexitime was an improvement over the old system; 4% felt it was not 91% of employees had an overall favorable attitude toward flexitime 38% of employees reported feeling more energetic and motivated when they arrived at work; 57% felt no change 42% of employees reported that flexitime contributed to their job satisfaction; 54% felt flexitime didn't affect satisfaction; 1% felt it detracted from satisfaction
Pitney Bowes $N = 220$	Employees and supervisors almost unanimously in favor of the program 66% of employees and supervisors reported improvements in job satisfaction, motivation, cooperation, and better information exchange
Sandoz, Inc., East Hanover, NJ $N = 42$ supervisors $N = 116$ employees	92% of employees felt the program should be made permanent; 4% felt it should not; 4% had no opinion 86% of employees felt free to use flexitime as their work load permits 76% of supervisors wanted to continue the program for their own benefit; 12% wanted to discontinue it 88% of supervisors wanted to continue the program for the employees' benefit; 12% voiced no opinion 82% of supervisors wanted to continue the program for the benefit of the division; 18% voiced no opinion 71% of employees felt morale had improved; 27% felt no change; 2% felt it was worse 71% of supervisors felt employee morale improved; 29% saw no change
SmithKline $N = 183$ supervisors $N = 274$ employees	83% of employees opposed returning to fixed work hours; 11% were neutral; 6% desired returning to fixed work hours 81% of supervisors reporting as employees opposed a return to fixed hours, while 9% desired a return to the fixed schedule 85% of supervisors reported an improvement in employee morale
State Street Bank $N = 128$	98% of employees wished to continue the program 63% of employees reported increased satisfaction with their job

Table 12-3 Membership Behavior—Withdrawal

Organization	Absenteeism	Tardiness
Berol Corporation $N = 88$ experimental $N = 78$ control	50% decrease in absenteeism compared to a preflexitime period 1.8 day reduction per year per employee in personal leave usage	Tardiness virtually eliminated
Control Data Corporation—results from employees on various schedules 58% on FWH $N = 286$ nonexempt employees $N = 100$ managers	16% of managers reported that sick leave usage decreased; 4% reported an increase; 80% saw no change 8% of managers reported a decrease in absenteeism; 69% reported no change; 23% reported an increase	47% of managers reported that tardiness decreased; 43% reported no change; 10% reported an increase
First National Bank of Boston $N = 125$	No change in absenteeism No change in turnover rate	Tardiness eliminated
Hewlett-Packard $N = 200$	51% of employees reported a reduction in absenteeism; 49% reported no effect 36% of employees reported a reduction in sick leave usage; 64% reported no effect	81% of employees reported tardiness was reduced; 4% reported an increase; 15% saw no effect
Metropolitan Life Insurance Company Study A $N = 884$ supervisors and managers Study B $N = 404$ clerical, professional, and supervisory employees	77% from Study A reported that employees take less personal time under flexitime; 13% reported no change; 10% reported an increase 50% from Study A reported a possible or definite reduction in 1 day absences; 45% reported no change; 5% reported no effect No significant change in short-term (5 days or less) absence in Study B	72% from Study A reported that flexitime reduced personal duties related to controlling tardiness; 14% reported that duties increased; 14% reported no change

Company		Tardiness
Occidental Life Insurance Company $N = 700$	75% decrease in partial-day absences 21% decrease in full-day absences	Tardiness virtually eliminated
J. C. Penney $N = 613$	17% of employees reported absenteeism had decreased; 73% had no opinion; 7% did not agree that it had decreased 86% of employees felt that use of personal days was not affected 28% of employees felt that partial-day absences had decreased or remained the same; 6% felt they had increased; others indicated no change.	50% of employees felt tardiness had decreased or remained the same; 6% felt it had increased
Pitney Bowes $N = 220$	Decrease in average absence rate of 1 hour per employee per month Decrease in absenteeism from 3.2% in 1974 to 2.7% in 1975 with trend continuing	Tardiness eliminated
SmithKline $N = 50$ exempt employees $N = 50$ nonexempt employees	14% decrease in single-day absences	
State Street Bank $N = 128$	No change in average use of sick days from 1974 to 1975 despite a high incidence of illness in 1975 due to flu epidemic	

ism rates. Of these measures, 4 indicated no change, while 7 measures described reductions in leave usage and absenteeism. The remaining 9 items were survey results, reporting the perceptions of employees and managers about changes in the amount of leave usage and absenteeism. Of the 9, 5 indicated no change and 4 described reductions in leave usage.

The aspect of leave usage which one would predict to be the most significantly affected by flexitime implementation is short-term leave usage—particularly absences of 1 day or less. When these are extracted from the data, the results are impressive. There were a total of 6 measures—3 from objective data and 3 from survey reports. Of the 6, 5 were positive; in fact, one company, Occidental Life, reported a 75 percent decrease in partial-day absences. The sixth report, which was based on objective data, indicated no change.

In the other reports, it is most likely that short-term absence—whether from sick leave usage or personal time off—were not differentiated from long-term absence. In order to evaluate the effects of flexitime on membership behavior, it is important to make this distinction, assuming, of course, that objective data are being collected and maintained in this category. Most organizations keep accurate records on absenteeism and tardiness, and these should be utilized wherever possible in the evaluation of the effects of flexitime on membership behavior. We should also note that although turnover is usually considered a form of membership behavior, it has been included as an expense associated with recruiting, which is an aspect of work environment in Table 12-1. Turnover seemed more relevant in this context, as it contributes to the work climate through the attitudes of employees expressed as a commitment to stay with the organization.

Tardiness.   Data on tardiness were reported in 8 organizations. As a rule, when full daily flexibility is permitted, tardiness is virtually eliminated since one can be late only by arriving after the beginning of core time. Of the organizations, 6 reported significant decreases in tardiness, 4 of which were objective measures. Two others, Control Data and J. C. Penney, did not report overwhelming changes. In J. C. Penney's case, since daily flexibility was not allowed, the traditional problem of tardiness continued. This may also be the situation at Control Data, where a variety of schedules were used, some of which may not have included daily flexibility.

Time Management

Time Management (Table 12-4) is similar to Attitudes (Table 12-2) to the extent that no objective measures were reported in this category. In the case of Time Management, however, the problem is not that the subject area is strictly a matter of self-evaluation, but rather that the subject reflects changes in the individual's life style outside of work. It is somewhat difficult for the organization to investigate the personal lives of its employees with respect to the effects of flexitime. Furthermore, the organization is probably less concerned with actual changes in work-nonwork fit, since this is outside the realm of organizational functioning, as long as attitudes are favorable.

Personal Time.   In 9 organizations, information was reported on the employees' personal use of time for a total of 16 measurements. Of the 16, 11 were positive, 5 were no change. The overall positive nature of these results indicates that employees' ability to engage in activities relating to family responsibilities, leisure pursuits, and personal business matters had improved. It is clear that a flexible schedule at work will make scheduling of other activities easier. The Bureau of Policies and Standards of the U.S. Office of Personnel Management found, in a pilot study on flexitime, that satisfaction with flexible schedules and their effects on personal time usage were related to the amount of planning an employee did in connection with his recreational and other personal activities. In other words, if leisure or other activities outside of work are important to the individual, flexitime is likely to result in a significant change. This also implies that some employees, for whom outside activities are less important, may need assistance, perhaps in the form of counseling or educational activities, to enable them to make full use of their time, thereby improving their work-nonwork fit and quality of life overall.

Transportation and Commuting.   In Chapter 13, it is explained that significant changes in transportation modes, length of commuting times, and expenses could only be expected as a result of a large scale, coordinated flexitime program within a metropolitan area. Since most metropolitan areas do *not* have extensive flexible hours programs, any small but consistent changes in a positive direction can be considered meaningful. Factors influencing transportation for employees would include location of employer (suburban or central business district), major mode of transportation (car or public transportation), and the work schedule of other nearby organizations. In 9 organizations, effects were reported of flexible schedules on transportation to and from work in 13 questions addressed to employees. The data are very favorable—11 out of the 13 were positive, 2 were no change—indicating that most employees did experience some improvement in commuting patterns. The general trend is clearly toward decreased commuting times—especially since the majority drive to work. One great benefit that is immediately available under flexitime, noted by Control Data employees, is decreased pressure to arrive on time during the commute, even if the actual time of the commute is not decreased.

Summary Table of Measurements

Table 12-5, Summary of Measurements, represents a compilation of the entries in Tables 12-1 through 12-4. Each entry has been categorized as positive, negative, or no change. Measurements have been separated according to whether they are objective or survey data, and the number of measures available tallied for each category. As mentioned earlier, there is no objective data for Attitudes (Table 12-2) or Time Management (Table 12-4). These results reflect directly the descriptions of results from Tables 12-1 through 12-4.

Summary Table by Organization

Table 12-6 summarizes the experiences of the 12 organizations in each of the categories presented in Tables 12-1 through 12-4. The overall experience of the organization was rated as positive (+), negative (−), or no change (=). The bases for categorizations were the results presented in the previous tables, supplemented by other information gathered from the organizations or their members. In cases where objective data were available, the symbol (0) appears on the table to indicate that objective measures were the basis of the rating decision, so that objective measures could be differentiated from survey results.

A quick look at Table 12-6 shows no negative ratings. It is unlikely that these judgments are overly lenient or biased. All organizations contacted were satisfied with their programs. The only criterion used in determining whether organizations should be included in this study

Table 12-4 Time Management

Organization	Personal Time Usage	Transportation
Berol Corporation N = 88 experimental N = 78 control	A significantly greater number of employees on flexitime reported a higher rating of improved personal life than those not on flexitime	
Control Data Corporation—results from employees on various schedules 58% on FWH N = 286 nonexempt employees N = 100 managers	59% of employees reported an increase in leisure time; 19% reported a decrease; 22% reported no change 74% of managers reported an increase in employee leisure time; 2% reported a decrease; 24% reported no change	57% of employees reported a decrease in driving time; 19% reported no change; 24% reported an increase 73% of employees reported decreased pressure in commuting; 19% reported no change; 13% reported increased pressure 72% of managers reported an decrease in employee driving time; 3% reported a increase; 25% reported no change
First National Bank of Boston N = 125	73% of employees with dependents reported that they accomplished more during leisure time 50% of employees without dependents reported that they accomplished more during leisure time	27% of employees reported a reduction in commuting time; others reported no change
John Hancock Life Insurance, Inc.	59% of employees felt flexitime had a positive impact on the amount of time available for personal use 47% of employees felt that scheduling of personal business was easier with flexitime	
Hewlett-Packard N = 200		93% of employees reported that traffic conditions improved; 1% reported worsened conditions; 6% reported no change
Occidental Life Insurance Company N = 700		43% of employees reported that commuting was easier; 54% of employees reported no change; 3% of employees reported that commuting was worse

198

J. C. Penney $N = 613$	47% of employees felt flexitime contributed to a feeling of control over their lives; 40% felt no effect 50% felt flexitime contributed to finding time for family or friends; 46% felt no effect 34% felt flexitime contributed to ease of making medical, dental, or other appointments; 61% felt no effect 25% felt flexitime contributed to ease of meeting personal responsibilities such as child care, car pools, etc.; 71% felt no effect 42% felt flexitime contributed to finding time for recreational or cultural pursuits; 54% felt no effect	36% of employees felt that commuting time to work improved; 54% felt no change 41% of employees felt commuting time from work improved; 53% felt no change 3% felt the cost of commuting was reduced; 93% felt no change
Pitney Bowes $N = 220$	Reasons for using flexible schedule were (in order of frequency) (1) personal business, (2) evening leisure time, (3) avoiding rush hours, (4) morning leisure time, and (5) more time with family	Employees used flexitime to avoid rush hour
Sandoz, Inc., East Hanover, NJ $N = 42$ supervisors $N = 116$ employees	80% of employees felt their personal freedom had increased; 18% felt no change; 2% felt it had decreased	General decrease in travel time reported with the exception of bus riders; 29% of bus riders reported an increase in travel time because of limited service outside of the normal rush hour; employees who drive or use car pools were most likely to report decreased travel time
SmithKline $N = 183$ supervisors $N = 274$ employees	82% reported an improvement in ability to attend to personal business; 16% reported no change; 2% reported an unfavorable impact	75% of employees reported that flexitime had a favorable impact on traffic congestion; 23% reported no impact; 2% reported an unfavorable impact
State Street Bank $N = 128$	70% of employees reported more time for leisure or family activities	59% of employees experienced reduced commuting time

Table 12-5 Summary of Measurements

Table	I Organizational Effectiveness			II Attitudes		III Membership—Withdrawal		IV Time Management	
Category	1 Productivity: Quality, Quantity, Services	2 Work Environment	3 Costs (Operating Costs, Not Start-Up Costs)	1 Morale and Job Satisfaction	2 Attitude toward Flexitime	1 Absenteeism	2 Tardiness	1 Personal Time Usage	2 Transportation
Objective Data	$N=9$ 4 positive 5 no change	$N=2$ 2 positive	$N=3$ 3 positive	N/A	N/A	$N=11$ 7 positive 4 no change	$N=4$ 4 positive	N/A	N/A
Survey Data	$N=27$ 19 positive 7 no change 1 negative	$N=35$ 16 positive 17 no change 2 negative	$N=2$ 1 positive 1 no change	$N=13$ 10 positive 3 no change	$N=21$ 21 positive	$N=9$ 4 positive 5 no change	$N=4$ 2 positive 2 no change	$N=16$ 11 positive 5 no change	$N=13$ 11 positive 2 no change

NOTE: N/A designates not applicable.

was that they had made a well-organized attempt to assess the effects of the flexitime program. We contacted many other organizations during our research, all of which were satisfied users of flexitime, but, unfortunately, having little or no data to support their claims.

Organizational Effectiveness.   The summary on organizational effectiveness indicates two important deficiencies in these reports. First, there is not enough objective data related to the impact of flexitime on effectiveness: less than half of the 12 organizations attempted to measure changes in productivity objectively. Second, there is a general lack of data on costs related to the implementation and the use of the program. The effect on productivity in 7 of the 12 organizations was no change and the other 5 noted a positive effect. The majority of organizations reported improvements in the work environment, and all 4 organizations who measured costs indicated positive effects. The reader should remember, however, that no organization attempted to assess the cost benefits, such as reduced overtime, in relation to other expenses which may have been incurred. Therefore, the bottom line on costs remains an unknown.

Attitudes.   All but one of the organizations reporting data in this area indicated a positive effect. As mentioned earlier, employees generally report a high level of satisfaction with flexitime and an improvement in morale. In addition to the direct advantages of the schedule itself, these results are usually attributed to the increased trust in employees expressed by management through the implementation of flexitime, a more relaxed work environment resulting from reduced commuting pressure, and the elimination of the tardiness problem.

Membership Behavior.   Absenteeism was most frequently reported using objective measures of the categories listed here. In 5 of the 7 organizations using hard measures, results were positive, providing strong support for the claim that flexible schedules can reduce leave usage. On tardiness, all organizations reported positive results. Under a system allowing daily flexibility, tardiness should be virtually eliminated. On other schedules, such as employee-chosen staggered hours, it is reduced, since the employee chooses a time that is convenient for him, although it may not be entirely eliminated.

Time Management.   Time management is another area in which flexitime should have a consistently positive effect, and, indeed, all entries in the tables support that claim. As mentioned earlier, the reports from the organizations do not necessarily represent unanimous agreement among employees concerning the benefits of flexible scheduling. The effects of flexitime on personal time management and transportation are dependent on the personal characteristics of employees as well as characteristics of the work situation. Therefore, rating an improvement noted by a limited percentage of employees as an overall positive effect, as long as the majority of the remainder indicated no change is probably justified.

CONCLUSIONS

Both Summary Tables 12-5 and 12-6 provide a positive picture of flexitime programs, especially with respect to its effects on attitudes, membership behavior, and time management. The effects on organizational effectiveness are equivocal, although there is little indication of any negative effects in this area, with the possible exception of minor communi-

Table 12-6 Summary Table by Organization

Organization	I Organizational Effectiveness			II Attitudes		III Membership		IV Time Management	
	Productivity	Work Environment	Costs	Morale and Job Satisfaction	Attitude toward Flexitime	Absenteeism	Tardiness	Personal Time Usage	Transportation
First National Bank Boston	+ (O)	ND	ND	ND	+	= (O)	+	+	+
Hewlett-Packard Corp. ND	+	+	ND	+	+	+	+	ND	+
State Street Bank Boston	= (O)	+ (O)	+ (O)	+	+	+ (O)	ND	+	+
Control Data Corp.	+	+	ND	+	ND	=	+	+	+
Metropolitan Life Insurance Co.	= (O)	+	+	+	+	= (O)	+	ND	ND
Berol Corp.	=	ND	+	+	+	+ (O)	+	+	ND

Pitney Bowes	= (O)	+	+	+	+	+ (O)	+	+	+
Occidental Life Insurance	= (O)	=	ND	ND	+	+ (O)	+ (O)	+	ND
SmithKline Corp.	+	+	+ (O)	+	+	+ (O)	ND	+	+
Sandoz, Inc.	=	=	ND	+	+	ND	ND	+	ND
J. C. Penney	=	=	ND	=	+	=	+	+	
John Hancock Life Insurance Co.	+	=	ND	+	+	ND	ND	+	+
Summary	$N=12$ 5+ 7=	$N=10$ 6+ 4=	$N=5$ 5+	$N=10$ 9+ 1=	$N=11$ 11+	$N=10$ 6+ 4=	$N=8$ 8+	$N=9$ 9+	$N=9$ 9+

+ indicates overall positive experience.
× indicates overall negative experience.
= indicates overall lack of effect or inconclusive results.
(o) indicates some or all measures based on objective data.
ND indicates no data reported.

cation problems. At the same time, these tables demonstrate the incomplete nature of many organizational assessment procedures and the need for a more objective and standardized system of analysis. Similar results were found in a recent review of the literature by Golembiewski and Proehl.[18]

All of the organizations contacted, even those without formal evaluations, indicated satisfaction with the programs they were using. If changes in existing flexitime programs were under consideration or had been implemented, they were in the direction of providing additional flexibility. Even a conservative evaluation of these results would indicate that flexible work schedules offer many possible personal and organizational benefits with little or no indication of any deterioration of the organization's ability to meet its short- and long-term goals.

NOTES

1. A comprehensive list of organizations employing different alternative work schedules was published by the National Council for Alternative Work Patterns (McArthy, 1978).

2. Cohen, A. R., and Gadon, H. *Alternative work schedules: Integrating individual and organizational needs.* Reading, Mass.: Addison-Wesley, 1978.

3. Swart, J. C. *A flexible approach to working hours.* New York: AMACOM, 1978.

4. Martin, V. H. *Hours of work when workers can choose: The experience of 50 organizations with employee chosen staggered hours and flexitime.* Washington, D.C.: Business and Professional Women's Foundation, 1975.

5. Nollen, S. D., and Martin, V. H. *Alternative work schedules: Flexitime.* An AMA Survey Report, New York, AMACOM, 1978.

6. This experience was reported by the director of Human Resources in a Journal article: Morgan, Frank T. Your (flex) time may come. *Personnel Journal,* February, 1977, *56,* No. 2, 82–85.

7. Sources: Control Data Corp. In-house publication, *Flexible hours,* May 1973; In-house publication, *Information about flexible work hours;* In-house publication, *Flexible work hours 3 year status report: Aerospace operations;* In-house publication, *Flexible work hours 3 year status report, microcircuits operations;* Gomex-Majia, Luis R., Hopp, Michael A., and Sommerstad, C. Richard. Implementation and evaluation of flexible work hours: a case study. *The Personnel Administrator,* February 1978.

8. White, Warren L., and Morre, Brian E. *An evaluation of flexitime* at the *First National Bank of Boston.* Working paper 76-39. The University of Texas at Austin: April, 1976.

9. Sources: Direct Contact and In-house report, John Hancock Mutual Life Insurance Company. *Flextime Survey Report,* Personnel Research-Personnel Operations. May 1978.

10. Flaherty, J. Personnel Manager, Hewlett-Packard, Waltham, Massachusetts. Presentation at the Boston Variable Hours Work Project. Boston, Massachusetts, July 1978. Robison, D., Hewlett-Packard tries flexitime: White collar production employees endorse flexible work schedules. *World of Work Report,* November 1978, *3,* No. 11, 89. Robison, David. Flexible work hours handbook. Hewlett-Packard, Palo Alto, California.

11. Schein, V. E., Maurer, E. H., and Novak, J. F. *Flexible working hours as an organizational development intervention.* Paper presented at the 83rd Annual Convention of the American Psychological Association, Chicago, Illinois, September 1975. Clarke, J. C., and Tafro, D. P. *Flexible starting times program evaluation.* Internal Personnel Research for Metropolitan Life Insurance Co., 1976.

12. Schein, V. E., Maurer, E. H. and Novak, J. F. Impact of flexible working hours on productivity. *Journal of Applied Psychology,* 1979, *62,* 463–465. Clarke, June C., and Tafro, Diana P. Flexible

starting times program evaluation. Internal personnel research for Metropolitan Life Insurance Co., 1976.

13. Best, J. Flexible work hours at Occidental. In proceedings from *New ways of working faire* prepared by The Center of the Quality of Work Life, UCLA. Los Angeles, March 1, 1977.

14. De Mayo, L. G. Final Report Flextime Surveys 1977 & 1978, J. C. Penney, Office Management, September 1978.

15. Corporate Communications, Pitney Bowes, Stamford, Conn. 11/18/77 #245A, and #245.

16. Source: In-house report, Sandoz, Inc., N.J. *Gliding work time: Corporate personnel dept.*

17. Mayoon, W. and Schnicker, L. Flexible hours at State Street Bank of Boston: A case study, *The Personnel Administrator,* 1976.

18. Golembiewski, R. T., and Proehl, C. W., Jr. A survey of the empirical literature of flexible work-hours: Character and consequences of a major innovation. *Academy of Management Review,* 1978, *3,* 837–853. Golembiewski, R. T. *The role of flexible work hours in organizations.* Paper presented at the 87th Annual convention of the American Psychological Association, New York, September 1979.

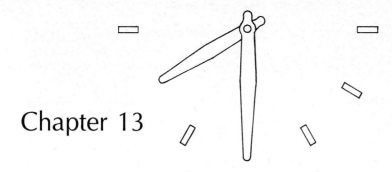

Chapter 13

Transportation

THE PRACTICAL ASPECTS OF FLEXIBLE SCHEDULES

The original stimulus which led to the invention of flexitime in Germany was a transportation problem. Workers in a particular organization found it nearly impossible to get to work on time because of traffic congestion. Flexitime was created to help alleviate this problem. For example, in a survey of 300 European firms published in 1976, it was found that while improvement in transportation was listed as the fourth most frequently noted benefit of flexitime, it was the *most* frequent response given as the initial reason for experimenting with the system.[1] Thus, despite all of the organizational and personal advantages associated with flexitime, its origins are associated with this very practical and pressing problem. Its rapid rate of acceptance and adoption in Europe reflects this practical consideration. It was much easier to "sell" the idea based on this aspect rather than on less tangible, difficult-to-prove benefits.

Although the personal and organizational benefits accruing through the implementation of flexitime are potentially significant, in this chapter we will consider the benefits of flexitime with respect to transportation and energy conservation, from a societal point of view. In order for these benefits to be realized, there must be an organized effort to change and coordinate the schedules of organizations in the central business districts and along major travel routes.

DEFINITION OF THE PROBLEM

The problem is illustrated, quite graphically, by the following pictures. The first was taken 8:30 A.M. in New York's Grand Central Terminal. The second was taken at the same location at 9:20 A.M.*

*The author wishes to acknowledge the assistance of The Port Authority of New York and New Jersey in securing the station photographs and their helpful comments.

(a)

(b)

Figure 13–1 Grand Central Terminal on a working day: *(a)* at 8:30 A.M. *(b)* at 9:20 A.M.

208

In the followng sequence of three photographs taken during the evening rush hour, attendance on a subway platform is seen to peak just after 5 P.M.. Photographs were taken at 4:30, 5:12, and 5:46 P.M.

A similar situation is presented in Table 13-1 below. These figures represent usage levels during the evening at a Boston train station.[2] Between 4:30 and 5:30 P.M., trains running on this line are loaded beyond any minimal level of comfort. Notice that in the period of a little over an hour between 4 and 5:01 P.M., ridership increases more than fourfold. However, the increase in cars available (from 16 to 20) is enough to handle only one-quarter of the ridership increase. Another example of increased peak hour demand is in London, where 3,500 buses are quite sufficient for the off-peak needs, but 5,500 buses are required during the rush hours.

The problem illustrated by these examples is known as *peaking* in the transportation sector and refers to the sudden increase in demand placed on public transportation systems for short periods of time in the morning and evening. A similar situation holds for our system of roads and highways. They suffer from peaking just as the mass transit system does. This phenomenon is most commonly known as the *rush hour*—although everyone knows that one thing you cannot do in any central business district is *rush* anywhere during this period.

The peaking problem places great strain on the transportation system and the people using it. Some of its effects are noticeable immediately. *Dwell time,* the time a bus or train is stopped at a station loading or unloading, increases. As a result, the schedule backs up and average speed through the system is reduced. The problem is shown graphically in Figure 13-3, which was produced as part of the Port Authority of New York and New Jersey Staggered Work Hours Project.[2] Because dwell time in a station doubled during the peak hour, average train speed was reduced by 50 percent.

This problem has been alleviated in the past by expanding the transportation system to accommodate the peak load. By now, however, this solution is unfeasible. Physical space for new highways and mass transit systems is unavailable. Moreover, it is becoming prohibitively expensive to fund such projects. One report from the Seattle Commuter Pool Program estimated costs of between $20 and $40 million to build 1 mile of freeway and of over

Table 13-1   Actual Peak Point Loads

Red Line—Southbound   (June 7, 1977)

	South Shore Line			
Time	People	Cars	Average/Car†	% Capacity
3:30–4:00 P.M.	915	16	57	38
4:01–4:30 P.M.	1,588	16	99	66
4:31–5:00 P.M.	2,749	16	172	114
5:01–5:30 P.M.	4,096	20	205	136
5:31–6:00 P.M.	2,946	20	147	97
6:01–6:30 P.M.	647	16	40	27

*   Count taken as trains leave South Station.
†   Normal capacity of South Shore cars is 151 passengers assuming all seats occupied and 2.5 sq. ft. of space for each standee.
SOURCE: Spred-Sked: A Work Rescheduling Program for Boston. The Massachusetts Bay Transportation Authority, Community Affairs and Marketing Department. September 1978.

(a)

(b)

Figure 13–2 A subway platform on a working day: *(a)* at 4:30 P.M. *(b)* at 5:12 P.M. *(c)* at 5:46 P.M.

(c)

$114,000 for a new bus. In addition to these practical problems, it is becoming appar-
ent that it is difficult to justify constructing the types of transportation systems necessary
to handle the peak load when this level of demand is in effect for two relatively short
periods a day. There is an alternative approach, and that is to distribute the demand
over a greater period of the day by varying the starting and quitting times of the work
force.

This idea has been widely supported in the transportation sector and has resulted in
the organization of transportation groups whose main purpose is to introduce and support the use of variable work schedules in the business districts that they serve. These
groups—including The Port Authority of New York and New Jersey Staggered Work
Hours Project, Seattle/King County Commuter Pool Program, the Toronto Variable
Work Hours Project, Boise Carpool, and Portland TRIMET—are responsible for a great
deal of the experimentation with, and use of, flexible schedules. They have encouraged
the major employers in their areas by offering help in setting up experiments with a
variable schedule. They emphasize to the organization that if the peak load demands on
the transportation system could be distributed over a longer period, workers would have
less trouble getting to their jobs. The benefits to the organization would include reduced
tardiness, more satisfied workers, and perhaps even improved productivity. Besides al-
leviating traffic and transit congestion, the planned use of flexible work schedules—as a
joint effort of the transportation sector, the government, and private industry—has other
beneficial effects, all of which follow from the more efficient use of mass transit and
highway systems.

MASS TRANSPORTATION BENEFITS

A major reason for encouraging the adoption of variable work schedules on a citywide basis is, as described above, to flatten out the peak demand curve over a wider range of time. For example, if 300,000 people use a specific subway line to get to work each day and all of them start work between 8:30 and 9:00 A.M., the system would have to transport people at a rate of 600,000 per hour. If those same people report to work between 7 and 10:00 A.M., the system's rate of transport can drop to 100,000 people per hour, assuming the rate of arrival is evenly distributed over the three hours. One immediate benefit would be a decrease in delays as a result of reduced crowding. Furthermore, when employees spend less time and energy commuting, they are more relaxed upon arrival. Another benefit to be gained from redistributing the peak demand period is decreased overloading, which means less wear and tear on the equipment. Perhaps most important, when the demand is less concentrated during a short time period the overall ability of the system to serve the public will increase. For example, if the absolute limit of a system is 300,000 people per hour, with an optimum (comfortable) rate of 250,000 people per hour, then the maximum passenger usage under a 1-hour peak period will be 300,000 people, with maximum discomfort for riders during this period. If, however, the peak demand period is extended to 3 hours, the system can transport 250,000 people per hour, or 750,000 people per peak period in relative comfort. Obviously, this can be an incentive for increased ridership—those who avoid mass transit because of its discomfort may be willing to switch from automobiles to subways, buses, or other mass transit forms. Increased ridership means additional energy savings and a reduction in pollution through a decrease in the number of automobiles on the highways.

It is important that the local transportation authority become involved in any project of this type so that it can adjust transit schedules to accommodate the transformed level of demand at rush hour, assuming, of course, that flexitime has been implemented on a large enough scale to cause such a transformation. If such coordination is lacking, those traveling outside of the former peak demand period will find the service inadequate, and their incentive to use mass transportation will be reduced.

Another type of mass transportation benefit is related to specific organization settings. Organizations located in large, high-rise office buildings and at suburban locations with large parking lots report improvements in the use of facilities under flexible schedules. Bottlenecks at elevators and parking lot entrances and exits are alleviated. The Port Authority of New York and New Jersey monitored waiting time for elevators as part of their evaluation of a flexitime system used at their office in the World Trade Center in New York City. Figure 13-4 compares the departure pattern of Port Authority (PA) employees leaving work via the elevator at various times in the afternoon *before* FWH to the pattern *after* FWH was introduced, and to the pattern for another firm in the same building which used a fixed schedule.

TRAFFIC BENEFITS

There are several very important benefits for society and the individual which can be realized by decreasing peak period use of the highways through an extension of the rush hour. The

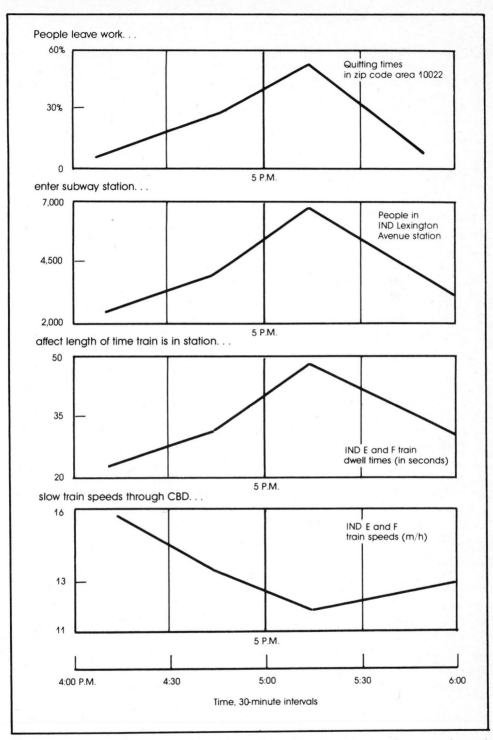

People leave work. . .

Quitting times in zip code area 10022

enter subway station. . .

People in IND Lexington Avenue station

affect length of time train is in station. . .

IND E and F train dwell times (in seconds)

slow train speeds through CBD. . .

IND E and F train speeds (m/h)

Time, 30-minute intervals

Figure 13–3 A case study of the peaking problem: IND E and F trains to Queens, afternoon peak period.

213

resulting improvement in the flow of traffic means that there are fewer bottlenecks and delays at points where traffic merges, enters, or exits. This may be especially true at back-up points such as bridges, tunnels, and tolls.

Improved traffic flow also means that cars travel at a higher rate of speed without having to stop and start frequently. When the national speed limit was set at 55 MPH, it was argued that a car operated at its optimal gas consumption rate at this speed. Further, a study by the Federal Energy Administration indicated that there is a 37 percent improvement in the gas consumption rate when a car in a stop-and-go traffic jam is compared to the same car in free-flowing traffic. Thus, an improvement in traffic flow implies not only a faster, more comfortable commute, but a possible saving in gasoline costs.

The potential exists not only for a reduction in transportation costs to the individual but also for a reduction in the national gasoline consumption rate. As a secondary benefit of any reduction in this rate, the Federal Energy Administration also states that if absolute demand for gasoline can be reduced, then the production process in the oil industry can place more emphasis on refining crude oil into fuel oil instead of gasoline. Because fuel oil is a more efficient energy source, there would be an increase in the total amount of energy extracted from our oil. The effects of flexible schedules alone may not be great enough to enable the oil industry to effect a major change; however, flexitime should certainly be considered a contributing factor in a national energy conservation program.

Another benefit of improved traffic flow is a reduction in air pollution along major highways, near bridges, in tunnels, and in other areas where traffic now tends to become congested during peak travel periods. Cars caught in stop-and-go traffic operate less efficiently and release more pollutants into the air per car than cars moving freely along a highway. The high concentration of cars in a congested area can create a buildup of pollutants in the vicinity. If implemented on a large scale, flexitime could contribute to improved air quality by improving traffic flow.

One side effect of flexible working schedules often reported is an increase in the use of car pools. Significant changes are limited to those situations where fully flexible working schedules are in use rather than staggered hours or a compressed workweek. Under flexible working schedules, a person is free to form a car pool with people in his neighborhood—or with his own family members—even if they work for different organizations or have different schedules, whereas under a rigid schedule, or the compressed or staggered systems, the individual is restricted to making arrangements with those who have very similar schedules, usually from the same company.

The implications for easing traffic congestion are clear: the more individuals who can be persuaded to share cars instead of driving alone, the fewer cars there will be on the road. In fact, some cities, such as Washington, D.C., have actually encouraged car pools by creating an express lane on the highways leading to and from the central business district for cars carrying four or more passengers.

Some people might argue that car pools tend to defeat the purpose of flexible hours, since the employee is then tied to the car pool schedule. However, the *important* fact is that if the employee agrees to a car pool schedule, he does it of his own choice. Most people using flexible working hours tend to choose a regular schedule that they are comfortable with and to follow that schedule more or less regularly. An employee could choose to form a car pool with people who follow a similar schedule and be very satisfied. When an occasion arises

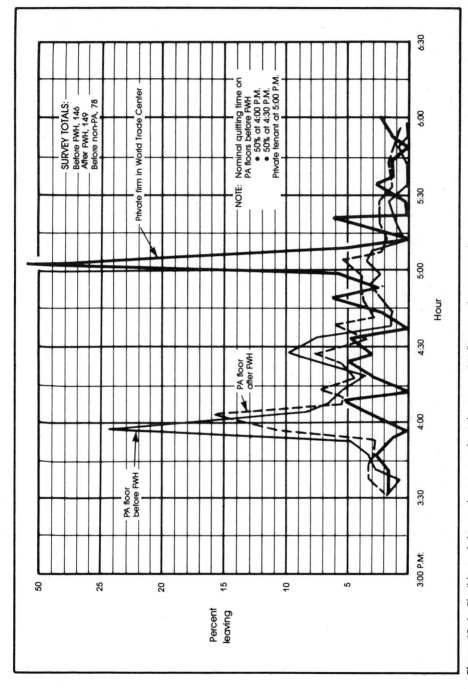

Figure 13–4 Flexible work hours: departures of employees on PA floor vs. departures of employees on non-PA floor.

215

in which an employee wishes to deviate from this pattern, he can make other transportation arrangements without being concerned about an assigned work schedule. Of course, when it is the employee's turn to drive, he has a certain obligation to the other members of the car pool, but that is a social obligation which was voluntarily undertaken and is not really related to organizational constraints.

Although these potential benefits are impressive, there is one drawback which should be mentioned. One could easily argue that improved traffic flow and decreased congestion may tempt people to switch from mass transportation to traveling by car, undermining the benefits gained. However, it is hoped that with the high cost of gasoline, the ease of forming car pools, and improvements in mass transit, individuals will not switch to driving their cars to work.

EXTENT OF THE PROBLEM

The problem of peaking on transportation systems is not limited to a few large congested urban areas. In November 1975, the Port Authority of New York and New Jersey reported the results of an international survey of cities which was conducted by their planning and development department. The results of this survey indicated that approximately 74 percent of United States cities (N=85) and 82 percent of non–United States cities (N=26) have problems with peak demand periods on their transit systems. Over half of these cities reported that the peak demand was related to work schedules in their central business district. Of the cities in the United States, only 10 percent reported that they had developed any program to promote flexible working schedules as a way to deal with the problem. In most (over 80 percent) of the cities, the absence of any program was the primary reason for the lack of attention in this area. The responses from non–United States cities indicates that 65 percent of those cities have tried a flexible work hours solution.

It is apparent from these figures that there is a great deal of potential for the use of flexible work hours. There is clearly a need for a national program to persuade municipalities of the potential real benefits of flexitime and to assist them in setting up and coordinating individual projects. Cities must be presented with a cost/benefit analysis of the expense of setting up a program of variable work schedules compared to the expense of (1) wasted fuel and increased pollution, (2) inefficient transit systems and decreased ridership, (3) loss of productivity from tardiness and high, short-term absenteeism, and (4) loss of revenue from firms and employees who leave the city to relocate because of all of the above factors. Results from individual organizations and the few citywide programs available are reported in the section to follow.

RESULTS FROM INDIVIDUAL ORGANIZATIONS

The results contained in reports by individual organizations who use flexitime confirm that the benefits we have described have been realized. Of 196 organizations on flexitime which participated in a survey by Nollen and Martin,[3] 97 percent reported that employee commuting improved under the new schedule, 3 percent indicated that there was no change, and none reported an increase in commuting problems. Improved commuting was the third most mentioned benefit of flexitime, behind increased morale and reduced tardiness (which are themselves indirectly related to easier commuting).

If we look at the table of results on transportation from the public sector (Table 10-4), we can observe some of the specific benefits that organizations have noted. For example, the Environmental Protection Agency, the Bureau of Health Insurance, and the Air University all reported increases in the number of employees participating in car pools. These are not large increases, but it must be noted that these improvements have been realized even though there has *not* been areawide implementation of flexitime. The implications for implementation on an areawide basis are significant. Employees of the U.S. Geological Survey and of the Navy Finance Center in Ohio report decreases in weekly gas consumption. The table contains many other entries concerned with workers' perceptions of the daily commute. All of the entries are positive and clearly support the claim that flexitime facilitates transportation to and from work.

RESULTS FROM ORGANIZED PROGRAMS

Most of the organized areawide projects do not have formal results available yet. However, there are some results reported from two large programs, one in New York City and one in Ottawa.

In 1970, the Port Authority of New York and New Jersey, along with the Downtown-Lower Manhattan Association, started a program to promote the use of staggered hours in their area.*[4] Within 2 years, there was a 25 percent reduction in the number of peak period passengers at three major downtown subway stations. The passenger volume at the Port Authority Trans-Hudson Terminal dropped by 1,000 (from 7,500 to 6,500) during its busiest quarter-hour period. Volume during the least used quarter-hour rose by 1,500 (from 3,100 to 4,600). Note that there was a decrease in the peak demand but no decrease in overall passenger volume.

In 1974 and 1975, the Port Authority experimented with a flexible hours schedule in its own office and reported a positive experience. It now promotes flexible schedules as well as staggered hours in the downtown area. A similar program exists for midtown Manhattan businesses.

In 1974, the Ottawa-Carleton Regional Transit Commission reported on the impact of the simultaneous introduction of flexible working schedules to some 35,000 government employees in their area (over 50 percent of the work force). It was found that prior to the introduction of flexitime, 29,800 people used the transit system to get to and from work daily and 54 percent of these riders were government employees.

A 6-month evaluation of the effects on the transit system revealed the following:[5]

1. Prior to flexitime usage, 73 percent of the passenger volume was handled during the 30-minute peak period in the morning. After flexitime, only 40 percent of the passenger volume was handled in that same period. Before flexitime, 68 percent of the passenger

*The author is thankful to Walter Colvin and Charles Fausti of the Port Authority of New York and New Jersey for their helpful comments.

volume was handled in the 30-minute afternoon peak period. After flexitime, this was reduced to 33 percent.

2. After the introduction of flexitime, the morning peak period increased from 60 to 90 minutes. The afternoon peak period increased from 45 to 105 minutes.

3. The average daily ridership of this system increased by 7,000. When this is combined with the extension of the peak periods, the result is an *increase* in ridership during peak periods of 8 percent—without the accompanying discomfort!

4. There was an increase of 24 percent in measures of manpower utilization of the transit operators. This was brought about by the ability of operators to make more than one run over their routes because of fewer delays.

5. After introduction of flexitime, management was able to reschedule several major bus routes and reduce the total number of buses used on each route, thereby saving on fuel and wear and tear on equipment.

These results offer dramatic evidence of the effect of flexitime on transportation. Such significant results were possible because, in this situation, *half* of the area's work force was placed on flexitime at one time. The effects were noticeable at once and attributed totally to the use of flexitime.

The evidence demonstrates that people will choose travel times in order to avoid the usual peak period when given the chance (see Table 10-4). Transportation personnel should note that most people choose earlier starting times (as noted in Chapter 9), and that transportation facilities and schedules will have to be adjusted accordingly.

SUMMARY

The need for a solution to transit problems is obvious to anyone who lives or works in a congested urban area. Survey results indicate that the problem is widespread, while the results of studies by individual organizations suggest that flexible working schedules can be a simple and inexpensive improvement in the peak load demand problem. The fact that those organizations which have implemented flexitime on their own initiative have experienced small improvements in this implies possibilities for significant improvements through coordinated citywide efforts. This conclusion is strongly supported by the reports from Ottawa and New York.

The results from other projects, such as the Boston Area Variable Work Hours Project and Portland TRIMET, should be available soon. It is hoped that they will lend further support to the concept.

NOTES

1. Jaeger, J. B., and Groushko, M. A. *Flexible working hours in Europe.* Brussels: Management Centre Europe, 1976.

2. Flexible Work Hours at the Port Authority of New York and New Jersey Planning and Development Department. December 1975.

3. Nollen, S. D., and Martin, V. H. *Alternative work schedules: Flexitime.* An AMA Survey Report. New York: AMACOM, 1978.

4. *Staggered Work Hours: A Report on International Practice.* The Port Authority of New York and New Jersey Planning and Development Department. November 1975. *Staggered Work Hours Study: Phase I—Final Report.* The Port Authority of New York and New Jersey. August 1977.

5. Bonsall T. A. *Flexible hours and public transit in Ottawa.* Presented at the Annual Conference of the Roads and Transportation Association of Canada. Toronto, Ontario. September 23–24, 1978.

PART

Flexible Working Hours and the Labor Force

4

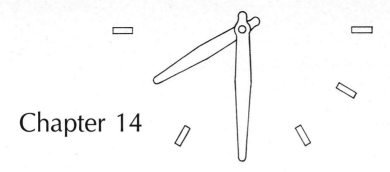

Chapter 14

First-Line Supervisors

INTRODUCTION

A critical factor in the success or failure of a flexible work hours system is the attitude of first-line supervisors toward the program. Flexitime, by its nature, requires a supervisory style which focuses on planning and coordination as opposed to monitoring. If this varies from the current supervisory style of the organization, upper management may be confronted with resistance to a flexitime program. Supervisors used to monitoring their employees may feel threatened by its implementation. Indeed, a number of organizations have reported first-line supervisor dissatisfaction with flexitime, for example, the Navy Finance Center in Long Beach, the General Radio Company in Concord, Massachusetts, a St. Louis bank, and a St. Louis Insurance Company.[1]

With flexitime, supervisors should be less concerned with time-keeping functions, and should be willing to spend more time on planning, scheduling, and coordinating functions; they will have to place less emphasis on employee control and develop a more participatory style of supervision. Since this may not be an easy adjustment for some first-line supervisors, the organization must be prepared to facilitate the process through orientation beginning *as soon as the decision is made to implement flexitime.* An orientation program for first-line supervisors should:

1. Involve supervisors in the planning and implementation of the system

2. Educate supervisors so that they understand their new roles and responsibilities

3. Provide an appropriate climate and necessary feedback for the supervisors, especially in the initial phase of the system's use, so that supervisors can adjust their behaviors in the appropriate directions

This chapter will explore in more detail the role of the first-line supervisor and review reported effects of flexitime implementation on supervisors.

THE IMPACT OF FLEXITIME ON THE ACTIVITIES
OF THE FIRST-LINE SUPERVISOR

The work activities of 251 first-line supervisors from 40 different plants of a major tire company were examined by a questionnaire.[2] Seven common factors which described the work activities of this varied sample emerged. Although some differences in the relative importance of a factor or the relative time spent on a factor were noted among different types of supervisory jobs, all factors applied to all jobs to some degree. The factors are (1) working with subordinates, (2) organizing work of subordinates, (3) work planning and scheduling, (4) maintaining efficient quality production, (5) maintaining a safe and clean work area, (6) maintaining equipment and machinery, and (7) compiling records and reports.

When these seven factors are examined in relation to the use of a flexible work hours system as opposed to a fixed hours system, it is apparent that the supervisor's job will be more complex under the flexible system. Factor 1, working with subordinates, would certainly be influenced. A supervisor may perceive a decrease in authority because he will not have control over (or, in some cases, even have to verify) employees' starting and quitting times. Some supervisors have objected to this aspect of flexible scheduling because they feel threatened by this loss of power.[3] Other supervisors, however, have welcomed flexitime because in many cases it eliminates the necessity for time recording—a source of friction with employees and a time-consuming, nonproductive task. The way in which a supervisor reacts will depend upon how much importance he attaches to the monitoring function and how well he has been prepared to accept the new system.

As to factors 2 and 3, organizing work of subordinates and work planning and scheduling, supervisors will no longer have the stability of a fixed schedule to work from when they are organizing and planning. Work will have to be organized and scheduled to the point that the supervisor's presence is not required at all times. The supervisor will have to increase his awareness and responsiveness to all levels of interaction with subordinates, since there may be less total time for interaction. Factor 7, compiling records and reports, may become more or less time consuming depending on the type of time-recording system installed. The remaining factors may be affected by a flexible schedule depending on the specific work situation.

While we do have some reports from organizations which have attempted implementation of flexitime, there is a dearth of empirical research concerning the nature and extent of the changes in first line supervisory orientation and practices. One of the few studies available is by Graf,[4] who had done some preliminary research into the general impact of FWH on the first-line supervisor's job. The research was based on 311 questionnaires returned from 508 supervisors working under flexitime. These first-line supervisors came from 40 different United States organizations using a wide variety of flexitime systems.

The questionnaire was distributed after the implementation of flexitime. It was not a before and after comparison, but represented the supervisors' after-the-fact analysis of changes in their jobs. Five managerial components were analyzed: planning, organizing, staffing, directing, and control.

According to Graf's results, these supervisors noted an increase in the amount of long- and short-term planning required on the job and a decrease in their own concern with direct control of employees. These supervisors also reported that there was a significant increase in the amount of both written and oral communication between themselves and employees *in spite of a decrease in the opportunity to interact.* It may be surmised that this perceived increase in level of communication implies a more participatory style of supervision.

Graf also found that supervisors had to generate more formal rules and regulations to ensure smooth work flow in their absence. Further, the results indicated that supervisors feel they are more actively involved in the employee appraisal process. A possible explanation for these results is the idea that supervisors perceive a decrease in their direct control over the work unit because of their inability to monitor *all* employees *all* the time under flexitime. The increase in rules and appraisal activity may represent a compensation in the form of *indirect* control. The supervisors must provide contingencies for the times when they are unavailable, and some form of guidance is needed. Additional rules and appraisals may help to fill this void.

This shift from direct to indirect control has implications for task autonomy provided to the employee. The focus on appraisals and less direct control of behavior through rules instead of monitoring requires a different style of supervision: instead of focusing on the *process* of behaviors utilized in performing a task, the supervisor is now concentrating on the *results* of those behaviors. In becoming more result or goal oriented, the supervisor must give the employee more autonomy to perform task activities in his own style. The addition of rules may indicate the reluctance of the supervisor to relinquish control over behavior —the degree to which he imposes new rules and regulations may be commensurate with his degree of discomfort with the change of focus. Perhaps the most important point, however, is that task autonomy may be increased for the employee. Flexitime, through its imposition of increased autonomy in work scheduling, forces the supervisor into a position of increasing task autonomy in his work unit.

It should also be noted that any increase in formal regulations, demands a reexamination of the specific task requirements during the implementation and planning stages of the flexitime program as well as an effective evaluation process. The implications of this system are more effective supervision based on an improved understanding, more accurate administration of the work process itself, and a fairer evaluation technique.

Another study measured the attitudes of first-line supervisors at SmithKline Corporation.[5] They reported for themselves as employees, and then reported as supervisors in terms of impact on their jobs. The researchers found that work attitudes were very much improved after implementation of flexitime when the supervisors reported as employees. When these individuals reported as supervisors, their attitudes did not show any improvement at all. The same effect was observed in the public sector, as can be seen in the tables presented in Chapter 9 showing the results of federal government experiments. This is indicative of the role conflict experienced by the supervisor. As an employee, he enjoys the benefits of the system, but as a supervisor he may encounter problems in the work unit resulting from flexitime. The result is that his overall attitude is less positive than that of the rank-and-file worker, who is accountable only for his immediate, discrete task.

The evidence thus far presented indicates that the job of a first-line supervisor is affected by the implementation of flexitime and that consequently changes in attitudes may result. If the changes in responsibilities are viewed as threatening or burdensome, supervisors' attitudes toward flexitime are more likely to be negative than are the attitudes of employees.

The question then arises how to overcome or avoid negative attitudes in order to achieve a successful shift in supervisory focus or style.

Cohen and Gadon[6] have suggested that the flexitime program itself, through the increased autonomy granted in scheduling, will create an atmosphere of trust sufficient to overcome these threatening aspects. They propose that "flexible scheduling is primarily a trust-inducing strategy for change rather than one that is trust-based." Further, an organization requires only enough trust between the workers and supervisors to try a flexitime experiment—the system will then generate enough trust to sustain itself.

Although these statements by Cohen and Gadon are made in the context of a discussion of organizational development programs, they may be misleading, especially in light of the evidence just presented. Although a successful flexitime program is most definitely based on mutual trust between supervisors and employees, it can only be a trust-*inducing* strategy in a climate where trust has already been well established. As part of a comprehensive effort by management to develop a climate of trust, flexitime will be trust-sustaining or even trust-inducing. However, as an isolated effort, flexitime cannot succeed as *the* method for increasing trust between supervisors and subordinates. The result of this will be negative attitudes toward the program and unwillingness to cooperate—and without active support and supervisory cooperation, any flexitime system is clearly doomed to failure.

We emphasize this point so strongly because of the tendency by organizations to take a statement such as that made by Cohen and Gadon and to decide to use a flexible system to "instill trust in the employee-supervisor relationship." This approach overlooks the complexity of organizational change. It is most important for implementors to understand that any intervention or new system must be consistent with the organization's climate in order to be successful. As pointed out by Byham,[7] systems, in and of themselves, do not change organizational behavior. Byham continues, "It is not the system that shapes the people, but the attention, training, and positive reinforcement that accompanies the system."

Within the context of flexitime, this means training and feedback for supervisors, beginning in the earliest stages of consideration, planning, and implementation. The implementation process itself is not sufficient to provide adequate positive reinforcement and feedback for behavioral and attitudinal change; the implementation of flexitime must be supplemented with involvement in the planning process and educational programs to encourage an organizational climate of attitudes receptive to the desired change. In a 1978 American Management Association survey, those organizations which involved supervisors in planning and implementation of a flexitime program had significantly fewer problems than those which ignored their supervisors.[8] Furthermore, reports from Hewlett-Packard Corp. and SmithKline (discussed in Chapters 11 and 12) are excellent examples in support of this approach.

TWO EXAMPLES OF FLEXITIME PROGRAMS AND THEIR EFFECT ON FIRST-LINE SUPERVISORS

The potential effects of a flexible work system on first line supervisors clearly deserve serious consideration by upper management before implementation of a flexitime system. The following examples (one positive and one negative) illustrate two differing approaches and their results.[9]

An East Coast utility company has reported that it attempted to implement flexitime. After a few weeks, several departments canceled the program and most others were seriously considering ending it as well. It seems that *after* flexitime was implemented, upper management decided that first-line supervisors were required to report to work at the start of the bandwidth and stay on the job until *all* employees finished their 8-hour day (typically a 10- to 12-hour day) in order to ensure that employees were supervised at all times. Evidently incidents had occurred under flexitime which made the company feel that constant and close supervision was necessary. Needless to say, the first-line supervisors felt that this was an unjust, undesirable arrangement. These supervisors, understandably, demanded an end to the project. It is clear from the description of this organization's experience with flexitime that they "plugged in" to the system without (1) any feasibility research, (2) programs to educate the employees and supervisors, or (3) consideration of changes in organizational processes so that hours were compatible with work flow.

The Hewlett-Packard Corporation in Waltham, Massachusetts, has had much success with a flexitime program which is used by a large number of its manufacturing employees and their supervisors. This organization developed flexitime as *part* of their overall organizational development program rather than as an isolated change. One assumption of upper management was that flexitime would be beneficial and acceptable to the rank-and-file employees. Another was that the major impact of the program would be on the first-line supervisors. As a result of this thinking, management conducted education programs for employees about the logistics of the system and its potential advantages. Employees were informed that time management would be a shared responsibility between themselves and supervisors.

Since management's assumption was that this premise of shared responsibility for time management would not be readily accepted by supervisors, special care was taken to ensure that supervisors did not feel their interests were being disregarded. Through many meetings and memos, supervisors were informed that they were not expected to be present during the entire bandwidth and that they were not expected to continuously supervise employees. They were encouraged to concentrate on planning and coordinating functions under the new system.

This reeducation process was conducted *before* the program was actually implemented. When the program was installed, problems were virtually nonexistent. Upper management was pleased to find that when there were problems in scheduling or in other areas, these problems were handled at the supervisor-worker level.

CONCLUSION

It is unfortunate that some organizations choose to proceed with a haphazard implementation of a flexitime program without sufficient understanding, or awareness, of the nature of the organizational climate and change which must accompany the system. When these aspects are overlooked, problems are bound to arise and they usually appear at the first-line supervisor level. Those organizations which held meetings with supervisors and managers and appointed an internal project director to oversee the flexitime experiment had significantly fewer problems with employee scheduling, work scheduling, and internal communication than those organizations that did not take such steps.

From this evidence and discussion, we can conclude that for several reasons it is *essential* to include supervisors at the earliest implementation stages of a flexitime program. First, supervisors are aware of information on task requirements and work flow that is necessary to the formation of the structure of the system. Second, supervisors serve as a source of information for the rank-and-file employees and, therefore, must be fully aware of the workings of the system. Third, supervisors must reorient their behavior toward a focus on planning and coordinating instead of on monitoring behavior. In order for this to happen, the climate of the organization must be supportive of these changes, encouraging the establishment of trust between supervisors and employees. Without this conducive atmosphere, the supervisors will not receive the positive feedback necessary to give them the incentive to accommodate and promote the flexitime system.

NOTES

1. Swart, J. C., *A flexible approach to working hours* New York: AMACOM, 1978. Hilgert, R. L. and Hundley, J. R. Supervision: The weak link in flexible scheduling? *Personnel Administrator,* 1975, *20,* 24–28.

2. Dowell, B. E. and Wexley, K. N., Development of a work behavior taxonomy for first line supervisors. *Journal of Applied Psychology,* 1973, *63,* 5, 563–572.

3. Partridge, B. E. Notes on the impact of flextime in a large insurance company. *Occupational Psychology,* 1973, *47,* 241–242.

4. Graf, L. A. *The impact of flexitime on the first line supervisor's job: A preliminary investigation.* Paper presented at the 38th Annual Meeting of the Academy of Management. San Francisco, California, 1978.

5. Golembiewski, R. T., Hilles, R., and Kagno, M. S. A longitudinal study of flexitime effects: Some consequences of an OD intervention. *The Journal of Applied Behavioral Science,* 1974, pp. 503–532.

6. Cohen, A. R., and Gadon, H. *Alternative work schedules: Integrating individual and organizational needs.* Reading, Mass.: Addison-Wesley, 1978.

7. Byham, W. C. Changing supervisory and managerial behavior. *Training and Development Journal,* 1977.

8. Nollen, S. D., and Martin, V. H. *Alternative work schedules: Flexitime.* An AMA Survey Report. New York: AMACOM, 1978.

9. This information was gathered by the author at the Conference on Variable Work Hours, June 21, 1978, at the Park Place Hotel in Boston, Massachusetts, sponsored by the Boston Area Variable Work Hours Project.

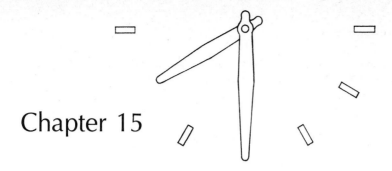

Chapter 15

Union Attitudes and Considerations

PRIMARY UNION CONCERNS

A primary concern of unions is to improve terms and conditions of employment through their increased power in negotiating collectively rather than singly. Negotiations usually involve the protection of workers against what are perceived as unfair industry practices and work conditions, as imposed by management. Tannenbaum defines unions as "organizations designed to protect and enhance the social and economic welfare of their members."[1] Within this context of protecting the worker, there are two primary aspects of union concern involving both protecting and maintaining the *economic* position of the worker: (1) the maintenance and increase in the level of employment, and (2) the financial well-being of the individual employee. Unfortunately, conflicts sometime arise in the implementation of these objectives. This conflict is reflected in the dichotomy between the goals of union leadership and union members at the employee level. Through an examination of these aspects, one may be able to better understand a union's position on flexitime and to help the organization overcome some of the union's apprehensions.

As mentioned above, major concerns of the union movement—especially of union leadership—have been the creation of jobs and the maintenance job security for those already employed. This concern has been aggravated by high unemployment levels and economists' predictions that joblessness will remain above 6 percent. Further, many union leaders fear increased productivity through advances in technology and automation as an additional threat to the work force. (A United Auto Workers' spokesman has projected that, while industry production levels will be 47 percent higher in 1990 than in 1976, employment will increase by only 5 percent because of improvements in productivity.)

In their efforts to combat the shrinking employment level (as measured by the high unemployment rate and the increasing ratio of productivity to man-hours), unions have adopted policies aimed at maintaining or expanding the number of available jobs. Three policies, in particular, have been adopted which influence attitudes toward flexitime: bargaining for the shorter workweek, limiting regularly scheduled overtime, and attempting to limit moonlighting. Each aspect, beginning with the shorter workweek, will be examined here in turn.

The Shorter Workweek

The Bureau of Labor Statistics's figures have shown a steady decline in hours worked per week from 41.1 in 1948 to 38.2 in 1976 for nonagricultural wage and salary workers.[2] Howard Young, a special consultant to the United Auto Workers, predicts that the average workweek will be 25 hours in 30 years.[3] One might predict that reduced work hours would create additional jobs, decreasing unemployment. However, Young adds that demand for output will not grow as quickly as the total labor force, offsetting the trend toward creating additional jobs and lowering unemployment.

The United Auto Workers union has been a leader in lobbying for a shorter week. According to Leonard Woodcock, former president of the UAW, "We should seek to cut hours for union members to increase the number of jobs available."[4] In their September 1976 contract negotiations, the UAW bargained for, and received, a shorter working year. Specifically, UAW members were granted 12 additional paid days off per year, in addition to the 33 they already had. The UAW also made it clear that they would give a high priority to the 32 hour workweek in the following year's contract negotiations. It should be noted, however, that the UAW is in a position to make such demands because of the highly automated nature of its industry and its strong economic position.

In a similar vein, the United Steelworkers of America is one of the first large organizations to adopt an employee sabbatical system. Their 1976–1977 Policy Statement, adopted by the International Wage Policy Committee, stated the following:

> It continues to be our belief that the most practical means of using collective bargaining to increase the job opportunities which are so needed in our two Nations is by negotiating a shorter work week without reduction in pay, accompanied by programs such as our extended vacation plans which result in a shorter work year. We assert that it is now time to move to a reduced work week with no loss of pay and without extending the normal work day.[5]

It should be noted here that the potential benefits of the shorter week are not confined to increasing employment levels. For the individual worker, the additional time for leisure, family activities, or moonlighting can be beneficial and has been responsible for the grass roots support this policy has received.

However, despite the support for the shorter workweek, certain unions and industries, as well as outside observers, disagree to some extent about its effectiveness. Economists, industry, and union representatives have attacked the shortened workweek on two fronts. First, most economists contend that over the long run, the cost of a shorter workweek, if not offset by increased productivity, would result in price rises, diminished demand, and further increases in unemployment. Some do admit, however, that the idea has value as a means of improving the predicted long-range unemployment problems.

Second, in rebutting the argument that increased automation leads to job losses, economists and others have pointed out that the total union work force in the automotive industry has remained static for years. The improvements in automation have offset the trend toward increasing absenteeism (whether authorized or not). For example, in 1970 General Motors found that on Mondays and Fridays the rate of daily absenteeism was as high as 10 percent of the work force. To avoid disruptions in the assembly process, two additional workers were required for every ten full-time jobs.[6]

Although the short week policy is not without controversy, it is clear that it has gained considerable support, and, further, that *it has serious implications for the adoption of flexitime.* Flexitime is viewed negatively by some unions because it may be considered a management compromise to a shorter workweek. In other words, unions feel that management may offer a rearranged schedule allowing employees to work fewer hours in one unit of time in exchange for more hours later, instead of granting them a permanent decrease in hours. Employee acceptance of and satisfaction with this "compromise" may delay, or even diminish, future chances for the shorter week.

In the context of employment levels, there is another aspect to flexitime which may create opponents. Because flexitime allows a better home-work fit, it may bring additional members to the work force who would normally be unable to work—specifically, women with families, the elderly, and students. While the benefits are significant for the individuals involved, the impact on the work force may be to increase unemployment. These individuals represent new entrants to the work force competing for an inadequate supply of jobs. Because these new entrants are less skilled and experienced, they may be willing to work for a lower salary than current jobholders, bringing down the salary level, increasing competition, and even decreasing job security for those currently employed at higher salaries. These are undesirable outcomes in terms of union objectives because they threaten the stable, skilled work force which is the foundation of the union movement.

Overtime

The establishment and maintenance of overtime premiums have always been an important focus of union concern and represent one of the most visible union achievements.

Overtime premiums were originally legislated as a means to actively discourage employers from requiring the employee to work hours beyond the normal workday. Union officials continue to oppose overtime on a regular basis as a reflection of their policy to maximize available jobs: regular overtime may imply the need for additional workers in the work area. On the other hand, they are extremely protective of hard-won overtime rights and view with suspicion, if not outright opposition, any suggestion which threatens these rights. Flexitime has been opposed on just this basis—that it decreases the need and frequency for overtime scheduling. For example, this attitude is expressed by Kenneth T. Blaylock, national president of the American Federation of Government Employees, in his statement before the Senate on the flexitime bill. While supporting flexitime in general, Blaylock commented:

> Our primary concern is that none of the rights American workers have fought for over the years, including the right to overtime pay after an eight hour day, be sacrificed in any effort to extend the scope of existing flexitime experiments.[7]

This policy is further supported by union employees, who view overtime pay as a supplement to their base pay, and would view its reduction because of flexitime as a loss of income.

This policy was reflected in the resistance by AFGE and other unions to the flexitime bill proposing the relaxation of these legal constraints to allow flexitime experimentation.

Flexitime threatens overtime payments not only because it extends the organization's workday—some unionists fear that management will attempt to pressure employees to arrange their work schedules in order to avoid having to pay overtime. An example is presented as a hypothetical case based on an actual situation in a British firm.[8]

> Employees in an office customarily work late Wednesday nights to accommodate a weekly rush of payroll work, but Mondays and Fridays are slack times. Before the introduction of flexitime, each worker put in 44 hours a week and was paid time-and-a-half for the four hours of overtime on Wednesday. Workers like long weekends, however, and so when flexitime was installed, most asked to have a portion of Monday or Friday off. Management agreed on the condition that the time be made up when the worker was needed—on Wednesdays. This was an entirely legitimate management policy, but it can be shown that most workers may have been worse off as a result.
>
> Assuming that each worker in this office made five dollars hourly, three alternatives need to be appraised. A: In the original situation, with 44 hours of work, everyone's weekly pay was $230 and all worked Wednesday nights but had a relatively easy time Mondays and Fridays. With flexitime the employer in effect offered the worker the following choice. B: In 40 hours of work for $200, the employee could work Wednesday nights and take either Monday morning or Friday afternoon off. Because overstaffing is eliminated on those days, however, the employee must exert himself more than before on the Mondays or Fridays he does work. C: Or, in 40 hours of work per week for $200 an employee could work a standard 8:00–4:30 five-day workweek, but again, because overstaffing is eliminated, each worker must exert himself more than before on Monday and Friday.
>
> Under flexitime, alternative A was no longer available to the worker, because the employer could meet his Wednesday night needs without offering overtime. Some workers, however, may well rank the three alternatives: A > B > C. These workers could be worse off under the flexitime system because their most preferred option is no longer available. In fact, where most employees have become dependent on overtime earnings to maintain their living standards, those made worse off by the system could constitute a majority of the work force.*

From the union perspective, flexitime may be opposed owing to overtime considerations.

Moonlighting

In their desire to maintain employment levels, some unions have taken positions against moonlighting, acting on the theory that an employee who holds two jobs is depriving an unemployed individual—especially one on the fringes of the labor force—of the opportunity to work. For example, the UAW has actively attempted to limit moonlighting by its own members, although this has been difficult to enforce. Flexitime has been criticized because it facilitates moonlighting by allowing the employee to schedule his hours to accommodate a second job. Some unions have placed themselves in an awkward situation, however, because the shorter workweek which they desire also encourages moonlighting. From this perspective, it is difficult to criticize flexitime.

*J.D. Owen, Flexitime: Some problems and solutions. *Industrial and Labor Relations Review,* 30: 157–158, January, 1977. Copyright © Cornell University. Used with permission.

Summary

In evaluating the union policies which hinder or limit flexitime implementation, one observes the genuine dilemma of union leadership trying to function in the current economy. Unions have focused on economic issues such as the maintenance and creation of jobs through a shorter week, limited overtime, and decreased moonlighting. This orientation toward the economic needs of the employee has taken precedence over quality of work life considerations such as flexible hours. According to one expert, "unions have been willing to experiment cautiously with quality of work life changes, but only if these are the side show. They will strongly resist any effort to move economic questions off center stage."[9] Thus, union leaders fear a quality of work life innovation such as flexitime not only because of its nontraditional nature but because they fear its implementation will impede or conflict with economic gains sought from management. The result of this strict economic policy is that individual interests may suffer. This can lead to differences of opinion between union members and union leadership, as, for example, the conflicting views on the purpose of overtime.

FLEXITIME AND UNIONS IN EUROPE

It is interesting to note that in Europe, where unemployment is much lower than in the United States, flexitime has been more favorably received and, in general, much more widely adopted. A group of union leaders who visited several countries in Europe to study alternative work patterns reported that, while the average number of weekly hours worked in European industry is greater than in the United States, flexitime is extensively utilized. For example, in Switzerland the typical workweek is still 45 hours, yet approximately 40 percent of the work force is on some form of flexitime.[10] This trend clearly reflects the different economic environments of the two countries. Because the employment rate is higher in the European countries, employers cannot easily expand their work force and, consequently, are not receptive to a reduction in work hours. On the other hand, European industry must be receptive to qualitative improvements in work life to maintain employees and to keep absenteeism and turnover to a minimum. Flexitime represents this type of qualitative alternative. In the United States, where there has been a surfeit of labor for the last 10 years, employers feel little incentive to offer qualitative improvements, and organized labor must place quantitative considerations as top priority.

Although many European unions view flexitime as a social benefit, chiefly because of reduced rush hour traffic congestion, there is some suspicion that flexitime is primarily benefiting management because of reduced tardiness and increased productivity.

In spite of these reservations, European unions are currently engaged in forming policies favoring flexitime, issuing specific bargaining guidelines, and adopting official positions on the issue. They have been forced into action by the popularity of flexitime and demands from workers at the local level—although these demands have at times conflicted with overall union policy. The involvement of European unions with the political system—in contrast to the United States, where union involvement in politics is usually confined to "bread and butter" issues—may have hastened the consideration of flexitime. In this respect, the European unions are now confronting issues which unions in the United States will have to deal with in the near future. The popularity and widespread implementation of flexitime in Europe has resulted in a work force educated in the concepts of alternative work schedules. As our work force becomes similarly educated, our unions will find themselves in a similar position.

AREAS OF AGREEMENT AND DISAGREEMENT BETWEEN MANAGEMENT AND LABOR

In a study completed by Katzell and Yankelovich,[11] labor-management relations were examined with respect to various aspects of productivity. Areas of agreement and disagreement between labor and management are summarized in the following lists.* In general, managers and union leaders agreed that improving the quality of working life was important and that cooperation between the two groups was possible, although union representatives tended to view management-initiated changes in these areas with suspicion.

Areas of Agreement

1.   Improving the quality of work life is a desirable management goal even if it doesn't increase productivity.

2.   Unions are suspicious of job enrichment but they will support it once they are confident that it isn't a productivity gimmick.

3.   It is possible for the union and management to cooperate on specific programs which will improve productivity.

4.   Workers who have experienced job enrichment almost invariably indicate greater satisfaction with their work.

5.   Unions are always suspicious of management sponsored programs for increasing productivity.

Areas of Disagreement

1.   By a greater than 2 to 1 margin over management, union leaders agree that the interests of management and workers are, by and large, in conflict.

2.   By an even greater margin, management assumes that unions are opposed to productivity improvements.

3.   Three times as many union leaders as managers make the assumption that few managers and supervisors are genuinely concerned about workers and their jobs.

4.   Union leaders hold the assumption that since jobs are scarce, a greater emphasis on productivity may jeopardize jobs.

It should come as no surprise, considering the nature of the management-union relationship, that union leaders felt that the interests of management and workers were in conflict. It is interesting that although managers did not agree with this conclusion, they did feel that unions were opposed to attempts at improving productivity, a primary management interest.

In a similar study, union activists were surveyed regarding their attitudes toward certain

*Adapted from Katzell, R., and Yankelovich, D. *Work, productivity and job satisfaction.* New York: Harcourt Brace Jovanovich, 1975. Copyright © 1975 New York University.

issues involving the work situation.[12] Specifically, the researchers sought to determine whether quality of work life issues were perceived as equal in importance to the more traditional economic issues. From a sample of 221 activists, they found that traditional bargaining issues such as earnings, fringe benefits, and job security were rated more highly in importance than quality of work issues, such as interesting work, supervisor ratings, and productivity. In general, they concluded that "there is a consensus among these union people concerning the importance of earnings, fringe benefits and safety, but much disagreement concerning the importance of issues such as 'interesting work' and 'better jobs.' " Perhaps even more disturbing are the union activists' perceptions concerning areas of common ground between management and the union. The data indicated that respondents tended to view quality of work life issues as areas where management and union objectives were completely different. On the other hand, except for earnings, activists reported similar objectives on the traditional issues. The researchers hypothesize that these results reflect the respondents' "lack of familiarity with the issues, uncertainty over the degree of potential conflict inherent in them, and apprehension concerning their personal and institutional impact."

The results from these two studies reflect the differing viewpoints and objectives of unions and management, but do encourage hope for cooperation between the two groups. However, it seems clear that unions will be hesitant to cooperate on joint ventures on quality of work life issues such as flexitime unless they are given a major role in determining the program specifications. In terms of productivity improvement or job enrichment programs, the major criteria for the successful implementation must be mutual trust and full acceptance of the objectives to be met. This requires some overlap in goals, or agreement that the particular goals or objective will be beneficial to both parties. To the extent that flexitime is viewed as a program for job enrichment, the implications are obvious. If such a program is introduced by management, it is likely to be viewed negatively by union representatives, especially if it is viewed as a "productivity gimmick" (see Table 15–1, item 2). Management must actively seek union opinion and participation in the earliest stages to overcome these forms of resistance. Furthermore, if the alternative work schedule is initiated by management, management must persuade the union that the objectives of the system are compatible with union goals. If this can be achieved, the agreement itself may represent a form of improvement in the quality of work life in terms of improved labor-management relations, in addition to being the means of securing the benefits offered by flexitime.

SURVEY RESULTS INDICATING UNION POSITIONS ON FLEXITIME

Other than magazine articles and a few policy statements, there has been little in the way of surveys of opinion on union positions toward flexitime in the United States. One exception, however, is the survey completed by J. Carroll Swart and Robert A. Quackenbush.[13] These researchers surveyed 42 union representatives (rate of return on their questionnaire was 22 percent). Of the 42 respondents, 23 of the unions were AFL-CIO–affiliated, and 19 were independent.* Although the small response rate raises questions about its representativeness, the survey does provide some indication of attitudes of union leadership toward

*In 1976 AFL-CIO claimed about 16,600,000 members, which constituted 74 percent of all union membership. This would appear to leave 26 percent unaffiliated with AFL-CIO.

flexitime. Three questions were posed regarding variations in work schedules, including the compressed workweek, flexitime with debiting and crediting options (carry-over), and flexitime without these options. Adding a fourth option of fixed hours, the researchers then asked the union representatives to rank their preferences. The results of the survey are described in the following section. Table 15-1 summarizes the data on the responses to the three questions.

1.   The first question (see Table 15-1, section I) represents union policies regarding the compressed workweek, in which overtime pay requirements apply only to hours worked in excess of 10 hours per day or 40 hours per week. It is interesting that the AFL-CIO affiliates tended to oppose the proposal, whereas independents were neutral or supported it. One might hypothesize that the AFL-CIO unions are less likely to consider alternatives which may threaten the overtime rights of their workers. Another possible explanation is that these unions may view the compressed week, like flexitime, as an undesirable compromise or trade-off to the shorter week and an acceptance of the status quo in terms of current hours worked per week.

2.   The second question asked for union views toward flexitime systems which allow the debiting and crediting of hours and in which overtime pay would be required only where the employer requests *in advance* additional work hours in excess of the standard number. Again, there was divergence of opinion between the AFL-CIO–affiliated unions and the independents. The AFL-CIO affiliates tended to oppose, while the nonaffiliates tended to support it. These findings reflect the same concerns as those reflected in the union reactions to question one. It seems that AFL-CIO affiliates are less willing to jeopardize overtime benefits for any form of trade-off, although they are clearly more receptive to this flexible scheme than to the compressed workweek, perhaps because it is less drastic in its reshuffling of the work schedule.

3.   The third question asked for union respondents' views toward flexitime programs which do not allow debiting or crediting, and in which existing overtime rules are not relaxed. Among the three systems, this received the most support from both the AFL-CIO affiliates and the independents; in fact, none of the independents opposed this option. Clearly this option is the least threatening to the unions surveyed. Even if this is the case, one must not overlook the fact that, for the AFL-CIO affiliates, the percentage opposing all of the options is still greater than the percentage in favor (see Table 15-1, section III). In fact, this is the case for all three of the proposals.

4.   Table 15-2 is a ranking of preferences by the AFL-CIO members, the independents, and their combined rankings. Added to the three options already described is a fourth option for fixed hours, in which overtime rules are not altered. Not surprisingly, considering the answers to the three questions above, there is little in common between the AFL-CIO affiliates' rankings and that of the independents. The AFL-CIO group ranked fixed hours as their first choice, while the independents ranked flexitime without debiting or crediting first. In general, it seems accurate to say that the unions avoid the options which would require a change in the overtime schedule. On the more promising side (for flexitime advocates), the flexitime scheme without debiting or crediting was ranked number one by the independents and number two by the AFL-CIO affiliates. In general, these results are consistent with

Table 15-1 Survey of Union Preferences*

Selection Alternatives	Compressed Workweek I			Flexitime with Debit/Credit II			Flexitime Without Debit/Credit III		
	AFL-CIO	Independents	Total	AFL-CIO	Independents	Total	AFL-CIO	Independents	Total
Oppose the program	74	5	43	65	21	45	35	0	19
Neither oppose nor support the program	26	63	43	22	32	26	39	47	43
Support the program	0	32	14	13	47	29	26	53	38

SOURCE: Swart, J. C., and Quackenbush, R. A. *Unions' views concerning alternative work schedules and proposals to alter federal overtime pay legislation.* Presented at the Industrial Relations Research Association Annual Winter Meeting, 1977, New York City. Used with permission.

* Total sample = 42 unions: AFL-CIO, N = 23; Independent union, N = 19. Figures are percentages of replies.

the general trends already observed: concern for protecting already established benefits—especially overtime rights—and avoidance of any scheme which would threaten other priorities, such as the shortened workweek. For instance, the rank of number one for fixed hours given by AFL-CIO affiliates may reflect a reluctance on the part of these unions to become involved in alternate schedules when top priority is creating and protecting jobs.

UNION CONCERNS ABOUT IMPLEMENTING FLEXITIME

Up till now, the policy issues relative to flexitime and the unions have been reviewed. Now some of the practical implications of implementing flexitime in a union environment will be considered.

Flexitime is subject to the same reservations and skepticism with which many management-oriented proposals are met, reflecting the traditional union-management antagonism. If flexitime is introduced by management, it is assumed by union members to be beneficial to management. Can it benefit the worker as well? Is the employee being taken advantage of by this new scheme? These reservations are reflected in the specific concerns expressed repeatedly by union members. These concerns include loss of overtime and paid time off, the use of time-recording systems, the exclusion of some groups from participation, and the level of union involvement in implementation and design. Each of these concerns is elaborated on in the following discussion.

A frequently expressed reason for opposing flexitime has been that it reduces overtime payments as well as paid time off to workers. One union official expressed his concern after a trip to Europe to investigate the possibilities of flexitime:

> There is no such thing as overtime with Flexitime. Workers who used to get a couple of hours off during the day, with pay, to visit a doctor, are no longer paid for those hours; with Flexitime, if you take a couple of days off because of a death in the family, you have to work 2 extra days to make up the time you lost.

As shown earlier, flexitime often reduces the amount of overtime worked per average worker. This, however, does not require the elimination of overtime, but rather, a careful scheme for determining when an overtime situation arises. Typically, the determination of extra hours worked is made by the employer instead of the employee, and overtime is defined as the number of hours worked in a day or week in excess of the standard. In the

Table 15-2   Ranking of Union Preferences for Four Alternative Work Schedules

Selection Alternatives	AFL-CIO	Independent
Fixed hours	1st	3rd
Flexitime with debiting and crediting options	3rd	4th
Flexitime without debiting and crediting options	2nd	1st
4-day, 40-hour workweek	4th	2nd

flexitime agreement negotiated by the Association of Scientific, Technical, and Management Staffs (a union) with two English insurance companies, the following detailed list of guidelines for the payment of overtime premiums was created:[14]

Guidelines for Overtime Payments

Overtime
In the first place, it should be reiterated that, where employees are asked to work longer than their standard hours, they should be compensated either by time off or payment: The Company has certainly no intention of using flexitime as a device for getting employees to work more than standard hours without compensation either in time or money. What remains to be defined, therefore, are the circumstances in which paid overtime is likely to be authorized. The following general guidelines are issued:

1. Paid overtime will normally be authorized only in advance, except in cases of extreme emergency.

2. It may be authorized for specific non-recurrent tasks of such magnitude as not to be coverable by the normal credit accumulation permitted under flexitime. (Such tasks could equally be requirements at short notice, a long term major project or a regular annual job beyond the normal capacity of the department or office.)

3. It may be authorized in an area where the work load is such that small, but constant, excess hours have to be worked leading to a steadily increasing credit beyond the flexitime rules. (Examples are departments or offices with shortages of staff or experience.)

4. The opinion of individual employees as to the necessity of overtime is not, in itself, sufficient and applications must be submitted formally to the official responsible.

5. It is not necessary for employees to have completed their standard hours for the period, plus the maximum credit hours before overtime can be authorized.

Concern was also expressed by this union about a decrease in paid time off for personal reasons. This, of course, will depend upon the individual organization and the agreement regarding personal leave. It is important to emphasize, however, that flexitime would not eliminate personal days for family emergencies or other problems of this nature; rather, it obviates the need to grant personal time off due to tardiness—because it eliminates the concept of tardiness itself.

One criticism related to the reduction in overtime is that of the intensification of work. For example, if overtime is reduced and productivity is increased under flexitime, one might conclude that employees are working harder. Such a generalization ignores other important factors. Some studies have reported that productivity has increased, but, for the most part, these increases have been attributed to decreased tardiness and absenteeism, better communication between employees and supervisors, and longer periods during the day without interruption (quiet time)—all factors which enhance employee effectiveness. Therefore, one cannot say that productivity, as a measure of output per unit time, has increased because of flexitime. What one can say is that output has increased because of the factors just described. Regardless of the cause of the increase in productivity, there is some argument to be made for employee participation in the benefits accruing to the organization.

Clearly, overtime and paid time off are major issues which must be resolved if flexitime is to be widely accepted within the union environment. Before this can happen, however, union leaders must evaluate what the true impact of flexitime on overtime and time off is likely to be for their organization, and what the accompanying benefits of flexitime will be. Most important, these issues must be confronted by both union and management representatives and resolved in the planning stages before effective implementation can occur.

Another aspect of flexitime which has been of concern to unions is the use of time-recording mechanisms. The punch clock has traditionally been the stigma of the blue-collar worker. Unions have expressed the opinion that the use of time-recording mechanisms may further widen the gap between white- and blue-collar workers, especially if time-recording mechanisms are required only for blue-collar or nonmanagement employees. The implication, unions feel, is one of untrustworthiness. Interestingly enough, union leaders have also noted that time recording required of white-collar workers is "an insidious encroachment on the rights and prerogatives that the office workers traditionally have enjoyed."[15]

This concern is certainly a valid one, and can be dealt with in two ways. First, in many flexitime systems, particularly those simple forms which do not allow banking of hours, a manual form of time recording is employed which relies on self-reporting by employees. Second, if time-recording devices are used in the more complex forms of flexitime, in which manual recording becomes difficult, they do not have to be of the punch clock variety. Cumulative recording devices are available which minimize the intrusion on one's privacy (see Chapter 19 for a further discussion), and this is, in fact, considered a helpful source of information for the employee as well as employer. Also, under certain situations in which debiting and crediting are allowed, manual time recording can become quite complicated and cumbersome. Finally, if time-recording devices are to be installed, they should be required for *all* employees on flexitime, regardless of rank in the organizational hierarchy.

A difficult and somewhat sensitive problem is posed by employees who cannot participate in a flexitime program because of scheduling limitations. Some unions have recommended that since such employees are prevented from realizing the benefits of flexitime, they should be paid a premium on top of their base salary. This would obviously have to be negotiated as part of the union contract. However, the employees should not have the *choice* between the premium or flexitime. One should also note that this recommendation from the unions represents a contradiction: while taking a position that flexitime is disadvantageous to the worker, they are requesting compensatory pay for those who cannot participate in the program!

Once the union has decided to accept the flexitime concept, a most important concern becomes that of union—or employee—involvement at the initial stages of design, implementation, and incorporation of the system into the contract. From the point of view of organizational change, any new system is more likely to be successful if those to be affected are included in the process of change. The systems that have been most successful in the European experience are those in which the employees were initially receptive, and in which employees and their unions participated directly in developing the programs. Along the same lines, several unions suggested that alternate work patterns should be started with small scale pilot programs before extending the system throughout the organization. This is certainly consistent with appropriate implementation practices (see Chapter 17).

Union spokesmen have also emphasized the importance of including flexitime in the collective bargaining agreement. This is necessary, both to protect the worker (and the employer) from abuse of the system, and to provide guidelines for conflict resolution. According to John Zalusky of the AFL-CIO,

> There will . . . be a need for contract language to ensure that the flexitime schedule is at the employees' option rather than his immediate supervisor's need. In addition, the union will also want some means of dealing with conflicting rights of workers to exercise the flexitime option, and some assurance that core time will be fixed.[16]

Note that this statement runs counter to the policy of some nonunionized organizations (e.g., SmithKline), which emphasize that the supervisor must have the option to dictate scheduling needs when work loads demand it. This is a possible area of conflict which will have to be carefully resolved for successful implementation.

This chapter concludes with a list of considerations for negotiations adapted and edited from different sources.[17] For the most part, these guidelines are useful, commonsense suggestions for collective bargaining issues. Patsy Fryman has concluded:

> Much will depend on the union's assessment of the employer and his motives. What certainly is true is that the trend towards increased flexibility in patterns of working hours is likely to continue and needs to be kept under firm control.
>
> It can also be seen from the foregoing that FWH should not be viewed in isolation from the developments taking place in management control techniques generally. Employers do not introduce change simply for the workers' benefit, and the need is for trade union representatives to assess carefully the relative advantages and disadvantages to their members. Effective negotiations depend on clear-sighted appraisal of all the circumstances.[18]

Fryman's conclusions are certainly consistent with the research studies presented on management-labor relations. They underline the critical nature of union involvement and reinforce the need for participation in the decision-making and implementation process, if a flexitime system is to be successful.

Considerations for Negotiation

1. FWH should not be introduced unilaterally by management. Union involvement is mandatory at the earliest stages if full cooperation is to be achieved.

2. The individual's right to choose his or her starting and finishing times should be made clear. Instances, *if any,* where management has the prerogative to dictate start or finish times must be carefully defined. In general, unions want to include contract language that assures that employees will not be coerced into electing schedules designed to satisfy production rather than personal needs.

3. There should be a limitation on the number of credit/debit hours in the settlement period. A good guide might be 15 hours/month or 5 hours/week. Excessive hours could have injurious effects on health.

4. Some collective bargaining agreements include higher rates of compensation for work performed after a given hour in the evening or on weekends. Employers are unlikely to establish systems that permit employees to choose these hours if such premiums apply.

5. Can union business, such as union meetings, be conducted during core time when all are present?

6. It may be necessary to introduce FWH on a group basis. Where this is the case, agreement on starting and finishing times should be agreed upon within the group whenever possible.

7. In the past, contracts frequently called for paid time off to vote, keep medical and dental appointments, or attend to other personal business that could not be conducted outside of working hours. The extent to which these privileges will continue under flexitime must be negotiated.

8. Inevitably, the nature of certain jobs prevents some employees from participating in a flexible hours program. Do these workers deserve something like a shift differential because their working conditions, relative to those in other parts of the organization, have been diminished?

9. In order to give maximum flexibility to individuals, and at the same time maintain production or service, it may be necessary for workers on flexible hours to cover for one another. To what extent will employees be allowed to work outside their job classification?

10. Flexitime often results in increased productivity because of decreased absenteeism and tardiness, improved morale, or more efficient scheduling. Will employees share in these gains, either through increased leisure, higher wages or a profit-sharing system?

11. Many employees object to time clocks—yet flexitime necessitates a time-keeping system that not only informs nonexempt employees of how many more hours they need to work in order to meet contract requirements but also maintains records sufficient to meet the requirements of wage and hour laws. Whether conventional time clocks, automatic time-recording devices, or manual systems are used is a matter for negotiation.

NOTES

1. Tannenbaum, A. S. Unions. In J. G. March (Ed.), *Handbook of organizations.* Chicago: Rand McNally, 1965.

2. Zalusky, J. Shorter hours—The steady gain. *AFL-CIO American Federationist,* January 1978.

3. Economy will force new limits on work week, UAW aide says. *Business Insurance,* October 31, 1977.

4. UAW's bargaining ploy—Cut hours to make jobs. *Iron Age,* February 9, 1976.

5. United Steelworkers of America, 1976–1977 International Wage Policy Statement and Collective Bargaining Program. Pittsburgh, Pa., 1976.

6. Gooding, J. *The job revolution.* New York: Walker, 1972.

7. Blaylock, K. T. Statement in hearing before the Committee on Governmental Affairs, United States Senate, 95th Congress, on S.517, S.518, H.R. 784, HR. 10126, pp. 220–224.

8. Owen, J. D. Flexitime: Some problems and solutions. *Industrial and Labor Relations Review, 30,* No. 2, January 1977.

9. Strauss, G. Managerial practices. In J. R. Hackman and J.L. Suttle (Eds.), *Improving life at work. Behavioral science approaches to organizational change.* California: Goodyear Publishing, 1977, pp. 297–363.

10. Miller, J. *Innovations in working patterns.* Report of the U.S. Trade Union Seminar on Alternative Work Patterns in Europe, Washington, D.C., 1978.

11. Katzell, R., and Yankelovich, D. *Work, productivity and job satisfaction.* New York: Harcourt Brace Jovanovich, 1975.

12. Kochan, T. A., Lipsky, D. B., and Dyer, L. Collective bargaining and the quality of work: The views of local union activists. In *Proceedings of the 27th Annual Winter Meeting of the Industrial Relations Research Association,* San Francisco, December 28–29, 1974.

13. Swart J. C., and Quackenbush, R.A. Union's views concerning alternative work schedules and proposals to alter federal overtime pay legislation. Industrial Relations Research Association Annual Winter Meeting, 1977, New York.

14. Miller, op. cit.

15. Miller, op. cit.

16. J. L. Zalusky, *Alternative work schedules: A labor perspective.* Paper presented to the National Conference on Alternative Work Schedules, March 1977. Also cited in *The Journal of the College and University Personnel Association,* 1977, *28,* No. 3.

17. Miller, op. cit. Nollen S.D., and Martin V. H. *Alternative work schedules.* Part 1: *Flexitime.* AMACOM Survey Report, 1978.

18. Ibid.

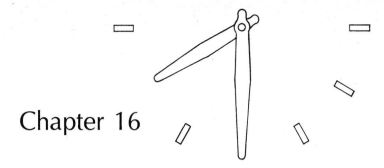

Chapter 16

Women at Work: Employment Trends and the Potential of Flexible Schedules

Flexible working hours can significantly influence family life and traditional male-female roles. More particularly, flexitime has specific implications for the dual role of women at home and in the work place. This chapter evaluates the implications of flexitime for women in terms of its advantages and disadvantages. Before proceeding further with this discussion, however, it is important to delineate a broader perspective on women in the labor force. Therefore, the first section of this chapter is devoted to the examination of recent trends in labor force participation rates of women, and the explanation of some of the reasons for these trends.

WOMEN IN THE LABOR FORCE

Demographics

In recent years, there has been substantial growth in female participation in the labor force. Some interesting statistics reflect this growth:

In 1977, women represented approximately 41 percent (39.8 million employees) of all jobholders in the United States—double the percentage in 1920.[1]

On the average, 45 percent of all women age 20 years or older were included in the labor force during 1977, compared to 76 percent of all men age 20 years or older.[2]

In 1976, wives were working in 49 percent of all families with husbands present.

In 1976, 72 percent of all working women had full-time jobs.[3]

In 1975, women within the labor force included 57 percent of all single women, 73 percent of those divorced or separated, 43 percent of those who were married with husbands present, and 25 percent of those who were widowed.

The rate of change in the number of females in the labor force between 1960 and 1974 was greatest in the married category—the number of entrants has tripled since 1940.[4]

Approximately 33 percent of all women with preschool-age children and 50 percent of all women with school-age children were working in 1977. This has doubled in the past 25 years.[5]

Increases in the participation rate of married women with children has surpassed the rate of increase for all wives and for wives with no children under 18. This trend is particularly significant for women with children under 6 years of age.[6]

These figures are intended to describe some of the important characteristics of women at work and the extent and nature of their participation in the work force. It is clear that female involvement in the work force is *neither* short-term *nor* capricious. Women are making serious commitments to pursue careers outside the home, even when preschool-age children are present. Proportionately more married women are entering the work force, and, in general, the ratio of working women to working men is approaching unity.

Naturally, this growth in labor force participation by women has had a significant impact on our economy and, as will be discussed at length in a later section, has been reflected in far-reaching changes in our cultural and social values. Values within organizations have also changed, and will continue to change as women attain higher levels of responsibility in traditionally male-dominated jobs.

Additional Questions

The late Hubert Humphrey has been quoted as saying, "One of the richest, under-utilized resources in America is the talent of its women. And this nation has for many years squandered this talent in shameful fashion." The truth of this statement is only too clear if one evaluates the occupational distribution of women in the work force. Of the women working, 5.5 percent are managers or administrators, compared to 15 percent of working men; 32 percent hold clerical jobs, compared to 6.4 percent of men; 1.4 percent hold craft-oriented positions, compared to 32.3 percent of men; and 21.3 percent are in service industries, compared to 7 percent of men.[8] Men have traditionally dominated engineering, medicine, law, industrial equipment sales, and other high-paying jobs.

When one compares the *distribution* of women in the work force in light of the number of women entering the job market in recent years (as described in the data presented in the previous section), the validity of Senator Humphrey's statement is apparent. It is important for management personnel in business organizations to understand not only how these statistics reflect the composition of the labor force but also the reasons for this state of affairs, if they are to fully utilize and benefit from the entrance and rise of women in the labor market. Specific questions which must be considered include the following: How many women who would like to work are not working and why? What conditions would facilitate their working? What problems do working women face? Would flexible working hours provide solutions to some of these problems?

Answers to these questions will help to determine the full impact of the participation of women in the labor force and to identify those organization and job conditions which can best serve the special needs of this group.

Unfortunately, only isolated studies are available concerning the number of women who wish to work outside the home but are unable to do so. Two such studies are briefly presented here. The first, a survey conducted in 1968, estimated that among unemployed housewives 18 to 49 years of age, 20 percent would unconditionally accept a part-time job if such were available. Some 47 percent of the women in this age group said they would accept part-time work if child-care facilities were adequate. Less than 10 percent stated a preference for full-time over part-time work.[9]

The second study, citing population survey data from 1967, found that 9 percent of women not in the labor force desired a regular job.[10] Of this group, 30 percent described family-related responsibilities and 12 percent cited child care as the primary factors preventing them from working. Among the other factors cited by these women as reasons for not joining the paid labor force at that time were: personal reasons (7.9 percent), health (16.4 percent), school (14.7 percent), intention to seek work soon (6.2 percent), and belief that it would be impossible to find work (13.4 percent).

Although some of these categories are ambiguous, it is clear that work force participation by women ten years ago might have been significantly greater if there had been job opportunities, adequate child care facilities, and ways to accommodate individuals with roles both at home and at work. It is in these areas that many changes have been occurring since 1967, resulting in the dramatic influx of women into the labor market in recent years.

REASONS FOR INCREASED FEMALE PARTICIPATION IN THE WORK FORCE

Changes in Value Systems

During the last decade there have been cultural and social transformations in the United States which have significantly altered attitudes toward women in the work force. In the past, "a women's place was in the home." She was (and often still is) encouraged, through an elaborate socialization process, to remain passive, nonassertive, other-directed, and nurturing. Her real worth was frequently measured by her attractiveness to the opposite sex.

This socialization process was reinforced and extended through the mass media—radio, television, literature, magazines, movies, advertising—which extolled the virtues of homemaking, child rearing, house beautification, cleaning, cooking, washing, and diapering.[11] All this was in the name of "convenient social virtue," which ascribed merit to any pattern of behavior, "however uncomfortable for the individual involved, that serves the comfort or well-being of, or is otherwise advantageous for, the more powerful members of the community."[12] Thus, "convenient social virtue" resulted in relegating women to domestic, menial, and personal service. In short, being a virtuous woman was synonymous with being a good homemaker.

Though discouraged from doing so, a woman could work if she had no other source of income; financial need was the only real excuse for not staying in the home. Yet, even with this excuse, working women were often considered less than virtuous! In contrast, the traditional work ethic places men in the role of provider. Masculinity is measured in terms of economic success. Failure as a provider could lead not only to poverty but also to social ostracism, divorce, and other personal disgrace.

However, in recent years a reduction in overall economic insecurity has accompanied a lessening of the guilt and fears caused by these role distinctions. Emphasis is now being placed on quality of living, on independence, and on flexibility in lifestyle. As a consequence, new cultural values and norms are developing, a result of which has been greater acceptance of working women, whether they are working for economic reasons or for self-fulfillment, whether they are single or married, whether they have children or are childless. In addition, men who choose to assist in child-rearing and homemaking activities are also receiving greater acceptance, making it easier for more women to work.

Changes in Role Stereotypes at Work

Not only have women had to contend with stereotypes in the home, but those women who did work have had to contend with a long list of stereotypes regarding their roles at work. To name only a few, men are intellectually superior, more emotionally stable, inherently more assertive, more faithful and loyal to organizations and to each other. Men value achievement, promotion, and meaningful work more than women do. In contrast, women are less career-oriented, less mature, less career-mobile, less assertive, less involved in the organization, and less willing to work long hours.[13]

Through their work performance, women are gradually dispelling some of these stereotypes, but the process is a long one. Helping to discredit these stereotypes are studies published by several organizations which set out to scientifically measure differences between men and women in terms of attitudes, aptitudes, and job performance. Such psychological research has failed to support the existence of the characteristics described by stereotypes. There are, of course, certain aptitudes and personality dimensions that differ between men and women (some as a result of socialization processes), but the work place stereotype of a typical man as compared to a typical woman is now becoming meaningless.[14]

One piece of research emanates from the Human Engineering Laboratory of the Johnson O'Connor Research Foundation. Since 1922, this foundation has been involved in a program of inherent aptitude assessment and measurement of acquired knowledge. During the past 50 years, it has measured the differences in the level of ability between men and women in a wide variety of areas including analytical reasoning, foresight, inductive reasoning, number memory, objective personality, and subjective personality. They have found *no* discernible sex difference. There was also no discernible difference in acquired knowledge, as measured by tests of English vocabulary. Women excelled in finger dexterity (handling, demonstrating, and assembling), verbal persuasion, abstract visualization, and accounting aptitude. Men excelled in physical strength, as measured by grip, and in structural visualization (demonstrated by assembly of three-dimensional puzzles). The conclusion which can be drawn from this research is that no occupation can be considered the *exclusive* prerogative of either sex, based on aptitudes.[15]

Another study investigated male-female differences in organizational behavior.[16] In the organization studied, no sex differences were found in career orientation, career priority, career mobility, career-family conflicts, job assertiveness, willingness to travel, and willingness to work overtime. Women in the study were found to be more likely to set career goals, and more likely than men to use mentors and role models. Findings such as these clearly contradict the traditional role stereotypes for women in business.

There is one area which warrants more extensive research—comparison of aptitude and performance between male and female managers and executives. Here, sufficient information is not yet available, since, in the past, few women have been given the opportunity to advance into these organizational levels. In the future, such research will be a significant factor in determining the extent of occupational and hierarchical segregation which will persist in organizations.

Women's Movement

Any discussion regarding changes in sex roles must pay attention to the contribution of the women's liberation movement and the growing influence of women's organizations on academic, professional, and community institutions. Actions by these groups have increased social awareness of sex discrimination and stereotyping, and have provided support to women trying to eliminate traditional sexual barriers. These organizations have taught women that they no longer need to feel guilty for working and no longer need to feel that the only justification for work is financial need. The implications of this are significant: women can feel free to pursue careers instead of jobs in which the only source of motivation is economic return.

Higher Education Levels

Perhaps as a result of changing cultural values, many women are seeking higher levels of education with the intent of entering the labor force at managerial and professional levels. Between 1960 and 1972, the number of women attending college rose from 1.2 million to 3.5 million. The Wharton School of Business has recently reported an increase in female enrollments from 5 percent to 26 percent over the last five years.[17] At New York University Graduate School of Business Administration, women composed approximately 9.7 percent of the total enrollment to the MBA program in 1970. In 1978, the percentage was 41 percent. Such trends have been noted throughout the country and reflect the career aspirations drawing women into professional, technical, and managerial jobs in increasing numbers.

Unfortunately, higher education levels have not always meant full utilization of this investment in human capital. *Human capital investment* is an economic theory which considers education and training as an investment in the individual, contributing to that person's worth in terms of potential productivity. From this point of view, women with college or graduate degrees who do not work or who are underemployed in relation to their educational level are wasting valuable resources or assets—valuable not only to themselves, but to society.

Decline in the Birth Rate

Also contributing to the rising rate of female involvement in the work force is the decline in birth rates during the last 15 to 20 years.[18] With fewer preschool children in the home, women have had greater opportunity to work. In addition, expansion of day care facilities and the resulting lower cost of day care are contributing factors.

Higher Divorce Rates

Changes in attitudes toward family life have also had an effect on employment participation rates. Not only are more women remaining single, but divorce rates have been climbing rapidly. The incidence of first marriages ending in divorce for women in their early twenties tripled from 2.1 percent in 1940 to 6.3 percent in 1970. For women in their early thirties, the rate rose from 6.3 percent in 1940 to 15.8 percent in 1970. As a result of such trends, increasing numbers of single or divorced women (many with children) are finding it necessary to support themselves through employment outside the home.

Legal Action

In keeping with the changes discussed above, various federal, state, and local laws have been enacted which are aimed at significantly improving employment opportunities and job conditions for women. Several of the federal laws are briefly described below:

Title VII of the Civil Rights Act of 1964.   This law prohibits discrimination on the basis of sex by employers of 15 or more employees, by employment agencies, and by labor unions. (State and local governments are considered employers.) Discrimination is prohibited in hiring, firing, compensation, fringe benefits, training, promotions, and all other terms and conditions of employment.

Equal Pay Act (1963).   This law makes it illegal to discriminate in the payment of wages on the basis of sex for equal work on jobs which require equal skill, effort, and responsibility under similar working conditions. This law applies to state and local government workers as well as to private sector employees.

Executive Order 11246 (1965).   This order imposes upon federal government contractors and subcontractors obligations parallel to those imposed upon employers under Title VII. In addition, there is a requirement that contractors take affirmative action to ensure equal employment opportunity.

Legal action taken under these and other laws in recent years has resulted in increased opportunity for female participation in the work force. Great strides have also been made towards providing nondiscriminatory terms and conditions of employment for women, once employed.

Also worth noting here is a recently enacted provision of the tax law which expanded the tax credit for child care expenses for working parents who qualify. Although its impact is yet to be measured, this law seems likely to encourage more women to work.

Inflation

One last factor which has received great attention in the 1970s is inflation. In an effort to keep pace with inflation and maintain real family income, more wives are entering the work force. By 1975, full-time working wives were providing 38 percent of family income (in families in which both husband and wife were employed). Wives working less than full time were providing 29 percent of their family income. One author claims that women entering the work force account for the "vital margin between insolvency and solvency."[19] It has been suggested that the purchasing power generated by the additional work force can make the difference for thousands of businesses on the verge of bankruptcy.

THE DECISION TO ENTER THE WORK FORCE

It should now be clear that the influx of women into the labor force is an important social and economic phenomenon. It demands a reevaluation of organizational practices and management policies as they affect and are affected by women's decisions to pursue careers. Challenges arising from these trends must be anticipated and solutions must be developed which will help improve the quality of work life. The relationship between work and home responsibilities of women must be given careful and thoughtful attention.

Kreps has investigated these relationships in a study of 1,600 wives. Three significant variables were identified which affect wives' decisions to work, namely, income of husband, wife's education level, and age. Presence of preschool children was accounted for in the age criterion. This study found that, generally, the higher the husband's income, the less a wife tends to seek work (although this decision is becoming less sensitive to income level). Also, the higher the education level of a woman, the greater her likelihood of working. The presence of preschool age children was found to discourage work, but this is less the case now as younger women with better education credentials enter the labor force.[20]

Other variables cited by the Kreps study included illness or unemployment of a husband, size of town of residence, race, a husband's attitude toward working mothers, whether a husband is self-employed, the size of a family, and the number of children in college. In addition, this study determined that participation rates and work life patterns of single, separated, widowed, or divorced women are quite different from those of married women.

A more comprehensive discussion of these variables is not intended here. However, the research has been briefly reviewed in order to emphasize the complexity of the decision-making process which leads women into the work force. The choice made by women is dependent upon many conditions or variables which differ from individual to individual. Nevertheless, common to most analyses has been an emphasis upon family-related factors —marital status, number and ages of children, family income, and presence of husband in the home—in women's decisions to enter or not to enter the work force. Sweet provides a classification of the personal criteria determining the commitment to work, based on various conditions of the woman's life stage and family situation:[21]

1. Enabling conditions, including number of children, ages of children, expectations of additional children, and current pregnancy

2. Facilitating conditions, including education and previous work experience

3. Precipitating conditions, including income of husband and wife, attitudes, life satisfaction, and need for accomplishment.

Other factors, not related to personal criteria, also influence a woman's decision to enter the work force. These include changing societal values and norms, the economic positions of various industries and business organizations, and government, as represented by its legislation. Each of these factors influences women to a varying degree in their decision making, thus influencing the ultimate composition of the work force. These societal factors and their impact on the decision-making process are summarized in Figure 16-1.

ADVANTAGES OF FLEXITIME FOR WOMEN

In this section, some generally accepted benefits which flexible working hours offer to women are reviewed. Although many of these advantages apply only to specific groups, one should not discount their overall significance. Taken together, the groups affected by these advantages constitute a broad spectrum of the female population.

Parent-child Relationships

Although advantages of flexitime apply to most groups of women, they *particularly* apply to women with children and to single parents, male or female. These individuals face limited alternatives. The ability to tailor individualized working schedules can help these individuals

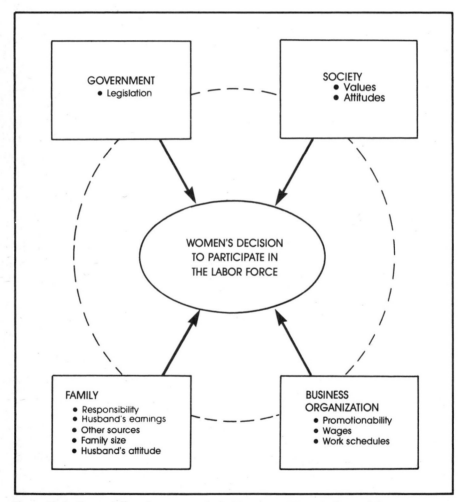

Figure 16–1   Factors influencing a woman's decisions to participate in the work force.

minimize the stress typically associated with juggling child-rearing and employment responsibilities. With flexitime, working mothers can adjust their time off to more closely coincide with that of their school age children, and they can be more readily available to take children to appointments, school functions, and club activities without being late or missing time from work.

If flexitime is available to both husband and wife, each parent can take a more active, balanced role in child-rearing activities. It is possible that such dual participation could result in an improved quality of family life. For example, a recent evaluation of the flexitime system in effect at the First National Bank of Boston suggested that flexitime substantially improved quality of life, especially among personnel with dependents.[22] Some 73 percent of employees with dependents as compared to 50 percent of employees without dependents indicated they enjoyed or accomplished more during leisure time; and most respondents reported more time available for family activities.

Child-Care Costs.   In addition, the potential exists through FWH for reducing child-care costs. Working parents, both on flexitime, can choose to stagger starting and quitting times to provide child care in the early mornings and late afternoons, reducing the hours that children must be cared for outside the home.

Single Parents.   Single parents face even greater need for flexibility in scheduling work and family activities, as they have no spouse with whom to share child-rearing demands. This is a growing problem. From 1962 to 1973, the number of women without husbands and with preschool-age children increased by 60 percent. In fact, approximately 17 percent of all children live with a single parent, most with their mothers.[23] In these cases, flexibility to deal with family crises, with minimum interference from job responsibilities, is of paramount importance.

The British Survey.   Though further quantitative research is needed in the area of flexitime and child care, some European studies reinforce the advantages outlined above. In a 1975 survey in two British government offices with flexitime systems, 100 employees were asked to indicate from a list of 18 different advantages those which they found applicable to their circumstances. Women with children under age 16 listed the highest number of advantages. These women indicated that they obtained more advantages from flexible working hours than did other categories of office workers.

Social Security Administration Survey.   In a study conducted at the Social Security Administration in Baltimore, Maryland, 350 employees in lower-grade clerically-oriented jobs were interviewed. The average subject was female, 25 to 30 years of age, single, widowed, or divorced, and a mother of 2 children between 5 and 12 years of age. Of the respondents, 90 percent reported greater ability to spend time with their families under flexitime. Of those with major responsibility for the care of one or more children, 82 percent said flexitime made caring for these children easier.[24]

Welfare

Dissatisfaction with work hour patterns may contribute to higher welfare rolls.[25] Poorly educated and underprivileged women on welfare may be discouraged from trying to locate employment when faced not only with the difficulty of finding any job but with the added conflict resulting from rigid working hours and home/family demands.

Career Continuity, Wage Differentials, and Reentry

Women should be able to compete more effectively with men under flexitime than under traditional work schedules. An October 1976, U.S. Department of Labor report indicated a substantial earnings gap between working women and working men.[26] According to the report, the average college-educated woman earns approximately the same wage as a male with an eighth grade education. A primary reason cited for this gap are patterns of discontinuous work related to child rearing. Interrupted careers make women less desirable in the job market and less likely to be considered in terms of career advancement. Flexible working hours may aid these women, during child-rearing years, to maintain continuous employment patterns. Perhaps as important, as a result of more continuous patterns of employment, the organization may begin to view the woman as a career-oriented employee.

For those women who do leave the labor force to start families, flexitime can aid them in returning to work more quickly if they choose to do so. With flexible working hours, these women may reenter the work force and still fulfill their child-rearing responsibilities without the constraints of rigid work schedules. This is an important aspect for their career development. *Career* is emphasized here. Many women have waited till their late twenties or early thirties to have their first child. After a brief hiatus, many expect to return to their careers.

Ms. Barbara Preiskel, a successful executive and board member of two large companies, stressed the importance of flexible scheduling for women with families in her comment to *The New York Times,* "A woman who can work only part time today may be a leader of industry in later years."[27]

Continuous employment may be evaluated from another point of view. According to a study conducted a few years ago by the Commission on Population Growth and the American Future, a mother, on average, would forgo $100,000 in earnings by staying out of the labor force until a child is 14. Of course, this varies with education level, ranging from $75,000 for a mother with elementary education, to $155,000 for a mother with postgraduate education.

Recruiting and Utilization of the Labor Pool.

More women are continuing their education in universities and professional schools and entering jobs which were previously the exclusive domain of men. These well-educated and qualified women will select companies which offer them the most opportunities to balance their various roles and responsibilities.

Corporations under pressure to meet the legal requirements imposed by various antidiscrimination laws will be in a far better competitive position to attract these women if they can offer options such as flexitime. Not only will recruiters have a more qualified applicant pool from which to choose, they will be hiring women whose job performance may be enhanced through personal flexibility.

Education

The educational advantages of flexitime are especially applicable to women. By making it possible to attend classes held during hours which may conflict with work schedules, flexitime can assist those women who are locked into low-paying, routine jobs because of a lack of vocational skills, as well as those who wish to obtain advanced professional degrees. With growing numbers of women returning to school after child rearing, flexitime may create conditions which allow them to simultaneously pursue advanced education and develop a career.

Community Participation

As women gain more influence, they are becoming more involved in community activities, and it is in the best interest of business and society at large to encourage this participation. One does not have to look far to find active groups of women organized to help improve education, employment opportunities, child-care facilities, government programs, and the cultural environment. In business and professional organizations, women are offering new perspectives and insights. Flexitime will aid in creating conditions which encourage this social awareness and contribution by working women.

Value of Work

An in-depth discussion of flexitime advantages specifically for women inevitably leads to the never-ending debate: to work or not to work. Although this is an important problem, a solution, if indeed there is one, will not be proposed here. However, there are two points on this topic which are important with respect to flexitime. The first is that flexible hours provide conditions which enable women who wish to work to enter the work force. To some of these women, a profession is not simply valued for economic reasons. It is valued because it contributes to their self-realization, personal development, and integration into society, and offers them interest, variety, responsibility, and an opportunity to contribute to society.

The second point is that work, for some women, is a type of insurance against separation, widowhood, or divorce—a chance to escape the degradation of dependency upon husband, family, or society, an opportunity to gain confidence and remain independent. Flexitime provides the opportunity to women who hold these values to act on them without sacrificing other responsibilities important to their lives.

DISADVANTAGES OF FLEXIBLE WORKING HOURS FOR WOMEN

After this overview of the benefits offered by FWH to women, it is fitting now to address some of the disadvantages or apprehensions which have been voiced concerning this subject.

Role Conflict

There can be no doubt that coordinating family responsibilities and career activities presents a challenge. To manage successfully, women must learn to carefully judge priorities among work, family, community, and leisure activities. This requires creativity, judgment, energy, and opportunity.

The well-being of working women who must juggle many responsibilities has become a subject of concern. Conflict appears inevitable. Home-related tasks and voluntary activities are generally still more acceptable for women than work and consequently cause less stress.

Women involved in these activities receive external role support, admiration, and intrinsic satisfaction. On the other hand, working women still venture outside traditional roles and may encounter increased role conflict, time pressure, prejudice, and discrimination.[28]

However, even with these conflicts, women working in full-time jobs are more satisfied with their work than full-time homemakers or part-time employees.[29] Also, women with no children who work full time are more satisfied with their health and physical condition than part-time workers or homemakers.[30] They also found that nonwork activities such as hobbies were the only areas in which full-time working mothers tended to be less satisfied.

Based on these studies, it appears that while working women may be under greater stress from role conflict, they may also derive compensating satisfaction in some dimensions of their lives from being employed. The overall impact of these influences on working women's health and well-being may be only minor. And flexitime may help alleviate stress by making coordination of the activities easier.

Overload

Trying to perform in more than one role may result in overload. FWH may draw some women into the work force with unrealistic expectations and aspirations. Women may initially assume too much responsibility without balancing or equalizing their roles and work load, thus experiencing greater tension, frustration, and physical exhaustion—the higher the expectations, the higher the risk of failure. Willingness of men to share household and child-rearing responsibilities when wives are working may help alleviate this problem.

The following question must be considered: With flexible working hours available, will women be pressured by family, friends, or society into working outside the home when, in fact, they are not prepared or willing to do so? Or stated another way, will expectations concerning possible higher real income create role conflict at home for women who choose not to work? Only more experience with flexitime and further research will adequately determine answers to this question.

Oversupply of Labor

A third apprehension voiced is that an oversupply of labor (especially in certain geographical areas) will result from the widespread implementation of flexitime. This could occur either by attracting more people (especially women) to the job market or by creating conditions which encourage moonlighting.[31] Studies of multiple jobholding indicate that workers on nonstandard hours are more likely to seek or hold more than one job.

Family Acceptance of Working Wife

If a man views work as his special sacrifice to his family to provide for their livelihood, then a working wife may present a threat. "If a man's role as he-who-makes-sacrifices-for-his-kid's-education-and-his-family's-material-well-being, grows less vital, the whole fragile bargain threatens to break down."[32] If the man cannot be the sole provider, sacrifice becomes meaningless.

These conclusions are supported by research which suggests that blue-collar workers suffer more discontent when other family members also work.[33] Findings such as these lead to the suspicion that working class men (blue-collar) may be less amenable to wives working than professional men. A class distinction may therefore exist regarding acceptance and use of flexible working hours.

Other Apprehensions

As women enter the work force under flexitime programs, they will have the least seniority. This situation may result in less than optimal working hours where group scheduling is necessary or choice of hours is based on seniority. Further, as new employees, they may be first to be laid off—last in, first out.

CONCLUSIONS

In this chapter, the composition of the female labor force, participation rates, cultural and social factors influencing these rates, and some specific reasons why women choose to work or not to work have been discussed. The patterns and trends noted may be summarized as follows:

1. Cultural values and norms, including the institutions of marriage and the family, are changing, creating norms more supportive of working women.

2. The government has enacted laws which have helped in securing equal opportunities for women in the work force.

3. More women desire to work, and are doing so.

These trends strike an optimistic note: it is becoming easier and more acceptable for women to seek employment. However, traditional customs and practices which take a male-dominated work force for granted persist within organizations: specifically, little flexibility in job design, highly structured task performance, and rigid hours. These are difficult conditions to impose upon a woman with a family who wishes to work. Further, many women expect that upon taking a job, they will continue to bear the primary burden of homemaking and child-rearing responsibilities. For all of the positive progress which has been made in the last decade, traditional roles in the home persist, and few women or men would agree to total elimination of a distinction between roles. (One study in the Chicago area, which preceded a national survey, revealed that women who work full time typically do 80 percent of the house chores as well.)[34]

Thus, in spite of relaxed norms and increased acceptance of working women, women with families face serious obstacles. Flexibility in job conditions is essential to these women if they are to join the work force. Types of flexibility suited to women with family responsibilities include alternate work schedules—especially flexitime. In particular, flexitime offers the woman an important means of weaving her career into the fabric of the business organization while simultaneously honoring her family responsibilities. However, business organizations have been slow to adapt to this influx of women, except where required by law to do so. Further, they have often regarded the requests for flexible schedules as special treatment—a view which cannot persist if women are to be fully incorporated into the work force.

These social, cultural, and legal factors favor constructing working conditions which adapt to women's needs and capacities as individuals. This does *not* mean special privileges for women. On the contrary, it means the institution of programs such as flexible working hours which benefit men, women, and their families.

In considering flexitime, it is essential to caution that it is not a universal panacea for problems facing working women, and it may not be appropriate nor helpful for all employees. Nevertheless, it is clear that for the majority of women, the advantages of flexitime far outweigh potential disadvantages. The participation of women in the labor force is a growing reality, and their need for flexible working conditions will persist in the future, as will the need of all employees for more extensive options in career planning.

NOTES

1. "Women—Their impact grows in the job market. *U.S. News and World Report,* June 6, 1977, pp. 58–59.

2. Current labor statistics: Household data. *Monthly Labor Review,* August 1978, *101,* 64.

3. Rosow, J. M. Changing attitudes to work and lifestyles. In D. Robison, *Alternate work patterns —Changing approaches to work scheduling.* Report on a conference cosponsored by the National Center for Productivity and Quality of Working Life and the Work in America Institute, Inc., New York, June 1976, pp. 5–8.

   ———. *The worker and the job—coping with change.* Englewood Cliffs, N.J.: Prentice-Hall, 1974, pp. 1–170.

4. Kreps, J., and Clark, R. *Sex, age and work, the changing composition of the labor force.* Baltimore: Johns Hopkins, 1975, pp. 1–82.

5. Rosenberg, G. S. Statement of The National Council for Alternate Work Patterns, before House Subcommittee on Employee Ethics and Utilization of the Committee on Post Office and Civil Service, July 8, 1977.

6. Kreps and Clark, op. cit.

   Smith, R. E. Sources of growth of the female labor force, 1971–1975. *Monthly Labor Review,* August 1977, *100,* 27–29.

7. Quoted in: Killian, R. A., *The working woman—a male manager's view.* American Management Association, Inc., 1971, p. 26.

8. Ginzberg, E. The changing American economy and labor force. In J.M. Rosow (Ed.), *The worker and the job—coping with change.* Englewood Cliffs, N.J.: Prentice-Hall, 1974), pp. 49–72.

9. Schonberger, R. J. Ten million U.S. housewives want to work. *Labor Law Journal,* June 1970, *21,* 374–379.

10. Sweet, J. A. *Women in the labor force.* New York: Harcourt Brace Jovanovich, 1973, pp. 5–40.

11. Yankelovich, D. The meaning of work. In J. M. Rosow (Ed.), *The worker and the job—coping with change.* Englewood Cliffs, N.J.: Prentice-Hall, 1974, pp. 22–47.

12. J. K. Galbraith, *Economics and the public purpose.* New York: Signet New American Library, 1973, pp. 29–32.

13. Mills, C. M., and Berryman, C. L. *Male/female comparisons of career development dimensions: Do females fit the stereotype?* Paper presented at the 38th Annual Meeting of the Academy of Management, San Francisco, California, August 1978.

14. Fenn, M. Female dimension: Barriers to effective utilization of women in the world of work. In B.A. Stead, *Women in management.* Englewood Cliffs, N.J.: Prentice-Hall, 1978, pp. 26–27.

15. Durkin, J. J., The potential of women. Human Engineering Laboratory/Johnson O'Connor Research Foundation, Inc., *Congressional Record,* Vol. 117, Part 23, 92nd Congress, 1st Session, Sept. 8, 1971, pp. 31088–89.

16. Mills and Berryman, op. cit.

17. Kreps and Clark, op. cit.

    Robertson, D., *Women business school academicians.* Paper presented at the 38th Annual Meeting of the Academy of Management, San Francisco, California, August 1978.

18. Easterlin, R. A., Population. In L. G. Reynolds, S. H. Master, and C. H. Moser (Eds.), *Readings in labor economics and labor relations.* Englewood Cliffs, N.J.: Prentice-Hall, 1978, pp. 15–21.

    Johnston, D. F., The U.S. labor force: Projections to 1990. *Monthly Labor Review,* July 1973, *96,* 3–13.

19. Janeway, E. Revising the economy—If women can't do it, no one can. *Working Woman,* October 1977, pp. 66–67.

20. Kreps and Clark, op. cit.

21. Sweet, op. cit.

22. White, W. L., and Moore, B. E. *An evaluation of flexitime at the First National Bank of Boston.* Unpublished paper, University of Texas at Austin, April 1976.

23. A. S. Grossman, Children of working mothers—March 1977. *Monthly Labor Review,* January 1978, *101,* 30–33.

24. Snyder, R. A. Flexitime research and the federal government: Some issues of concern for agency decision-makers. U.S. Civil Service Commission, February 1976.

25. Schonberger, R. J. Inflexible working conditions keep women unliberated. *Personnel Journal,* November 1971, pp. 834–845.

26. Changing Patterns of Work in America, 1976. U.S. Congress, Senate Subcommittee on Employment, Poverty and Migratory Labor of the Committee on Labor and Public Welfare, hearings, 94th Congress, 2nd Session, April 7 and 8, 1976.

27. Klemesrud, J. Women executives: View from the top. *The New York Times,* March 11, 1979, p. 50.

28. Hall, D. T., and Gordon, F. E. Career choices of married women: Effects on conflict, role behavior, and satisfaction. *Journal of Applied Psychology,* 1973, *53,* 42–48.

29. Hoffman, L. W., and Nye, F. I. *Working mothers.* San Francisco: Jossey-Bass, 1974, p. 209.

30. Allen, R. E., and Keaveny, T. J. *The effects of work and family status on the attitudes of married women.* Paper presented at the 38th Annual Meeting of the Academy of Management, San Francisco, August 1978.

31. Hedges, J. N. Flexible schedules: Problems and issues. *Monthly Labor Review,* February 1977, *100,* 64.

32. Yankelovich, op. cit.

33. Sheppard, H. L., and Herrick, N. Q. *Where have all the robots gone? Worker dissatisfaction in the 70's.* New York: The W. E. Upjohn Institute for Employment Research, The Free Press, 1972, pp. 25–28, 114–117.

34. Schwartz, E. B., and MacKenzie, R. A. Time management strategy for dual career women. *Business Quarterly,* Autumn 1977, *42,* 32–41.

    Stead, B. A. *Women in management.* Englewood Cliffs, N.J.: Prentice-Hall, 1978, pp. 1–362.

Hall, D. T., and Hall, F. S. *The two-career couple.* Reading, Mass.: Addison-Wesley, 1979.

Wertheim, E. G., and Glasbert, A. *Women office workers: The relationship of attitudes and expectations to job performance and other behavioral responses to temporary work.* Paper presented at the 37th Annual Meeting of the Academy of Management, Kissammee, Florida, August 1977.

PART

Considerations for Effective Implementation

5

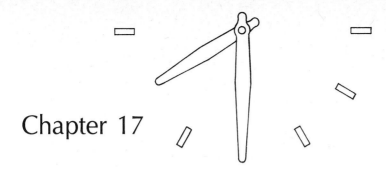

Chapter 17

Flexible Working Hours as an Organizational Change

Principles of Organizational Change

The achievement of the objectives of a planned change depends on many variables, including the environment in which the firm is operating, the structure of the organization, the adequacy of planning and control, the type and style of decision-making strategies used by management, and an effective management approach and practices which are consistent with the prevailing organizational climate. The moderating effects of these variables necessitates their consideration in any change to be implemented. Further, since these variables have different levels of influence in each organization, each change process is always unique.

Organizational change is primarily aimed at improving some aspect of effectiveness, although the process can take different forms. Improving effectiveness can be approached by attempting to change individual behavior directly or by changing organizational structure and processes. The implementation of an FWH system involves both approaches. Certain aspects of flexitime may be viewed as structural change while other aspects are intended to affect directly individual employee attitudes and behavior. Ultimately, however, employee behavior is affected by structural changes, and new attitudes may be formed as a result of these changes. We are thus differentiating indirect and direct effects of flexitime on individual behavior and attitudes. It is important that management view the system in this light as a structural change altering work processes directly as well as altering the attitudes and motivational systems of individual employees. The influence flexible working hours may have on improving organizational climate can be viewed within an organizational development (OD) framework which aims at improving trust, interpersonal communications and job involvement.

Although the consequences of the implementation of flexible working hours include, as we have seen, an improved organizational climate, it is imperative that the prevailing climate be sufficiently conducive or receptive to the change—that is, a climate which can accommodate changes which assume trust between employer and employee and the willingness by employers to grant more autonomy and control to individual employees. Elements of an appropriate climate include participatory decision making and supportive first-line supervisors. In some organizations, the preparation of a receptive climate will be the necessary first stage of the change strategy, although organizations with more appropriate climates should also evaluate the implications of flexitime and the reception it will receive from employees at all levels. Flexible working hours as a planned structural intervention in the form of changed schedules and work processes cannot therefore be divorced from its closely associated effect as an organizational development (OD) tool. In describing the stages for implementing flexible working hours, factors which reflect both approaches will be considered.* Because the implementation of flexible working hours affects nonmanagement employees most significantly—it is usually this group which has least personal discretion in job activities—the process of planning and implementation should include active representatives from the employees and first line supervisors. The following *assumptions* should be kept in mind during the planning stages:

• Individual and organizational goals are not necessarily incongruent. The degree of compatibility will be reflected in the climate and receptiveness to the system—hence the importance of a supportive organizational climate.

• The organization is an open system with subunits which are interdependent, interacting entities. Within this context, cooperative rather than competitive behavior is essential.

• Individuals want self-control and flexibility, especially when attempting to balance work and nonwork domains.

• It is essential for an effective organization to be highly adaptable to environmental changes, and to changes in employee needs and values.

• Individuals should be considered as continually growing and developing entities. This requires the acceptance of individual differences.

These assumptions should be the underpinnings of any change seriously considered by the organization.

Whether the basic model for the change process borrows from the literature on *structural change* or *organizational development* (OD), the following *principles* should provide a basis for an implementation strategy for flexible working hours:

• Implementation should be based on applied management and behavioral science, anchored in theory and experimentation, considering individuals as whole people in both the work and nonwork environments.

• It should be based on data obtained through feasibility and pilot studies conducted *within* the organization.

• It should have clear, identifiable goals, and criteria for measuring the achievement of these goals.

*FWH has been referred to by a few researchers as a structural organizational development intervention (Golembiewski, Hilles and Kango, 1974; Schein, Maurer and Novak, 1977).

- It should be fully endorsed by top management.
- It should include inputs and ideas from lower-level employees in the organization.
- It should be viewed as an aspect of organizational functioning—that is, a systematic and on-going process.

These principles should constitute the basic approach of members of the planning committee and the coordinators of the program. The purpose of this chapter is to help coordinators and planners cover all important factors and stages necessary to ensure the successful implementation of an FWH system. The assumptions and principles for implementation described are essential for a successful program. Because of the unique character of each organization, there is no single, optimal technique for flexitime implementation. Consequently, the material to follow is presented in an abbreviated form of checklists and reminders; it is left to the reader to determine which aspects are applicable to his or her organizational situation, based on the variables mentioned earlier.

The stages of implementation to be described are making an initial consideration of the program, forming a task force, conducting a feasibility study, planning the program itself, defining an evaluation process, conducting a pilot study, and finally, implementing the change on a companywide basis.

INITIAL CONSIDERATIONS

The initial idea for flexitime may come from any of a number of sources, such as the personnel department, a group of employees, or a highly placed executive. Top management may then consider the idea, weigh its apparent advantages and disadvantages, and appoint an individual to pursue the idea further. This individual may be an internal consultant, such as a personnel representative, or an employee, perhaps the originator of the idea, or an outside consultant. His initial task will be to acquire information on the topic and to review programs in other similar firms. The consultant must also compile a list of possible goals or reasons for adopting flexitime, along with an evaluation of the objectives of a flexitime program for the particular organization, for presentation to top management. These objectives could include (from results experienced by other organizations):

- Improved employee attitudes
- Improved quality of work life
- Improved commuting and transportation to and from work
- Improved interpersonal relations at home and/or work
- Decreased withdrawal behavior
- Decreased turnover
- Decreased absenteeism
- Elimination of tardiness
- Increased productivity
- Increased utilization of facilities and equipment

- Increased hours of availability to clients

- Increased ability to attract and recruit presently unavailable segments of the workforce —for instance, women with families

This represents a comprehensive list of possible outcomes; the planners should be selective in choosing those outcomes which are particularly desirable or feasible for their organization. For instance, if turnover is a problem, flexitime may be viewed as a means of diminishing it.

FORMATION OF A TASK FORCE

A project director (often the internal consultant or the originator of the idea) and committee members should be appointed to the task force. Members may include managers, nonmanagement employees, and union representatives. The decision to include employees and union representatives should be carefully considered. On the one hand, these groups should be included early in the planning and implementation process in order to encourage participation and commitment to the change. On the other hand, premature inclusion may raise expectations about the system which may not be met—especially if the organization is equivocal about the program. The decision not to go ahead may affect morale if employees have been actively involved in the initial planning. One guideline for employee involvement is to seek participation at the point when the employee's work unit is under consideration for implementation. If one flexitime schedule is to be implemented for an entire organization, involvement would come earlier in the process; if each department or work unit is to establish its own schedule, involvement would not be necessary until the decision for the work unit is to be made. This differentiation also has implications for the level of participation possible. In the former case, participation may be limited to a few employee representatives; in the latter, close to full participation from all employees in the decision-making process may be possible, depending upon the size of the work unit. Of course, this will require support and coordination from the union if employees are unionized. Once a task force has been formed, it should begin its work by conducting a feasibility study, based on the objectives defined by management.

FEASIBILITY STUDY

The objective of a feasibility study is to determine whether flexitime can be implemented without permanently disrupting organizational functioning. Given the objectives for flexitime, the committee must evaluate the extent to which work flow, technology, and work-unit functioning will be affected by changing arrival and departure times. The goal should be to examine work conditions in the context of *as flexible a schedule as possible.*

It should be noted that a purpose of the feasibility study is not to examine the preferences of employees. With this in mind, a survey to ask employees if they would like flexitime is not recommended. Not only can this be taken for granted, based on the survey data presented in this book, but it serves only to raise expectations which may not be met. Surveys are appropriate later in the implementation process—specifically, in the evaluation of the system with respect to changes in attitudes—but not at this point. Employee preference can be inferred from demographic variables such as age, sex, and marital and family status (number and age of children).

The focus of the investigation on the feasibility of flexitime should be its effect on work processes. Before continuing, however, a note of caution must be injected. Many managers, upon considering flexitime for their organization, reject it out of hand for any type of highly automated, interdependent work units, such as an assembly line. Although a flexitime schedule may present difficulties in implementation, some form of flexibility is usually possible, although it may need to be limited to variations for individual groups or teams of employees. Extra consideration should be given to these employees because the monotonous nature of their jobs is usually related to a greater orientation toward the nonwork domains and leisure activities. Even a small degree of autonomy in work scheduling may help to improve quality of life aspects through better planned leisure time and reduced or more convenient commuting. With this in mind, the following issues should be addressed in the feasibility study:

1. Identify and describe your work force.
    - Total number of employees to be affected (workers and supervisors)
    - Personnel characteristics
    - Task functions and work load characteristics for each functional department, including the following:
    - Interdependence of work flow within and between departments
    - Amount and times of contact with public and customers
    - Peak work load periods
        Within a day
        Within a week
        Within a month
    - Size of work force necessary in peak periods
    - Frequency of meetings and their timing
    - Schedule of incoming supplies, materials, and telephone calls
    - Schedule of outgoing products
    - Interdepartmental communications
    - Administrative functions
    - Need for supervisory coverage and presence

2. Consider any legal or contractual constraints (see Chapter 18).

3. Those organizations in which a high level of openness is the norm may wish to investigate employee preferences for FWH, preferred arrival and departure times, present mode of transportation, and possible changes under flexitime. However, the caution about raised expectations should be kept in mind.

4. Consider environmental conditions and support services. Support services staff should be consulted about the potential changes in their operations resulting from flexitime schedules, including:

- Cafeteria hours
- Safety and security services
- Medical services
- Switchboard hours
- Elevators
- Maintenance
- Power—electricity, gas, coal
- Heating or air-conditioning
- Cleaning and janitorial services

5. Identify those whose participation in the program will be limited or entirely prevented.
    - Define possible problems resulting from this and consider solutions.
    - Consult with supervisors of those potentially restricted.
    - Explore possible alternatives in work processes, including group instead of individual determination of schedule. This may be effective in assembly line situations, especially if sufficient in-process inventory can be provided between groups of workers to allow some degree of independent functioning.

6. Write a report with conclusions and recommendations. Present it to management (steering committee) for evaluation and approval.

PLANNING THE PILOT STUDY

Assuming that the presentation of the feasibility study to the steering committee has resulted in a go-ahead for a pilot study, the careful designing and planning of the study should begin. The original committee which conducted the feasibility study may continue with the pilot study, although it may be necessary to expand the committee because of the additional workload. In planning the pilot study, the following points should be considered:

1. Choose an appropriate department for the pilot study.
    - Consult with the supervisors and managers in the proposed department in order to solicit full cooperation.
    - Obtain approval and support from union representatives.
2. Set the timing for the pilot study, including dates for initial implementation, and the length of the study (6 months is usually considered optimal).
3. Establish system definitions and features:
    - Bandwidth
    - Core times
    - Flexbands
      Morning
      Evening
      Lunch
    - Settlement period

- Carry-over—debit and credit hours allowed
- Leave (time off) allowable during core time
  ½ day
  full day

4. Establish overtime policy and guidelines
5. Decide on a time-recording system
6. Consider potential transportation or parking difficulties
7. Consult with plant service personnel
8. Decide how the pilot study results will be evaluated.

EVALUATION

The subject of evaluation is covered in detail at this point, as it is critical to the decision-making process. The considerations described here also apply to the ultimate evaluation of flexitime after companywide implementation. It is included as part of the planning of the pilot study as it is imperative that the method for gathering and analyzing results be decided *before implementation.*

The effects of any planned organizational change must be carefully measured and monitored for the following reasons: first, in order to evaluate whether the goals set in planning the change have been achieved; second, in order to provide feedback for any alterations or improvements in the implemented change; and third, to identify unexpected effects, either positive or negative, which may result from the change. In field research such as change introduced to an organization, measurement of effects may not be so straightforward, however. In comparison to laboratory experimentation in which variables may be optimally controlled and the isolation of causal relationships is more feasible, field research is less "scientific." In the field, no change can operate in isolation, which makes the investigation of the effect of planned change more difficult. It requires a rigorous plan of study and evaluation utilizing the knowledge available in the fields of organizational behavior and research methodology. Organizations considering implementing flexible working schedules should employ the skills of an expert, even if it is necessary to obtain an objective outside consultant. The results of any objective research evaluation should be divorced, wherever possible, from the subjective impressions and sometimes unwarranted conclusions of managers or participants. The research design should optimally employ experimental and control groups, and provide for the collection of data both before and after implementation.

Data collection processes will not be described here in detail; this is better left for the individual organization with its unique attributes, technology and structure to plan. Instead, the variables which should be considered important criteria for evaluating the effects of flexible working hours will be delineated. These criteria coincide closely with the items in the tables describing results from the public and private sectors in Chapters 10 and 12. It was seen earlier that flexitime may improve organizational effectiveness as well as the individual's quality of work life. The objectives of the study should therefore be to research and evaluate variables in both of these broader categories. With respect to organizational functioning, measures of performance and withdrawal behavior should be investigated.

With respect to the individual, changes in employee behavioral patterns such as departure and arrival times and commuting patterns, and in attitudes toward the organization and toward the particular flexitime system are relevant. The organization should also evalute the success of monitoring systems used under the new working schedules such as time-recording devices and the maintenance of attendance information.

One point should be emphasized: measurements of these variables can be based either on objective or subjective measures, or both. Certain variables, such as job attitudes, are based, by definition, on the subjective reports of individuals. Other variables, such as productivity, should include both categories—evaluations of objectively measured criteria for productivity, and subjective reports from supervisors and employees. Consideration of absenteeism offers opportunities for accurate, objective measures, since most organizations keep information on this subject over a period of time and changes should be relatively easy to evaluate. In general, although both techniques offer valuable and needed information, the organization should make the utmost effort to collect objective information whenever and wherever possible.

One important aspect of the research methodology requires attention—the reliability of the information offered through questionnaires and subjective reports. Questionnaires are particularly useful for obtaining information about attitudes toward the organization, toward members of the organization, and toward the planned change itself. Usually a guaranteed anonymity for respondents is a necessary condition for an accurate and honest response to questionnaires or surveys; any identifying information that does not jeopardize anonymity should be included on a questionnaire. Information such as biographical data (e.g., sex, age, marital status, family composition, salary, and work experience) is valuable in order to enable comparisons of changes in behavior and attitudes among different subgroups to be made. Flexitime may not affect all groups equally. In general, the more accurately an employee can be described demographically, the more conclusive can be an analysis of results for comparative and longitudinal studies.

Organizational Effectiveness

Because any changes in organizational effectiveness are critical to the evaluation of flexitime, all possible resources should be utilized to detect any such changes including objective data, evaluations by supervisors, and employee reports. Although membership behavior is one component of the overall evaluation of the organizational effectiveness level, this category will be presented separately. Criteria for evaluating changes in effectiveness include:

1. Productivity
   - Output volume (quantity)
   - Quality of work performed
   - Utilization of equipment (time span)
   - Machine down time
   - Unit productivity, that is, labor cost per unit output
   - Service to public—deliveries, telephone availability, etc.

- Necessary attendance levels during peak work periods
- Overtime wages
- Increases in hours of availability to customers

2. Additional Responsibilities of Supervisors
   - Work scheduling and planning
   - Maintaining work flow
   - Problems in monitoring, controlling, and supervising performance
   - Customer complaints
   - Supervisor-worker relations

3. Communications
   - Interdepartmental communication
   - Intradepartmental communication
   - External communications

4. Costs
   - Implementation of system including a time-recording system
   - Physical plant and energy consumption
     Gas
     Coal
     Electricity
   - Support personnel
     Elevators
     Maintenance
     Security
     Cafeteria

Attitudes

Most organizations are well acquainted with employee attitude surveys. Many of the variables which are usually included in such surveys are applicable here as well. In addition to changes in job attitudes such as job satisfaction, the attitudes toward different aspects of the new system should be surveyed:

1. Job Satisfaction Components
   - Supervisor
   - Organization and management policy
   - Physical conditions
   - Co-workers as a supportive group
   - Effectiveness of teamwork
   - Recognition and feedback from peers and supervisors
   - Satisfaction with work itself
   - Autonomy and responsibility
   - Overall job satisfaction

2. Satisfaction with Flexitime
   - The span of flexbands and core time
   - Bandwidth

- Lunch breaks
- Time-recording system
- Commuting changes
- Overtime availability
- Grievances
- Attitude of employees not included in system
- Attitude to the implementation process itself

Membership Behavior (Withdrawal)

Membership behavior should be assessed using objective measures, such as changes in leave usage, absenteeism, and tardiness. The one area that is limited to measurement by opinion is the amount of abuse of the system, since abuses are not usually recorded. The question of abuse should always be asked in terms of comparison to past abuses under the old work schedule, because in some companies, lax attitudes towards work hours may be an organization problem which predates the implementation of flexitime. Aside from abuse, other criteria for evaluating membership behavior can be measured objectively. These include the following:

- Turnover
- Ease of recruiting and hiring new employees
- Absenteeism
- Leave usage
- Tardiness
- Time and attendance records
- Administration of records
- Injuries and accidents
- Credit/debit accumulation
- Attendance during peak work periods
- Cooperation with peers and supervisors in attendance record keeping

Time Management

Changes in the individual's use of his time are at the heart of the flexitime concept. There is an almost endless list of possible criteria for measuring changes in this area. These are a few of the basic categories which should be considered:

- Ability to plan and use leisure time
- Ability to make use of educational opportunities or facilities
- Ability to conduct personal business and schedule medical and dental appointments without conflict
- Easing of child-care responsibilities

- Ability to spend more time with family
- Ability to participate in community and social events
- Easing of commuting stress
- Changes in mode of transportation and length of commute
- Changes in gasoline consumption if driving to work
- Changes in congestion at parking lots, elevators, lockers, etc.

Implications for the Community

Depending on the size of the workforce on flexitime as a percentage of the local community, it may be possible to measure changes in the following:

- Highway utilization and traffic congestion
- Mass transportation availability and scheduling
- Participation in car pools
- Availability of recreational facilities
- Availability of health and social services

PILOT STUDY—TRIAL PERIOD

The purpose of the pilot study is to test the suitability of flexible work schedules in the organization. It should provide statistical information on the behavioral and attitudinal criteria defined in the evaluation stage to enable the organization to make the decision regarding the adoption of the system on a companywide basis. If the decision is to go ahead, then the pilot study also helps to determine the most suitable system through the experience already obtained, and to identify potential problems.

The pilot program includes three major stages: planning phase, implementation phase, and the evaluation phase. Evaluation has been described in detail as part of the planning stage in order to emphasize the importance of defining criteria and determining how they will be measured ahead of time. Of course, the actual evaluation itself will be conducted at the end of the pilot study, when all data have been collected. In addition to the items delineated in the planning sections, the following list includes considerations for trial period implementation.

1. Set goals for the pilot study.
2. Select a department for the pilot in which the criteria for evaluation can be identified.
3. Set a period for the trial (3–6 months is typical).
4. Appoint a coordinator, and possibly a departmental committee, from the pilot department who will participate in subsequent phases of implementation.
5. Choose an appropriate flexitime schedule for this department and its subunits, considering obstacles and variations.

6. Choose time-recording systems and records procedures.

7. Review policies for absenteeism, and leave and overtime usage.

8. Review the decisions made thus far and obtain final approval from the department head and top management.

9. Inform the rest of the company (usually via memo) of the pilot study, its purpose, and the requirements for a successful outcome.

10. Prepare guidelines and information sessions for participants.

11. Review the following:
    - Company policy
    - FWH definitions and general system description
    - The actual schedule to be implemented

12. Conduct supervisor orientation sessions addressed to the special needs of this group, including monitoring and control issues.

13. Conduct a review, in detail, of the data collection and evaluation procedures.

14. Plan a system for handling complaints or disputes.

15. Meet with employees to iron out details.

16. Start pilot study.

MAKING A DECISION

At the conclusion of the pilot study and the evaluation process, an extensive report should be made to top management, presenting the findings according to the criteria originally determined. The process of decision making may include the following steps:

1. Report to top management and union officials the results and recommendations of the study.

2. Reevaluate features and consider alternatives.

3. Decide on organizationwide implementation—go ahead, or drop the program.

4. Obtain approval and commitment from union officials.

5. Decide on level of departmental autonomy in determining schedules.

6. Communicate decisions to department heads.

COMPANYWIDE IMPLEMENTATION

At this stage, enough information has been collected to ensure effective policy guidelines for top management. Decisions regarding the system itself, time recording, and policies concerning absenteeism and overtime, grievance procedures, and record keeping should have been made. Once these aspects are determined, the task of companywide implementation is reduced to two key processes: *coordination and communication.* In order to facilitate these processes, certain activities may be helpful:

1. A central coordinator should be named.

2. A local coordinator should be named for each independent subunit participating in the pilot.

3. All employees should be informed about the implementation. Usually written documents precede group meetings at local levels. Endorsement of top management and the union, if relevant, should be made clear.

4. Separate educational programs should be prepared for employees, supervisors, and managers on the implications of flexitime for job performance. Union representatives (stewards) should also have a special educational session if a union is involved.

5. Once the program has been implemented,
- Monitor and evaluate progress
- Prepare periodic reports and evaluations
- Provide periodic feedback to management and supervisors.

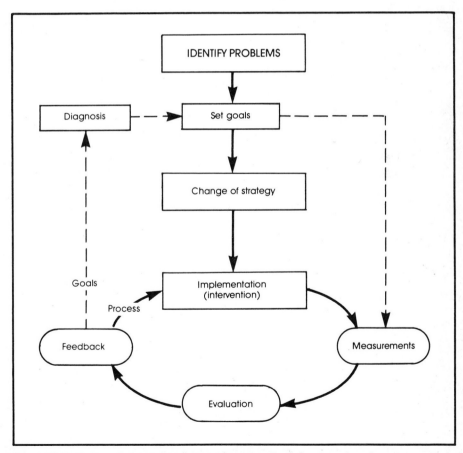

Figure 17–1   System of on-going evaluation of organizational change goals and processes.

SUMMARY AND CONCLUSIONS

The implementation of an organizational change should be considered a process within the organization, rather than a one-time intervention. Once goals have been set, and criteria for their measurements determined, measurement and evaluation should be an on-going process. If the resulting feedback does not meet the criteria for organizational effectiveness, the *goals* of the program must be redefined, or the *process* by which the change has been effected reconsidered. This process is described in Figure 17-1.

In this chapter, an exhaustive list of considerations for implementing flexitime has been presented in an abbreviated form. Not all of these considerations will apply to every organization. Further, in terms of the steps described in the process of implementation, some firms will skip stages while others will repeat the same stage several times.

Each organization must determine its own criteria for effectiveness, and the means of measuring these criteria. However, as emphasized earlier, it is imperative to plan the measurement and evaluation process *before* beginning the pilot study. Finally, this process should be modified and incorporated into the permanent evaluation systems of the organization.

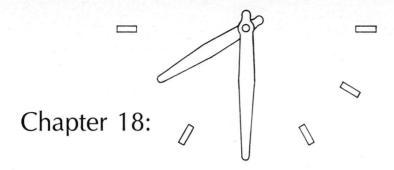

Chapter 18:

Legal and Contractual Considerations*

LEGAL ASPECTS OF FLEXITIME

INTRODUCTION

The American worker is covered by a vast and complex set of federal, state, and local laws, rules, and regulations governing his employment. One or more of these is likely to affect the design and implementation of a flexitime system.

As has been seen in previous chapters, there are many possible variations in the structure of a flexitime system, ranging from a limited flexible workday to almost unlimited flexibility. Although the choice of any particular variation will be dictated largely by organizational and operational considerations, certain aspects of a flexitime model will have to be structured with reference to the applicable laws regulating hours of work. And even after a model is chosen, one must be ready to deal with the laws which regulate the *method* of implementing such a system for employees.

Most of the laws which affect the operation of flexitime are those which establish a maximum work period and mandate the payment of wage premiums for work in excess of those maximum work periods. On the federal level, these overtime laws include the Fair Labor Standards Act (FLSA), the Contract Work Hours Act, the Walsh-Healy Act, and U.S. Code Title 5. Other laws affect the implementation of flexitime. For example, the National Labor Relations Act imposes certain restrictions upon employers who implement substantial changes in terms and conditions of employment where there is a union involved.

As we will see from the discussion later in this chapter, each of the laws has a limited application. Which law, if any, applies is a function of various elements of the employment relationship. Is the employee employed in the public or private sector? If in the private sector,

*This chapter was written by Gerald Schilian, Esq., an attorney specializing in employment law. Mr. Schilian and Deborah Watarz, Esq., who is also an employment law specialist, functioned as legal consultants for this book.

is he engaged in work on a public job or contract? If in the public sector, is he employed by the federal government, a state government, a city or town government, or some other public or quasi-public entity? What is his level of responsibility? What is his salary level? What industry is the employer engaged in? What is his gross volume of business? Are the employees unionized? Is there a collective bargaining agreement in effect? Is there a union organizing drive?

This chapter does not attempt to describe every aspect of every existing law. It does offer a reasonably comprehensive summary of the federal law as it relates to flexitime. (Analysis of state, and local law is far beyond the scope of this book.) The intention here is to provide a manager with sufficient knowledge to be able to identify potential legal problems and to communicate with a reasonable degree of sophistication with his legal consultant. Such consultation is recommended at the earliest planning stages, so that potential problems can be identified and the system designed accordingly.

Legal Regulation of Hours of Work

Background

Traditionally, most organizations have resolved the problem of scheduling hours of work by the assignment of fixed schedules. Although the current standard 5-day workweek of between 35 and 40 hours represents a substantial reduction from the 6-day, 72-hour week which prevailed at the turn of the century, the concept of fixed scheduling has remained. The law reflects this tradition. The various laws regulating hours of work have institutionalized fixed scheduling by mandating the payment of wage premiums for work in excess of 40 hours in a week and, in some cases, 8 hours in a day.

Although some maximum hours laws date from the late nineteenth century, the principal elements of the maximum hours laws that exist today are derived from the anti-Depression legislation of the 1930s. These laws were adopted for reasons which were sound at the time of their enactment. They served to curb the exploitative practice of some employers who demanded 10 or 12 hours of work for 8 hours pay. Moreover, during times of recession and depression, the maximum hours laws encouraged employers to spread the limited available work among a greater number of workers.

In 1937, President Roosevelt launched a major attempt to secure broad federal wage and hour legislation. In a message to Congress, he stated that "to conserve our primary resource of manpower, Government must have some control over maximum hours, minimum wages, the evil of child labor and the exploitation of unorganized labor." Out of that message grew the Fair Labor Standards Act of 1938 (FLSA). As originally passed, the FLSA mandated a maximum work week of 44 hours, a minimum wage of 25 cents per hour, and severe restrictions on the use of child labor in covered employment in the private sector. Many jobs and industries were excluded or exempted. Today, this law still exists. It is the cornerstone of wage and hour regulation. Coverage has been broadened, although there are still certain exclusions and exemptions, a discussion of which is found later in this chapter.

Of course, the minimum wage has been substantially increased, but the 40-hour workweek, which became effective shortly after the passage of the original act, remains, with time and one-half payable after 40 hours.

Current Status of Maximum Hours Legislation

During the 1930s, the principal focus of protective legislation was private sector employment. For the most part, employees of federal, state, and local governmental entities were not yet covered by laws regulating hours of work. Today, in its regulation of wages and hours of private sector employees, the FLSA continues to have an impact on more workers than any other law controlling hours of work. Moreover, there is now also a proliferation of legislation regulating wages and hours of public employees as well.

Those provisions of the FLSA relating to maximum hours and overtime, which are of interest to us in this chapter, have been applied primarily to the private sector. However, in 1961, amendments to the FLSA extended its coverage to persons employed in enterprises having a traditionally private character, *even though such enterprises were governmentally owned or operated.* In 1966, amendments further extended coverage to certain federal employees and to employees of state and local hospitals and educational institutions. The Supreme Court of the United States affirmed the validity of this extension.*

In 1974, the FLSA was again amended to extend its coverage to other federal, state, and local employees, and there was another court challenge. This time, however, the Supreme Court† held unconstitutional the congressional application of minimum wage and maximum hour rules to state and local government employees. Therefore, only federal employees‡ and a very limited number of state and local employees engaged in operations having a traditionally private character remain covered by the FLSA. All other public employees are not covered.

Since the FLSA wage and hour rules are not generally applied to employees of state and local government, these entities have full authority to make their own rules without federal interference. This means that state and local governments have greater latitude to take advantage of the full range of flexitime options. (Unless, of course, state or local laws or union contracts otherwise restrict them.)

ANALYSIS OF THE COVERAGE OF SPECIFIC LAWS

General

Following the discussion of the general implications of the FLSA, it is necessary to alert the reader to the main criteria used to determine its coverage. A single private sector employer may find that some of its employees are governed by one law, some of its employees by a second law, and still others by no law at all. Such a company could construct different flexitime models for the different classifications of employees. For example, employees covered by a law requiring the payment of overtime premium after 8 hours worked in any day may be restricted to flexibility within the 8-hour workday. For those covered by FLSA,

---

Maryland v. Wirtz, 392 U.S. 183 (1968)

†*National League of Cities v. Usery,* 426 U.S. 833 (1976), which overruled *Maryland v. Wirtz*

‡In addition to the FLSA, federal employees are covered by United States Code, Title 5, Chapter 55, entitled *Pay Administration,* providing for overtime after 8 hours worked in a day *and* after 40 hours worked in a week, shift premiums for work performed after 6 P.M. and before 6 A.M., on Sundays, holidays, and the like. However, a 1978 law authorizes a limited exception to these provisions for the purpose of experimenting with flexitime and compressed workweek models. This will be discussed later.

which requires the payment of overtime premiums after 40 hours worked in a week, a flexible workweek may be constructed and debit or credit hours carried so long as the account is balanced at the end of the week. Finally, those employees not covered by any law could be permitted to bank debit and credit hours from any one accounting period to another. SmithKline Corporation has implemented such a three-tiered system.

Even under the FLSA, if an organization is already on a workweek of less than 40 hours, limited banking could be easily achieved by authorizing employees to work up to 40 hours. An organization on a 35-hour workweek, for example, could legally permit an employee to work up to 40 hours in a week without paying an overtime premium, so long as there is no contrary union contract. The Equitable Life Insurance Company has implemented such a system.

In the sections that follow, the principal federal laws regulating hours of work to determine who is covered are analyzed. Since FLSA is the most broadly applicable of these laws, it is examined first.

Fair Labor Standards Act

Inclusions.   The FLSA provides that its overtime regulations apply to any employee who "in any work week is engaged in commerce or in the production of goods for commerce, or is employed in an enterprise engaged in commerce or in the production of goods for commerce."* To determine who is covered, we must first ascertain whether the employee or his employer is engaged in commerce. The term *commerce* means trade, transportation, or communication among the states or between any state and any place outside the state.† (If no such commerce exists, Congress does not have the constitutional authority to legislate.)

An employee is deemed to be engaged in commerce if he works on goods, any part of which is intended for interstate commerce, even though it cannot be determined that the particular goods on which the particular employee worked were, in fact, those goods which were sent out of state. Thus, in an enterprise in which some goods are produced for local distribution and similar goods are produced for sale outside the state, all employees working on the goods are deemed to be in interstate commerce, and they are potentially covered by the FLSA. However, they are still subject to exclusion from coverage based on other considerations discussed below.

There are also monetary requirements which must be met. The FLSA provides that an employer is engaged in commerce if it has employees engaged in commerce and does gross annual business in excess of $275,000.* (This minimum standard will increase on July 1, 1980, to $325,000, and on July 1, 1981 to $362,500.) The act specifies that laundering and cleaning enterprises, construction and reconstruction operations, as well as hospitals and various kinds of health-care facilities are engaged in commerce regardless of the dollar volume of business. On the other hand, businesses regularly employing only the owner, parents, spouse, children, or other members of the immediate family of the owner are excluded from coverage regardless of the dollar volume of business.

*Section 7 (a)(1) 29 USC 207 (a)(1)
†Section 3 (b) 29 USC 203 (b)
*Section 3 (s) USC 203 (5)

In general, most private employers are covered by the FLSA, and all of their employees are thus covered unless specifically exempted. The specific exemptions and exclusions will be discussed next. Courts have interpreted the act as broadly as possible to cover as many people as possible.

Exemptions.   The Fair Labor Standards Act sets forth specific classifications of employees who are exempt from the overtime provisions. Probably the most important exemption is that for employees employed in bona fide executive, administrative, or professional positions. Detailed rules defining these so-called "white-collar exemptions" have been promulgated by the U.S. Department of Labor, which is in charge of implementing the FLSA. The white-collar exemptions cut across industry lines and apply to some number of employees in virtually every enterprise.

Executive Exemption.   An executive employee is one whose primary duties consist of (1) management of the enterprise or a department or subdivision thereof, (2) regular direction of the work of two or more other employees, (3) authority to hire or fire or to effectively recommend same, (4) regular exercise of discretionary powers, and (5) spending of not more than 20 percent of work time on nonexecutive duties. To qualify for an executive exemption, an employee must be earning a salary in excess of certain minimums set forth in Department of Labor regulations.

Administrative Exemption.   The administrative exemption applies to an employee whose primary duties consist of office work not of a manual nature, who earns more than specified salary minimums, and whose work (1) is directly related to management policies or general business operations of the company or its customers, (2) requires him to customarily and regularly exercise discretion and independent judgment, (3) includes regular assistance to an executive, execution of special assignments, or performance of certain specialized work, and (4) does not involve the spending of more than 20 percent of work time on nonadministrative duties.

Professional Exemption.   In creating a test to determine whether an employee fits within the professional category, the Department of Labor regulations again set minimum salary standards, as well as stipulating that (1) the employee's primary duties require either advanced knowledge in science or learning of a type customarily acquired by a prolonged course of specialized and intellectual instruction, or require original and creative efforts in a recognized field of artistic endeavor, (2) the work demands consistent exercise of discretion and judgement, (3) the work is predominantly intellectual and varied in character, and (d) the employee spends not more than 20 percent of his work time on nonprofessional work. Doctors, lawyers, registered nurses, along with certain pilots and flight engineers have been found to be exempt from the FLSA coverage.

Other Classification Exemptions.   Some other groups of employees are also exempt, for example, "outside salesmen" if they (1) are employed for the purpose of making sales or obtaining orders or contracts for services for which the customer will pay, (2) customarily and regularly spend their time in such work away from the employer's place of business, and (3) are required to spend not more than 20 percent of work time on nonsales activities. There is also an exemption for apprentices. Such exemptions are granted, where appropriate, on a case-by-case basis.

Exclusions.   In addition to providing employee exemptions, the FLSA provides for employer exclusion from coverage. If an employer is excluded, *all* his employees are excluded from coverage. The following are examples:

Industrywide Exclusions.   In some instances, employees in an entire industry are excluded from the FLSA coverage, for example, the taxicab industry and all employees of specified seasonal businesses. Table 18-1 provides a more detailed description of various exempt industries. Certain employees are not covered by the FLSA because their employment is regulated under another federal law, as previously noted. An example of such a law is the Motor Carrier Act of 1935, which authorizes the U.S. Secretary of Transportation to regulate employment in trucking and busing industries. The secretary's regulatory authority extends to employees who are employed as drivers, drivers' helpers, mechanics, and loaders in interstate bus, trucking, and related operations, when their work directly affects the operational safety of motor vehicles. Employees will be exempt even though they spend only a small portion of their workweek in these roles. These employees are exempt from the FLSA because the secretary has the power to regulate them. The secretary need not have actually formulated regulations.

Railroad employees, too, are excluded from the FLSA coverage.* Such employees are subject to provisions of the Interstate Commerce Act. This exclusion may not apply to employees of nonrailroad businesses operated by the railroad company. Thus, for example, in a company that owns a hotel and a railroad, hotel employees may be subject to the FLSA while the railroad employees are not.

The FLSA provides a further exemption for employees of air carriers subject to the provisions of the Railway Labor Act. As is the case for railroads, all employees of the air carrier will be exempt from the overtime provisions of the FLSA, except those who are employed in activities wholly unrelated to the air transportation business.

Because of the legal definitions described above, within the same company some employees may come under the FLSA rules while others may be subject to regulation by the Department of Transportation or the Interstate Commerce Commission. Other employees may be free from maximum hour restrictions.

The fact that in many instances, transportation industry employees are not covered by maximum hour rules, combined with the unique nature of their industries, has led to the creation of scheduling arrangements resembling flexitime, although not so labeled.

Small Business and Specialized Exclusions.   Certain small retail or service establishments are excluded if more than 50 percent of the annual dollar volume of business of such establishments derives from within the state in which the establishment is located. Amusement and recreational establishments operating less than 7 months per year, or which do more than two-thirds of their annual business within a 6-month period, are also excluded. Fishing and sea farming (mariculture) are businesses excluded, as well as certain types of agricultural enterprises. Small newspapers, small independently owned public telephone companies, radio or television stations located in certain small towns, seamen, and baby-sitting operations are similarly specifically excluded from FLSA coverage.

Summary.   The above recital of inclusions, exclusions, and exemptions from the maximum hour provisions of the FLSA should not be construed as definitive. Its purpose is merely to

*Section 13(b)(2); 29 USC 213(b)(2)

identify for the manager who is creating a flexitime model which of his employees may be covered and which may not. The U.S. Secretary of Labor has issued detailed regulations and advisory opinions which, together with decisions of the courts concerning the application of the act, give substance to the skeletal structure of the statutory language and serve to better define the manner in which the law is applied to any specific enterprise.

In order to evaluate the limits of the FLSA coverage, an employer should obtain legal advice. In the final analysis, the Secretary of Labor has the power to "define and delimit" the FLSA coverage, and reference must be made to the published regulations and determinations. *Most private industry employers should assume that at least some employees are covered by the maximum hour provisions of the act.*

The 26-Week and 52-Week Contract Exceptions.   Because of a little-known provision of the FLSA, a partial exception to the standard 40-hour workweek is available in certain instances where a collective bargaining agreement with a bona fide labor union provides for semiannual or annual limitations of hours of work. These contracts are generally negotiated in industries having unusually high seasonal work load demands followed by slack periods. In order to qualify for this exception, the contract must conform to strict rules which are set forth in the FLSA and the regulations which have been established by the Secretary of Labor.

26-Week Contract Exception.   Under the FLSA, the 26-week contract exception permits employment for up to 56 hours per week without the payment of overtime premiums. The employer, however, is burdened with a concomitant obligation to limit the sum of all hours worked by any employee during the 26-week period to 1,040 hours; this averages out to 40 hours per week. Thus, employees covered by a 1,040-hour contract may work many hours in some weeks and few hours in others during the 26-week period so long as they average no more than 40 hours per week by the end of the period. During the other half of the year, the employees, if they work, are treated as any other employee covered by the act.

The 26-week contract must satisfy the following conditions:

1.   It must be a written contract negotiated and signed by a bona fide union representing the employees of the employer and certified as genuine by the National Labor Relations Board.

2.   The contract must provide that covered employees will not work more than 1,040 hours in any period of 26 consecutive weeks; there can only be one such period of 26 consecutive weeks within a period of 52 consecutive weeks.

3.   It must provide that the employer pay an overtime premium of time and one-half for all hours worked in excess of 12 in a day or 56 in a week.

4.   If the employer violates any of the rules, it will be required to pay time and one-half for all hours worked in excess of 40 in each week of the 26-week period.

52-Week Contract Exception.   In contrast to the 26-week contract, the 52-week contract does not impose a maximum number of weekly hours beyond which additional work would be paid for at a premium. (However, there is nothing to prohibit the union from negotiating such a premium.) The 52-week contract guarantees that each covered employee will be paid for a certain minimum number of hours (1,840) during the contract year,

Table 18-1 Maximum Hour Law Exemptions (FLSA)

Industry or Occupation	Overtime Exemption
Airlines	Exemption except for employees engaged in activities not necessary to or related to air transportation.
Amusement and recreational establishments	Exemption if (a) establishment doesn't operate more than 7 months during calendar year, or (b) its average receipts during any 6 months of prior calendar year don't exceed one third of its average receipts for the other 6 months of the year. 1977 amendments added organized camps or religious or nonprofit educational conference centers as exempt establishments, but specifically deny exemption to concessioners in national parks, refuges, and forests, with exception of facilities operating in these areas that are directly relating to skiing.
Auto, farm implement, boat, aircraft dealers	Exemption for salesmen, partsmen, and mechanics primarily selling or servicing autos, trucks, or farm implements, if employed by nonmanufacturer primarily selling to ultimate consumer. Exemption for salesmen primarily selling trailers, aircraft, or boats if employed by nonmanufacturer primarily selling to ultimate consumer.
Drivers and drivers' helpers	Exempt if making local deliveries and compensated on trip-rate basis.
Foreign employment	Exemption for services performed within a foreign country.
Forestry or logging	Exemption if employer has 8 employees or less.
Gasoline stations	Exemption for stations with annual sales of less than $250,000.
Holly-wreath manufacture	Exemption for homeworkers engaged in making of wreaths composed principally of natural evergreens.
Hospital and nursing homes	Hospital may use work period of 14 days, rather than 7 days, in computing overtime if employees agree in advance and 1½ times regular rate is paid for hours over 8 per day, and 80 in 14-day period. Otherwise, overtime rate applies after 40 hours per week.

Industry or Occupation	Overtime Exemption
Hotels, motels, and restaurants (Other than those qualifying for retail-service exemptions)	Exemption for hotel, motel, and restaurant employees (other than hotel maids and custodial employees) provided they are paid 1½ times regular rate for hours over 44 hours per week effective January 1, 1976. Exemption is repealed effective January 1, 1979.
Motion picture theaters	Exemption.
Motor carriers	Exemption for employees whose hours of service are subject to regulation by Department of Transportation.
Newsboys delivering newspapers to the consumer	Exemption.
Newspapers	Exemption for employees of paper with 4,000 or less circulation, major part of which is in county in which paper is published or in contiguous counties (paper may be printed elsewhere).
Petroleum distributors	Exemption for any employee of independently owned and controlled local enterprise engaged in wholesale or bulk distribution of petroleum products, *provided* he is paid 1½ times the *statutory* minimum rate for work between 40 and 56 hours per week and 1½ times his *regular* rate all work in excess of 12 per day and 56 per week.
Professional, executive, and administrative personnel	Exempt if they meet regulatory tests.
Radio and TV broadcasters	Exemptions for announcers, news editors, and chief engineers of radio or TV station whose major studio is located in (1) city of 100,000 or less that is not part of a metropolitan area of more than 100,000, or (2) city of 25,000 or less, even in such metropolitan area if it is located at least 40 airline miles from principal city in area.
Railroad, steamship companies	Exemption for employees of employer subject to Part I of Interstate Commerce Act, i.e., common carriers engaged in (a) transporting passengers or property wholly by rail, or partly by rail and partly by water when both are used under common

Industry or Occupation	Overtime Exemption
	control, management, or arrangement for continuous carriage or shipment; or (b) transportation of oil or other commodities, except water and natural or artificial gas, by pipeline or partly by pipeline and partly by railroad or water.
Retail-service establishments (other than laundry–dry-cleaning establishment, hospital, nursing home, school for handicapped or gifted children, preschool, elementary, or secondary school, or college	Exemption if (a) more than 50% of establishment's annual sales is intrastate, and (b) at least 75 percent of its annual dollar sales is not for resale and is recognized as retail in the industry. Under the 1977 amendments to the FLSA, the test for coverage of employees of enterprises comprised of one or more retail or service establishments is raised to $362,500 in three steps as follows: •July 1, 1978 $275,000 •July 1, 1980 325,000 •Dec. 31, 1981 362,500
Retail commission salesmen	Exemption provided employee's regular rate (including salary and commissions) is more than 1½ times the statutory minimum, and more than half his compensation comes from commissions.
Retail-manufacturing units (e.g., bakeries, ice-cream parlors, candy shops)	Exemptions for establishments if (a) it meets tests for retail-service establishments, (b) it is recognized in industry as retail establishment, (c) more than 85 percent of its dollar volume of annual sales is made intrastate; (d) the goods are made or processed and sold in the same establishment.
Seamen	Exemption for all seamen, whether on U.S. or foreign vessels.
Substitute parents for institutionalized children	Exempt if employee and spouse are substitute parents for children residing in private nonprofit educational institutions, receive jointly cash wages of $10,000 annually, and reside in the same facilities as the children receiving free room and board.
Taxicab drivers	Exemption for drivers employed by taxicab company.
Telephone exchanges	Exemption for employees of independently owned telephone company that has fewer than 750 stations.

SOURCE: Reprinted by special permission from *Labor Relations Reporter.* Copyright © 1978 by the Bureau of National Affairs, Inc., Washington, D.C.

whether or not such a minimum is actually worked. Until such time as the employee has worked that minimum number of hours, he may work any number of hours in any week all at straight time. Once an employee reaches the guaranteed minimum number of hours, he must be paid the overtime premium for all hours worked in excess of 40 hours in any week. At such time as the employee has worked in excess of 2,080 hours in the 52-week period (an average of 40 hours per week), *all* hours worked thereafter must be compensated at the rate of time and one-half. To retain the exception, the employer may not permit an employee to work in excess of 2,250 hours in any given year. As with the 26-week contract, there must be a collective bargaining agreement with a bona fide union. The 52-week contract must also conform to the following rules:

1. It must provide a minimum annual employment guarantee of either 1,840 hours or 46 weeks of work.

2. It must provide an absolute limit of 2,250 hours of work during the year.

3. It must provide that, at such time as a covered employee works more than the minimum number of hours guaranteed, he receives time and one-half for hours worked in excess of 40 in any week from that point to the end of the 52-week period.

4. It must provide that covered employees receive time and one-half for all hours worked during the 52-week period in excess of 2,080 hours.

Few union contracts have adopted either this or the 26-week formula. Under appropriate circumstances, however, and with appropriate controls, these exceptions to the standard FLSA workweek could easily be adapted to fit within the flexitime framework. Where properly applied, a 26- or 52-week contract could facilitate the implementation of an advanced flexitime model.

Child Labor Provisions of FLSA.   The FLSA contains a provision which prohibits producers, manufacturers, and dealers from shipping or delivering for shipment in commerce any goods produced in an establishment situated in the United States where *oppressive child labor,* as that term is defined in the act, is practiced. In general, the various industry exemptions described above do not apply to the child labor section. Since the FLSA's child labor restrictions limit the hours that children subject to the act can work, any employer hiring such children must restrict the application of flexitime for its minor employees to legally permissable limits.

What is oppressive child labor? The act defines it as the employment of minors under the age of 16 in any occupation, although the Secretary of Labor may permit the employment of children between the ages of 14 and 16 in industries other than mining and manufacturing, so long as such employment is confined to periods which will not interfere with the schooling of the minors and will not interfere with their health or welfare. The employment of minors between the ages of 16 and 18 is permitted except where the Secretary of Labor finds that such employment is particularly hazardous and detrimental to the health and well-being of the child.

In occupations where minors between the ages of 14 and 16 are permitted to be employed, the Secretary of Labor has restricted such employment to (1) outside of school hours, (2) not more than 40 hours in any week in which school is not in session, (3) 18 hours in any week in which school is in session, (4) 8 hours a day when school is not in session, and (5) 3 hours in a day when school is in session. The employment of such children is also limited to the hours between 7 A.M. and 7 P.M.

Organizations employing significant numbers of students of any age should find flexitime helpful in dealing with the recurring scheduling crises arising from the demands of school-work. The various nonemployment related demands on a student's time—such as the need to study for examinations, to do research, write papers—often cause stress in the employment relationship. The employer must run his business; the employee wishes to be a successful student. The ability to apply flexible work scheduling within the framework of the employer's business needs could be a key factor in reducing such strains. The limitations of the law, however, must be observed.

Laws Affecting Employees of Private Employers Engaged in Work for the Federal Government

General.   There are a number of federal laws which establish employment standards for private employees engaged in various activities on behalf of the Federal Government. These include the Walsh-Healy Act, the Davis-Bacon Act, the Copeland Antikickback Act, the Contract Work-Hours and Safety Standards Act, and the Service Contract Act. These laws set minimum standards for wages, overtime, and other terms and conditions of employment for specified employees. Because the concern here is with flexitime, the discussion will be restricted to those laws that limit or restrict the hours that an employee may work at straight time rates of compensation.

The Walsh-Healy Act.   The Walsh-Healy Act requires the payment of overtime premiums to covered employees for hours worked in excess of 40 hours in one week or 8 hours in one day. This act is far more restrictive than the Fair Labor Standards Act, which only requires the payment of an overtime premium after an employee works 40 hours in a week. Under the FLSA, an employer may utilize a flexible week by which employees can work more than 8 hours on any day so long as they work no more than 40 hours in the week. Walsh-Healy restricts flexitime to a flexible day of not more than 8 hours.

Who is covered by the Walsh-Healy Act? The general rule is that all employees who actually work on federal government contracts in excess of $10,000 are covered. In many cases, employees of a subcontractor which furnishes materials or articles to a prime government are also covered. The Walsh-Healy Act itself excludes "open market" purchases, contracts for perishables including dairy, live stock, and nursery products, purchases of certain agricultural and farm products, contracts with common carriers for carriage of personnel and freight, and contracts for the furnishing of services by radio, telephone, telegraph, and cable. The Secretary of Labor has administratively excluded contracts (1) for public utilities, (2) for materials, supplies, articles, or equipment manufactured wholly outside the United States, (3) covering purchases against the account of a defaulting contractor, and (4) awarded to sales agents for the delivery of newspapers, magazines, or periodicals by the publishers. In addition, there have been partial administrative exemptions granted for certain contracts for the purchase of coal, goods on the commodity exchange, and export merchandise.

Contracts for construction or public works are not included under Walsh-Healy, although they are covered by the provisions of the Davis-Bacon and Contract Work Hours Standards acts, which are discussed in the next section. Contracts for the rental of real or personal property are also excluded, as are contracts exclusively for services. The Walsh-Healy Act applies only to employees engaged in or connected with the manufacture, fabrication, assembling, handling, supervision, or shipment of material, supplies, articles, or equipment required under the contract. Walsh-Healy does *not* apply to employees who perform only office or custodial work. As with the FLSA, it does not apply to any employee employed in a bona fide executive, administrative, or professional capacity or as an outside salesman.

In contrast to the FLSA, Walsh-Healy does not have general applicability to all employees of an employer. Only those nonexempt employees who *actually* perform work on the materials that are the subject of the federal contract are so covered. Thus, it would not be unusual for an employer to have one group of employees covered by Walsh-Healy while others are only covered by the FLSA. Moreover, Walsh-Healy coverage would only be applicable during the period of time that the goods for said contract are being manufactured. Once they are shipped, it no longer applies.

Laws Covering Federally Financed Construction.   While the Walsh-Healy Act provides wage and hour regulations for employees of private employers engaged in the manufacturing or furnishing of materials to the federal government, companies doing federal construction work are governed by other laws. For example, the Davis-Bacon Act requires an employer engaged in federal construction to pay covered employees at the minimum rate prevailing for that kind of work in the geographical area, together with applicable prevailing fringe benefits.

The Contract Work Hours Act establishes maximum hours standards for laborers and mechanics engaged on federal construction contracts of over $2,000. It mandates payment of an overtime premium of at least one and a half times the basic rate of pay to such employees for each hour worked in excess of 8 hours in any day and 40 hours in any week. The impact of the Contract Work Hours Act on flexitime is the same as that of the Walsh-Healy Act. The restrictions only apply to those employees who are actually engaged on the federal construction project and only for the time that they are so engaged.

Here again, one may be faced with the possibility that groups of employees within the same organization will be subject to different degrees of overtime restrictions. The organization seeking to introduce flexitime must therefore be cognizant of the different rules and design its system accordingly.

PUBLIC EMPLOYMENT

General

The previous sections dealt with the laws which, for the most part, affect employment in the private sector of the economy. It was seen that, in order to determine which, if any, of the laws apply to a particular situation, it is necessary to examine (1) the nature of the employer's business, (2) the job that the employee is performing, and (3) his function within the organization. In general, these same factors apply when we analyze the laws affecting public sector employment. With respect to the public sector, we must examine (1) the nature of the government entity, (2) the employee's job, and (3) the employee hierarchy within the agency.

Nature of the Government Entity.   When one uses the term *public employee,* the image most often conjured up is that of the dutiful civil servant, sitting at a desk and processing paper. Although many government employees do just that, rarely do we stop to realize that government operations in the United States require a full range of employee services and abilities. Almost every occupational title found in the private sector has its public sector counterpart.

The framework of most governments generally consists of the traditional branches—executive, legislative, and judicial. Normally, the agencies which perform most of the public services of government and which employ most of the government's employees are attached to the executive branch. In the federal government, executive agencies include the cabinet level departments, their subsidiary bureaus, and other entities. The laws governing conditions of employment for public employees frequently exclude employees of one or another of the branches, departments, bureaus, or agencies for various reasons. Consequently, in analyzing the impact of any law covering public employees, we must determine which agencies are included.

As will be more fully discussed in a later section, the basic terms of employment for most federal employees, including salary schedules and overtime, weekend, holiday, and shift premiums, are governed by federal law—Title 5 of the U.S. Code. Nonfederal public employees are not covered. Each state has its own version of a civil service law setting forth, in varying degrees of detail, the employment conditions for its employees. In some states, the civil service law applies to municipalities and other political as well as state subdivisions. Elsewhere, each locality sets its own rules. There are literally hundreds of state and local statutes governing employment conditions for employees of those entities. A detailed analysis of them is far beyond the scope of this book. The discussion will, therefore, be restricted to the law governing federal employees.

The Employee's Job.   As in private industry, the public employee's job may determine whether he is covered by any particular law. As an example, employees working in the laboring crafts may be covered by so-called *prevailing rate* laws. Such laws mandate that specified classifications of employees receive the wages and benefits prevailing for similar employment in private industry in the geographic area. On the other hand, public safety employees, such as police officers and fire fighters, are often excluded from any restrictive legislation. Creation of a flexitime system for any particular governmental employer requires analysis as to whether particular employees fall under the protection of statutes applicable to that employer.

In all probability, it will be found that a different flexitime model will have to be designed for each government agency. In some cases, a multilevel model, as in the SmithKline approach, may be necessary within an agency.

Employee Hierarchy within the Agency.   Although the term *public employee* encompasses almost everyone on the government payroll up to and including the President of the United States, laws regulating public employment usually recognize the distinction between higher-level jobs (such as supervisors and managers) and rank and file employees. Frequently, as in private industry, higher-level employees are excluded from legislative coverage. Consequently, where, for example, the law provides for cash payment of overtime premiums, such premiums may only be payable to lower-level employees.

Laws Affecting Flexitime for Federal Employees

The statutory regulation of terms and conditions of employment for most federal employees is contained in Title 5 of the U.S. Code, which establishes the general structure of the federal civil service. Chapter 55 of that Title, *Pay Administration,* sets forth salary schedules and provides for overtime premium pay.* Insofar as they affect flexitime, the essential elements of the premium pay provisions of Title 5, include:

1.   An overtime premium of time and one-half for hours worked in excess of 8 hours in a day and 40 hours in a week

2.   A 10 percent night differential for time worked between 6 P.M. and 6 A.M.

3.   A premium of 25 percent for work on Sunday if not overtime

4.   Double time for work on a holiday even if not overtime

As with the private sector, not all federal employees are subject to these provisions. To demonstrate the complexity of determining the coverage of the law and, hence, the need for professional analysis of this subject too, the following examples are given. Coverage of this law extends to employees of executive branch agencies, military departments, judicial branch agencies, the Library of Congress, the botanic garden, the Office of the Architect of the Capitol, and the District of Columbia government. Among those excluded are judges, agency heads, employees of the D.C. Board of Education, police and fire Departments and U.S. park police, prevailing wage employees, and Tennessee Valley Authority and Federal Land Bank employees.

Insofar as overtime is concerned, the premium is paid only on salary earned up to the basic G.S. 10 salary level. For monies earned above the basic G.S. 10 rate, time and one-half of the basic G.S. 10 rate, only, is paid. Nonmanagement air traffic controllers receive time and one-half up to G.S. 14. All prevailing-rate employees get time and one-half for work over 40 hours in a week and 8 hours in a day.

The overtime provisions of Title 5 limit the use of flexitime to within the 8-hour day. Even within the flexible day, there is further restriction in the choice of the bandwidth because of the night differential to be paid for hours worked after 6 P.M. The Sunday and holiday premiums prevent the easy incorporation of Sundays and holidays into any flexitime scheme. Despite these restrictions, as was seen in Chapter 10, limited flexitime has been successfully introduced in many federal agencies.

LAWS AFFECTING FLEXITIME IMPLEMENTATION

General

Laws regulating hours of work, such as those discussed above, have impact only on the design of a flexitime system. Once a suitable system has been designed, however, other laws may influence the process of introducing it into the organization. In general, the laws which

*On September 29, 1978, President Carter signed the Federal Employees Flexible and Compressed Work Schedules Act of 1978 ("Flexitime Act") which permits federal agencies to experiment with a full range of flexitime and compressed workweek models for three years notwithstanding any legal restrictions. The Flexitime Act's provisions are fully discussed later in this chapter.

affect system implementation are those labor laws, such as the National Labor Relations Act (NLRA), which require negotiation about proposed changes in terms and conditions of employment of unionized employees or those which a union is in the process of organizing. Implementing flexitime where unions are involved requires the additional step of union negotiation prior to the implementation of the system.

As with maximum hours laws, these labor laws exist at the federal, state, and local level, both in the private and public sectors. In the private sector, the NLRA covers most employers. Many states have adopted state labor relations acts which assume jurisdiction over private employers that are excluded from NLRA coverage. With respect to government employment, many states have adopted laws authorizing state and local public employees to negotiate collectively. Federal employees are governed by yet another labor relations statute.

The following discussion will be limited to the requirements of the NLRA, since that law has the widest application. Review of flexitime implementation procedures for federal agencies is reserved for the section on new legislation.

National Labor Relations Act

The National Labor Relations Act* is the principal law covering labor relations in private industry in America. The NLRA establishes the National Labor Relations Board (NLRB) as the impartial federal agency to resolve specified labor-management issues. The NLRB has jurisdiction over employers with operations "affecting commerce." It has established minimum economic standards to determine whether an employer falls under its jurisdiction.

NLRB jurisdictional standards vary somewhat based on the nature of the employer's operations, but a typical example is the standard applied to a retail establishment—it must do at least $500,000 in gross annual business, with at least $50,000 of sales or purchases flowing into or out of the state where its principal place of business is located. All employers meeting the NLRB's jurisdictional minimums are covered by the NLRA, except federal, state, and local governments, federally owned corporations, any Federal Reserve bank, persons subject to the Railway Labor Act, and certain industries which the NLRB has administratively excluded. Even in organizations subject to NLRB jurisdiction, managerial, confidential, and supervisory employees are excluded from coverage.

Insofar as flexitime is concerned, one's interest in the NLRA is limited to the *employer's duty to bargain.* NLRA makes it an unfair labor practice for any employer to refuse to bargain collectively with the representatives of its employees. In instances where employees who are to be given the right to have flexible working hours are represented by a labor union or where a union is in the process of organizing, the employer is obligated to bargain over the proposed changes. Cases interpreting the duty to bargain have held that an employer may not unilaterally make substantial changes in existing terms and conditions of employment where a union is involved, unless it has first bargained over the proposed changes. The rationale behind the rule is that unilateral changes could result in an undermining of the union's authority as employee bargaining agent. Needless to say, any proposed change which would be in violation of a term of an existing collective bargaining agreement could not be implemented, unless the union agreed to modify the contract.

*29 USC 151 et seq.

As an example, assume there is a labor contract which provides that an overtime premium be paid for all hours worked over 40 in one week. If management designs a flexitime system which permits employee flexibility within the 40-hour period but which does not permit the carrying over of hours from week to week, the system would not violate the contract. Nevertheless, the union would probably still have a right to negotiate. Although flexitime may be viewed as beneficial to the employees, many significant details of the system might be of concern to the union and its membership. For instance, the new scheduling could affect the number of hours of paid overtime, breaks, lunch periods, and other working conditions as well as security and safety procedures.

The duty to bargain, however, does not imply that the parties must reach agreement. So long as the employer is not contractually prohibited from making a proposed change, its obligation is to advise the union that it intends to make the change and offer to negotiate. If the union does not request negotiation or pursue meaningful bargaining, it may be deemed to have waived the right to object. If the union and the employer engage in good faith negotiations but reach an impasse on the items to be changed, the employer will have fulfilled its duty to bargain and may then unilaterally implement those changes over which there is an impasse.

Because of the lack of existing case law, it is not known at present to what extent flexitime-related changes will be subject to the duty-to-bargain rules. Certainly, an extensive flexitime system giving employees wide latitude in determining their work hours, including the right to work a longer than standard day, would require negotiation. It is strongly suggested, however, that since flexitime is viewed as a substantial benefit to employees as well as to management, and since the involvement and cooperation of employees is essential to success with the flexitime program, management should make every effort to involve employee unions at the earliest possible planning stages. In many cases, bringing the union into the planning phase of a flexitime system will help to allay any fears and suspicions which might otherwise seriously obstruct the effectiveness of the program. Moreover, the union's firsthand knowledge of employee needs and attitudes could well result in their making positive contributions which will increase the probability of the flexitime system's success.

NEW PROMISE FOR FLEXITIME IN LEGISLATION

As has been seen, the requirement that wage premiums be paid for overtime work imposes severe financial limitations on the design of a flexitime system. In most cases, employers would not want to grant their employees the authority to schedule overtime for themselves if such overtime will be compensated at time and one-half. Consequently, where laws such as Fair Labor Standards, Walsh-Healy, and the Contract Work Hours Act apply, employers will generally design a flexitime model which limits flexibility to nonpremium hours.

These laws have deep roots in America's industrial relations history. Despite increasingly favorable interest in the new, innovative work scheduling techniques, it will probably be a long time before the old laws will be modified to accommodate flexitime. One can readily understand the resistance of many unions to any change that would result in an employee working more than 8 hours without a wage premium. Unions have fought long and hard for such benefits as the 8-hour day. They would be reluctant to agree to a system that could jeopardize employee rights to overtime premiums. Some union leaders feel that management could use the more advanced forms of flexitime to return to exploitative overtime practices. And, with more options available, the difficulties of enforcing existing wage and hour regulations would increase.

The United States Congress has considered flexitime to be of sufficient importance to warrant passage of legislation waiving wage and hour controls to allow for federal flexitime experiments. The U.S. Office of Personnel Management will supervise those experiments.

Since 1974, a number of bills authorizing flexitime for federal employees have been introduced. These efforts culminated in the Federal Employees Flexible and Compressed Work Schedules Act of 1978, which finally passed Congress in 1978. At the signing ceremony, President Carter stated that he felt that the introduction of more flexible work alternatives will "benefit, among others, persons with children, students and the older or handicapped worker." He also expressed hope that "flexible work schedules will increase government productivity and responsiveness to public needs, and provide a new pool of talent for government services."

With respect to flexitime, the new law generally provides as follows:

1.   A 3-year trial period for flexitime experiments is authorized.

2.   The Office of Personnel Management is to develop experimental programs for federal agencies which cover a sufficient number of positions and sufficient range of work time alternatives to provide an adequate basis on which to evaluate the desirability of maintaining flexitime in the executive branch.

3.   Where a union is the exclusive representative of agency employees, the flexitime program may not be implemented unless it is included in a bargaining agreement.

4.   No employee may interfere with any other employee in the exercise of his rights under any flexible scheduling program then in effect.

5.   Core time and flexible bands will be established. If ordered in advance, overtime may be required and compensated in the traditional fashion. Full-time employees may carry over up to 10 credit hours from one biweekly accounting period to the next.

6.   Part-time employees may also be included in the experiments and may carry over credit hours from one accounting agreement to the next.

The new law constitutes a major step forward for the advocates of flexitime. If necessary funds are to be appropriated to enable the Office of Personnel Management to properly conduct and evaluate the experiments, the result will be the first large-scale, comprehensive analysis of sophisticated flexitime models in America. If the experiments are successful, flexitime will undoubtedly become a permanent option for government agencies. Private industry, too, should then become increasingly interested in adopting flexitime.

CONCLUSION

Flexitime represents a radical change in traditional concepts of employee scheduling. For this reason, as well as the legal and social inertia of existing practices, movement toward adoption of flexitime in America has been slow. However, the legal restrictions are not so great as to completely prohibit flexitime. Despite shortcomings, flexitime experiments have generally been successful. Employers must sometimes be creative, as SmithKline, with its three-tiered system of different levels of flexibility for Walsh-Healy, FLSA, and exempt employees. At the same time, they must take care to properly design the system to prevent future problems.

The recently passed federal legislation will facilitate further experimentation with flexitime. If these experiments are successful, it can be anticipated that it will become increasingly more acceptable both in the public and private sectors. As a result, further modification to existing law by federal, state, and local government will be achieved.

LABOR CONTRACTS AND NEGOTIATIONS

INTRODUCTION

We have previously examined the statutory restrictions on flexitime. With respect to hours, the Fair Labor Standards Act, the Contract Work Hours Act, and other similar laws mandate the payment of wage premiums for work in excess of 40 hours per week and, in some cases, for work in excess of 8 hours per day. With respect to implementation where unions are involved, the National Labor Relations Act and other labor relations statutes mandate negotiations concerning those aspects of the proposed flexitime system that would constitute substantial changes in terms and conditions of employment.

Another central consideration in designing the flexitime system is the impact the system will have on existing personnel policies. Virtually every employer has some policy, whether formal, informal, loose, or rigid, defining the structure of the work relationship. Where a union represents employees, the personnel policies will usually be embodied in a written collective bargaining agreement. These personnel policies often provide for benefits greater than the minimum available by law. They create restrictions upon an employer's freedom in addition to those found in statutes.

Personnel policies often include rules regarding such items as wage schedules, hours of work, reporting times, overtime premiums, holiday premiums, vacations, leaves of absence, lunches, breaks, work incentives, and the like. These items are generally referred to as *terms and conditions of employment*. The implementation of flexitime will clearly have some impact on existing terms and conditions of employment. In those areas where substantial changes have to be made, such as hours of work and overtime, an entirely new set of rules may have to be developed. However, organizations should make every effort to limit changes to the fewest possible and only to those clearly related to flexitime. Any change will necessarily create some degree of confusion and upset. Keeping changes to the minimum should make transition to flexitime easier and avoid any accusation that the introduction of flexitime is an excuse for diminishing other terms and conditions of employment.

Where employees to be covered by flexitime are represented by a union, the requisite personnel policy changes will probably be the subject of negotiations. Of course, any new policy which is *contrary* to a provision in an existing labor contract may be implemented only if the union agrees to change the contract. On the other hand, where there are no applicable provisions, changes may be made without union agreement after management has offered to negotiate with the union and an impasse is reached. (See previous section.) Even where there is no union, management should understand that the existing terms and conditions of employment constitute an informal contract with employees and should make every effort to involve employees in the planning stages of flexitime.

The following sections review a number of the specific terms and conditions of employment which, in one form or another, prevail in most organizations and which are affected by flexitime. The analysis must necessarily be limited to a general identification of problem areas. However, each individual organization must create a system to fit its own unique circumstances.

Hours of Work

Full Time

The flexitime system need not change existing policies regarding hours of work. The number of hours worked in a given period can remain the same, although starting, quitting, and break time may vary. An organization that currently works a 40-hour week can continue to work a 40-hour week; an organization that works 35 hours per week or 37½ hours per week can continue with those hours. The following section from an agreement between the Hotel Association of New York and the New York Hotel and Motel Trades Council is typical of a general clause that would need no substantial modification to accommodate limited flexitime.*

> The working hours per week on which the minimum wage is predicted shall be 40 hours within 5 days of the week for captains, hostesses and all tip classifications covered by this agreement, and 35 hours in 5 days of the week for all non-tip classifications covered by this agreement.

However, where a collective bargaining agreement specifies that hours of work commence at a particular time and end at a particular time, or where shifts with specific hours are set forth, the language will have to be revised to accommodate flexitime. An example of such an inflexible provision is:

> Seven hours shall constitute a day's work between the hours of 8:30 A.M. and 11:55 A.M. and from 12:30 P.M. to 4:00 P.M., 5 days a week, except Saturday, Sunday and Holidays. (Building Trades Employers Assoc., and Laborers)

Many collective bargaining agreements specify the standard to be a 40-hour workweek of 8-hour days. The following agreement is typical:

> The normal schedule of hours shall consist of 8 hours per day and 40 hours per week, Monday through Friday. (True Temper Corp., and Steelworkers)

---

*All contractual provisions quoted in this chapter are extracted from a 1974 United States Department of Labor study entitled *Hours, overtime and weekend work,* USDL BLS Bulletin (1425-15). Although many of the contracts cited have now expired, their language is illustrative of what still prevails. Written personnel policies found outside of collective bargaining agreements often contain similar language to the contract provisions quoted in this chapter.

Such a provision would not require modification for a flexitime model in which the employee works an 8-hour day and which offers flexibility only as to the time of arrival and time of departure. Where the employer is contemplating a system incorporating the flexible week or carry-over, a provision limiting the normal workday to 8 hours would have to be changed.

Part time

In general, contract provisions specifying hours of work refer to hours for full-time employees. However, increasing numbers of employers are utilizing part-time and job-sharing procedures. The nature and structure of part-time work vary from organization to organization and even within a given organization, and the attitude of unions toward part-time work varies from acceptance to rejection.

As with full-time work, contract provisions covering part-time work range from loose to restrictive. Typical examples are:

> Regular part-time employee is a regular employee whose normal assignment of work is less than the normal basic work week. (General Telephone Co., of Philadelphia, and IBEW)

and:

> The normal workweek for part-time employees shall be at least 20 hours but less than 40 hours of work on not less than 4 days in each week. (R.H. Macy & Co., and Retail Clerks)

Part-time arrangements include: working less than 8 hours five or fewer days a week; working less than five 8-hour days per week; working 40 or more hours per week for only a portion of the year, or any combination of the above. These arrangements constitute what could be called *regular part-time* as distinguished from casual employment.

By their nature, part-time arrangements within an organization tend to be far more flexible than full-time. One reason for this is the fact that employees don't have to worry about payment of overtime premiums which normally are not legally mandated until the employee works in excess of 40 hours in any particular week. And labor contracts often allow payment of reduced benefits for part-timers. Consequently, employers may have fewer adjustments to make for part-time employees within a flexitime system.

Many unions oppose the use of part-time labor because it reduces the number of full-time employees. Consequently, part-time labor should be of particular concern to any union if there is a possibility that the introduction of flexitime could undermine the rights, privileges, or benefits of full-time workers. Adequate definitions and realistic restrictions ensuring a reasonable degree of mobility among part-timers and full-timers are essential to prevent friction and to increase the possibility of flexitime success.

Limitation of Employer's Freedom to Make Changes

Where organizations have employees on a variety of work schedules, applicable collective bargaining agreements frequently contain provisions restricting the employer's ability to effect unilateral changes in scheduling. Some agreements require an employer to give advance notice of any scheduling change, others mandate that the employer consult with the union, and still others require that the union give prior approval to such changes. A few agreements even provide for wage premiums as penalties where scheduling changes are made without proper notice. Some typical examples of such provisions follow.

Notification prior to change of schedule:

> The employer must establish a regular starting time, then if the employer desires to change the established starting time, the employee(s) must be notified before the regular workday of any change in the established starting time for the following day. (Area Underground Contractors Assn., and Operating Engineers)

No scheduling change unless agreed to by the union:

> The employer shall arrange for starting time for work as is convenient to his operations and shall prepare a schedule showing the starting time for each employee and a copy shall be delivered to the union and to the shop steward. The starting time shall not be changed during the full term of this agreement unless mutually agreed to by the union and the employer. (N.Y. Area Industrial Refuse Collecting Contractors, and Teamsters; Exp. November 1975)

Limitation on the number of hours by which a schedule can be changed:

> The employer shall post, not later than Thursday, the schedule of days off and the starting times for the week immediately following. One week's notice shall be given of any change in the starting-time of more than 2 hours. In case of an emergency, the starting-time may be changed for 1 day only in a week by more than 2 hours, but a change in the starting-time shown on the posted schedule may be made for 1 day only in any one week, and only in case of an emergency.
>
> Except for bona fide relief men, an employee's starting-time shall not vary more than 2 hours earlier nor 2 hours later than the posted starting-time for the first day of the week. (Relief men —12 hours between shifts.) (Associated Milk Dealers, Chicago, and Teamsters)

Penalty of pay premium for employer violation of notification provision:

> When 24 hours or more notice before the start of work on a changed daily tour is given, the changed tour shall be the employee's scheduled tour and he shall be compensated at the basic straight-time rate, plus applicable premiums. When less than 24 hours notice before the start of work on the changed daily tour is provided, the following shall apply:
> Straight time compensation will be paid for all hours worked in the changed tour that coincides with the regularly scheduled tour. A non-scheduled tour premium of one-half ($\frac{1}{2}$) the basic straight-time rate will be paid for all hours worked that did not coincide with the regularly scheduled tour. (General Telephone Co., Michigan, and IBEW)

Obviously, many contractual restrictions on scheduling of work would have to be modified to accomodate a flexitime system, as the requirement that rigid schedules of days off and hours of work be maintained is incompatible with flexible scheduling. Such changes, however, may be strongly resisted by unions for historical reasons. Many contractual scheduling restrictions were developed by unions because of employer abuse of the right to schedule work time. When the employer unilaterally changed schedules without prior notice, the employees felt that their personal time was being infringed upon. Employees wanted to know, with some degree of predictability, what their work schedule would be so that they could plan the other aspects of their life. Unions fear that employers will use flexitime, which should be and is looked upon by employees as a benefit, as an excuse to return to old habits.

PREMIUM PAY RULES

Overtime

The U.S. Department of Labor's 1974 study of hours, overtime, and weekend work clauses in major collective bargaining agreements, cited above, reviewed 1,690 contracts, each of which covered 1,000 or more employees. Of those 1,690 agreements, only 34 did not contain a provision for overtime pay premiums (U.S. Dept. of Labor, BLS Bulletin 1425-15, p. 9).

Contractual overtime provisions tend to be somewhat more complex than the simple statutory mandates. Overtime practices vary from employer to employer; the complexities often derive from union and management attention to particular labor relations problems within their organizations. Consequently, of the collective bargaining agreements which provide for overtime, many have one or a combination of the following provisions:

1. Double-time pay premiums

2. Overtime premium of time and a half for an initial period of overtime work in a given day, with one or more higher premiums to be paid on a graduated scale for additional hours worked in that day (e.g., time and a half for the first 2 hours of overtime in any day, double time for the next 2 hours and double time and a half for all hours worked in excess of 12 in any day)

3. Graduated overtime premiums for work in excess of a certain specified number of weekly hours

4. Premium pay for working through lunch periods

5. Meal allowances, paid meal and rest periods during an overtime tour

6. Absolute limitations on the number of overtime hours any employee may work in a day or week

7. Advance notice by the employer to the employee that he will be required to work overtime

8. Guaranteed minimum number of overtime hours

9. Prohibitions on compensatory time off

10. Minimum time off between shifts (i.e., a minimum of 12 hours off before an employee may be required to come back to work)

11. Regulation of the distribution of overtime work (e.g., overtime must be distributed either on the basis of seniority, rotation, or some other system)

12. Compulsory overtime, as opposed to the right of the employee to refuse to work overtime

13. Restrictions on the eligibility of certain groups, such as probationary, temporary, and part-time workers to work overtime

Some examples of typical overtime provisions found in collective bargaining agreements follow:

1. Hours during which overtime premiums are to be paid:

i. Simple provision:

Time and one-half an employee's regular rate of pay will be paid for all hours worked in excess of 40 hours in a work-week. (West Point Pepperell-Lindale and Textile Workers; Exp. December 1975)

ii. Detailed Provision:

Wherever the word 'overtime' is used in this agreement, it means time during which an employee shall have worked for an employer (a) in excess of 7 hours in any period of 24 consecutive hours; (b) in excess of 35 hours in the regular payroll week; (c) before or after the regular working hours; or (d) on any Saturday or on any paid holiday or paid half-holiday mentioned in . . . this agreement. (Knitted Outerwear Manufacturers, Pennsylvania, and ILGWU; Exp. June 1975)

2. Graduated overtime premium based on the number of hours worked:

When an employee actually works more than 16 hours in a 24 hour period beginning with the starting time of a designated shift, he shall be paid at the overtime rate for all hours worked, beginning with the first hour, until he has had a rest period of 8 consecutive hours. The meal time taken during the first 8 hours will count as time worked towards the 16 hours but not for pay purposes. (Georgia-Pacific Corp., Crosset Division, and Paper Workers; Exp. June 1974)

3. Meal and break periods:

i) Premium pay for working during the meal period:

Employees may be required to work during a part of or all of their lunch period, in which case they shall be paid 30 minutes at time and one-half, or a total of 45 minutes. However, should an employee be required to work during his regular lunch period, such time will be allowed him to eat his lunch within the limits of the 4th and 6th hours after commencement of his work shift, without deduction in pay. (Kennecott Copper, Utah, and United Steelworkers; Exp. June 1974)

ii. Breaks during overtime period:

In the event employees are required to work overtime on regular work days and said overtime amounts to 2 hours or more, such employees shall be allowed a 5-minute break immediately prior to commencement of the overtime work. If said overtime amounts to 4 hours or more, such employees shall be allowed an additional 10-minute break upon the completion of 2 hours overtime. (Pacific Car and Foundry Co., and United Auto Workers; Exp. August 1974)

iii. Meal Allowance:

Supper money in the amount of $2.50 shall be paid to all employees after 10 hours of work. (Master Builders Assoc., Pennsylvania, and Teamsters; Exp. May 1973)

4. Prior notification of overtime:

Insofar as practicable and consistent with production requirements, the company will make every effort to notify employees scheduled . . . for daily overtime 2 hours prior to the end of their shift. (Bendix Corp., Kansas City, and Machinists; Exp. August 1975)

5. Limitation on overtime:

Overtime shall not exceed 3 hours per week, except by permission of the union. (Building & Construction Contractors, Madison, and Carpenters; Exp. March 1973)

6. Minimum overtime:

An employee who works overtime will be guaranteed a minimum of 2 hours of work or 2 hours of pay at his overtime rate. (Aerodex, Miami, and Teamsters)

7. Allocation of overtime:

Overtime will be distributed by rotation within a classification, as equally as reasonably possible among the employees in the department scheduled to work overtime. The individual employer will not be required to schedule an employee for overtime unless he has previously satisfactorily performed the assigned work. (Furniture Manufacturers of Southern California, and Carpenters)

8. Employee's right to refuse overtime:

Employees shall accept overtime work unless they have a reasonable or justifiable excuse to refuse such work. (Wire and Metal Manufacturers, New York, and Teamsters)

Looking at the above examples, it appears that in most instances there will have to be some modification of contructual overtime provisions to accommodate flexitime. How much modification is required will be determined by the scope of the flexitime model as well as the needs of the organization and the desires of the workers involved.

It is presumed that in some cases the introduction of flexitime may result in a reduction of the need for traditional overtime work. Such reduced need is the result of many factors, including the availability of some portion of the work force for more hours during the workday than previously and the fact that the employees will be at work when they are most productive.

Premium Pay for Weekend Work

Most employees work the traditional 5-day week from Monday through Friday. But in many industries work on Saturdays, Sundays, or both is necessary. Even where weekend work is not a standard practice, there may be an occasional need for someone to work a Saturday or a Sunday. Since weekend time off is of great importance to American workers, premium pay for weekend work provides a necessary inducement and/or compensation for requiring employees to work those days. The U.S. Department of Labor study mentioned earlier reports that over 90 percent of major American collective bargaining agreements have provisions for weekend work that reflect the work patterns of the employer. For example, a distinction is often made between weekend work after completion of a 5-day week (overtime) and weekend work as a part of a regular 5-day schedule. In addition, contracts frequently make provision for the manner in which weekend work is assigned or distributed; e.g., an employee may be permitted a choice as to whether or not his 5-day schedule includes a Saturday, based on seniority.

Where weekend work is overtime, an employee may have a contractual right to refuse to work. Distinctions may be made between Saturday and Sunday work, Sunday work generally carrying a higher premium. An example of a weekend work provision follows:

> All time worked in excess of a regular work day or the regular work week, or before the start or after the end of the regular work day and all work performed on Saturdays, Sundays and Holidays, shall constitute overtime and shall be paid at double the straight time rate except that all such overtime on jobbing and repair work shall be paid at one and one-half times the straight time rate. (Industrial Contractors, California, and Plumbers)

Where the weekend work is part of the work week, a different provision may apply:

> When Sunday is scheduled as part of an employee's regular five day workweek, if no half-time or full-time premium applies to the time worked, a premium of 25 percent of the employee's straight-time rate shall be paid for such time worked on Sunday. (Consumers Power Co., and Utility Workers)

Weekend work may be deemed a benefit to be offered to senior employees:

> In case of overtime on Saturday, Sunday or Holidays, the oldest seniority employee holding seniority on a designated seniority line, group or department on which the overtime occurs shall be entitled to the overtime. Said employee shall operate the job of his choice of those running that day provided he is qualified to run the job. However, if an employee's regular job runs on overtime and he is not displaced by an older seniority employee, said employee must run his regular job. (Teletype Industries, and United Auto Workers)

It may also be considered a burden which can be refused:

> Under no circumstances shall an employee be required to work a seventh day in any workweek. (Metropolitan Garage Board of Trade, and Teamsters)

The extent to which the introduction of flexitime has impact upon weekend premiums is directly related to the employer's manning requirements and the level of flexibility offered. In an organization such as a department store, which normally operates on weekends, rules that regulate the selection and compensation for weekend work should not be affected by the advent of flexitime, unless the system permits employees who are not regularly scheduled for Saturday work to make up time on a Saturday. Similarly, if the employer's operation is normally limited to a 5-day, Monday through Friday schedule, and if weekend work occurs only at the specific request of management, employees will not have the option to make up time on weekends and existing rules should not be affected.

However, where an employer wishes to give weekend flexibility to employees who normally work only Monday through Friday, a number of systems-design and implementation problems arise. For example, should a Monday–Friday employee who decides to work a Saturday under flexitime get a work premium? If the weekend work is desirable, how do you protect the interests of those workers who are regularly scheduled for such work? If it is undesirable, how do you ensure adequate staffing on weekends? Certainly, it is not difficult to design rules to resolve these questions. What is most urgent is that these questions be identified and satisfactory solutions be devised in advance of flexitime implementation.

Although there are several ways to handle the situation of weekend premiums, it would probably be easier for the organization to avoid such issues during the initial introduction of flexitime by limiting flexibility to the employee's regularly scheduled workdays. An extension of flexitime to other days should be introduced only after the initial period of experimentation.

Shift Differential

When an organization requires work during evening, late night, or early morning hours, wage premiums are often paid to employees who work the nontraditional hours. The theoretical basis for the payment of shift differentials is similar to that for weekend premiums. It is extra money for working at times when most others are off. An example of a contractual provision for shift premiums follows:

> Section 1. Employees whose regular schedule requires them to work a shift beginning at approximately midnight and ending at approximately 8 A.M. (A Shift), or a shift beginning at approximately 4 P.M. and ending at approximately midnight (C Shift), shall be paid 25 cents per hour above their basic rates of pay for the hours worked on the shift. (Monsanto Company, and IUE)

Here, too, a number of problems arise when flexitime is introduced, which parallel the problems of weekend premiums. On the one hand, employees who do not normally work during premium-pay hours may want to extend their work day into such hours for reasons other than wages. On the other hand, the employer does not want to incur premium-pay liabilities for employees who voluntarily work these hours. Some compromise will have to be reached to accommodate both sides.

Miscellaneous Contract Provisions

Most collective bargaining agreements provide for such benefits as holidays, vacations, and sick leave. In addition, some contracts require compensation for time off for events such as jury duty, the death of a family member, the conduct of union business, blood donations, and the like. Lunch and periodic coffee breaks are also incorporated into labor agreements. Such benefits are not limited to unionized employees. Nonunion employers usually provide at least some of these benefits.

The flexitime system should be designed so as not to alter such benefits. As has been said before, in approaching the problem of accommodating employee fringe benefits to a flexitime model, the general rule to follow is to design a system which will cause the least possible change to existing employee benefits.

Conclusions

The aim here has been to alert the parties concerned to many of the issues which arise when changes are made in personnel policies upon implementation of a flexitime system. The difference between how unionized employees and nonunionized employees are handled is a matter of form. Unionized employers will have to negotiate solutions through their unions and deal with potential or organized union opposition to flexitime implementation. However, the terms and conditions of employment previously discussed which must be analyzed and changed in order to implement flexitime will have to be dealt with, whether inside the negotiating forum or outside it.

It is fair to guess that where the existing labor-management relationship is characterized by hostility and suspicion, the union will view proposed changes in overtime, weekend, holiday, and shift premiums and the other contractual fringe benefits with skepticism. In such cases, it may be necessary for the parties to introduce flexitime even more gradually and on a more limited experimental basis than would otherwise be necessary. The union, its members, and management could then test the sincerity of the other side while they learn to feel more comfortable with flexitime and to appreciate its advantages. It is likely that once the union is shown that flexitime works and that it is beneficial to its membership, opposition will diminish.

Generally, the hours of work and overtime provisions of any collective bargaining agreement will be those most subject to flexitime renegotiation. The complexity of these negotiations will be dependent on many factors, including the number of employees involved, the variety of classifications, the number and distribution of work locations, the number of shifts worked, and the historic and present state of the labor-management relationship. We advise that *the union be brought in at the earliest planning stages.* These complexities should then be resolved with less difficulty. And even where there is no union, it would be advisable to obtain input from first-line supervisors concerning each of the terms and conditions of employment discussed here.

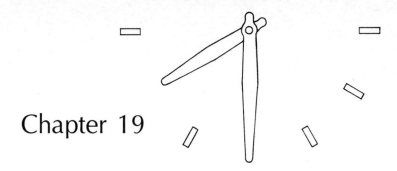

Chapter 19

Time-Recording Systems

INTRODUCTION

A time-recording system is necessary to provide an accurate record for both employee and the employer of the actual hours the employee has worked within a specified period of time. Management has the responsibility to ensure that the employee has worked the contracted number of hours and that the laws governing the minimum and maximum number of working hours are enforced. Time recording also provides a basis of information which can be used in the settling of disputes over credit or debit balances. For the employee, the time-recording system should provide an accounting system of the number of hours worked to date within the settlement period and the balance of hours still required. Thus, the time-recording system should be considered a source of information that is useful to both the employee and the employer, rather than a monitoring device. The systems used under flexitime should not be equated with the more traditional form of time recording—namely, time clocks. Although time clocks are one of the alternatives available under flexitime, such devices contradict the intent of the time-recording systems utilized for flexitime and are usually used only during transitional periods when converting to flexitime.

In common among time-recording systems used to record flexible hours is the fact that the *employee* has more responsibility for maintaining the record, unlike the standard hours system where the supervisor is usually responsible for record keeping. With the additional autonomy and control over work hours provided under flexitime comes the responsibility for self-reporting. Clearly, the mutual trust between employer and employee implicit in a flexitime system would be undermined if the employee did not have some participation in the reporting process itself. A system that claims to allow freedom of choice is severely limited if each choice is strictly monitored; the monitoring process itself becomes a form of control. In an environment of mutual trust, the employer must grant the employee some level of autonomy or freedom of choice; and, in return, the employee must fulfill his responsibility through some form of time recording. Ideally, the levels of trust and responsibility granted should be shared by both sides. For example, decreased control through a less structured time-recording system implies greater autonomy for the employee, but it provides greater possibilities for taking advantage of the system. More responsibility is placed upon the employee to fulfill the level of trust granted by the employer through accurate reporting. In sum, the decision by the employer to implement flexitime represents a commitment to trust his employees and to delegate additional responsibilities. After the choice of the actual FWH system, the choice of a time-recording system represents the second major vehicle for putting this commitment into practice. Much of the goodwill created through the willingness to implement flexitime can be negated through the inappropriate or inconsistent choice of a time-recording system.

The fact that employees have more responsibility for their own record keeping is also a reflection of another aspect of flexitime: that is, the elimination of the concept of tardiness, with corresponding benefits for employees and supervisors. Once time recording is no longer necessary to control punctuality, supervisors are freed from the unpleasant and time-consuming task of monitoring arrivals and departures. Note that this benefit of flexitime further enhances the opportunities for mutual trust to develop by eliminating much of the monitoring required of most supervisors under fixed hours. It also removes this *negative association* from the time-recording system.

Time recording-systems used with flexitime vary in the amount of participation required of the employee, and in the type and quantity of information returned to the employee and to the organization by the system. This variation is chiefly a function of the organizational climate within which the system is implemented, the mechanical/electronic sophistication of the time-recording mechanism, and the complexity of the flexitime system itself. Some aspects of organizational climate have already been described —in particular, the role of mutual trust in determining the level of responsibility granted to employees (as reflected in the choice of a time-recording system). As for mechanical/electronic complexity, one can generalize by stating that the more complex the system, the more information is provided to the organization and to the individual. On the other hand, simpler systems (especially manual ones) require greater levels of participation from employees.

The other major aspect for consideration in the choice of a time-recording system is the *flexitime schedule itself.* The more variations possible within the flexitime scheme, the more difficult and cumbersome time recording becomes. For example, under a flexitime system which has a fixed lunch period and does not allow the debiting or crediting of hours, quitting time is strictly determined by starting time. Thus, time recording is relatively simple, and, excluding other factors, some form of a manual system would be appropriate. On the other hand, consider the following situation, where debiting and crediting is allowed, and where the lunch hour is flexible:

Starting Time	Lunch Begins	Lunch Ends	Quitting Time
8:14 A.M.	12:32 P.M.	2:04 P.M.	5:47 P.M.

How much time has the employee put in on this particular day? What is the total number of hours he has worked so far this week? Obviously, under such a system, keeping track of hours worked can become quite a burden. An automatic means of time recording would benefit employees as well as the employer in this situation.

Time recording was earlier described as a major indication of the level of trust granted by the employer under flexitime. The degree of flexibility in the flexitime system becomes a complicating factor, however, as just shown. Fortunately, time-recording mechanisms have been devised which can keep track of complicated records with a minimum of intrusion upon the employee's autonomy. The following section is a description of the various types of time-recording systems available: manual systems, time clocks, cumulative meters, and computerized systems. The level of mechanical sophistication of each system is described, and its relationship to the type of flexitime system with which it is most compatible. For each type of system, a list of considerations for implementation and samples of actual forms used by organizations installing such systems are included.

MANUAL SYSTEMS

Honor System

The honor system, as the name implies, is a system of mutual trust in which no form of formal recording is required. Management fully trusts the employee to work the appropriate number of hours. One would expect to find such systems in very small organizations, composed mainly of professionals, high-level sales personnel, or employees who have a share of the business. In such organizations, employees are expected to be highly motivated and dedicated to organizational goals. Within this context, the concept of a flexitime system itself becomes almost redundant. Because employees are considered to be self-motivated, they are given the freedom to schedule their own work time. Under flexitime in such an environment, there may well be neither prescribed core hours, nor maximum nor minimum work hours per day.

Abuses of the honor system could result in serious losses for the organization, not to mention the undermining of trust, and the withdrawal of the privilege from all employees. The level of autonomy granted to employees on an honor system is possible only in an organizational environment where employees are fully trusted by management and by each other (the importance of the latter is not to be underestimated). Further, each employee must have his own job tasks which he can perform independently of fellow workers. Such a system (or lack thereof) can function well only in the types of organizational climates described. It is also clear, however, that this level of responsibility and autonomy is appropriate for this environment, and that a more structured arrangement may be counterproductive.

Recording by Exception

Reporting by exception is a variation of the honor system. An exception-reporting system is one in which only *exceptions to the standard workweek or accounting period are reported.* Typical exceptions include overtime, paid or unpaid absences such as illness or personal time off or vacation. If no exceptions are reported during the accounting period, no entries are made on the employee's personnel record, and the employee is paid for the standard period.

Under flexitime arrangements which do not allow daily banking, an exception would be reported whenever the hours worked in a day are greater or less than the required daily hours. Debiting and crediting on a daily basis where hours must be resolved at the end of the week would require exception reporting when hours worked at the end of the week do not total to the required amount. No exception would be reported, however, in the case in which hours are debited and credited from day to day. In a flexitime scheme in which banking is allowed between accounting periods (e.g., week to week) and no reckoning is required as long as debit or credit hours are kept within certain limits, the administration of exception reporting becomes more complicated. The criterion for reporting is no longer a disparity between required hours and hours worked. The employee must report any exceptions strictly on the basis of criteria for determining overtime, leaves of absence, or vacation. (In most cases, such determination would occur through some form of interaction with the supervisor.)

Because exception reporting becomes more complicated under systems allowing banking between accounting periods and thus places a greater burden on the employee, it is not usually recommended in these cases. Most typically, the exception system is used in conjunction with flexitime models requiring the employee to resolve his hours on a daily or weekly basis.

One firm (SmithKline) distributes a time-recording form to employees each week for their own use. Employees are requested to keep the form in their desk, locker, or in their personal possession, to complete it on a daily basis, and to total cumulative hours worked for the week. (In this firm, most employees are allowed debit and credit hours within the workweek.) At the end of the week, if they have worked the appropriate number of hours, they may dispose of the form. The firm emphasizes the importance of completing the form each day in order to avoid unauthorized overtime situations. If there is an exception to report, the employee submits the form to the appropriate manager or supervisor. (A sample of the form appears in Chapter 11, Figure 11-2.) A more complicated form would be necessary for a flexitime system with double core periods. This problem is discussed later in the chapter.

The chief advantage of such a system is that it reflects a great deal of trust between management and nonmanagement, while providing some formal system of record keeping. Further, this type of system is not limited to very small organizations, as one might think. SmithKline, the firm described in our example, has successfully implemented this time-recording system for over 2,000 employees, at all levels within the organization.

Disadvantages include employee attempts to cheat the system and difficulties for supervisors in keeping track of who is present and who is absent. With no central reporting place, supervisors have no quick way to determine who is actually on the job, unless employees are grouped within the same work area. The other disadvantage, of course, is the difficulty of using this system under a flexitime model with banking between accounting periods. On the whole, however, companies have reported satisfaction with it. As important, employees have been very positive, and have responded to the level of trust granted by management by making the system work.

Manual Recording Systems

The key to a manual time-recording system is a daily or weekly log sheet on which each employee's starting and stopping times, and hours worked are recorded. This information is then compiled by settlement period and by group or department for accounting and statistical purposes.

Although it is usually considered that manual recording systems delegate much responsibility to the employee for his own record keeping, the actual level of autonomy exercised in such systems can vary a great deal. Some manual entry systems allow the employee to exercise little or no discretion, while others place so much trust in the employee that they amount to an honor system. Of course, the less responsibility delegated to the employee, the greater the burden placed on the supervisor.

The key element in a manual recording system is the time-recording form completed by employees. The amount of information required on the form and the procedures for handling the form will reflect the degree of responsibility delegated to the employee. The following section is a series of questions which the implementor should consider when designing a manual time-recording system.

1. Is the form to be designed for a single employee or a group of employees? Who will maintain the form? Who will administer it? Forms designed for individual employees are typically completed by the employee over a specified period of time or an accounting period. The form is usually maintained by the employee and submitted on a periodic basis for supervisory review and accounting records. The amount of freedom given to the employee in the maintenance of his record can vary from complete autonomy, where the employee is responsible for maintaining his own record, to more restrictive systems in which the supervisor monitors each entry. Corresponding to these degrees of freedom are various types of forms.

Individual time-recording forms vary in complexity, depending on the level of flexibility available, and the amount of information required on the forms in addition to arrival and departure times.

Figure 19-1 represents a typical example of a simple form, maintained by the employee, containing space for 5 weeks of information. Note that this form includes space for debit and credit hours, because the system in which it is utilized allows banking. In the example, an employee has recorded a balance forward of +2.00 hours (top right hand corner), but has debited 1.45 hours for the first week of work (week 1, right column) for a new balance of +0.15 (2.00 − 1.45). Note also that on this particular form the employee records the total time worked each week in hours and minutes.

Another consideration in the design of an individual form is its administration. For example, if the form is to be completed over the course of several weeks, as the sample in Figure 19-1, will supervisory interference be required during this period? The systems designer must decide how frequently the employee will submit his form, as well as what special circumstances require special approval—e.g., personal time off, sick leave, vacations plans.

Forms designed for a group of employees are usually simpler and contain less information per employee than the individual forms. Forms of this type are maintained by the supervisor. However, the privacy granted the employee can be increased or decreased by the administration of the form. For instance, a requirement for the supervisor's initials beside each entry decreases privacy. Alternatively, firms may want to have employees initial their own entries at the end of each day, verifying that the entry is correct, and that the employee assumes full responsibility for that entry.

The location of the form also affects privacy. In order to maximize privacy, the form

MANUAL TIME RECORDING

Dept. _Personnel_	Name _E. Weity_		Employee number _282_						

Settlement period	From _w/c 5th Feb._	To _w/c 26th Feb._	Contracted Hours _4_ wks X _37.5_ h = _150_	Balance b/p _+2.00_					

Week No.	Day	Start A.M.	Finish A.M.	Start P.M.	Finish P.M.	Daily min. worked	Weekly h min	Period h min
1	M	9.00	12.32	1.30	4.30	392		
	Tu	9.20	12.50	1.32	4.30	388	35.45	+0.15
	W	9.05	1.00	1.35	5.05	445		
	Th	8.30	12.40	1.30	5.00	460	-1.45	
	F	8.50	12.45	1.45	5.30	460		
2	M							
	Tu							
	W							
	Th							
	F							
3	M							
	Tu							
	W							
	Th							
	F							
4	M							
	Tu							
	W							
	Th							
	F							
5	M							
	Tu							
	W							
	Th							
	F							
		(a)	(b)	(c)	(d)	(e)	(f)	(g)

Employee signature		Approved by	

Figure 19–1 Example of a manual time-recording sheet.

should be posted on a wall or bulletin board near the entrance to the work area, so that the employee can log his entries without being under the scrutiny of the supervisor. Some supervisors, however, may wish to keep the form at their desk. Although this decreases privacy, it does allow the supervisor to instantly determine who is present and who is absent —important information in certain work situations. Locating the form at the supervisor's desk also prevents any possibility of exaggerating entries on the time sheet.

2. For what amount of time will the form be used? Possibilities are a day, a week, or one month.

3. Will the form be used for individual or group reporting? Individual forms can usually be used for a greater time period than group reporting sheets, simply because of the amount of space available on the sheet. A single form for a work group is usually limited to one day, or a week at most.

4. Within each day, when must the employee sign in and out? For example, will the employee be required to sign in and out for lunch? This question will be largely determined by the level of flexibility allowed. Flexible lunch hours usually require midday entries as well as arrival and departure times. This will also affect the location of the form. If frequent postings are made, the supervisor may not want the form on his desk because of the constant flow of traffic as employees sign in and out.

5. How will irregularities in work time be recorded? Irregularities would include sick leave, paid or unpaid time off, overtime, and vacations. These must be entered for full reconciliation of the time sheet, regardless of whether banking is allowed. Also, as mentioned earlier, one must decide when supervisory interference is required, and what constitutes a special circumstance and what is routine.

6. Besides entries pertaining to work time, what additional information will be required on the form? Most forms request information such as employee identification number, the dates of the settlement period, department, supervisor, an employee signature, and space for approval by a manager. Some forms become multipurpose when information such as billing hours or account assignments are included.

7. In what increments will time be recorded? In manual systems, if time is not recorded to the minute, it is usually rounded to the nearest 5-, 10-, or 15-minute interval. The advantage to rounding is that it makes calculations of total time worked much simpler for the employee to perform. Recall the earlier example of the difficulty an employee would have in trying to determine hours worked under a manual recording system with no rounding. Under simple flexitime systems, such as individually chosen staggered hours, a chart can be devised to aid in determining hours worked.

Whether or not a chart is used, however, the employer must decide whether he will allow rounding when reporting hours worked. The disadvantage is that employees tend to round in a direction to favor themselves, resulting in losses in production time for the company. For example, suppose that an employee arrives at 9:07 A.M. and rounds his arrival to the nearest quarter hour, 9 A.M.—this would be correct under a 15-minute interval reporting system. Then, at lunch, he leaves at 11:57 A.M., but records it as 12 noon. Again, this is consistent with company policy. On this particular day, however, the employee has not worked 10 minutes for which he is paid. Over the course of 50 weeks, a typical work year, rounding 10 minutes per day adds up to 41 hours, or, roughly a week's worth of work. In a company with many employees, this could add up to a significant amount of time.

In those systems where rounding is allowed, firms have alleviated the problem just described by ruling that employees must always round *ahead* to the nearest reporting period. For example, under a quarter-hour system, an employee arriving between 11:46 A.M. and 12 noon would record their arrival time as 12 noon. This gives the company the advantage rather than the employee. However, it could have the negative effect of encouraging employees to delay the start of work till the time actually recorded. Employee behavior during this period may be nonproductive and even disruptive. In such a situation, one of the traditional benefits of flexitime—the decrease in disruptive behavior before settling down to work—can be negated.

8.   What are the procedures for handling the form? To whom will it be submitted and how often? Who receives copies? Usually these forms find their way to the accounting or personnel department. Traditionally, the supervisor collects attendance sheets and compiles the information, often on another form, for submission to other departments. Under flexitime, these procedures do not usually change significantly. However, it is worth considering other possibilities in the spirit of giving employees as much autonomy and privacy as possible. For example, employees might submit their own time sheets directly to the payroll department, as long as a system could be devised for recording absences such as vacation or illness in the employee's personnel record. An alternative would be to have employees take responsibility for compiling the payroll record from individual forms. This could be delegated to a senior employee or employees could take turns. Again, these are suggestions for increasing employee participation and responsibility consistent with the objectives of flexitime, but the full extent of the impact on other departments, such as payroll or accounting, must be considered in order for the system to be successful.

9.   How much additional bookkeeping will the system require? Manual time-recording requires that someone reconcile hours worked on a periodic basis. This task will vary in difficulty depending upon the complexity of the flexitime system in use. One must decide, regardless of the type of system, whether the individual will balance his own account, and, if so, how often. The supervisor's degree of responsibility for his employees' work time must be determined at the same time. Clearly, the greater the control the supervisor feels he must have over employee work habits, the less responsibility will be granted to employees for maintaining their own records. The approach taken by the supervisor is a matter of leadership style, as well as of task demands. Those supervisors who do not feel that they can delegate any of these responsibilities to employees must be able to make their own time available for these activities.

Summary of Manual Systems

An important aspect of the decision about a time-recording system and the form to be used with it is the level of privacy and autonomy to be granted the employee. This is reflected in the type of form—whether it is an individual or groups form—in the information to be reported on it, in the degree of supervisory interference, and in the administration of the reporting process. A decision regarding one of these considerations cannot be made independently of the others; each consideration should be consistent with overall policy as well as with the other decisions. Specifically, the decision to utilize a manual system should reflect policy decision to grant employees more personal freedom.

The means of time recording must be consistent with the flexitime system itself. Both must reflect the climate of the organization. If there is a discrepancy between these aspects, it is unlikely that the flexitime system or the time-recording method—as the most visible symbol of the flexitime scheme—is likely to work. This should serve as a caution to implementors: the best-laid plans for maximizing the autonomy and responsibility granted to employees can be negated by supervisors who administer the system in a way counter to its original intent.

ELECTROMECHANICAL SYSTEMS

Time Clocks

The simplest form of mechanical recording system is the traditional time clock, used with clock cards. Each employee has his own clock card, usually kept in a rack beside the time clock, which is used to clock in upon arrival and clock out when departing. Figure 19-2 is an example of a typical time card altered slightly for a flexitime system. The top portion of the card is completed by the employee or supervisor and represents an accounting of the actual hours worked for the week, standard weekly hours, balance brought forward from the previous period, and any resulting carry-forward. Time entries start at the bottom portion of the card opposite the row labelled (on the right) "Flexible start". From the example, this employee started on Monday at 9 A.M., on Tuesday at 8:30 A.M., and so forth. Notice that if the employee arrives or departs during core periods, these entries must be manually logged (see Tuesday and Friday). Since lunch is also flexible, the employee in this example must clock in and out during lunch as well as in the morning and evening. The bottom portion of the card is a manual reckoning on a day-by-day basis of total hours worked. Portions of hours are recorded in tenths, where one tenth of an hour is 6 minutes. The manual reconciliation of hours required represents one of the major drawbacks of the time clock system. Although this system does provide a mechanical (and thus highly accurate) system of recording hours, it does not significantly reduce the paperwork and administrative costs associated with a manual system. Considered in these terms, a time clock can be expensive when administrative and equipment costs are totaled.

There is, however, a more serious problem associated with time clocks. The time clock is traditionally associated with factories and assembly lines, while flexitime is most typically implemented in a white-collar, office environment. Predictably, office workers have resented and actively protested against the use of the time clock because it retains the stigma of the blue-collar environment, even though associated with the benefits of flexitime. In some cases, it has been reported that once employees become involved with the flexitime concept, the time clock is no longer objectionable. For this to occur, it is imperative that *all* employees, including management, be required to clock in and out to avoid the stigma felt by lower-level employees of reduced status or privilege.

Implementation of a time clock system requires a series of decisions similar to those which must be made for a manual system. For instance, who will reconcile the individual

Week ending Sept. 21/79

NAME Miss S. Primps

37.0 Standard hours

34.4 Actual hours

Difference	2.6	✳ —
B/F from previous period		+ —
C/F to next period	2.6	✳ —

≥ 16.5		≥ 17.0	⊨ 17.5	⊔ 18.0	Flexible finish
	⊨ 16.0				Core
≥ 14.0	⊨ 13.5	≥ 13.5	⊨ 13.0	⊔ 14.0	(Lunch)
≥ 13.0	⊨ 12.0	≥ 12.0	⊨ 12.0	⊔ 13.0	
				⊔ 10.0	Core
≥ 9.0	⊨ 8.5	≥ 8.0	⊨ 9.1		Flexible start
4.0	3.5	4.0	2.9	3.0	17.4 (A. M. total)
2.5	2.5	3.5	4.5	4.0	17.0 (P. M. total)
6.5	6.0	7.5	7.4	7.0	34.4 Total

Figure 19–2 Example of a time card. *(Adapted from a form created by Selectime, Inc.)*

employee time cards—the supervisor or the employee? How will this information be transcribed onto personnel records and by whom? Where should the time clock be placed? It is important to have enough clocks in a work area or floor to prevent long lines and traffic jams at popular hours for coming and going. Finally, how important is it for the supervisor to know who is available and who is not? Time clocks provide no instant means for the supervisor to determine the whereabouts of employees. If the work area is large or spread out, this can cause problems.

The time clock method serves mainly to remove the burden of accurate recording from the employee and minimize initial capital investment in recording equipment. However, it does not necessarily reduce administrative costs. Because of the negative stigma attached to the use of time clocks, and because of the lack of privacy in arrivals and departures under this system (actual arrival and departure times are recorded), time clocks are usually considered the least popular mechanical system. The high administrative costs, plus the availability of more up-to-date, less objectionable systems have made the use of time clocks rare. Firms which have used this method often do so because they already have time clocks in use, or because they are inexpensive. Still, most organizations using time clocks for flexitime have employed them during either pilot studies or transitional periods.

Cumulative Meter (Totalizers)

The concept of time recording using a cumulative meter has been the most popular and successful of the electromechanical recording systems used by companies implementing flexitime. The meter system provides a cumulative record of the amount of time worked for each employee within a settlement period. It is often chosen by firms instead of manual recording systems because it provides an accurate record for legal and contractual requirements concerning wages and hours worked. However, the benefits of this system extend far beyond this consideration.

Although the equipment varies in sophistication and complexity, a basic system usually consists of a master time clock, and some version of an individual time counter for each employee. Employees are given a badge, key, or credit card which is used to activate their counter. Total hours worked are then accumulated over the course of the settlement period for each individual employee. Master clocks can usually be programmed to stop recording outside of the daily bandwidth or during the required lunch hour to discourage working at those times. They are set back to zero at the end of the settlement period.

It is important to note that only total hours worked to date are recorded. Unlike the time clock, they do not record start and stop times. For this reason, cumulative meters are often acceptable to employees who find the use of the time clock objectionable. Acceptance of the cumulative meter concept is enhanced by the fact that these meters were primarily designed for firms on flexitime. Unlike the time clock, they have no history of previous negative associations.

Cumulative meters are most frequently chosen by firms who have decided to implement flexitime systems allowing much variation. In systems which allow a flexible lunch hour, debiting, crediting, and banking, a manual system can become quite cumbersome, as has been demonstrated. Although manual systems are associated with liberal flexitime systems and are consistent with the concept of maximum autonomy for the employee, the administrative burden can outweigh the intrinsic advantages for the employee as well as for the employer. In these situations, the cumulative meter becomes an acceptable alternative, as they have been carefully designed with the goals of flexitime in mind. They attempt to maintain the employee's privacy and minimize the intrusion on his work habits, avoiding the pitfalls of the time clock system. Thus, the cumulative meter can be the exception to the rule that manual systems are most suitable in climates of maximum flexibility and autonomy.

Under cumulative meter systems, some administrative paperwork is still required. On a periodic basis, the meters must be read and the employee's status recorded, including debit or credit hours. Usually, this is done at the end of the week or settlement period, and is called a *Working Record.* Typically, total hours worked each week are recorded for each employee, as well as the debit or credit status for the week and for the month (the settlement period).

An important decision is who will record this information. Some firms assign the supervisor this responsibility, some have supervisors share this task by rotating responsibility for several work groups among them, and others have the employee log his own record on the sheet. This form provides the supervisor and the individual employee with his own working time status at any point within the settlement period. Its use helps to insure that no one violates the flexitime rules or the hour and wage laws.

Provision must also be made for the recording of exceptions to the normal work pattern such as illness, vacation, or overtime. Figure 19-3 is an example of a form called a *diary sheet,* which serves this purpose. This form differs from the working record because it is used to record the activities of one employee for a single week. Note, on the right hand portion of the page, that only exceptions to the flexible day are recorded. This is consistent with the policy to respect the employee's privacy to the greatest extent possible. Note, also, the entry for Thursday of week 3—1 hour is deducted because the employee forgot to deactivate his meter when he went to lunch. The left hand side of the page is a balancing of hours using the information from the meter and the diary sheet. At the bottom, the form is signed by the employee and approved by the manager or supervisor. Again, the decision must be made as to who will maintain this form.

Some firms have combined these two forms, the working record and the diary sheet, in order to reduce paperwork. This is certainly feasible, but one must keep in mind the objectives of the system. Adding the diary sheet information to the working record means that the employee will have his personal transactions reported with other employees. Again, this decreases privacy and may cause problems for the personnel department. Adding the working record to the diary sheet may be more feasible if supervisors are given this responsibility, but this creates extra work for them.

There are several manufacturers of this type of equipment. The equipment developed by two of the firms specializing in this area will be described here in order to provide the reader with a better understanding of this type of system.

FLEXTIME CORPORATION.   The Flextime Corporation, a subsidiary of J. Hengstler KG, has copyrighted the term *Flextime* for their product line. Hence, the common use of the word *flexitime* to refer to the system itself. The basic Flextime component consists of a master control unit which is a clock, programmable to fit the flexible working schedule to

		DIARY SHEET		
		Hrs.	Reason	Dept. Head
Name ___S. Primps___	M	Week 1		
	Tu	2:00	Visit to auditors	E.W.
Personnel No: ___101___	W			
	Th			
Department: ___Accounts Dept.___	F			
		Week 2		
4 or 6-week period ending Friday ___4 week/24th February 1973___	M			
	Tu	7:50	1 Day Holiday	E.W
	W			
	Th			
	F			
Contracted hours (4 x 37½) ___150:00___		Week 3		
	M			
	Tu			
Total adjustment hours ___16:00___	W			
	Th	- 1:00	Left key in meter over Lunch Period	E.W.
Revised contracted hours ___134:00___	F			
		Week 4		
	M			
Actual hours recorded on meter ___135: 60___	Tu			
	W	7:50	Sickness	E.W.
Credit or debit brought forward from last month ___+ 2:00___	Th			
	F			
		Week 5		
credit or debit to be carried forward to next month ___+ 3.60___	M			
	Tu			
	W			
Employee signature ___S. Primps___	Th			
	F			
Department head signature ___E. Weits___			Other adjustments	
Date ___24/12/79___		16:00	Total adjustment hours	

Figure 19–3 A diary sheet for use with a cumulative meter system.

be implemented. Attached to the control unit are automatic personal time totalizers—time counters for each employee in the work area. The counters are contained in units of eight and are attached to the master control unit, as shown in Figure 19-4. One control unit can support up to 72 individual counters, in multiples of eight. The master clock with the appropriate number of counters is usually placed in a convenient location within the work area.

A key is used to activate each time totalizer. When the employee inserts the key, his totalizer continues to record his accumulated hours from the last time that the key was used. In the illustration, it is possible to see the counters to the left of the name and the slot for the key to be inserted. The keys are often used for other functions, such as security clearance

Figure 19–4 Master control unit (8-position).

when entering and leaving the building. The employee would wear the badge or keep it with him at all times when the badge is not inserted in the counter. Under the clock face is a small calendar with each day of the month listed, and the number of hours the employee should have worked at the standard number of hours per day. This allows the employee to compare at a glance the hours on his counter with the calendar on a particular date to see how far ahead or behind he is in hours worked.

Flextime Corporation also provides an additional piece of equipment which can be helpful. Figure 19-5 shows a light display, connected to the master control unit, which indicates who is present at the work site. When an employee inserts his key into his time totalizer, the light next to his name goes on at the light display. When the employee removes his key, the light goes off. Flextime recommends this device, in particular, for switchboard operators so that phone calls will not put through to an employee if he is not present. The firm actively discourages the use of this device by managers to monitor employees. They rightly feel that this type of monitoring may at times defeat the purpose of flexitime implementation.

Flextime estimates the purchase cost of this equipment at approximately $60 per employee, but this can vary, depending upon the number of employees involved, the number of master control units required, and any extra features included with the system.

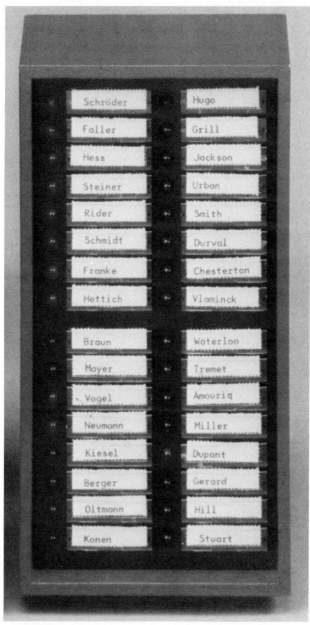

Figure 19–5 Light display.

INTERFLEX, INC.   Interflex may be considered a major competitor of the Flextime Corporation, and it has also enjoyed considerable success in the field of flexitime equipment. This equipment is very similar to the Flextime equipment. Perhaps the major difference is that Interflex utilizes credit-card-sized ID badges to activate the time counters, while the Flextime badge is not a standard shape or size. The Interflex system is divided into modules of 4, 8, or 16 counters per unit. As in the Flextime system, one control unit can accommodate 72 counters. In both systems, time is recorded in hundredths of an hour. This can be confusing to employees, at first, and often employers provide a conversion sheet which translates hundredths to minutes.

Advantages.   Cumulative meter systems have been popular with both employers and employees because they provide an accurate, always up-to-date record, while maintaining employee privacy. The master control unit and counters provide the employee with an up-to-the-minute accounting of hours worked in the current settlement period. It can be used by supervisors to determine at a glance who is present and who is absent from the work station by the presence or absence of keys in the meter. The light display would provide this information at a remote location.

Additional advantages include the fact that since an employee can activate his individual counter with only his own key, the possibility of fraud or of activating an absent co-worker's counter is reduced. Further, the key can be modified to serve as a company pass badge or ID when the employee is away from his work station. With this innovation, security is improved. Perhaps most important, because the meter does not indicate starting and stopping times, it does not have the negative connotations associated with the more traditional time clock. The meter is consistent with the principles of flexitime because it does not measure punctuality or tardiness—it measures only the cumulative amount of time worked. For this reason, it is not viewed as an intrusion of privacy by employees.

Disadvantages.   One of the most common problems associated with cumulative meters is employees who forget to activate or deactivate their meters when arriving or departing. This is usually a problem during the introductory period. To alleviate this problem, several actions may be taken: (1) make the supervisors accountable for the responsible use of keys by employees (a possible alternative, but undesirable); (2) display notices in prominent places, such as exits, as reminders; (3) reprimand employees who leave the meter running and make an entry on their attendance record. Some firms penalize the employee by debiting up to ½ hour from the cumulative time worked; and (4) shut off the meter at the end of the bandwidth and/or during required lunch breaks to limit the accidental accumulation of hours.

Perhaps the major disadvantage of the meter system is that it can be expensive to install. Individual counters are required at each work site where employees are on flexitime. However, the increased capital costs are somewhat offset by a commensurate decrease in administrative costs.

In conclusion, cumulative meters have proven to be an alternative acceptable to both management and employees. As emphasized earlier, however, successful implementation requires a time-recording system consistent with the policies underlying the flexitime system. An advantage of the cumulative meter is that it is acceptable to employees working under very flexible systems, but it can be used in more restrictive environments as well.

COMPUTER-BASED SYSTEMS

Computerized attendance-recording systems represent the state of the art in time recording. Each employee has his own personalized plastic badge, similar to a credit card, which he inserts into a data terminal designed to read the coding on the badge. The computer then logs the time worked. This information is provided periodically to management and employees in the form of a computer printout or through on-line access via a terminal. By modifying the input data station, employees can record authorized absences, overtime, and time spent at different company sites. In addition, depending upon the sophistication of the program, the computer may perform any or all of the following functions relating to time recording:

1. Calculate total employee hours
2. Verify and report core time infringements
3. Print credit and debit hours for each employee
4. Analyze work patterns and provide a database of information
5. Report daily absences

In addition to information relating to time recording, a computer system can be linked to other computer programs in order to serve multiple functions. Some of these functions might include:

1. On-line security systems
2. Calculation of pay and issue of paychecks, if linked to the payroll system
3. Inventory control and maintenance
4. Production control
5. A database of personnel records

Clearly, such systems have great potential in terms of the centralization and control of information pertaining to the activities of the employee at work. Management must carefully evaluate what information is really necessary to effectively manage the work unit. Too much information is not only wasteful and unnecessary, but a true invasion of the employee's privacy.Several firms manufacture computer systems for flexitime. Most also provide other features such as security systems or payroll data. Because of the range of complexity of these systems, it is impractical to describe a typical system. The Interflex 2112 system, illustrated in Figures 19-6 and 19-7, however, may serve as a good illustration of an advanced system. The following is an excerpt from the company's manual:

Time-recording Procedure and Feedback to Employees

Upon arrival at work, employees insert their ID-badges into the assigned Terminal and push the "IN" button. The badge number is then transmitted to the 2112 Controller, which checks validity of the badge, proper time zone and use of the assigned Terminal. If all checks are positive, the Controller sends a message back, which includes the new status "IN" and the display of the employee's accumulated hours for the current payperiod. All these routines take only a fraction of a second, with a delay hardly noticeable to the user.

Inside the Controller, following a valid transaction "IN", an individual time account will start to accumulate time until it is de-activated when the employee punches out, or when the shift assignment calls for the end of the time accumulating period automatically.

If the Controller finds any portion of an employee transaction invalid (wrong button pushed, wrong terminal used, invalid badge, error in data transmission, etc.), the user will be immediately alerted by the Terminal's built-in buzzer and the status display on the dot-matrix.

The dot-matrix (Figure 19-7) therefore is an important part of the communication between user and the microprocessor.

Communication between System Operator and 2112 Controller

While the 2112 microprocessor communicates with the employee via display of status and accumulated hours, the operation of the 2112 Controller was designed to be equally simple and communicative.

The dot matrix alerts the system operator of any incorrect entries and the digital display allows verification of all transactions prior to execution.

A third aspect is that the whole command structure is based on two numeric digits, which makes communication almost as simple as by voice.

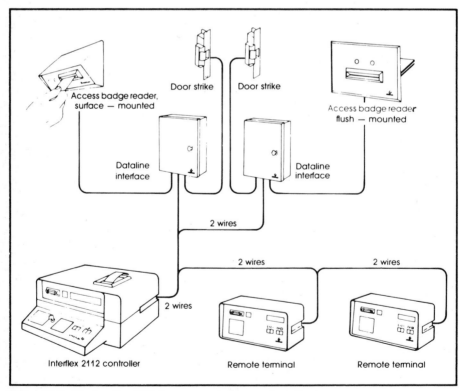

Figure 19–6   The Interflex 2112 System, stand-alone configuration.

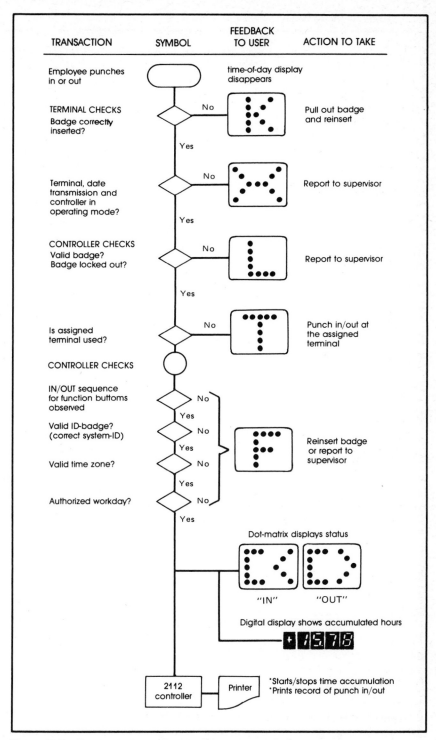

Figure 19–7 Communication at the Interflex remote terminal.

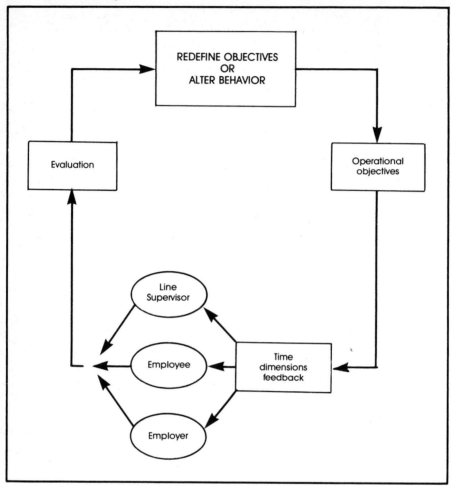

Figure 19–8   The time-recording system as a feedback mechanism.

When considering a computer system, the firm must first determine whether existing computer facilities can be utilized, and if so, to what degree. For instance, a firm may have processing time available for a flexitime program on its in-house computer. Alternatively, peripheral equipment such as terminals and printers may be available. If the firm decides to purchase hardware from one of the time-recording manufacturers, compatibility with internal computers and peripheral devices should be determined. The decision to use a computer-based system almost always represents a major capital investment. In order to be successful, a thorough investigation of the requirements of the system, and of the interface between new and existing equipment is necessary.

Many considerations have been presented for the decision maker. Because costs will always be a major factor in any decision of this nature and are outside the scope of the concerns presented here, this discussion has concentrated on guidelines relating to successful implementation.

SUMMARY

Perhaps the most important consideration in selecting a time-recording system is that of consistency. The operational objectives or requirements defined for the time-recording system must be consistent with management's objectives and concerns regarding the flexitime plan itself. These requirements can be thought of as the types of information or feedback required. Time-recording systems can provide feedback to three levels of users of the system: employers, employees, and supervisors. Each of these groups might use the system for different purposes and to obtain different kinds of information.

Employers may utilize statistical information reflecting membership behavior (e.g., levels of absenteeism). In addition, certain types of more sophisticated time-recording systems may provide information about payroll, customer billings, inventory levels, and even production control.

Employees may obtain their personal status with respect to hours worked and any absences over a given period of time.

Supervisors may obtain information regarding the status of their work unit vis-à-vis organizational regulations and objectives concerning membership behavior, as well as information about the availability of employees in the work unit at any given moment in time.

The feedback process, described in Figure 19-8, involves obtaining the information from the time-recording system and evaluating it against organizational criteria, such as regulations concerning absenteeism, or the flexitime schedule itself. As a result of the evaluation, the employer, employee, or supervisor has the option of altering behavior, or changing the objectives of the program. As an employer or supervisor, the behavior of others is evaluated; as an employee, self-behavior is under scrutiny. When viewed as a mechanism for feedback and a source of information for the employee as well as management, time-recording systems should be less threatening to employees.

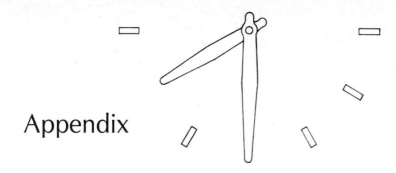

Appendix

Selected List
of
Companies Using Flexitime*

Number of Employees Listed When Available

AIL. (Division of Culter-Hammer, Inc.), Deer Park, New York

Agfa-Gevaert Inc. (425), Teterboro, New Jersey

American Airlines, Inc. (1,036), Lake Success, New York

American Bar Association (80), Washington, D.C.

American Fletcher National Bank, Indianapolis, Indiana

American Geophysical Union (65), Washington, D.C.

American Hofmann Corporation, Lynchburg, Virginia

American Management Association Headquarters, New York, New York

American Orthodontics Corporation (100), Sheboygan, Wisconsin

American Physical Therapy Association, Washington, D.C.

American Psychological Association (51), Washington, D.C.

American Standard, Inc. (200), New York, New York

American Sterilizer Company—Jamestown, N.Y., Division (40), Jamestown, New York

Anheuser-Busch, Inc., St. Louis, Missouri

Associated Corporation of North America, South Bend, Indiana

Baltimore New Directions for Women, Inc. (29), Baltimore, Maryland

Bank of California, N.A. (100), San Francisco, California

*Files from the National Council for Alternative Work Patterns, Inc., Washington, D.C., provided a major source of the listings offered here. Other sources of this list were various published materials and personal contacts.

NOTE: Federal and state agencies have been excluded from this list.

Bankers Life Insurance of Nebraska, Omaha, Nebraska

Bankers Security Life Insurance Society (184), Washington, D.C.

Bell Canada, Montreal, Quebec, Canada

Berol USA, Ville Le Moyne, Quebec, Canada

Berol USA—International Headquarters (200), Danbury, Connecticut

Blue Cross/Blue Shield of Arkansas (134), Little Rock, Arkansas

Blue Cross/Blue Shield of Kansas (800), Topeka, Kansas

Blue Cross/Blue Shield of Kansas City (200), Kansas City, Missouri

Blue Cross/Blue Shield of Michigan (500), Detroit, Michigan

Blue Cross/Blue Shield of Minnesota (978), St. Paul, Minnesota

Blue Cross/Blue Shield of Nebraska (115), Omaha, Nebraska

Blue Cross/Blue Shield of Southwest Virginia (275), Roanoke, Virginia

BOMCO, Inc. (60), Glouchester, Massachusetts

Boonton Electronics Corporation (156), Parsippany, New Jersey

Bristol Myers Company, Hillside, New Jersey

Bristol Tennessee Electric System, Bristol, Tennessee

CF Industries, Inc., Chicago, Illinois

Catalyst, New York, New York

Centrico, Inc., Northvale, New Jersey

Chicopee Manufacturing Company (161), New Brunswick, New Jersey

Chicopee Mfg. Company (18), Benson, North Carolina

Chicopee Mfg. Company—Milltown Administration (100), Milltown, New Jersey

Chicopee Mfg. Company—New Jersey Facilities (400), New Brunswick, New Jersey

Child Welfare League of America (75), New York, New York

Church School Publications, Nashville, Tennessee

City and County of Honolulu, Department of Civil Service (3,500), Honolulu, Hawaii

City of Baltimore, Baltimore, Maryland

City of Berkeley (500), Berkeley, California

City of Inglewood, Inglewood, California

Coca Cola Bottling Company of Chicago, Chicago, Illinois

College and University Personnel Association (10), Washington, D.C.

Commonwealth of Massachusetts—Division of Personnel Administration (1,500), Boston, Massachusetts

Connecticut Mutual Life (1,400), Hartford, Connecticut

Continental Inc. (80), Seattle, Washington

Continental Telephone Corporation, Bakersfield, California

Control Data Corporation (23,000), Minneapolis, Minnesota

Cornell University (46), Ithaca, New York

Degussa Corporation, Teterboro, New Jersey

Department of Motor Vehicles (6,500), Sacramento, California

Design Dynamics Ltd., Oakville, Ontario Canada

De Sota Inc., Des Plaines, Illinois

Digital Equipment Corporation, Maynard, Massachusetts

Dillingham Corporation, Honolulu, Hawaii

District of Columbia Public Library (40), Washington, D.C.

Domain Industries, Inc., New Richmond, Wisconsin

Dymo Industries Inc., Berkeley, California

East-West Gateway Coordinating Council (75), St. Louis, Missouri

Ellerbe Associates (520), Bloomington, Minnesota

EM Labs, Inc., Elmsford, New York

Employee Development & Community Affairs, Chicago, Illinois

Equibank N.A., Pittsburgh, Pennsylvania

Equitable Life Assurance Society of the United States, New York, New York

Equitable Trust Company (200), Baltimore, Maryland

Erico Products, Inc., Solon, Ohio

Erie Mfg. Company (70), Milwaukee, Wisconsin

Erie Mining Company, Howit Lakes, Minnesota

Exxon Corporation—MCS Department (450), Florham Park, New Jersey

F. L. Smidth & Company (20), Lebanon, New Jersey

Fiat—Allis Construction Machinery, Inc. (200), Deerfield, Illinois

Fidelity Union Life Insurance Company, Dallas, Texas

Fingerhut Mfg. Corporation, Minnetonka, Minnesota

First Bank (100), New Haven, Connecticut

First National Bank of Boston, Boston, Massachusetts

First Union Corporation (66), Charlotte, North Carolina

First Union National Bank, Charlotte, North Carolina

Flex Time Corporation, New York, New York

Frito-Lay, Inc., Irving, Texas

General American Life Insurance (800), St. Louis, Missouri

General Electric Company, Syracuse, New York

General Foods Corporation—The Technical Center (650), Tarrytown, New York

General Motors Corporation (8,000), Detroit, Michigan

General Radio Company, Concord, Massachusetts

General Telephone of California (600), Santa Monica, California

Graco, Inc., Franklin Park, Illinois

Group Health Association Inc. (40), Washington, D.C.

Group Hospitalization Inc. (1,450), Washington, D.C.

Guardian Life Insurance Company of America (890), New York, New York

Guidance and Control Systems, Woodland Hills, California

Gulf & Western Manufacturing Company—E. W. Bliss Division (200), Hastings, Michigan

Hammond Organ Company, Chicago, Illinois

Hartford Insurance Group (175), Seattle, Washington

Hartford Steam Boiler Inspection and Insurance Company (70), Chicago, Illinois

Harvard College Library, Cambridge, Massachusetts

Hecon Corporation (185), Tinton Falls, New Jersey

Hercules Inc. (2,000), Wilmington, Delaware

Hewlett-Packard Company (20,000), Palo Alto, California

Hewlett-Packard Company (1,650), Colorado Springs, Colorado

Hewlett-Packard Company (1,300), Waltham, Massachusetts

Hewlett-Packard Company (540), Avondale, Pennsylvania

Highway Users Federation (45), Washington, D.C.

Honeywell, Inc., Waltham, Massachusetts

Honeywell, Inc. (3,200), Minneapolis, Minnesota

Ideal Corporation (65), Brooklyn, New York

Ideal Industries, Inc. (225), Sycamore, Illinois

Indiana University Library (85), Bloomington, Indiana

Illinois Tool Works (2,500), Chicago, Illinois

Industrial Indemnity Company (2,200), San Francisco, California

Industrial National Bank (150), Providence, Rhode Island

Insurance Services Office (1,000), New York, New York

International Group Plans, Inc. (200), Washington, D.C.

Iowa Department of Job Service (600), Des Moines, Iowa

J. C. Penney Company, Inc. (1,500), New York, New York

Jewel Food Stores, Melrose Park, Illinois

John Hancock Mutual Life Insurance Company (1,138), Boston, Massachusetts

Johnson & Johnson, Corporate Headquarters (55), New Brunswick, New Jersey

Kellogg Company (100), Battle Creek, Michigan

Kellogg Company of Canada Ltd., Don Mills, Ontario, Canada

Kingsbury Machine Tool Corporation (854), Keene, New Hampshire

Koss Corporation, Milwaukee, Wisconsin

Lever Bros. Company (1,200), New York, New York

Levi Strauss & Company (300), San Francisco, California

Lincoln National Life Insurance Company (5,237), Fort Wayne, Indiana

Litton Industries, Inc., Beverly Hills, California

Lufthansa German Airlines (300), East Meadow, New York

Mabuhay Vinyl Corporation, Makati, Rizal, Philippines

Maryland Automobile Insurance Fund (400), Annapolis, Maryland

Maryland National Bank, Baltimore, Maryland

Maryland National Bank, College Park, Maryland

Massachusetts Mutual Life Insurance Company (2,600), Springfield, Massachusetts

Massachusetts Rehabilitation Commission (220), Boston, Massachusetts

Medenco Inc., Houston, Texas

Meredith Corporation, Des Moines, Iowa

Metropolitan Life Insurance Company, New York, New York

Metropolitan Life Insurance Company (500), Tampa, Florida

Monsanto Company, Akron Marketing & Research Center (125), Akron, Ohio

Montgomery Ward & Co., Headquarters, Chicago, Illinois

Monumental Life Insurance Company, Baltimore, Maryland

Motorola Inc., Scottsdale, Arizona

Mountain Bell (1,000), Denver, Colorado

Mutual of New York, New York, New York

National Shawmut Bank of Boston, Boston, Massachusetts

Nestle Co., Inc., White Plains, New York

New England Mutual Life Insurance Company (500), Boston, Massachusetts

New York City License Bureau, New York, New York

New York State Department of Motor Vehicles (1,500), Albany, New York

North America Reinsurance Company, New York, New York

North American Car Corporation—Tiger Leasing Group (225), Chicago, Illinois

Northern National Gas Company, Omaha, Nebraska

Office of State Personnel North Carolina State Government (12,000), Raleigh, North Carolina

Ohio National Life Insurance Company (230), Cincinnati, Ohio

Onan Corporation, Minneapolis, Minnesota

Overly Mfg. Company (60), Greensburg, Pennsylvania

Pacific Gas & Electric Company (519), San Francisco, California

Pacific Telephone (1,000), Los Angeles, California

Pacific Telephone (1,050), San Francisco, California

Paul Revere Life Insurance Company (750), Worcester, Massachusetts

Pennsylvania Power & Light Company (2,375), Allentown, Pennsylvania

Pfizer, Inc. (1,850), New York, New York

Phoenix Mutual Life Insurance (1,100), Hartford, Connecticut

Pioneer Electronics of America (125), Long Beach, California

Pitney Bowes, Inc. (800), Stamford, Connecticut

Polysius Corporation (90), Atlanta, Georgia

Port Authority of New York and New Jersey (500), New York, New York

Prince George's County Department of Licenses & Permits (140), Hyattsville, Maryland

Prince George's County Memorial Library (385), Hyattsville, Maryland

Prudential Insurance Company of America (2,000), Newark, New Jersey

Readers' Digest Association Canada Ltd., Montreal, Quebec, Canada

Red Owl Stores, Inc., Hopkins, Minnesota

Reuben H. Donnelley Corporation (350), Oak Brook, Illinois

Riley-Stoker Corp. (500), Worcester, Massachusetts

S. C. Johnson & Son, Inc., Racine, Wisconsin

St. Paul Companies, Inc. (7,000), St. Paul, Minnesota

San Diego County Probation Department (740), San Diego, California

Sandoz, Inc. (480), East Hanover, New Jersey

Schlitz, Jos., Brewing Company, Milwaukee, Wisconsin

Scott Paper Company (1,500), Philadelphia, Pennsylvania

Searle Diagnostics, Inc. (1,096), Des Plaines, Illinois

Sears, Roebuck & Company, Chicago, Illinois

Seattle First National Bank (261), Seattle, Washington

Security Life of Denver (130), Denver, Colorado

Shell Development Company, Houston, Texas

Shell Oil Company (4,000), Houston, Texas

Sieber & McIntyre, Inc., Chicago, Illinois

Signode Corporation, Glenview, Illinois

Simpson Electric Company, Elgin, Illinois

SmithKline Corporation (2,150), Philadelphia, Pennsylvania

Social Security Administration, Baltimore, Maryland

Southern Insurance Underwriters, Inc. (36), Atlanta, Georgia

State of Colorado (3,400), Denver, Colorado

State of Illinois (900), Springfield, Illinois

State of Iowa—State Comptroller's Office (2,000), Des Moines, Iowa

State of Maryland (1,000), Baltimore, Maryland

State of New Jersey—Department of Civil Service (900), Trenton, New Jersey

State of Oregon—Department of General Services (10,000), Salem, Oregon

State Personnel Board (600), Sacramento, California

State Street Bank & Trust Company (139), Boston, Massachusetts

Sun Co., Inc. (700), Philadelphia, Pennsylvania

Sun Oil Company, Philadelphia, Pennsylvania

Sun Shipbuilding & Dry Dock Company (450), Chester, Pennsylvania

Sunbeam Corporation, Chicago, Illinois

Sundstrand Data Control, Inc. (650), Redmond, Washington

Tally Corporation (300), Kent, Washington

Teachers Superannuation Commission, Willowdale, Ontario, Canada

Tele-Direct Limited, Montreal, Quebec, Canada

Tenneco, Inc., Houston, Texas

Thermo Systems Inc. (TSI Incorporated), St. Paul, Minnesota

Title Insurance Company—Minnesota, Minneapolis, Minnesota

Transcontinental Gas Pipe Line Corporation (800), Houston, Texas

Unigard Insurance Group (11,350), Seattle, Washington

United Insurance Company of America, Chicago, Illinois

United Life and Accident Insurance Company (350), Concord, New Hampshire

United Services Life Insurance Company (150), Washington, D.C.

Universal Oil Products Company (VOP Inc.), Des Plaines, Illinois

University National Bank (80), Rockville, Maryland

University of Florida Libraries (100), Gainesville, Florida

University of New Hampshire (150), Durham, New Hampshire

Vaughan & Bushnell Mfg. Company, Hebron, Illinois

Westfield Companies, Westfield Center, Ohio

Westinghouse Electric Corporation (2,800), Pittsburgh, Pennsylvania

White Pine Copper Company, White Pine, Michigan

Xerox Corporation (15,000), Rochester, New York

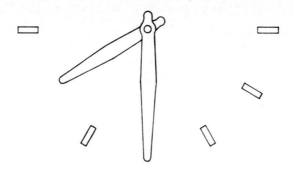

Selected Bibliography

Allenspach, Heinz. *Flexible working hours.* Geneva: International Labour Office, 1975.

———Flexible working time: Its development and application in Switzerland. *Occupational Psychology,* 1974, *46,* No. 4, 209–215.

———Working hours per week and day. *New patterns for working time.* International Conference. Paris, 26–29 September 1972. Supplement to the Final Report. Paris: Organization for Economic Cooperation and Development, 1973, pp. 83–96.

Baum, Stephen J., and Young, W. McEwan. *A practical guide to flexible working hours.* Park Ridge, New Jersey: Noyes, 1974.

Bolton, J. Harvey. *Flexible working hours.* Wembley, England: Anbar Publications Ltd., 1971.

Cambell, A., Converse, P. C., and Rodgers, W. *The quality of American life.* New York: Russell Sage Foundation, 1976.

Caulkin, S. The flexible working age. *Management Today,* March 1976, pp. 81–85.

Cohen, A. R., and Gadon, H. *Alternative work schedules: Integrating individual and organizational needs.* Reading, Mass.: Addison-Wesley, 1978.

Committee on Alternative Work Patterns and National Center for Productivity and Quality of Working Life. *Alternatives in the world of work,* Winter 1976, Washington, D.C.: 1976.

Davis, Herbert J., and Weaver, K. Mark. *Alternate workweek patterns: An annotated bibliography of selected literature.* Washington, D.C.: National Council for Alternative Work Patterns, 1976.

Elbing, A. O., Gadon, H., and Gordon, R. Flexible working hours: It's about time. *Harvard Business Review,* January-February, 1974, pp. 18–33.

Elbing, A. O., Gadon, H., and Gordon, J. R., Flexible working hours: The missing link. *California Management Review,* Spring 1975, *17,* 50–57.

Elbing, A. O., Gadon, H., and Gordon, J. R., Time for a human time-table. *European Business Review,* Autumn 1973, *39,* 46–54.

Evans, Archibald A. Work and leisure 1919–1969. *International Labour Review,* January 1969, pp. 35–59.

Fiss, Barbara. *Flexitime at the Bureau of Policies and Standards: A handbook for supervisors and employees,* Washington, D.C.: U.S. Civil Service Commission, 1975.

————*Flexitime—A guide,* U.S. Civil Service Commission. Superintendant of Documents, U.S. Government Printing Office, Washington, D.C. (Stock No. 006-000-00809-7; Cat. No. CS1.74: F 63), 1975.

————Government tests flexitime. *Civil Service Journal,* January-March, 1977, *17,* No. 3, 1–6.

Glickman, Albert S. and Brown, Xenia H. *Changing schedules of work: Patterns and implications.* Kalamazoo, Michigan: W. E. Upjohn Institute for Employment Research, 1974.

Golembiewski, R. T., Hilles, R., and Kagno, M. S. A longitudinal study of flexitime effects: Some consequences of an OD intervention. *The Journal of Applied Behavioral Science,* 1974, pp. 502–32.

Golembiewski, R. T. and Proehl, C. W., Jr., A survey of the empirical literature on flexible work hours: Character and consequences of a major innovation. *Academy of Management Review,* 1978, *3,* 837–852.

Hedges, Janice N. Flexible schedules: Problems and issues. in special flexitime report in *Monthly Labor Review,* February 1977, *100,* 62–74.

————How many days make a workweek? *Monthly Labor Review,* April 1975, *98,* 29–36.

————Work schedules and the rush hour. *Monthly Labor Review,* July 1975, *98,* 43–47.

Holley, W. H., Jr., Armenakis, A. A., and Field, H. S., Jr. Reactions to a flexitime program: A longitudinal study. *Human Resource Management,* Winter 1976, pp. 21–23.

International Conference on New Patterns for Working Time, Paris, 1972. September 26–29, Final Report. Organization for Economic Cooperation and Development, 1973.

Katzell, R. and Yankelovich, D. *Work, productivity and job satisfaction.* New York: Harcourt Brace Jovanovich, 1975.

Keppler, Bernhard. European industries. In David Robison, *Alternative work patterns—Changing approaches to work scheduling.* Report of a Conference Cosponsored by the National Center for Productivity and Quality of Working Life and the Work in America Institute, Inc.: New York, 1976.

Levine, E. L. Self Assessment for Personnel Selection: Bane or Boon. *Public Personnel Management,* 1978, *7,* (July–August), 230–235.

Levinson, D. J. *The seasons of a man's life.* New York: Ballantine Books, 1978.

Mahoney, T. A. The rearranged work week: Evaluations of different work schedules. *California Management Review.* Summer 1978, *20,* No. 4, 31–39.

Martin, Virginia H. *Hours of work when workers can choose: The experience of 50 organizations with employee chosen staggered hours and flexitime.* Washington, D.C.: Business and Professional Women's Foundation, 1975.

McCarthy, Maureen E. *The extent of alternative work schedules in state government.* Washington, D.C.: Committee for Alternative Work Patterns, 1977.

Miller, J. *Innovations in working patterns.* Report of The U.S. Trade Union Seminar on Alternative Work Patterns in Europe. Washington, D.C.: 1978.

Morgan, F. T. Your (flex) time may come. *Personnel Journal,* 1977, *56,* 82–83.

National Council for Alternative Work Patterns. *National Conference on Alternative Work Schedules: Resource packet.* Chicago, March 1977.

National Council for Alternative Work Patterns. *National Directory of Organizations Using Alternative Work Schedules.* Washington, D.C., 1978.

New Patterns for Working Time. International Conference, Final Report, Organization for Economic Cooperation and Development, Paris, 1973.

Nollen, S. D., and Martin, V. H. *Alternative work schedules: Flexitime.* An AMA Survey Report, AMACOM: New York, 1978.

Owen, J. D. Flexitime: Some problems and solutions. *Industrial and Labor Relations Review,* January 1977, *30,* No. 2.

Owen, J. D. *Working hours: An economic analysis.* Lexington, Mass.: Lexington Books: 1979.

Poor, Riva, (Ed.). *4 days, 40 hours: Reporting a revolution in work and leisure.* Cambridge, Mass.: Bursk and Poor, 1970.

Schein, E. H. *1978 career dynamics: Matching individual and organizational needs.* Reading, Mass.: Addison-Wesley, 1978.

Schein, E., Maurer, H., and Novak, F. Impact of flexible working hours on productivity. *Journal of Applied Psychology,* 1977, *62,* 463–465.

Sheppard, H. L., and Herrick, N. Q. *Where have all the robots gone? Worker dissatisfaction in the 70's.* New York: the W. E. Upjohn Institute for Employment Research, the Free Press, 1972, pp. 25–28, 114–117.

Snyder, R. A. *Flexitime research and the federal government: Some issues of concern for agency decision-makers.* U.S. Civil Service Commission, February 1976.

Swart, J. Carroll. *A flexible approach to working hours.* New York: AMACOM, 1978.

U.S. Comptroller General, *Contractors use of altered work schedules for their employees—How is it working?* PSAD-76-124, Washington, D.C.: U.S. Government Accounting Office, April 7, 1976.

U.S. Congress. House Committee on Post Office and Civil Service. *Alternative work schedules and part-time career opportunities in the federal government: hearings before the subcommittee on manpower and Civil Service on H. R. 6350, H. R. 9043, H. R. 3925, and S. 792.* 94th Congress, First Session, 1975.

U.S. Congress. Senate Committee on Labor and Public Welfare. *Changing Patterns of Work in America, 1976.* Hearings before the Subcommittee on Employment, Poverty, and Migratory Labor. 94th Congress, Second Session, 1976.

U.S. Geological Survey, Branch of Management Analysis and Branch of Personnel. *Planning for implementation of flexible working hours.* Interim Report, Reston, Virginia, 1975.

Wade, Michael. *Flexible working hours in practice,* New York: Wiley, 1973.

Walker, James. Flexible working hours in two British government offices. *Public Personnel Management,* July–August 1975, *4,* No. 4, 216–222.

Yankelovich, D. Work values and the new breed. In C. Kerr and J. Rosow (Eds.), *Work in America: The decade ahead.* New York: Van Nostrand, 1979.

Zaluski, J. L. Alternative work schedules: A labor perspective. Paper presented to the National Conference on Alternative Work Schedules, March 1977. Also cited in the *The Journal of the College and University Personnel Association,* 1977, *28,* No. 3.

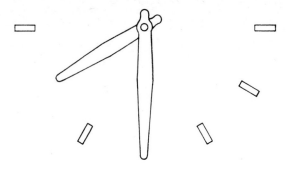

Index